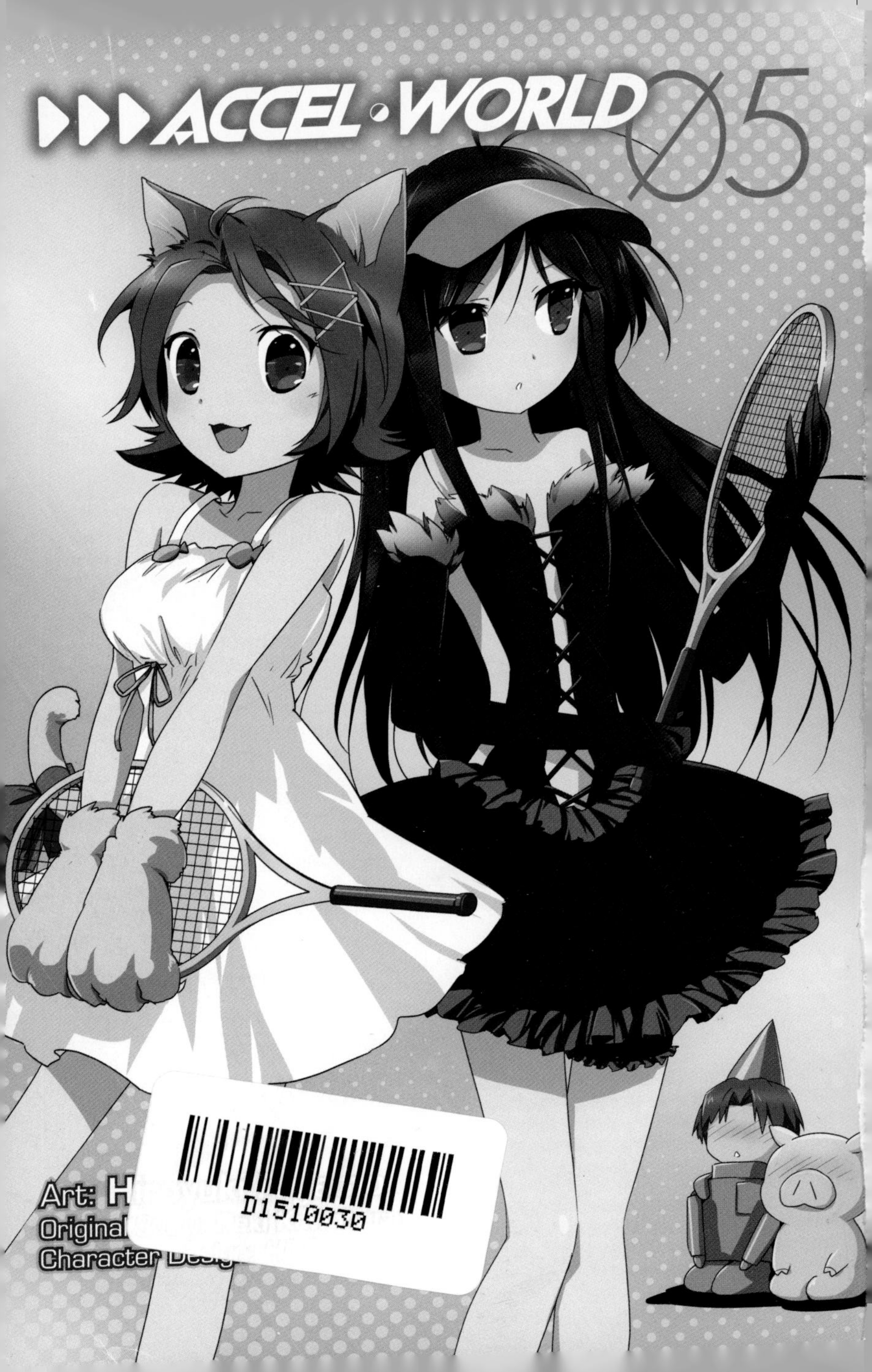
ACCEL·WORLD
05

05

accel world

art:
hiroyuki aigamo
original story:
reki kawahara
accel world 10: elements &
accel world 03: the twilight marauder
character design:
hima

characters

■ Kuroyukihime = Umesato Junior High School student council vice president. Trim and clever girl who has it all. Her background is shrouded in mystery. Her in-school avatar is a spangled butterfly she programmed herself. Her duel avatar is the Black King, "Black Lotus."

■ Haruyuki = Haruyuki Arita. Grade Seven at Umesato Junior High School. Bullied, on the pudgy side. He's good at games but is shy. His in-school avatar is a pink pig. His duel avatar is Silver Crow.

■ Chiyuri = Chiyuri Kurashima. Haruyuki's childhood friend. A meddling, energetic girl. Her in-school avatar is a silver cat.

■ Takumu = Takumu Mayuzumi. A boy Haruyuki and Chiyuri have known since childhood. Good at kendo. His duel avatar is Cyan Pile.

■ Niko = Yuniko Kozuki. Grade Five girl who pretended to be Haruyuki's cousin to get in direct contact with him. Her real identity is the Red King, ruler of the Red Legion. Her duel avatar is Scarlet Rain.

contents

key words

■ Neurolinker = A portable terminal that connects with the brain via a wireless quantum connection, and which supports all five senses with enhanced images, sounds, and other stimulus.

■ Brain Burst = Neurolinker application sent to Haruyuki by Kuroyukihime.

■ Duel avatar = Player's virtual self, operated when fighting in Brain Burst.

■ Burst points = Points required to use the power of acceleration. To obtain them, players must win duels against other duel avatars. If a player loses all their points, Brain Burst is forceably uninstalled.

■ Legion = Groups, composed of many duel avatars, with the objective of expanding occupied areas and securing rights. The Seven Kings of Pure Color act as the Legion Masters.

■ In-school local net = Local area network established within Umesato Junior High School. Used during classes and to check attendance. Umesato students are required to always be connected to it.

■ Global connection = Connection with the worldwide net. Global connections are forbidden on Umesato Junior High School grounds, where the in-school local net is provided instead.

■ Enhanced Armament = Items such as weapons or personal armor owned by duel avatars.

■ Normal Duel Field = The field where normal Brain Burst battles (one-on-one or tag matches) are carried out.

■ Unlimited Neutral Field = Field for high-level players where only duel avatars at level four and up are allowed. The game system is of a wholly different order than that of the Normal Duel Field.

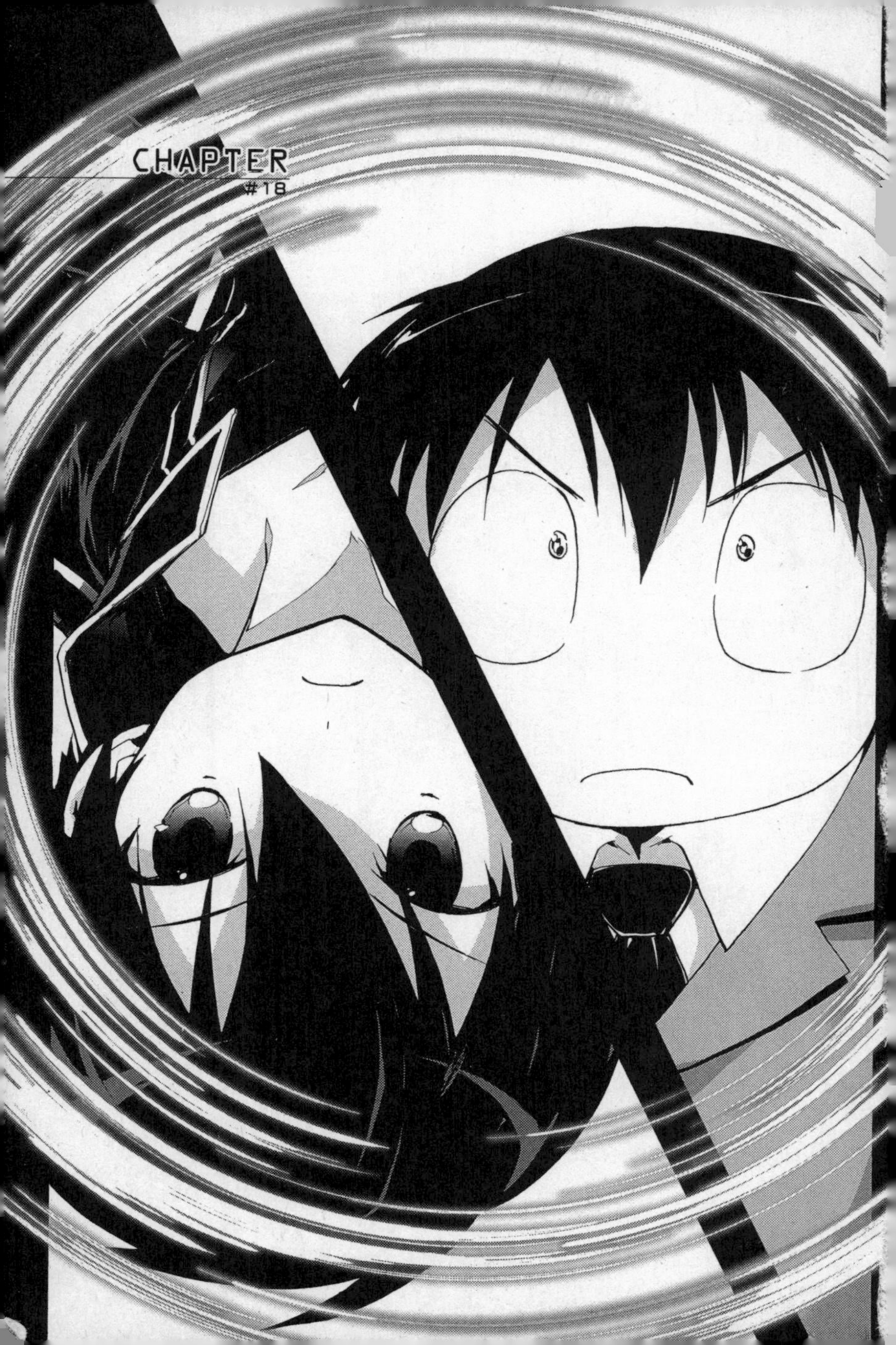
CHAPTER
#18

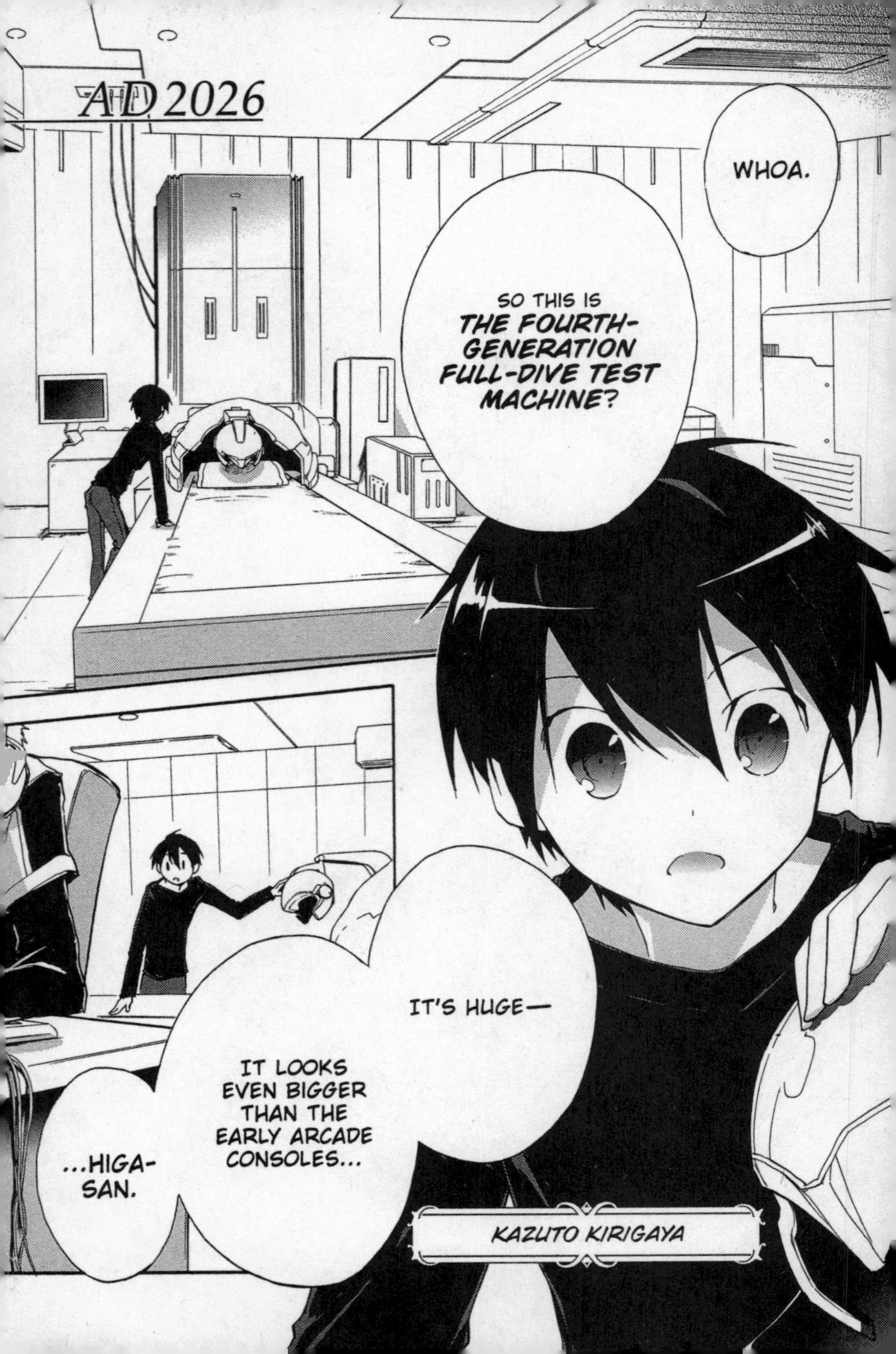
AD 2026
WHOA.
SO THIS IS THE FOURTH-GENERATION FULL-DIVE TEST MACHINE?
IT'S HUGE—
IT LOOKS EVEN BIGGER THAN THE EARLY ARCADE CONSOLES...
...HIGA-SAN.
KAZUTO KIRIGAYA

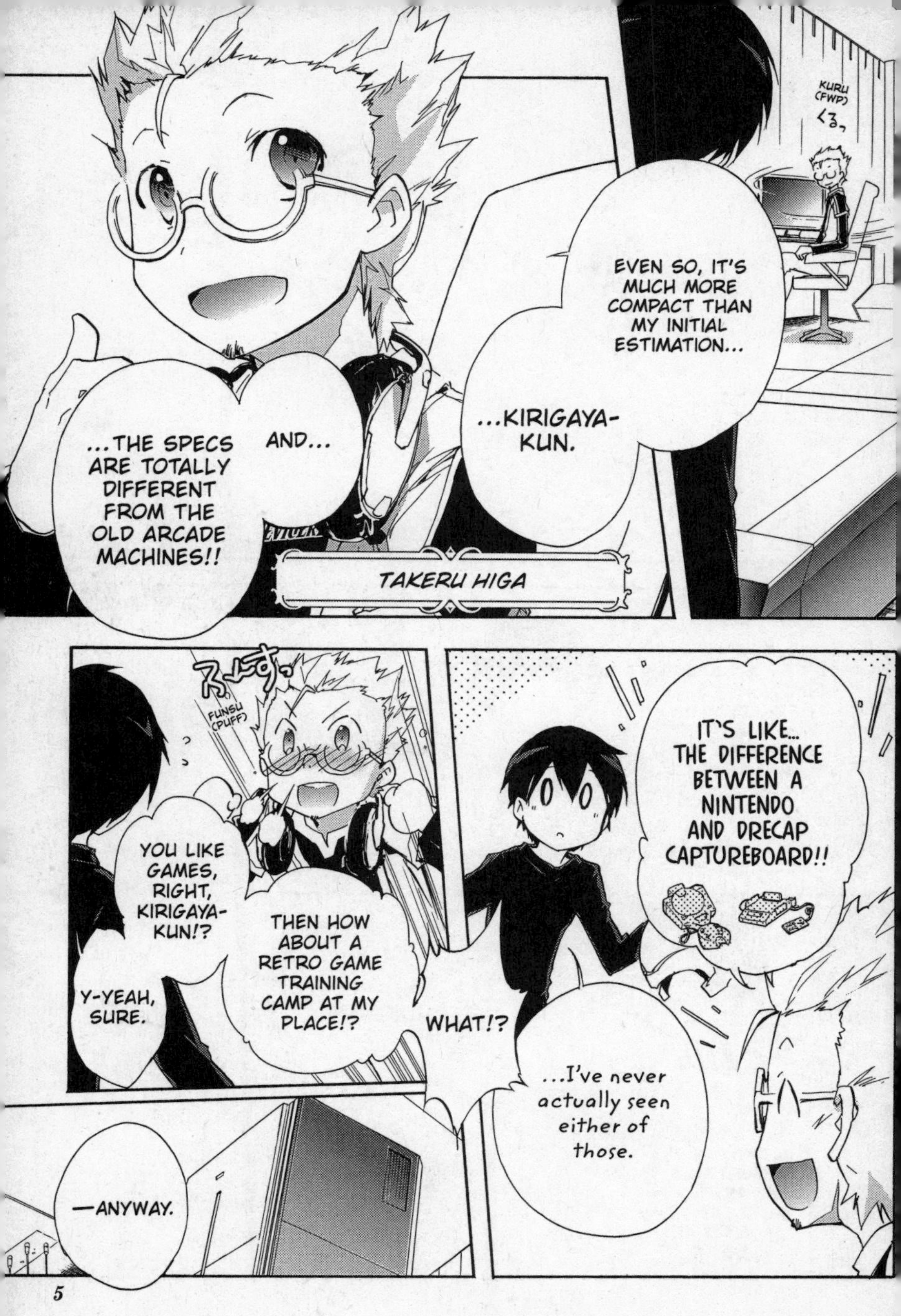
KURU (FWP)
くるっ
EVEN SO, IT'S MUCH MORE COMPACT THAN MY INITIAL ESTIMATION...
...KIRIGAYA-KUN.
AND...
...THE SPECS ARE TOTALLY DIFFERENT FROM THE OLD ARCADE MACHINES!!
TAKERU HIGA
IT'S LIKE... THE DIFFERENCE BETWEEN A NINTENDO AND DRECAP CAPTUREBOARD!!
WHAT!?
...I've never actually seen either of those.
ふんすっ
FUNSU (PUFF)
YOU LIKE GAMES, RIGHT, KIRIGAYA-KUN!?
THEN HOW ABOUT A RETRO GAME TRAINING CAMP AT MY PLACE!?
Y-YEAH, SURE.
—ANYWAY.

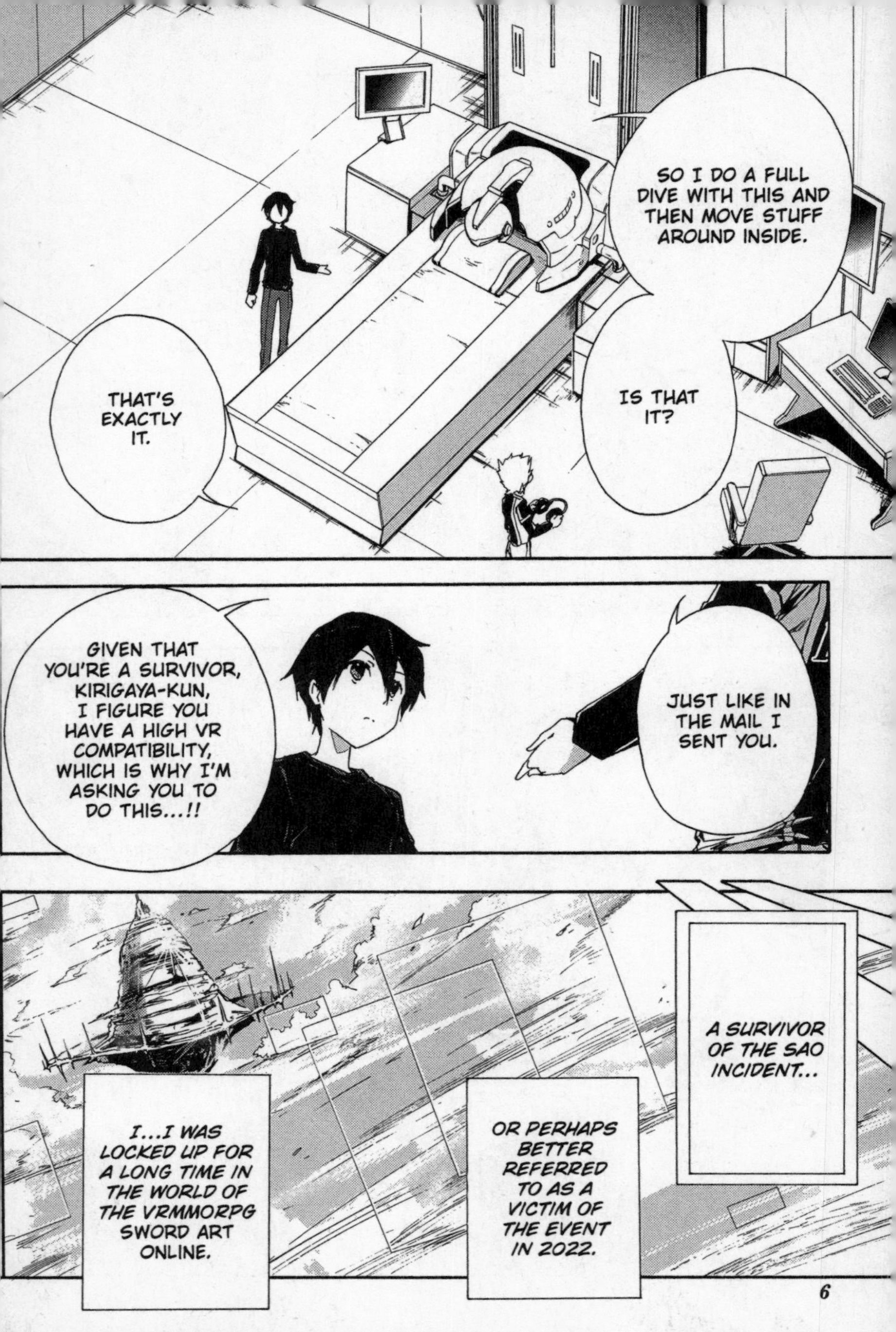
SO I DO A FULL DIVE WITH THIS AND THEN MOVE STUFF AROUND INSIDE.
IS THAT IT?
THAT'S EXACTLY IT.
JUST LIKE IN THE MAIL I SENT YOU.
GIVEN THAT YOU'RE A SURVIVOR, KIRIGAYA-KUN, I FIGURE YOU HAVE A HIGH VR COMPATIBILITY, WHICH IS WHY I'M ASKING YOU TO DO THIS...!!
A SURVIVOR OF THE SAO INCIDENT...
OR PERHAPS BETTER REFERRED TO AS A VICTIM OF THE EVENT IN 2022.
I...I WAS LOCKED UP FOR A LONG TIME IN THE WORLD OF THE VRMMORPG SWORD ART ONLINE.

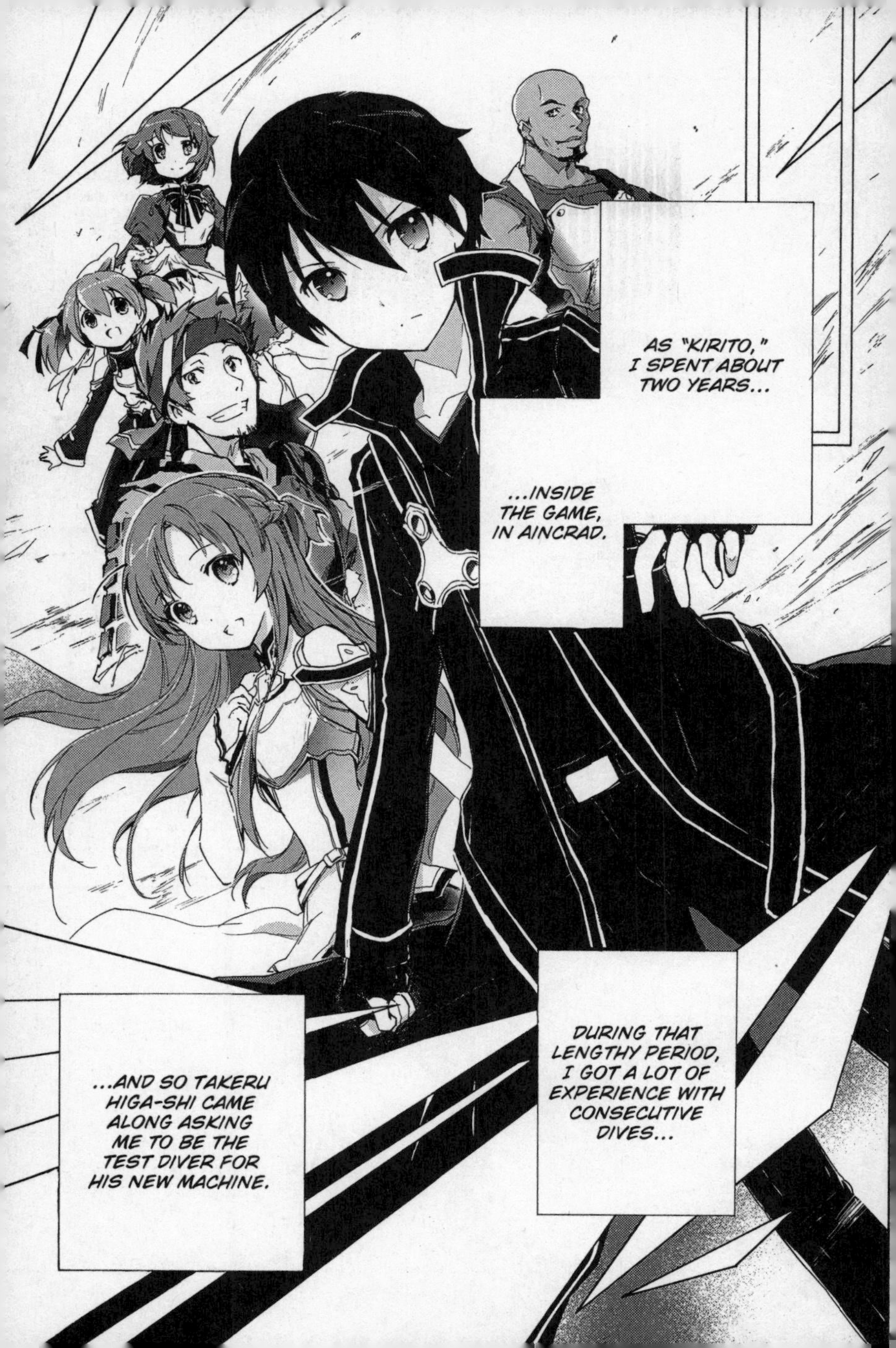
AS "KIRITO," I SPENT ABOUT TWO YEARS...
...INSIDE THE GAME, IN AINCRAD.
DURING THAT LENGTHY PERIOD, I GOT A LOT OF EXPERIENCE WITH CONSECUTIVE DIVES...
...AND SO TAKERU HIGA-SHI CAME ALONG ASKING ME TO BE THE TEST DIVER FOR HIS NEW MACHINE.

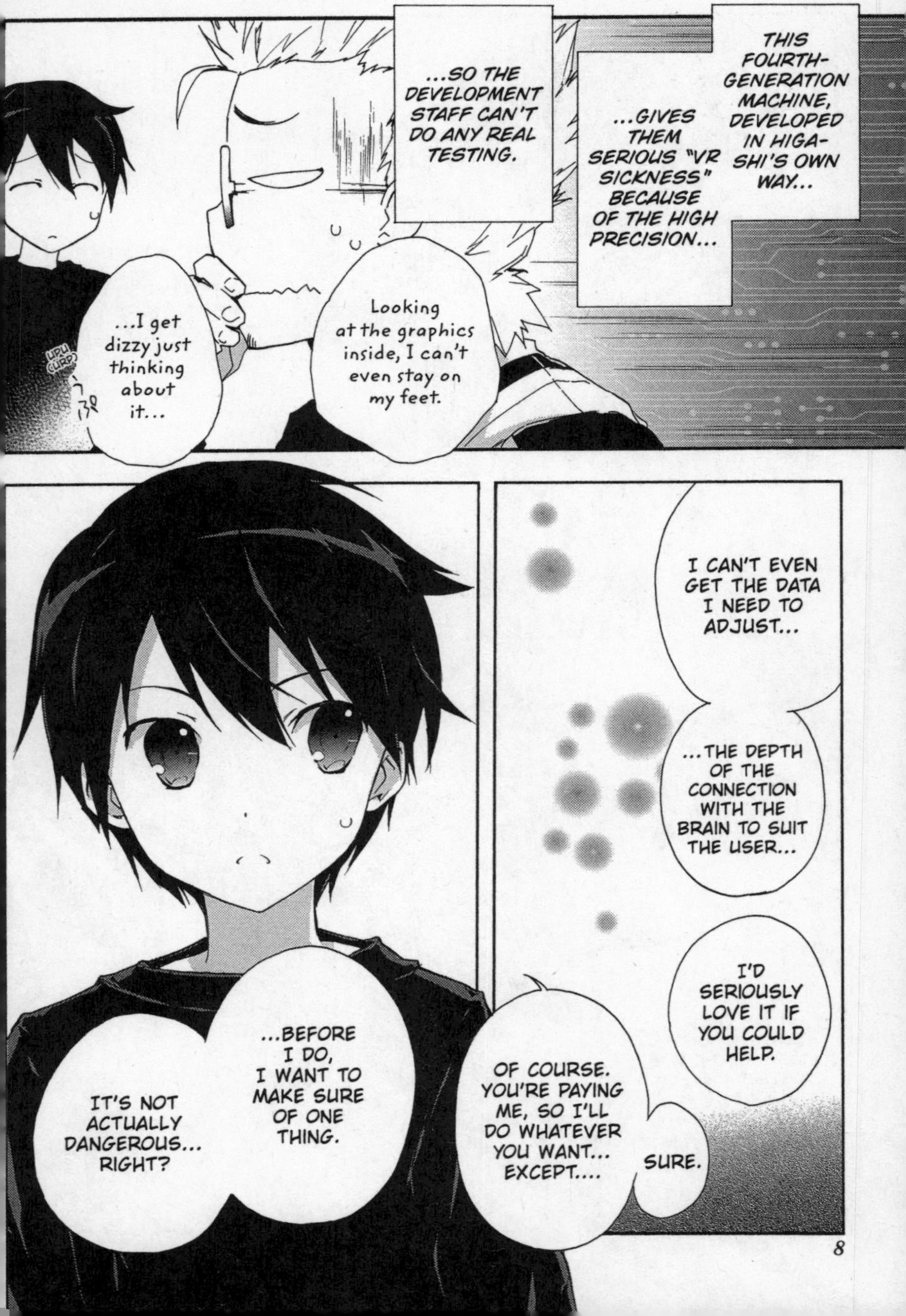
THIS FOURTH-GENERATION MACHINE, DEVELOPED IN HIGASHI'S OWN WAY...
...GIVES THEM SERIOUS "VR SICKNESS" BECAUSE OF THE HIGH PRECISION...
...SO THE DEVELOPMENT STAFF CAN'T DO ANY REAL TESTING.
Looking at the graphics inside, I can't even stay on my feet.
...I get dizzy just thinking about it...
I CAN'T EVEN GET THE DATA I NEED TO ADJUST...
...THE DEPTH OF THE CONNECTION WITH THE BRAIN TO SUIT THE USER...
I'D SERIOUSLY LOVE IT IF YOU COULD HELP.
SURE.
OF COURSE. YOU'RE PAYING ME, SO I'LL DO WHATEVER YOU WANT... EXCEPT....
...BEFORE I DO, I WANT TO MAKE SURE OF ONE THING.
IT'S NOT ACTUALLY DANGEROUS... RIGHT?

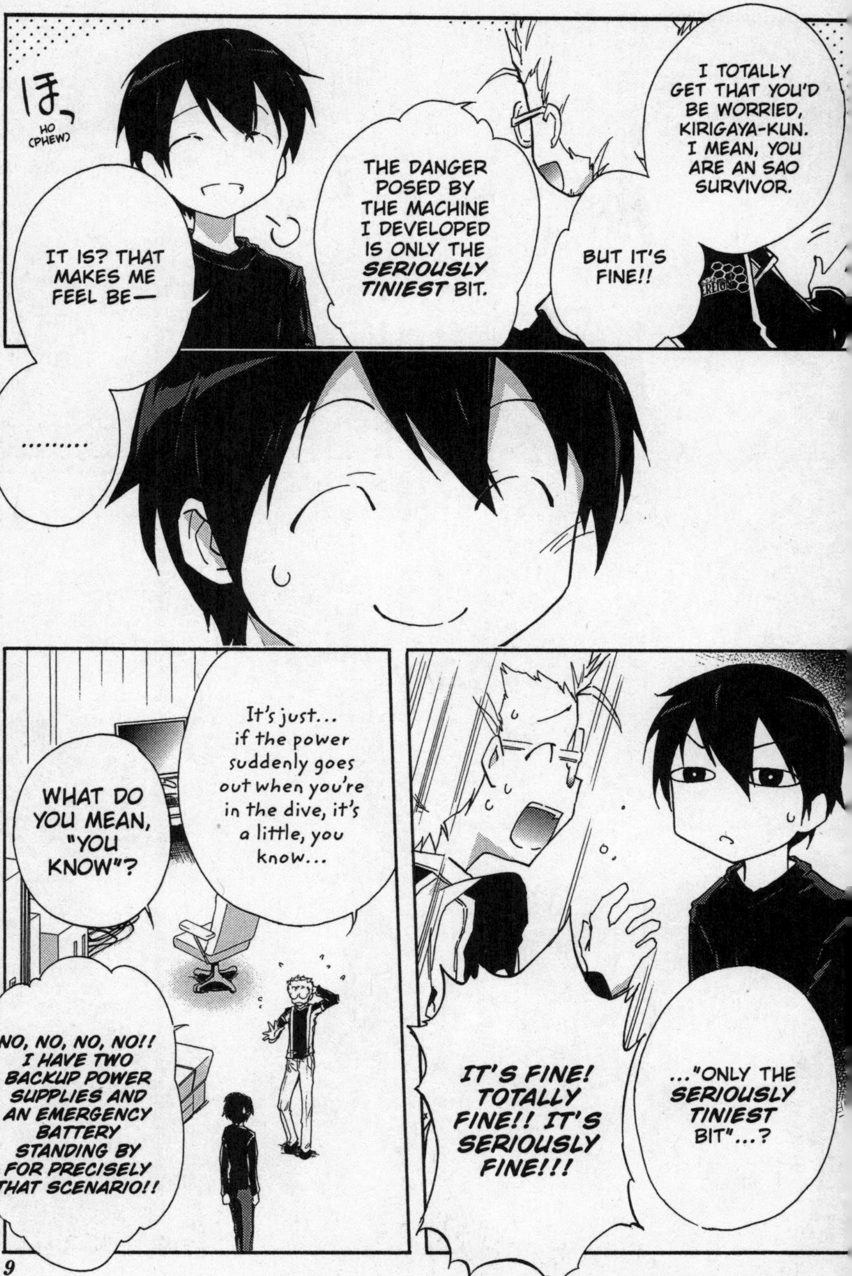
I TOTALLY GET THAT YOU'D BE WORRIED, KIRIGAYA-KUN. I MEAN, YOU ARE AN SAO SURVIVOR.
BUT IT'S FINE!!
THE DANGER POSED BY THE MACHINE I DEVELOPED IS ONLY THE SERIOUSLY TINIEST BIT.
ほっ
HO (PHEW)
IT IS? THAT MAKES ME FEEL BE—
....
..."ONLY THE SERIOUSLY TINIEST BIT"...?
IT'S FINE! TOTALLY FINE!! IT'S SERIOUSLY FINE!!!
It's just... if the power suddenly goes out when you're in the dive, it's a little, you know...
WHAT DO YOU MEAN, "YOU KNOW"?
NO, NO, NO, NO!! I HAVE TWO BACKUP POWER SUPPLIES AND AN EMERGENCY BATTERY STANDING BY FOR PRECISELY THAT SCENARIO!!

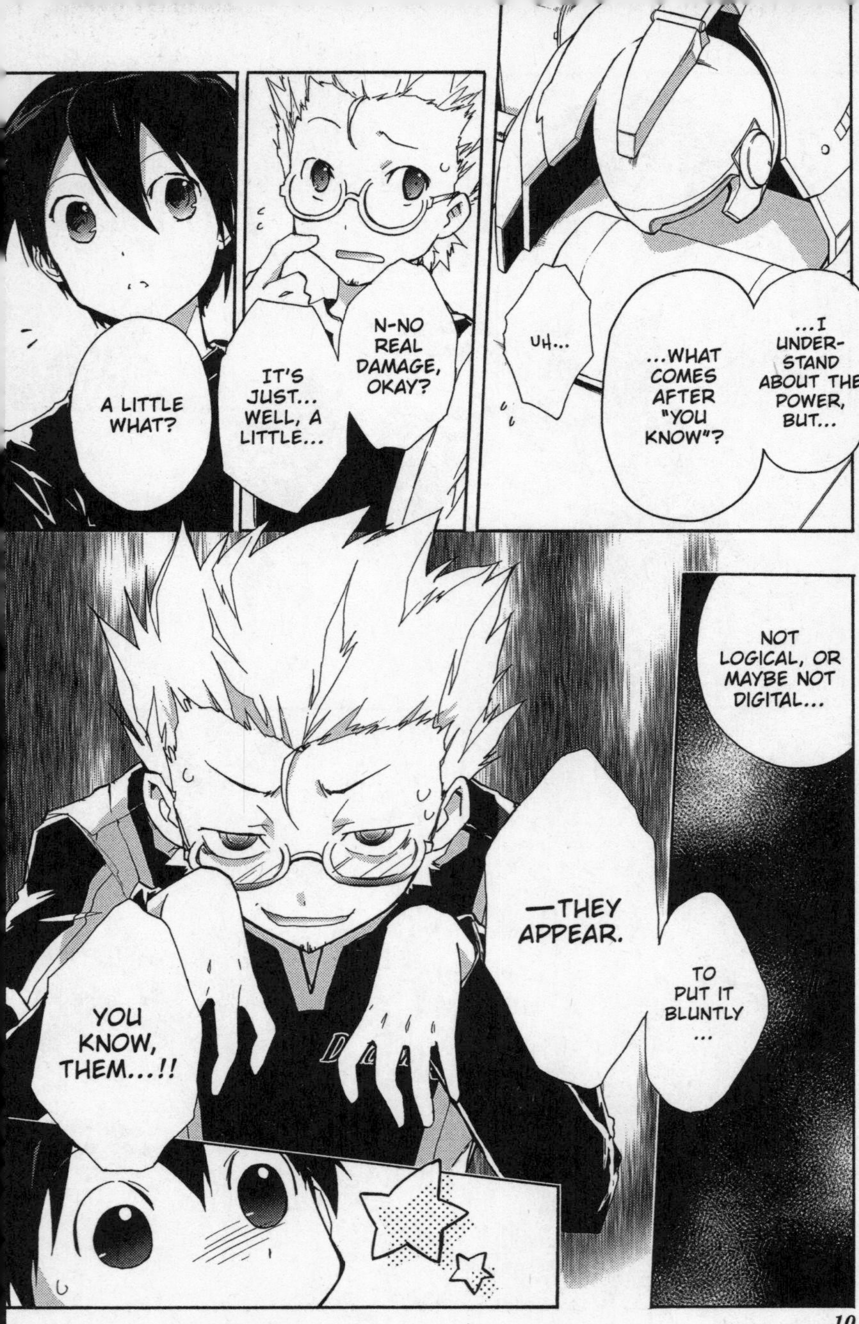
...I UNDER-STAND ABOUT THE POWER, BUT...
...WHAT COMES AFTER "YOU KNOW"?
UH...
N-NO REAL DAMAGE, OKAY?
IT'S JUST... WELL, A LITTLE...
A LITTLE WHAT?
NOT LOGICAL, OR MAYBE NOT DIGITAL...
TO PUT IT BLUNTLY ...
—THEY APPEAR.
YOU KNOW, THEM...!!

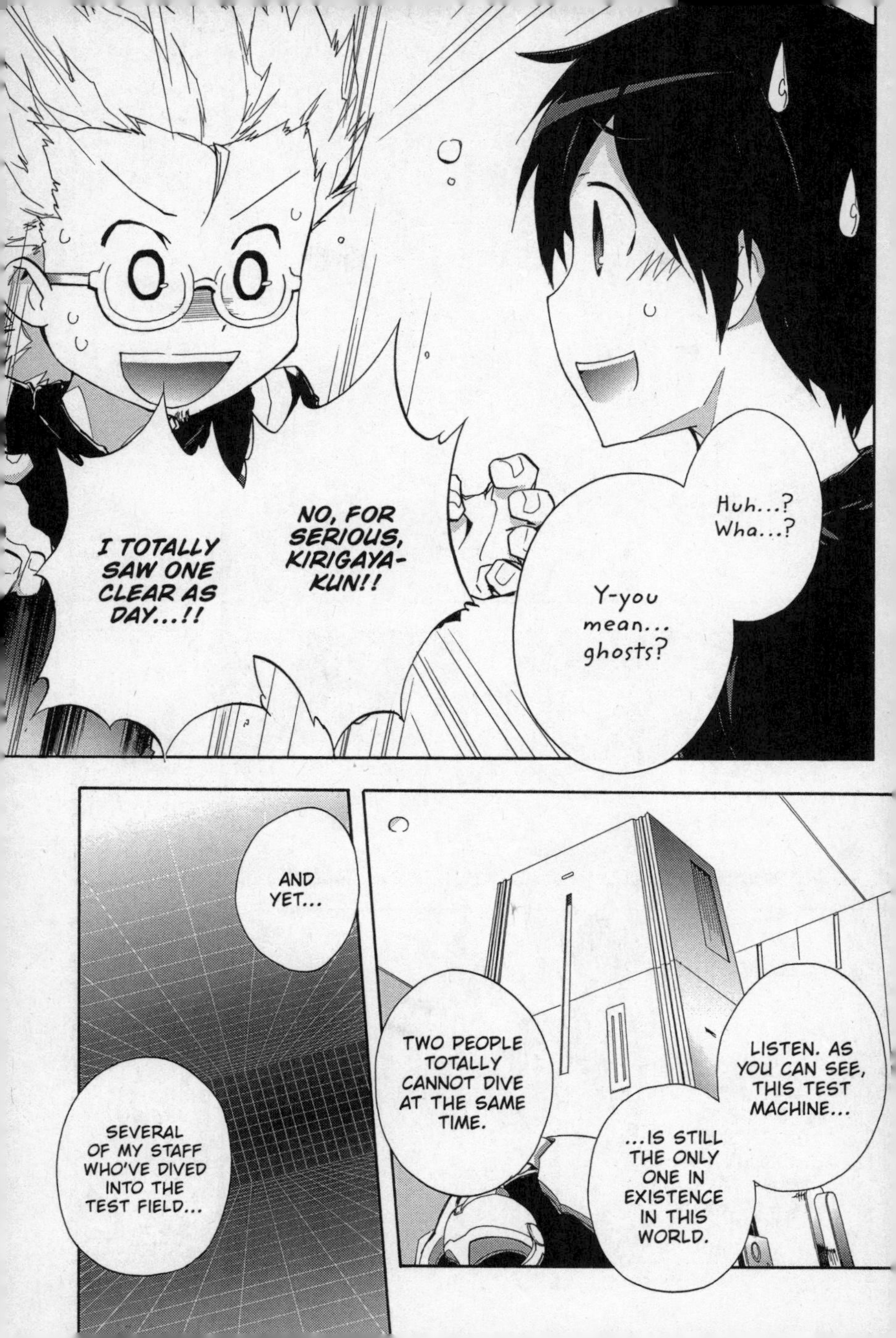
Huh...? Wha...?
Y-you mean... ghosts?
NO, FOR SERIOUS, KIRIGAYA-KUN!!
I TOTALLY SAW ONE CLEAR AS DAY...!!
LISTEN. AS YOU CAN SEE, THIS TEST MACHINE...
...IS STILL THE ONLY ONE IN EXISTENCE IN THIS WORLD.
TWO PEOPLE TOTALLY CANNOT DIVE AT THE SAME TIME.
AND YET...
SEVERAL OF MY STAFF WHO'VE DIVED INTO THE TEST FIELD...

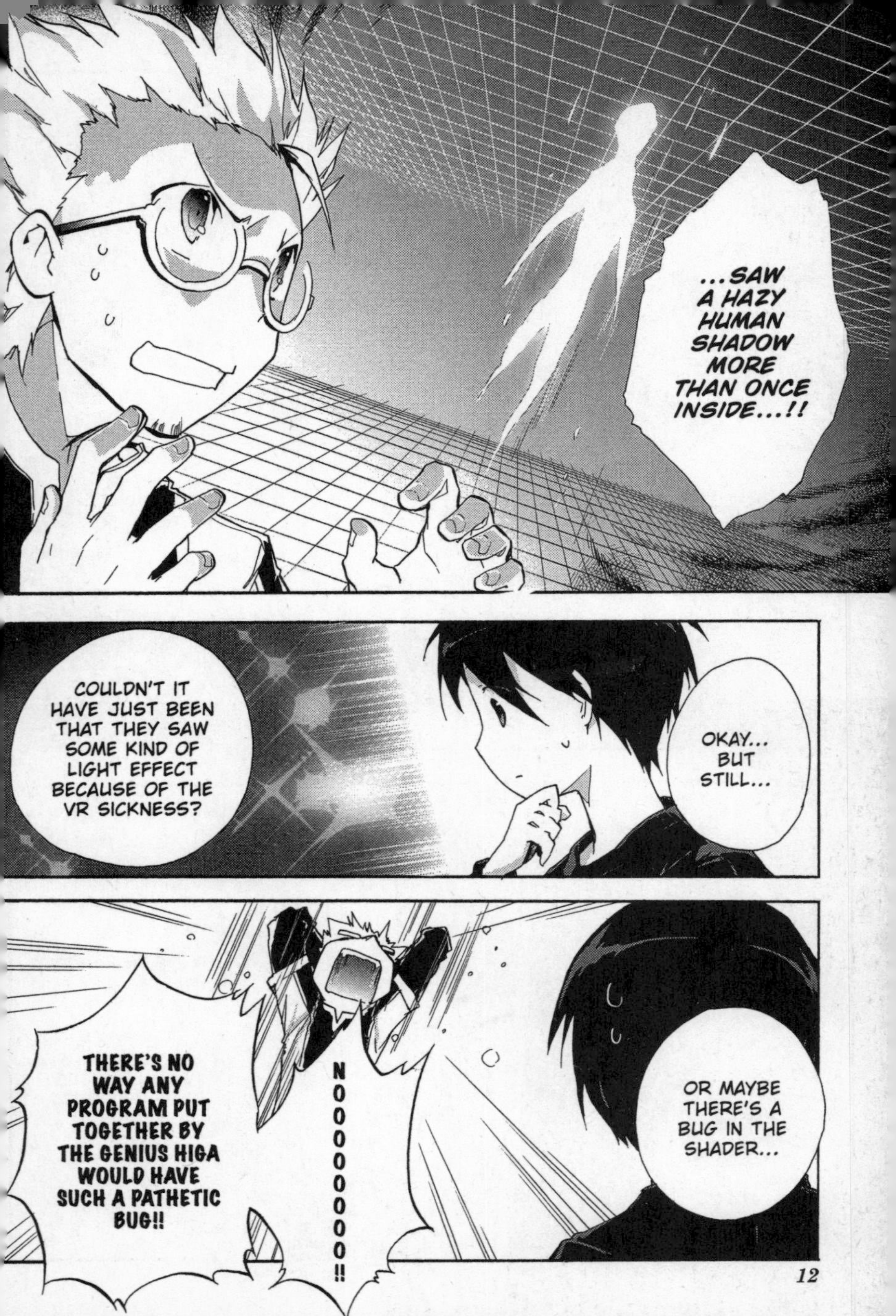
...SAW A HAZY HUMAN SHADOW MORE THAN ONCE INSIDE...!!
OKAY... BUT STILL...
COULDN'T IT HAVE JUST BEEN THAT THEY SAW SOME KIND OF LIGHT EFFECT BECAUSE OF THE VR SICKNESS?
OR MAYBE THERE'S A BUG IN THE SHADER...
NOOOOOOOOOO!!
THERE'S NO WAY ANY PROGRAM PUT TOGETHER BY THE GENIUS HIGA WOULD HAVE SUCH A PATHETIC BUG!!

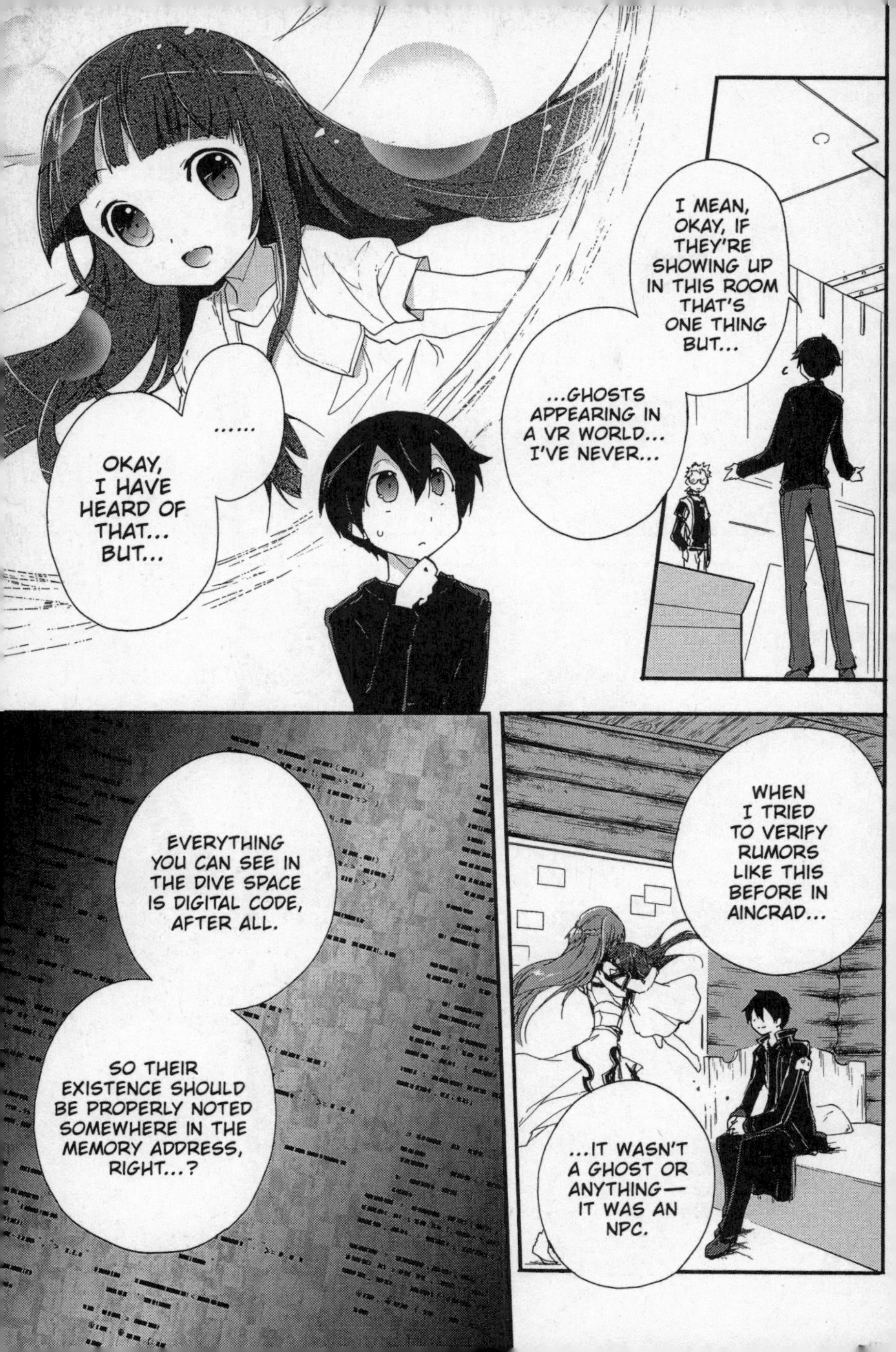
I MEAN, OKAY, IF THEY'RE SHOWING UP IN THIS ROOM THAT'S ONE THING BUT...
...GHOSTS APPEARING IN A VR WORLD... I'VE NEVER...
......
OKAY, I HAVE HEARD OF THAT... BUT...
WHEN I TRIED TO VERIFY RUMORS LIKE THIS BEFORE IN AINCRAD...
...IT WASN'T A GHOST OR ANYTHING— IT WAS AN NPC.
EVERYTHING YOU CAN SEE IN THE DIVE SPACE IS DIGITAL CODE, AFTER ALL.
SO THEIR EXISTENCE SHOULD BE PROPERLY NOTED SOMEWHERE IN THE MEMORY ADDRESS, RIGHT...?

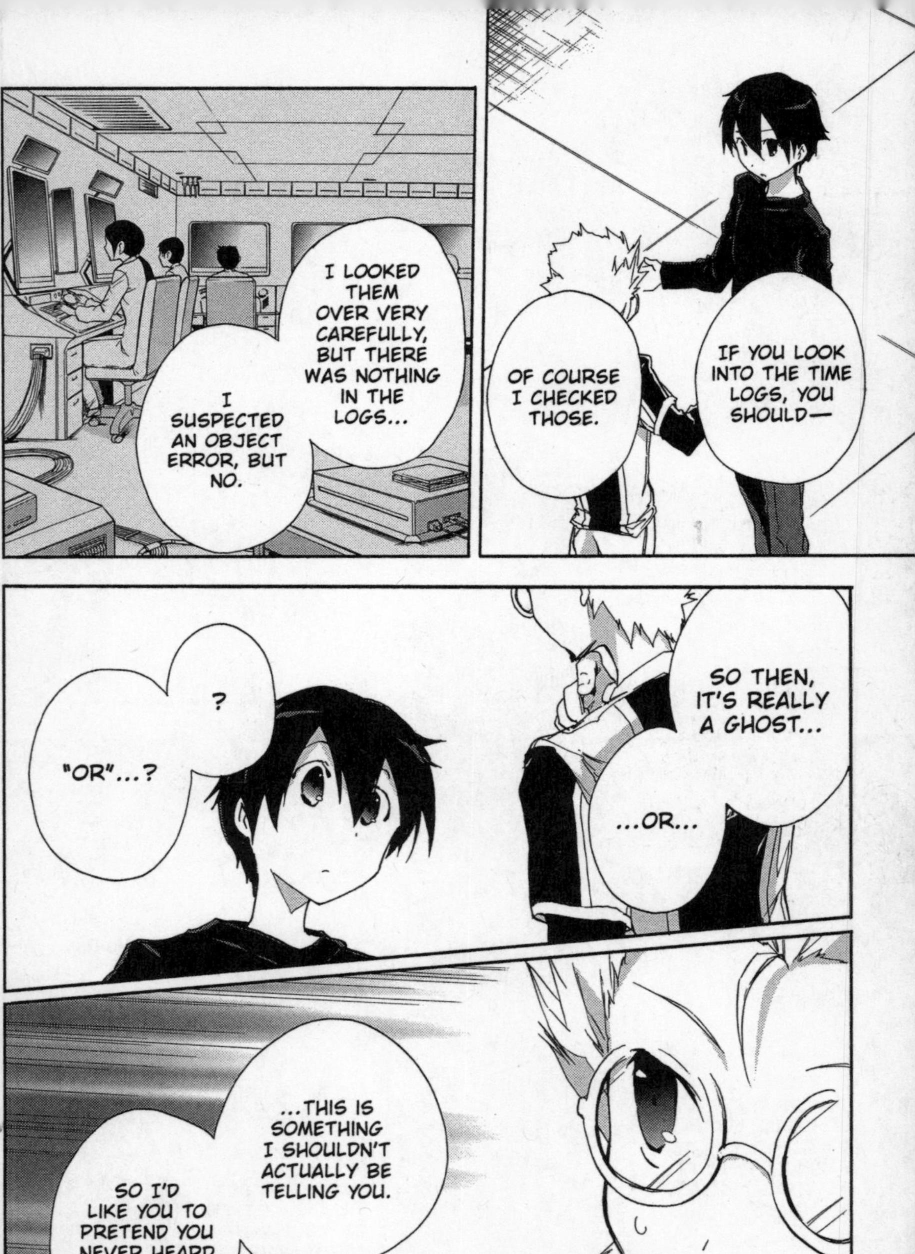
IF YOU LOOK INTO THE TIME LOGS, YOU SHOULD—
OF COURSE I CHECKED THOSE.
I LOOKED THEM OVER VERY CAREFULLY, BUT THERE WAS NOTHING IN THE LOGS...
I SUSPECTED AN OBJECT ERROR, BUT NO.
SO THEN, IT'S REALLY A GHOST...
...OR...
?
"OR"...?
...THIS IS SOMETHING I SHOULDN'T ACTUALLY BE TELLING YOU.
SO I'D LIKE YOU TO PRETEND YOU NEVER HEARD IT.

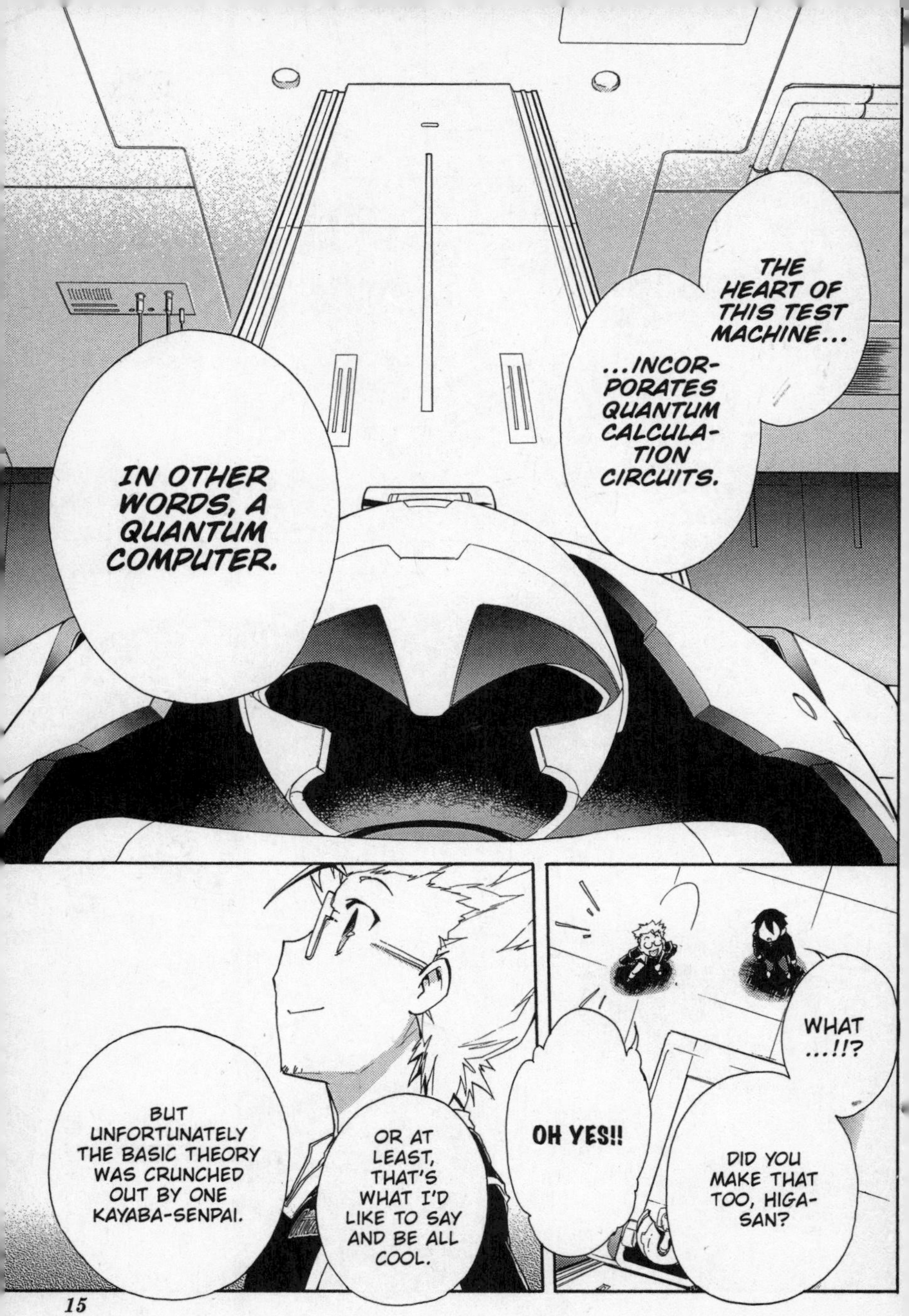
THE HEART OF THIS TEST MACHINE...
...INCORPORATES QUANTUM CALCULATION CIRCUITS.
IN OTHER WORDS, A QUANTUM COMPUTER.
WHAT ...!!?
DID YOU MAKE THAT TOO, HIGA-SAN?
OH YES!!
OR AT LEAST, THAT'S WHAT I'D LIKE TO SAY AND BE ALL COOL.
BUT UNFORTUNATELY THE BASIC THEORY WAS CRUNCHED OUT BY ONE KAYABA-SENPAI.

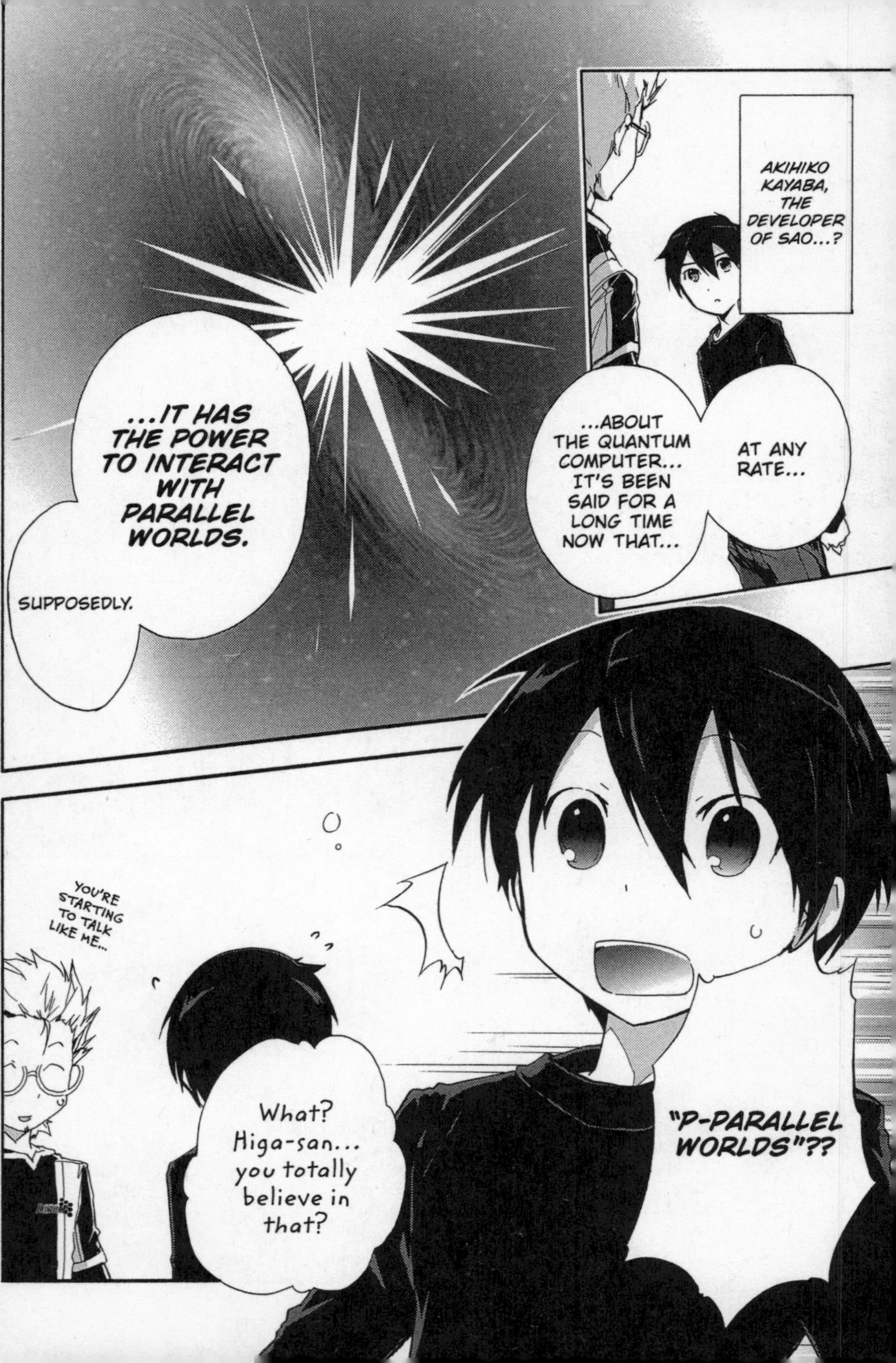
AKIHIKO KAYABA, THE DEVELOPER OF SAO...?
AT ANY RATE...
...ABOUT THE QUANTUM COMPUTER... IT'S BEEN SAID FOR A LONG TIME NOW THAT...
...IT HAS THE POWER TO INTERACT WITH PARALLEL WORLDS.
SUPPOSEDLY.
"P-PARALLEL WORLDS"??
What? Higa-san... you totally believe in that?
YOU'RE STARTING TO TALK LIKE ME...

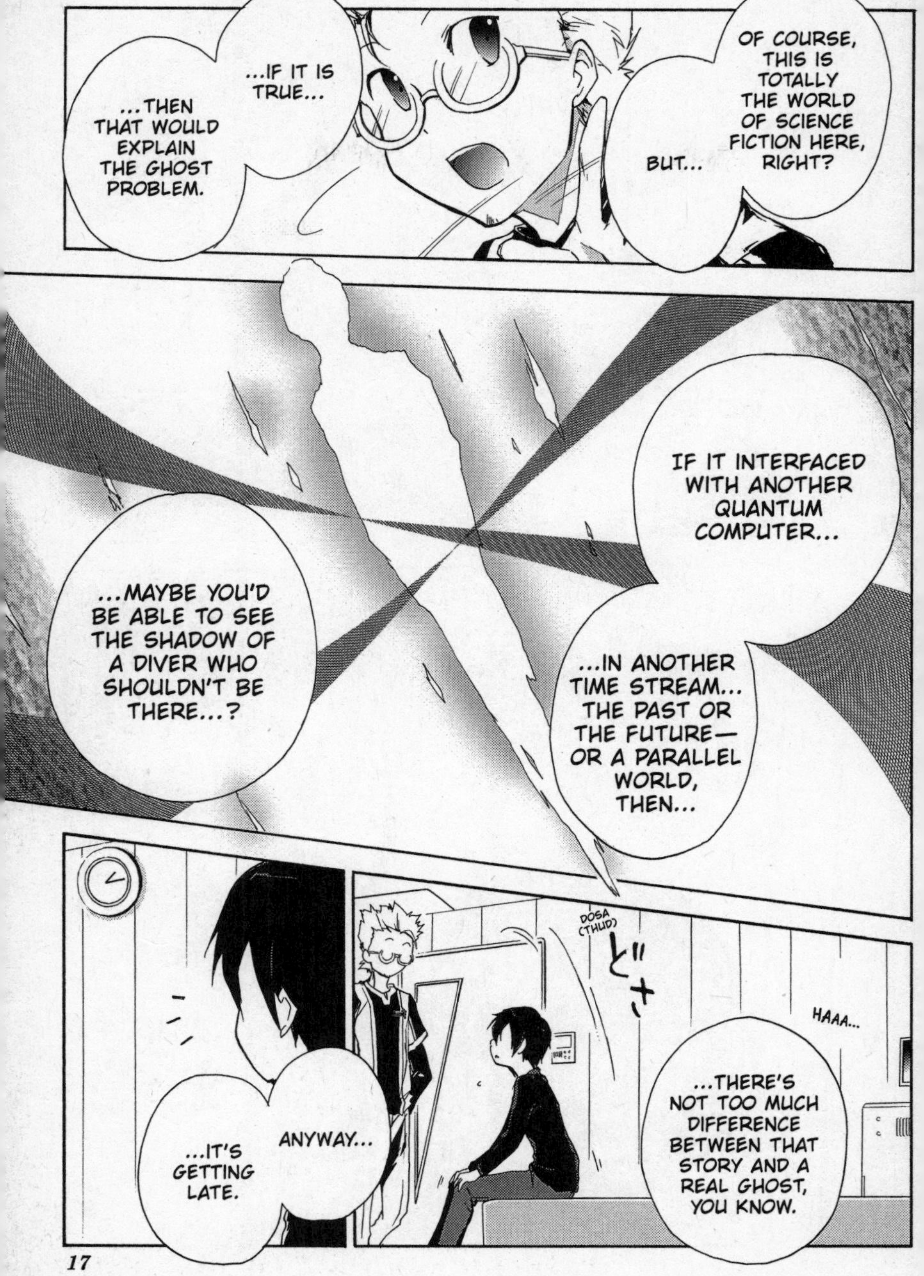
OF COURSE, THIS IS TOTALLY THE WORLD OF SCIENCE FICTION HERE, RIGHT?
BUT...
...IF IT IS TRUE...
...THEN THAT WOULD EXPLAIN THE GHOST PROBLEM.
IF IT INTERFACED WITH ANOTHER QUANTUM COMPUTER...
...IN ANOTHER TIME STREAM... THE PAST OR THE FUTURE— OR A PARALLEL WORLD, THEN...
...MAYBE YOU'D BE ABLE TO SEE THE SHADOW OF A DIVER WHO SHOULDN'T BE THERE...?
HAAA...
...THERE'S NOT TOO MUCH DIFFERENCE BETWEEN THAT STORY AND A REAL GHOST, YOU KNOW.
DOSA (THUD)
どさ
ANYWAY...
...IT'S GETTING LATE.

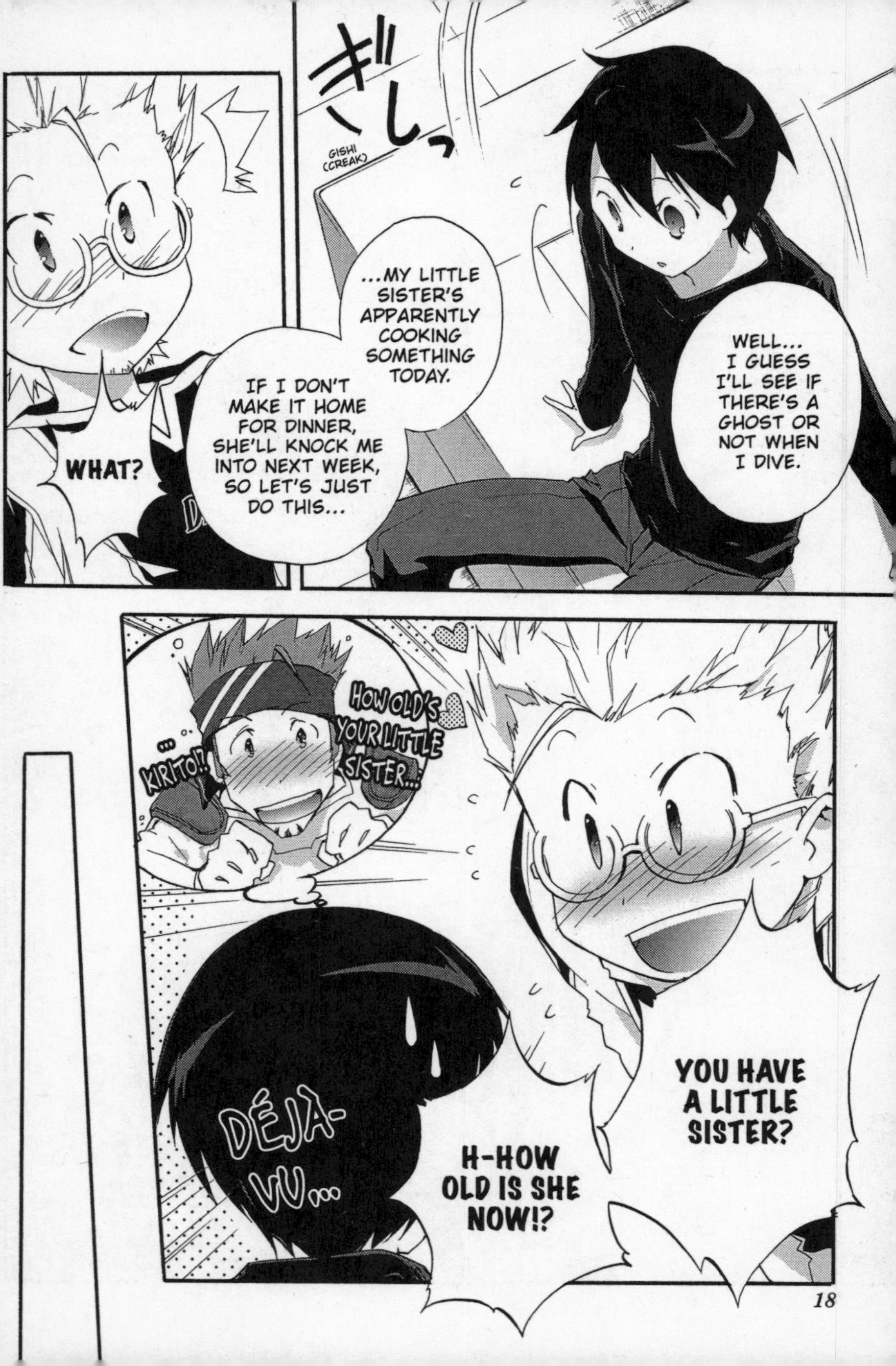
ぎしっ
GISHI (CREAK)
WELL... I GUESS I'LL SEE IF THERE'S A GHOST OR NOT WHEN I DIVE.
...MY LITTLE SISTER'S APPARENTLY COOKING SOMETHING TODAY.
IF I DON'T MAKE IT HOME FOR DINNER, SHE'LL KNOCK ME INTO NEXT WEEK, SO LET'S JUST DO THIS...
WHAT?
YOU HAVE A LITTLE SISTER?
H-HOW OLD IS SHE NOW!?
HOW OLD'S YOUR LITTLE SISTER...
...KIRITO!?
DÉJÀ-VU...

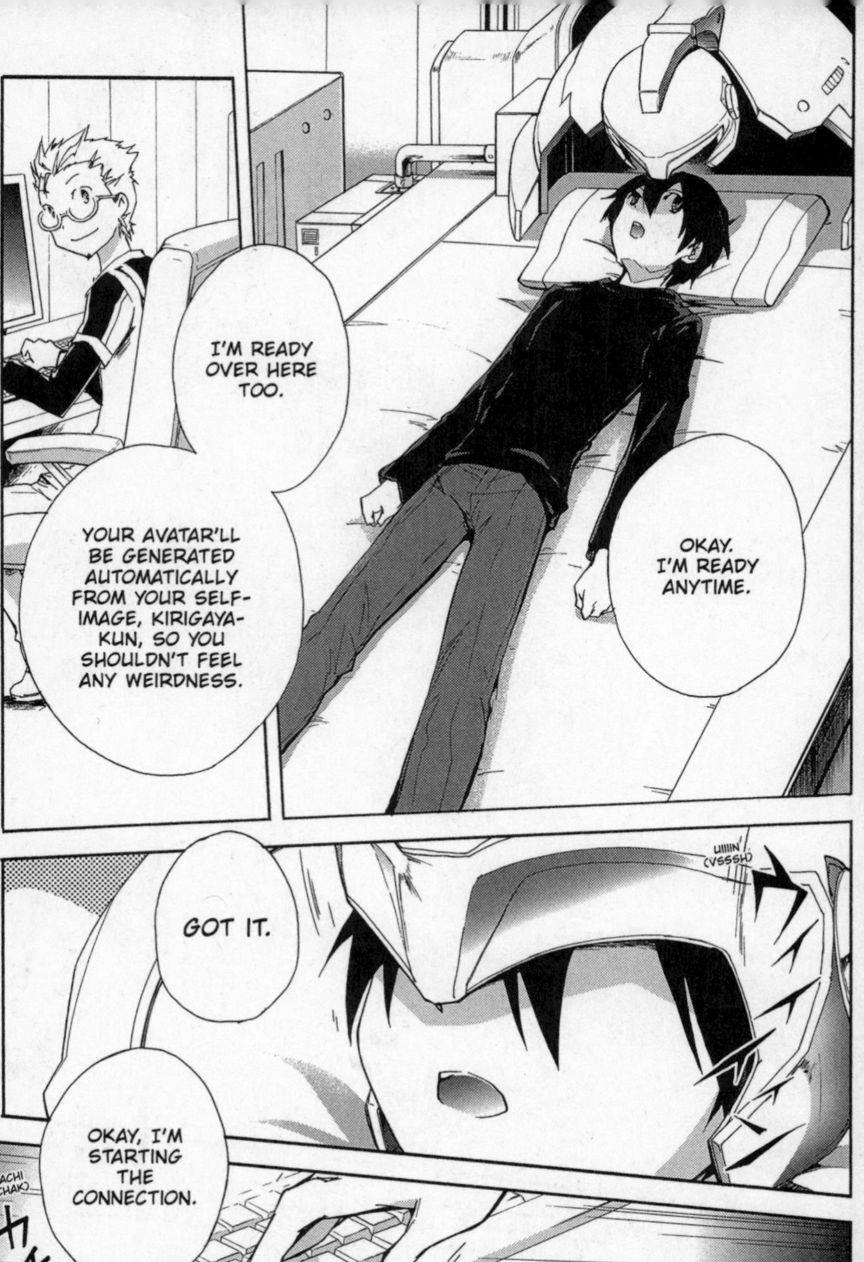
I'M READY OVER HERE TOO.
YOUR AVATAR'LL BE GENERATED AUTOMATICALLY FROM YOUR SELF-IMAGE, KIRIGAYA-KUN, SO YOU SHOULDN'T FEEL ANY WEIRDNESS.
OKAY. I'M READY ANYTIME.
UIIIN (VSSSH)
GOT IT.
OKAY, I'M STARTING THE CONNECTION.
KACHI (CHAK)
カチッ

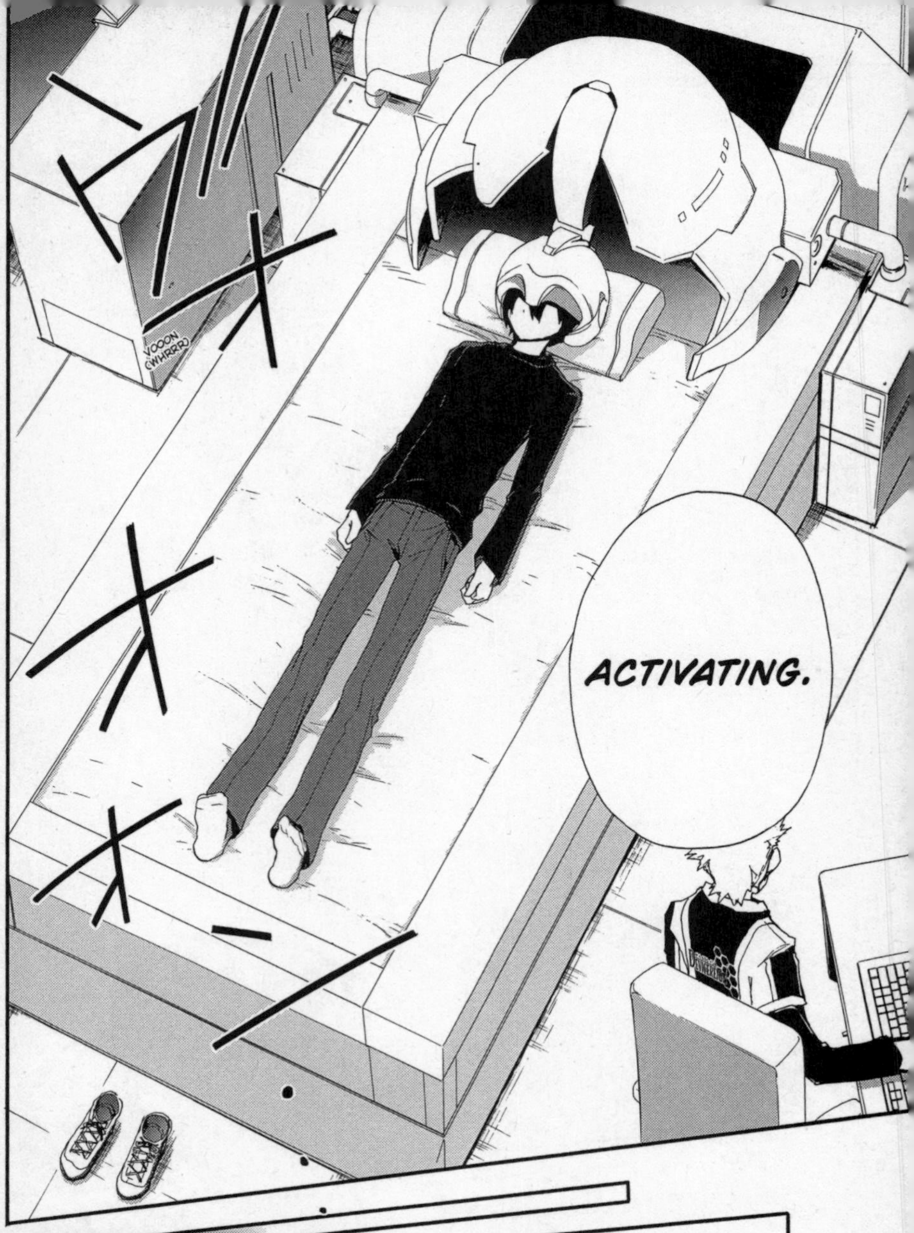
ACTIVATING.
VOOON
(WHRRR)

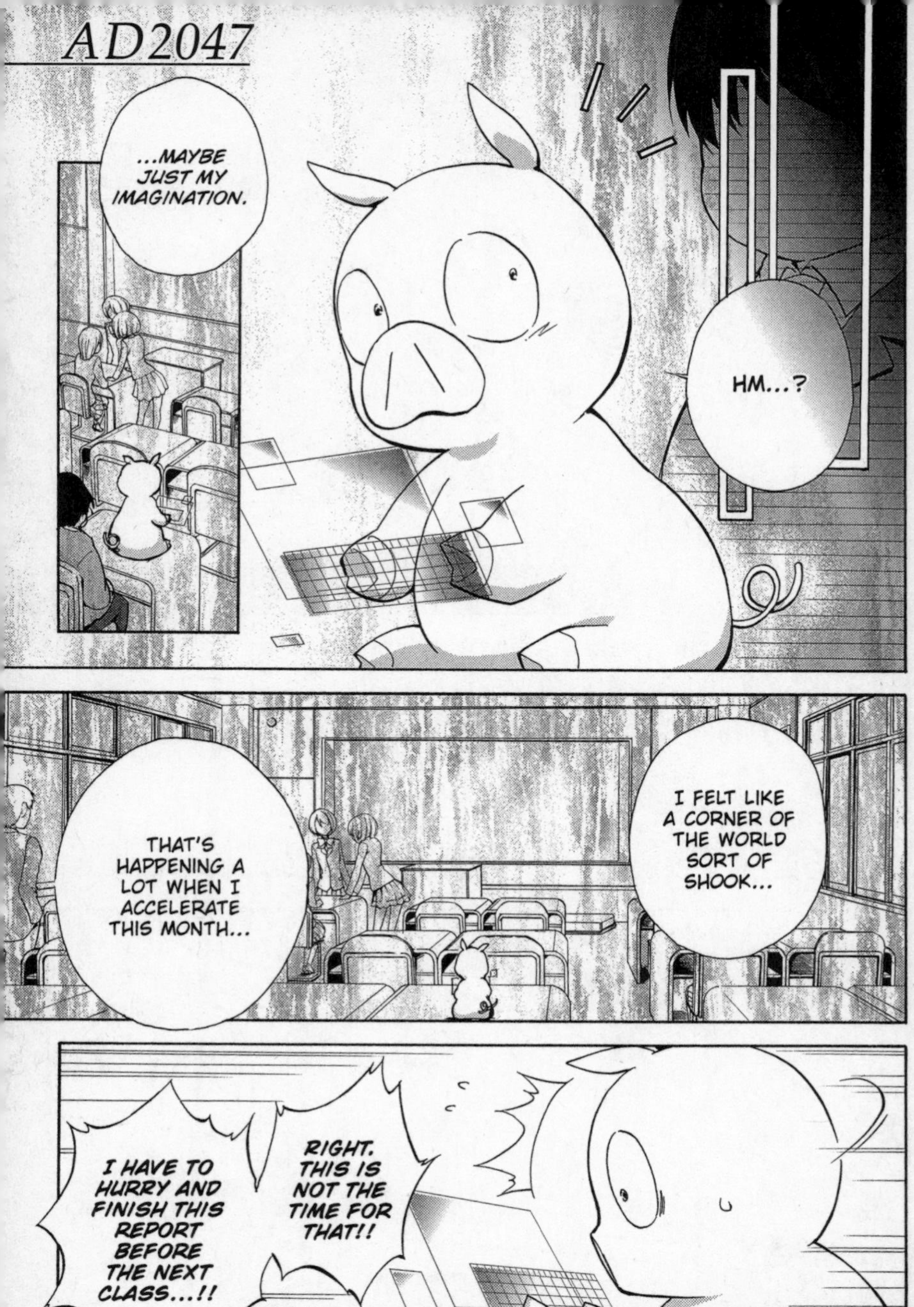
HM...?
...MAYBE JUST MY IMAGINATION.
I FELT LIKE A CORNER OF THE WORLD SORT OF SHOOK...
THAT'S HAPPENING A LOT WHEN I ACCELERATE THIS MONTH...
RIGHT. THIS IS NOT THE TIME FOR THAT!!
I HAVE TO HURRY AND FINISH THIS REPORT BEFORE THE NEXT CLASS...!!

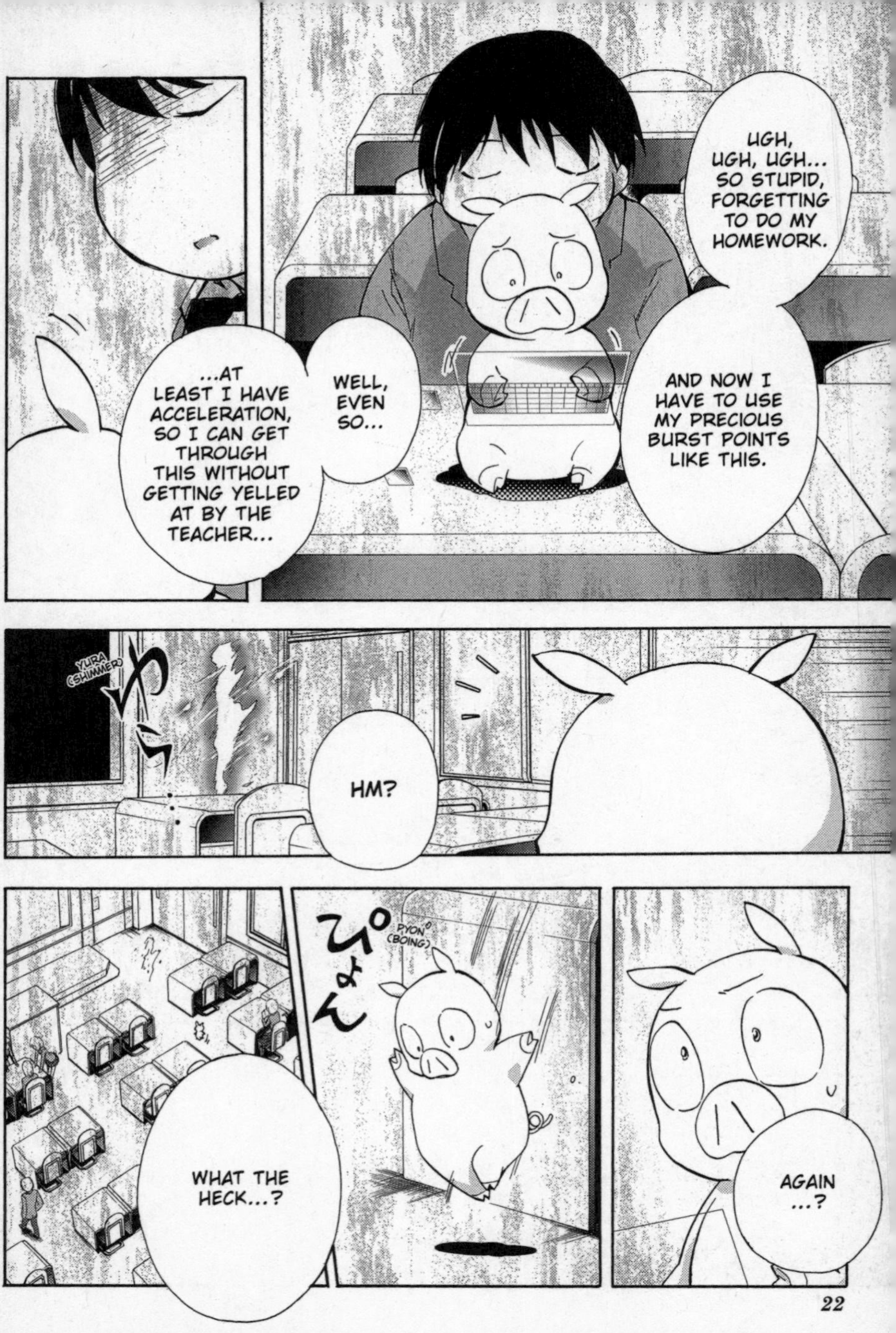
UGH, UGH, UGH... SO STUPID, FORGETTING TO DO MY HOMEWORK.
AND NOW I HAVE TO USE MY PRECIOUS BURST POINTS LIKE THIS.
WELL, EVEN SO...
...AT LEAST I HAVE ACCELERATION, SO I CAN GET THROUGH THIS WITHOUT GETTING YELLED AT BY THE TEACHER...
HM?
YURA (SHIMMER)
AGAIN ...?
PYON (BOING)
WHAT THE HECK...?

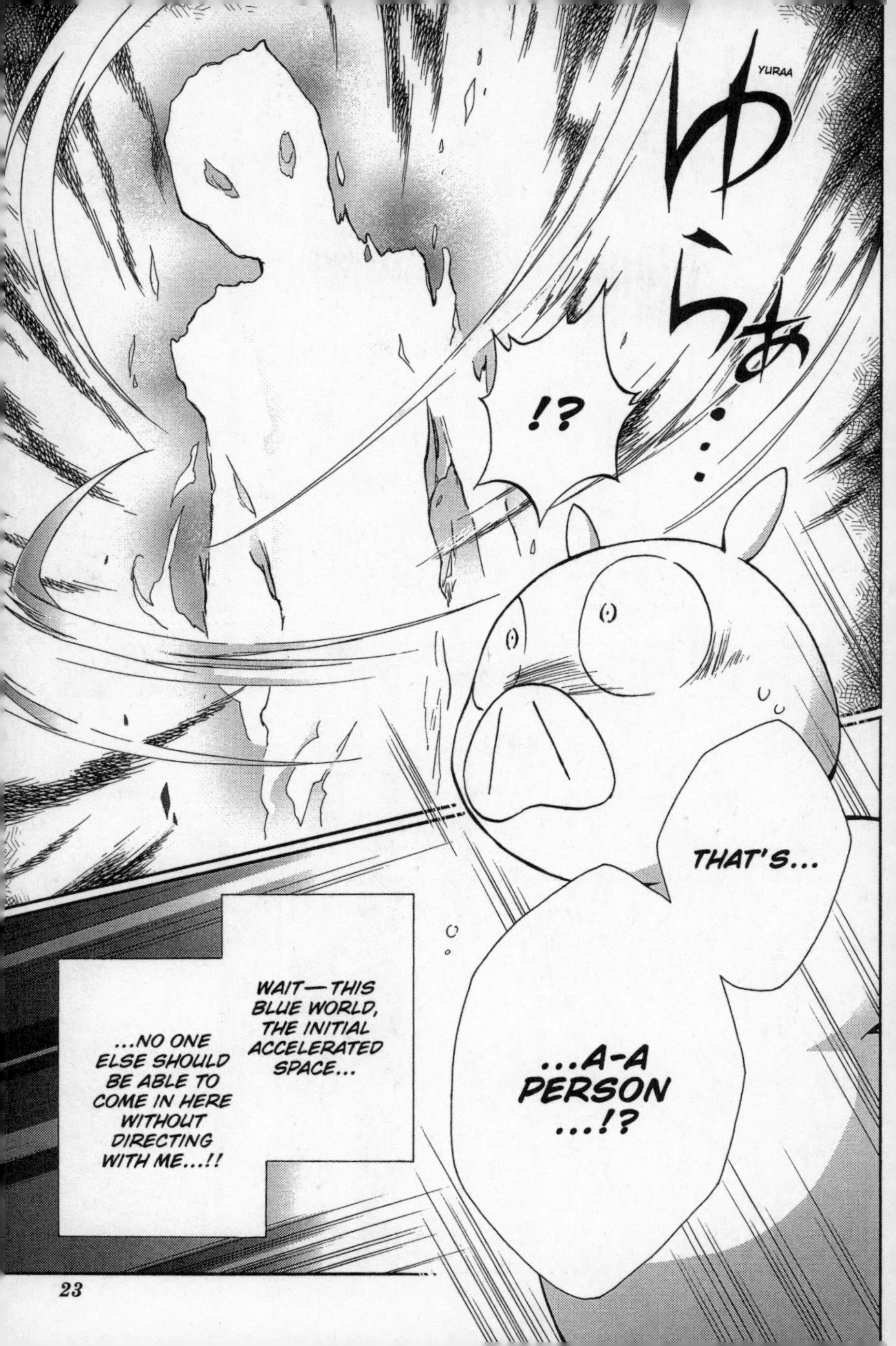
ゆらぁ…
YURAA
!?
THAT'S...
...A-A PERSON ...!?
WAIT—THIS BLUE WORLD, THE INITIAL ACCELERATED SPACE...
...NO ONE ELSE SHOULD BE ABLE TO COME IN HERE WITHOUT DIRECTING WITH ME...!!

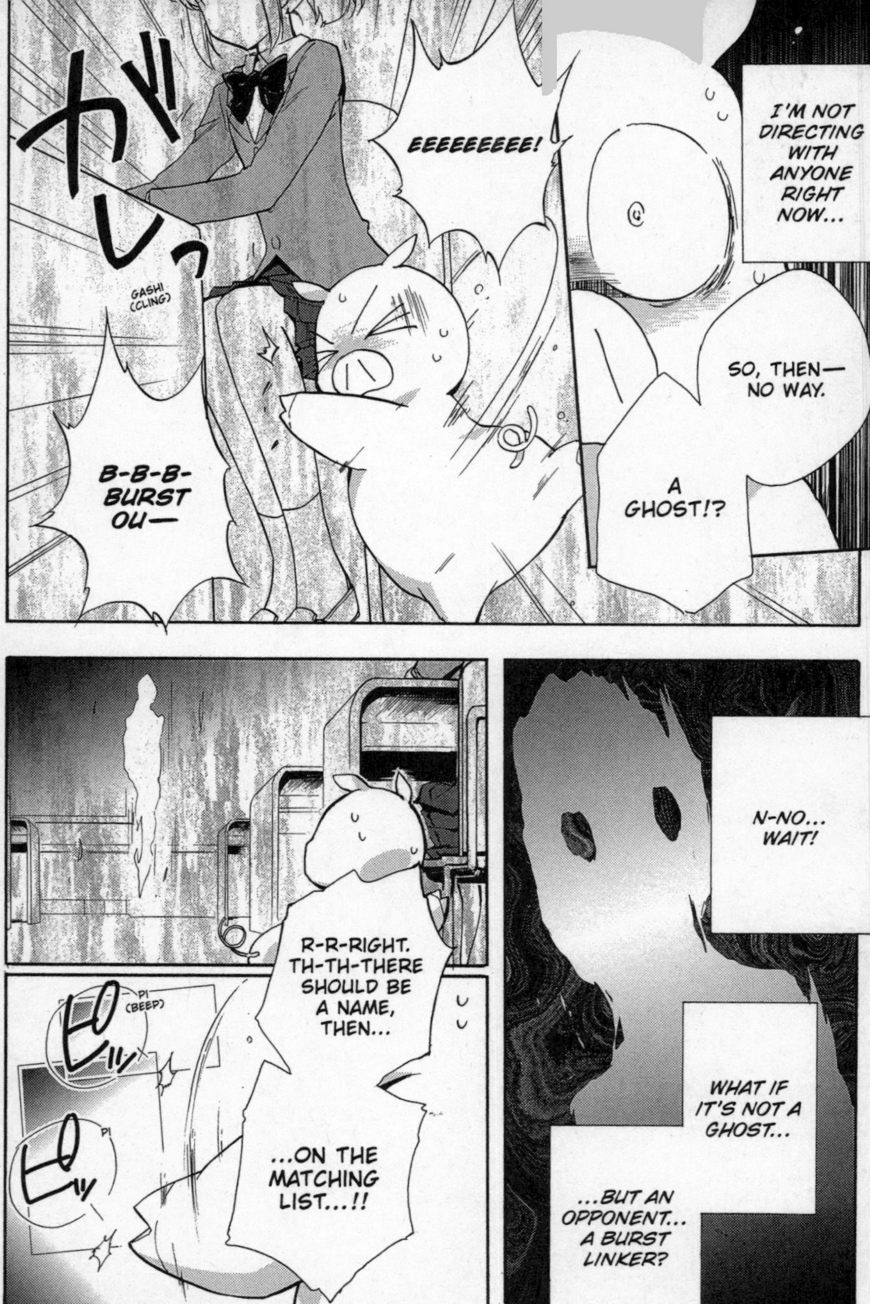
I'M NOT DIRECTING WITH ANYONE RIGHT NOW...
SO, THEN— NO WAY.
A GHOST!?
EEEEEEEEE!
GASHI (CLING)
B-B-B-BURST OU—
N-NO... WAIT!
WHAT IF IT'S NOT A GHOST...
...BUT AN OPPONENT... A BURST LINKER?
R-R-RIGHT. TH-TH-THERE SHOULD BE A NAME, THEN...
...ON THE MATCHING LIST...!!
PI (BEEP)
PI

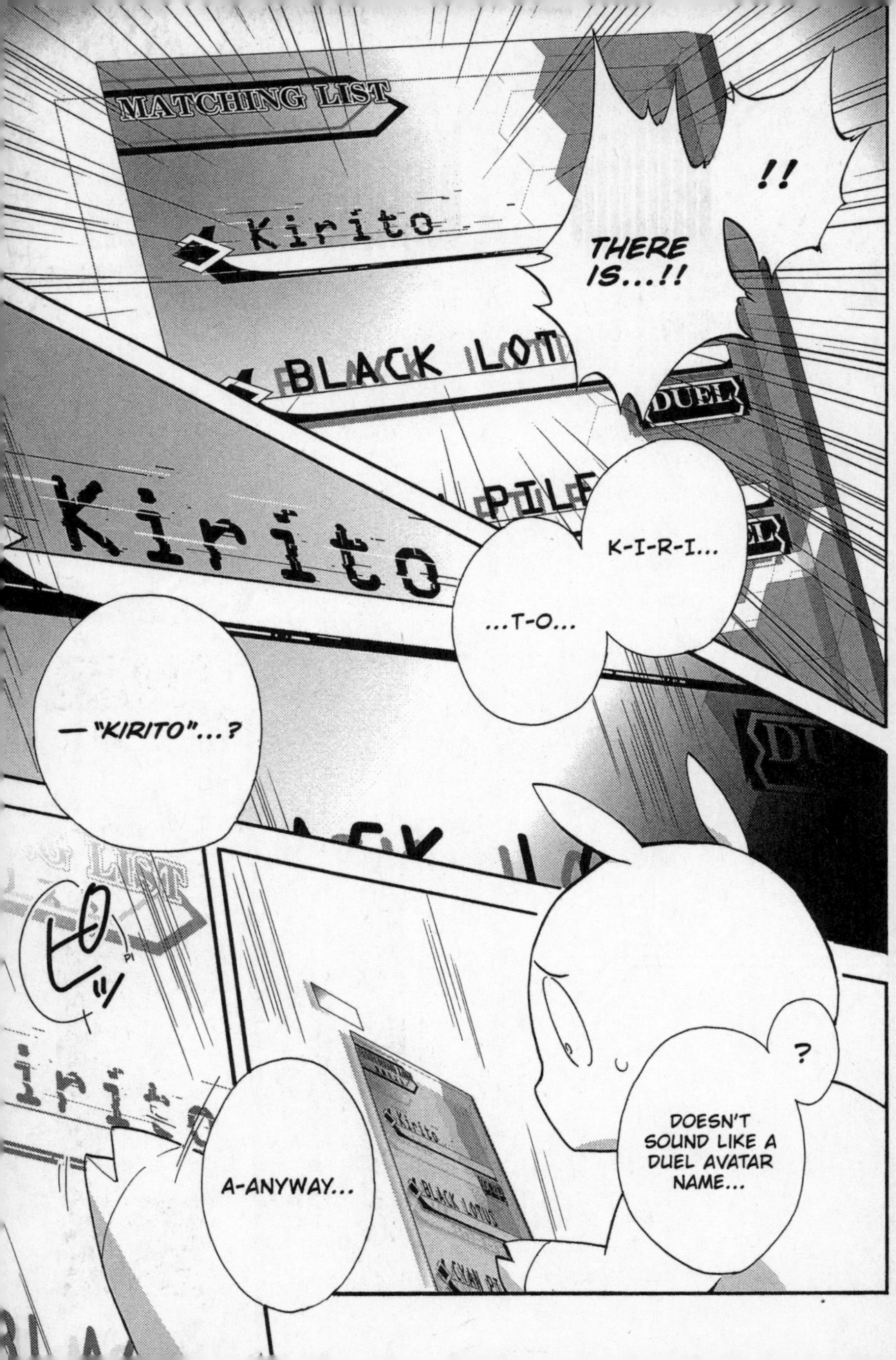
!!
THERE IS...!!
MATCHING LIST
Kirito
BLACK LOT
DUEL
PILE
K-I-R-I...
...T-O...
—"KIRITO"...?
PI
?
DOESN'T SOUND LIKE A DUEL AVATAR NAME...
A-ANYWAY...

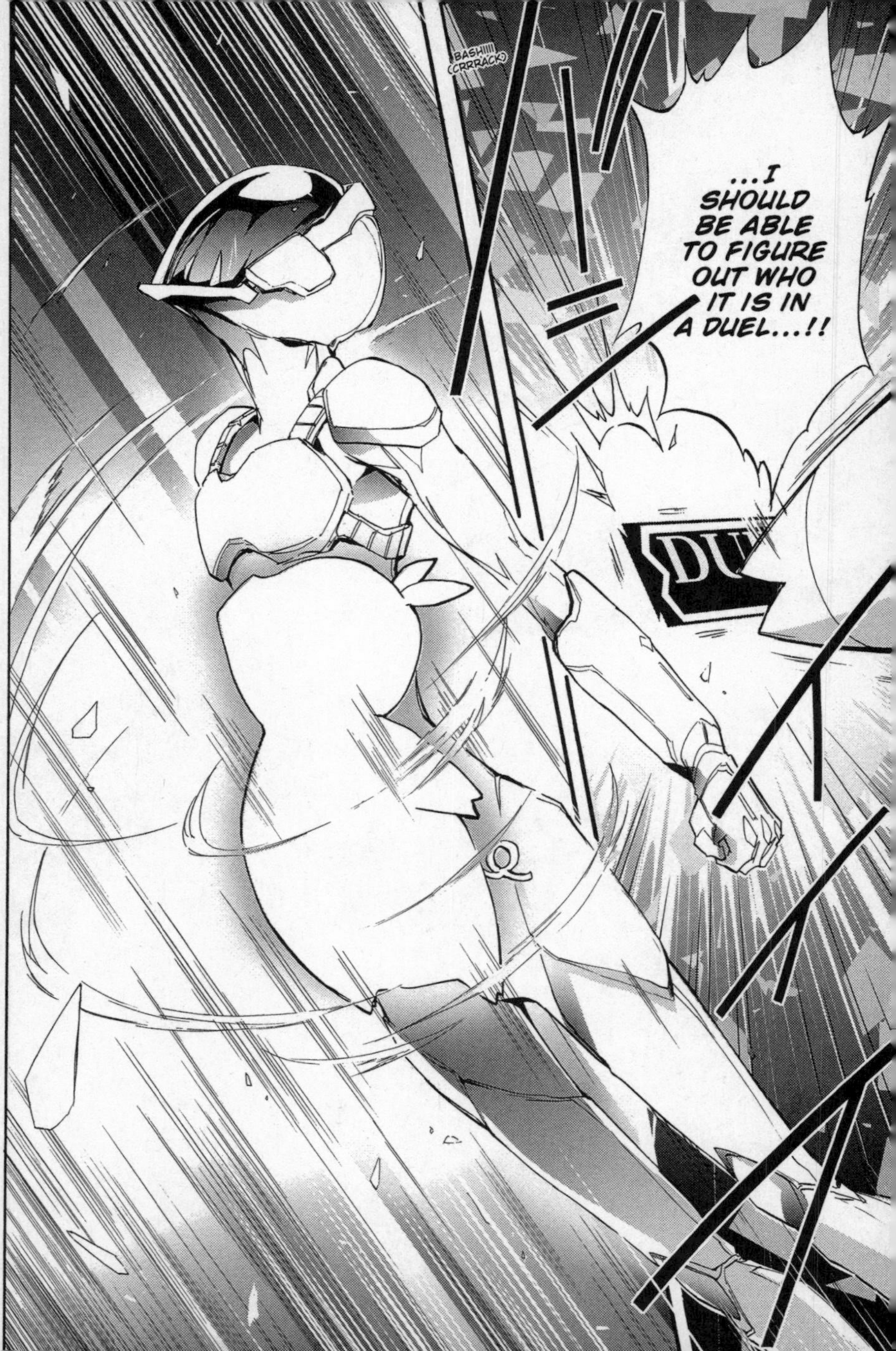
BASH!!!!! (CRRRACK)
...I SHOULD BE ABLE TO FIGURE OUT WHO IT IS IN A DUEL...!!
DU

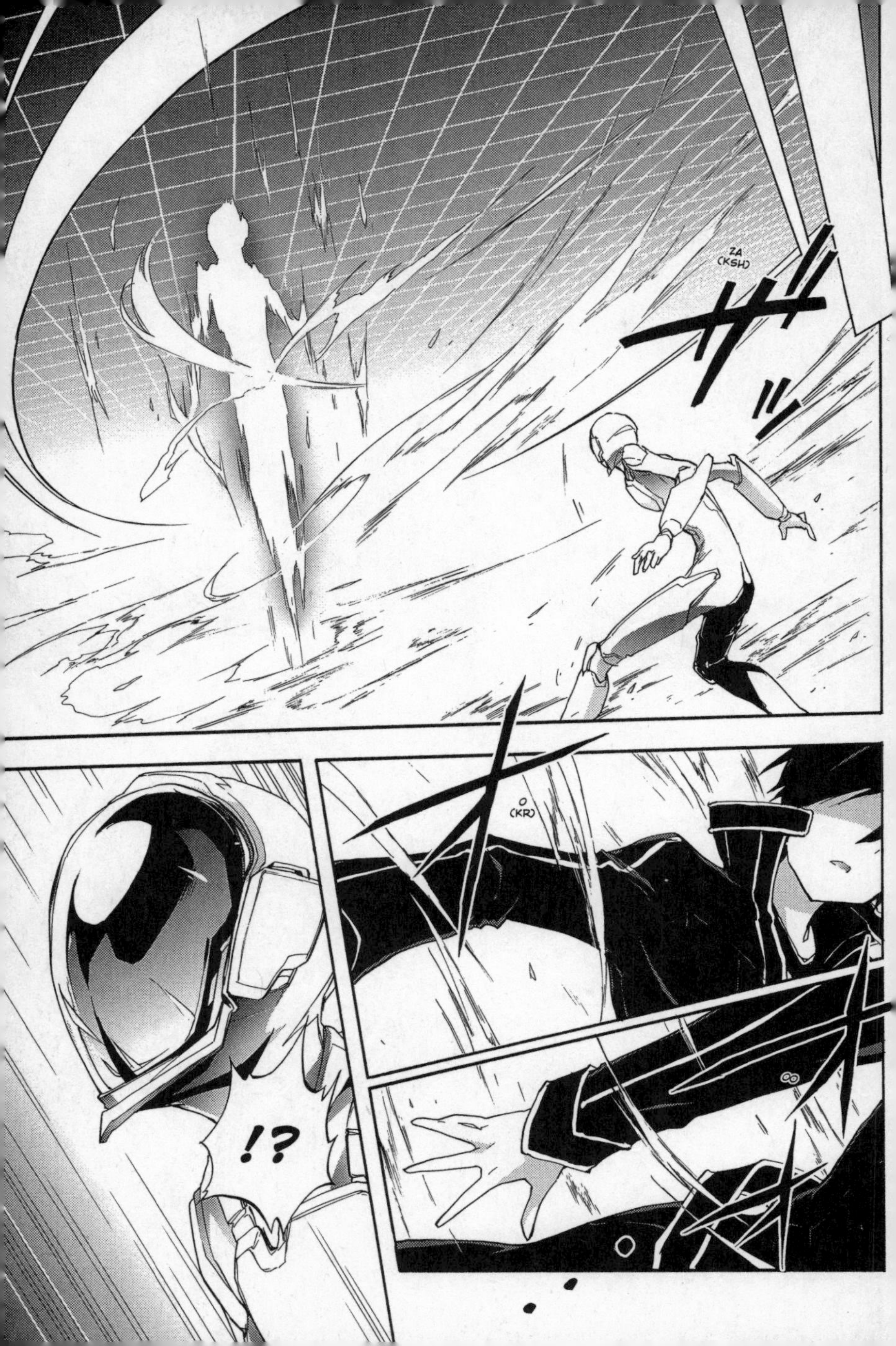
ZA
(KSH)
O
(KR)
!?

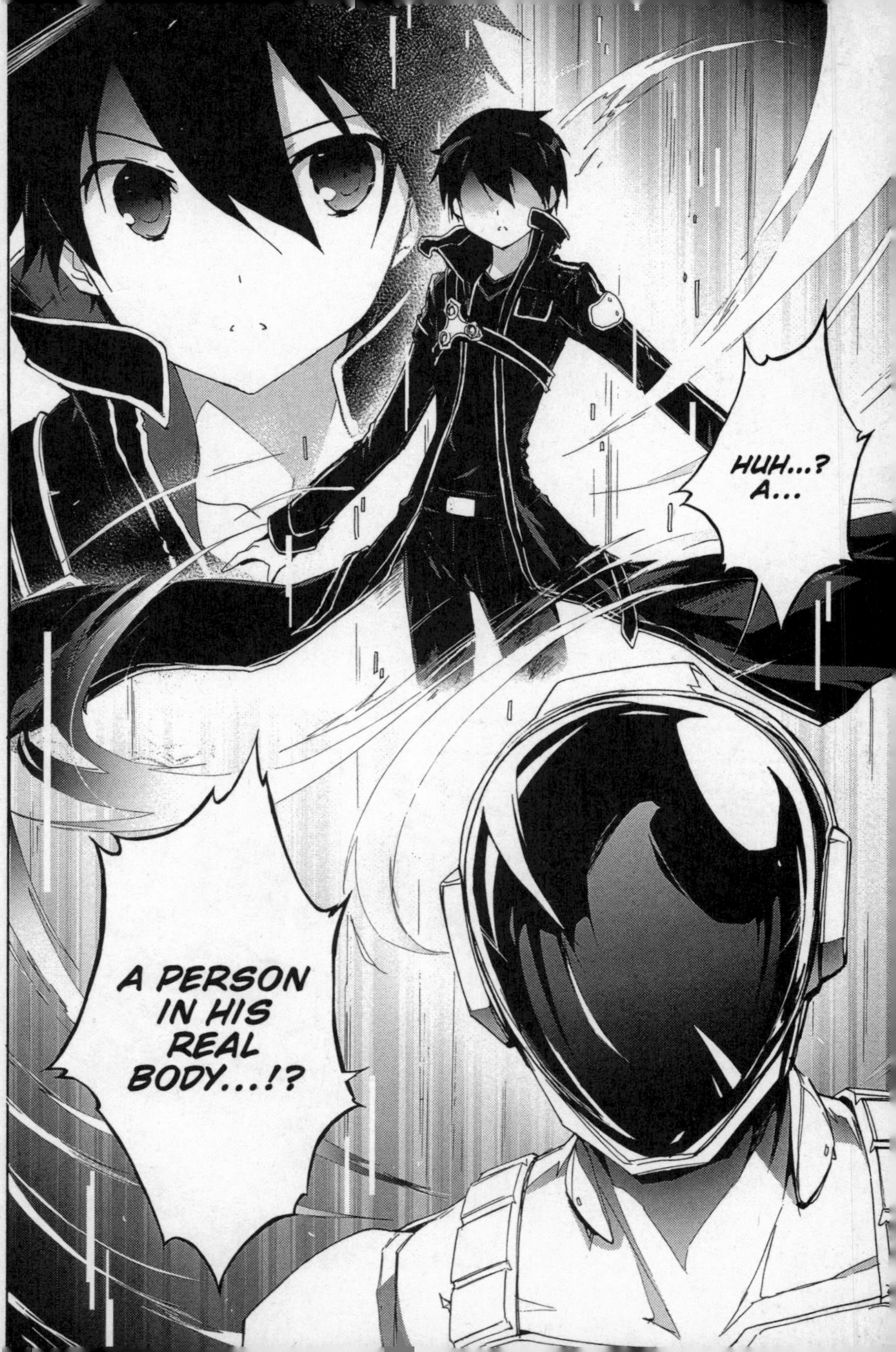
HUH...? A...
A PERSON IN HIS REAL BODY...!?

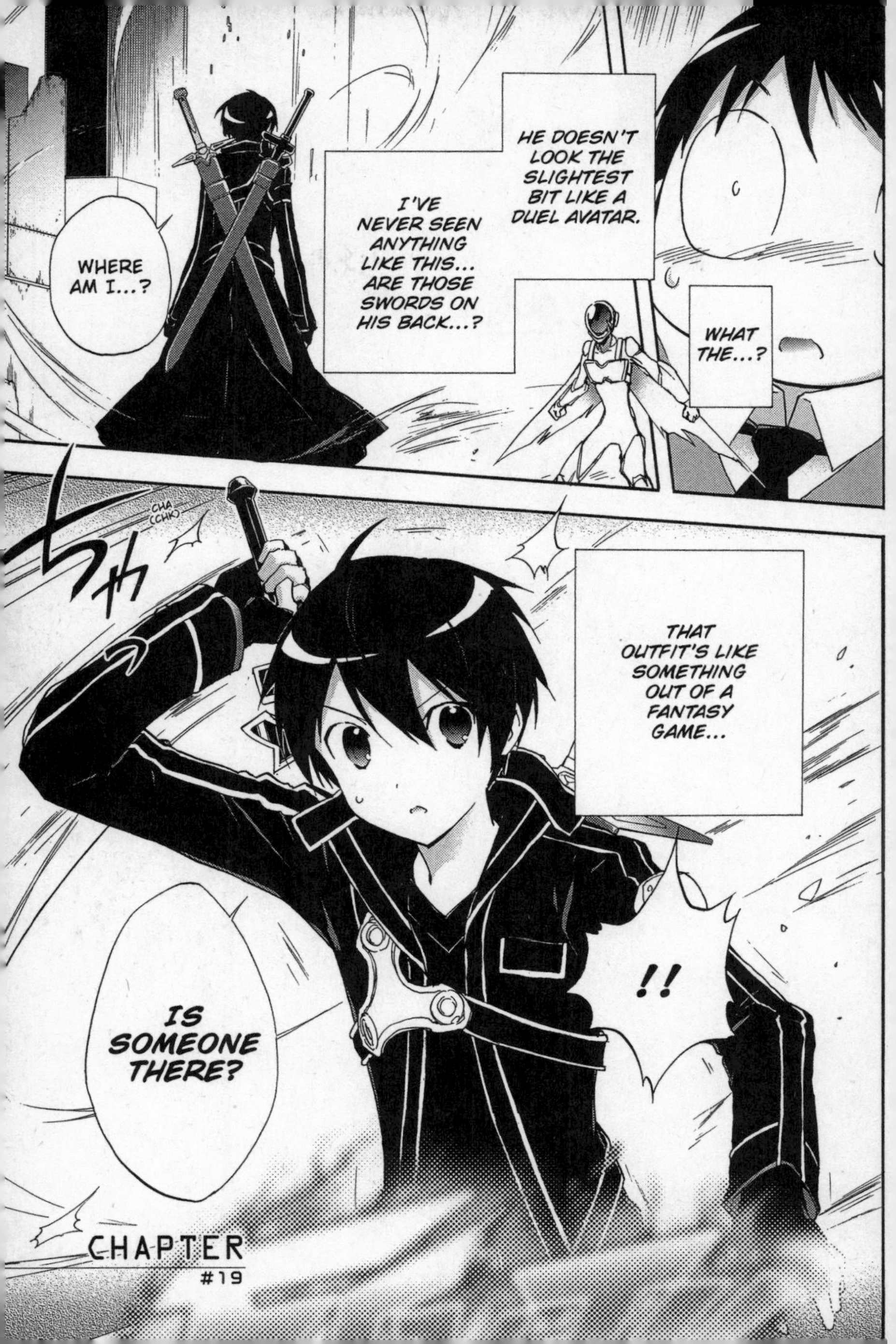
WHAT THE...?
HE DOESN'T LOOK THE SLIGHTEST BIT LIKE A DUEL AVATAR.
I'VE NEVER SEEN ANYTHING LIKE THIS... ARE THOSE SWORDS ON HIS BACK...?
WHERE AM I...?
THAT OUTFIT'S LIKE SOMETHING OUT OF A FANTASY GAME...
!!
CHA (CHK)
ちゃ
IS SOMEONE THERE?
CHAPTER
#19

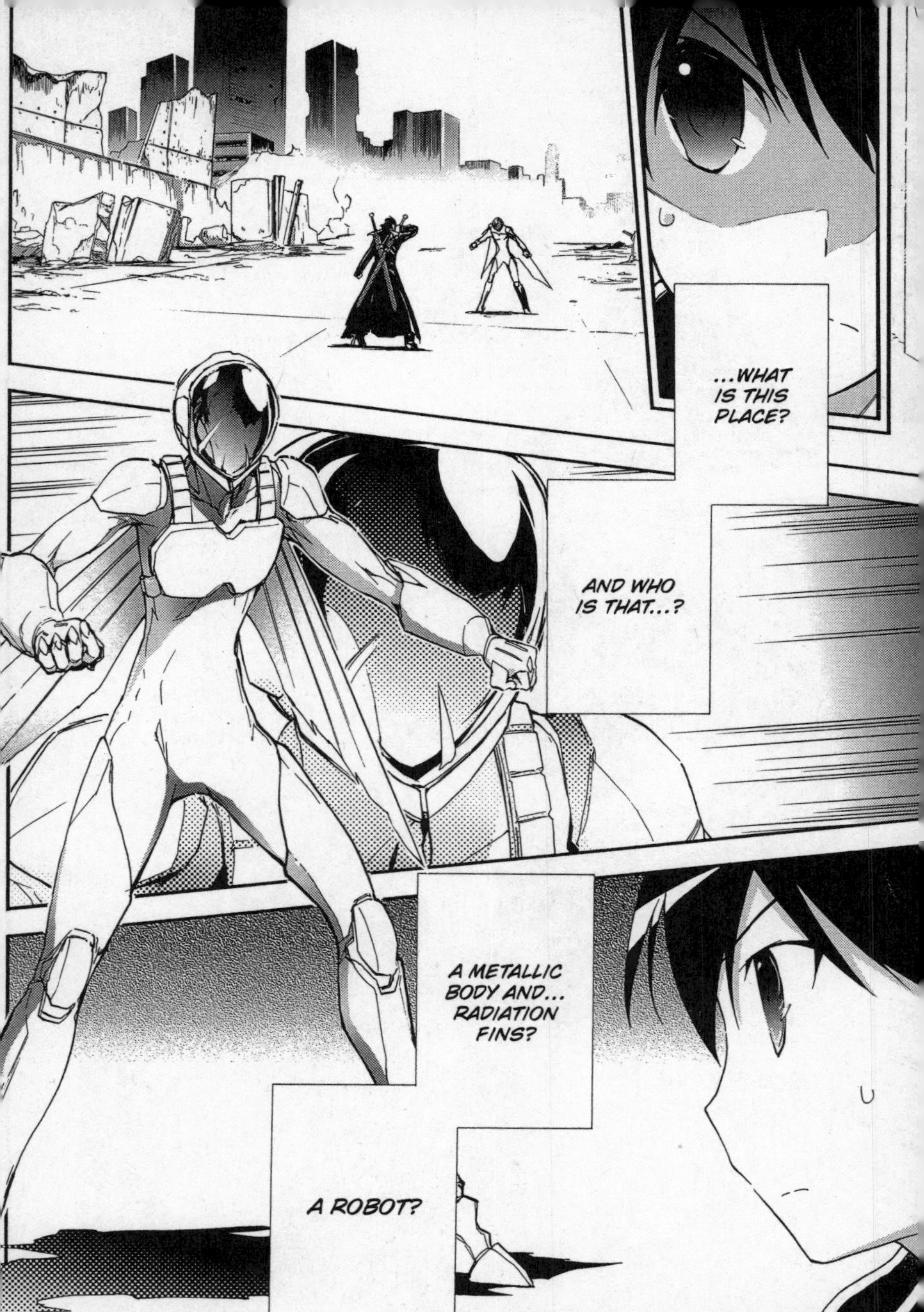
...WHAT IS THIS PLACE?
AND WHO IS THAT...?
A METALLIC BODY AND... RADIATION FINS?
A ROBOT?

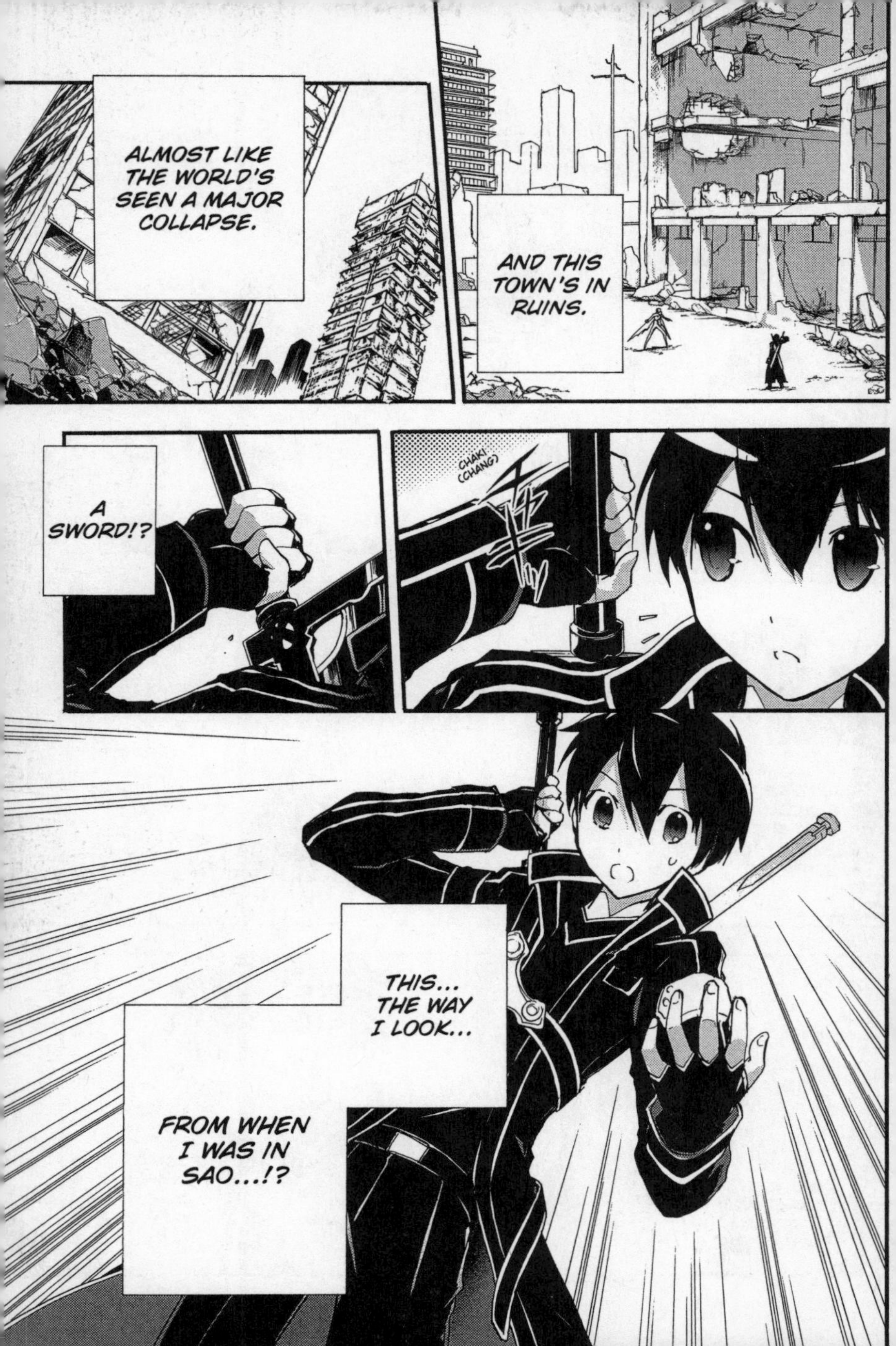
AND THIS TOWN'S IN RUINS.
ALMOST LIKE THE WORLD'S SEEN A MAJOR COLLAPSE.
CHAKI (CHANG)
A SWORD!?
THIS... THE WAY I LOOK...
FROM WHEN I WAS IN SAO...!?

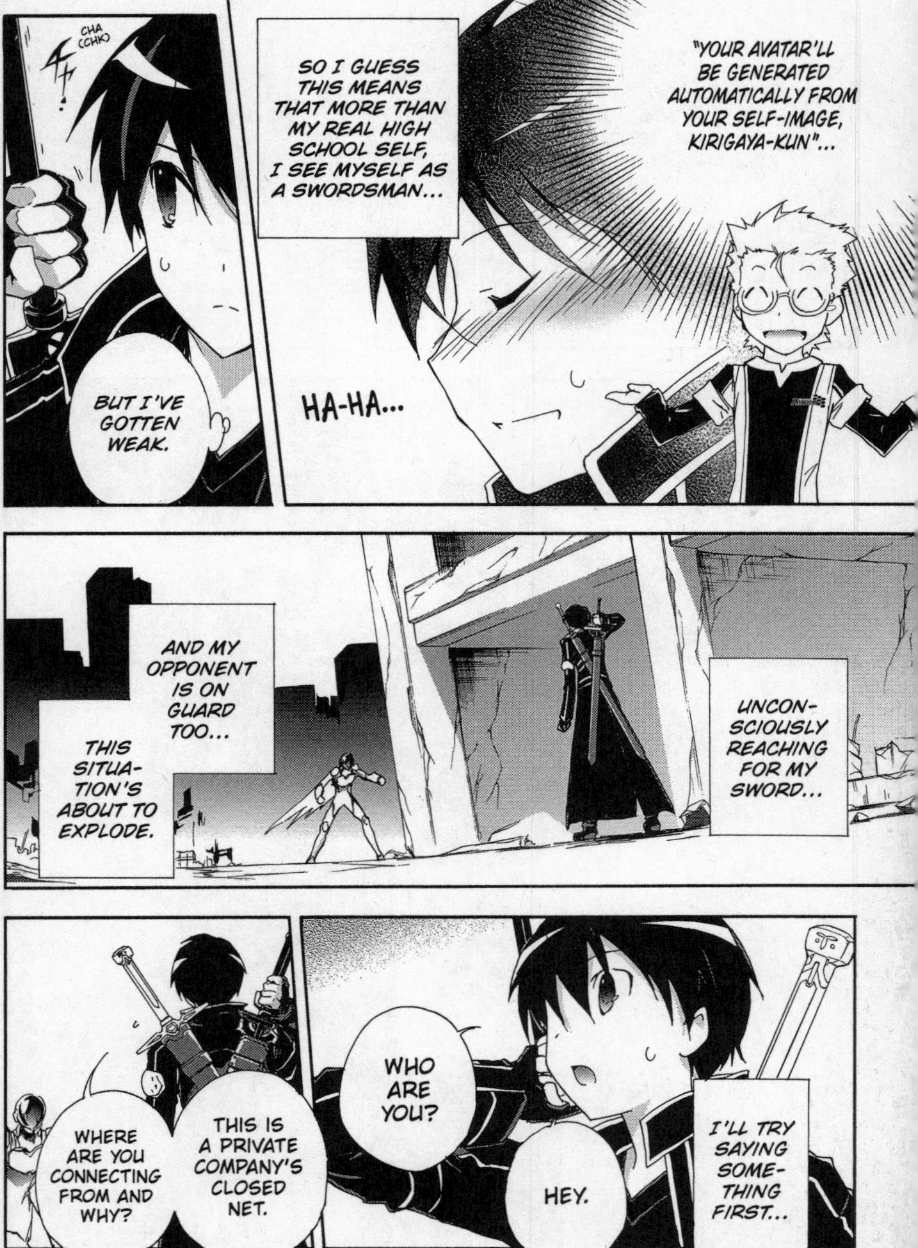
"YOUR AVATAR'LL BE GENERATED AUTOMATICALLY FROM YOUR SELF-IMAGE, KIRIGAYA-KUN"...
SO I GUESS THIS MEANS THAT MORE THAN MY REAL HIGH SCHOOL SELF, I SEE MYSELF AS A SWORDSMAN...
HA-HA...
CHA (CHK)
BUT I'VE GOTTEN WEAK.
UNCONSCIOUSLY REACHING FOR MY SWORD...
AND MY OPPONENT IS ON GUARD TOO...
THIS SITUATION'S ABOUT TO EXPLODE.
I'LL TRY SAYING SOMETHING FIRST...
HEY.
WHO ARE YOU?
THIS IS A PRIVATE COMPANY'S CLOSED NET.
WHERE ARE YOU CONNECTING FROM AND WHY?

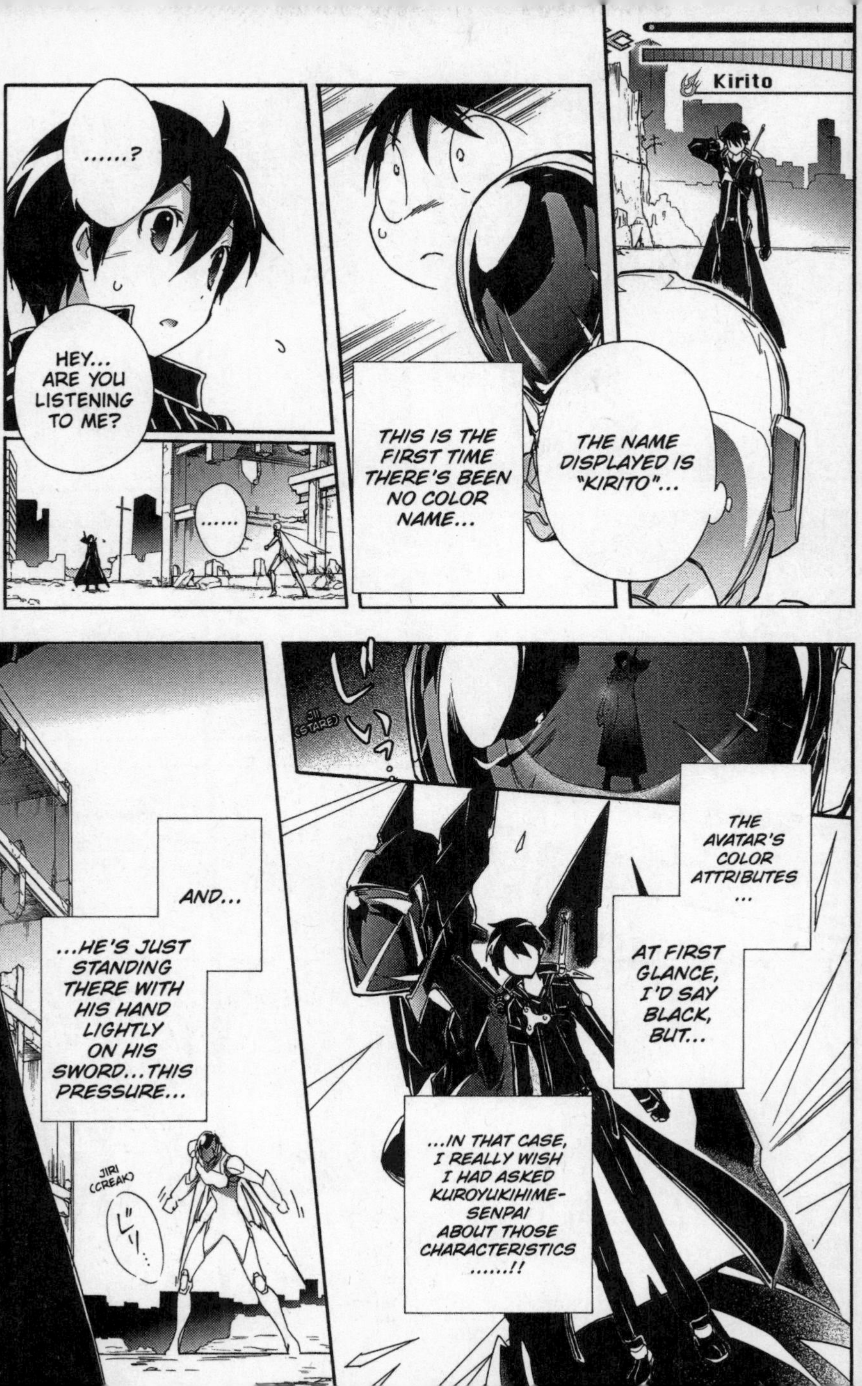
Kirito
THE NAME DISPLAYED IS "KIRITO"...
THIS IS THE FIRST TIME THERE'S BEEN NO COLOR NAME...
......?
HEY... ARE YOU LISTENING TO ME?
......
JIRI (STARE)
THE AVATAR'S COLOR ATTRIBUTES ...
AT FIRST GLANCE, I'D SAY BLACK, BUT...
...IN THAT CASE, I REALLY WISH I HAD ASKED KUROYUKIHIME-SENPAI ABOUT THOSE CHARACTERISTICS ......!!
AND...
...HE'S JUST STANDING THERE WITH HIS HAND LIGHTLY ON HIS SWORD...THIS PRESSURE...
JIRI (CREAK)

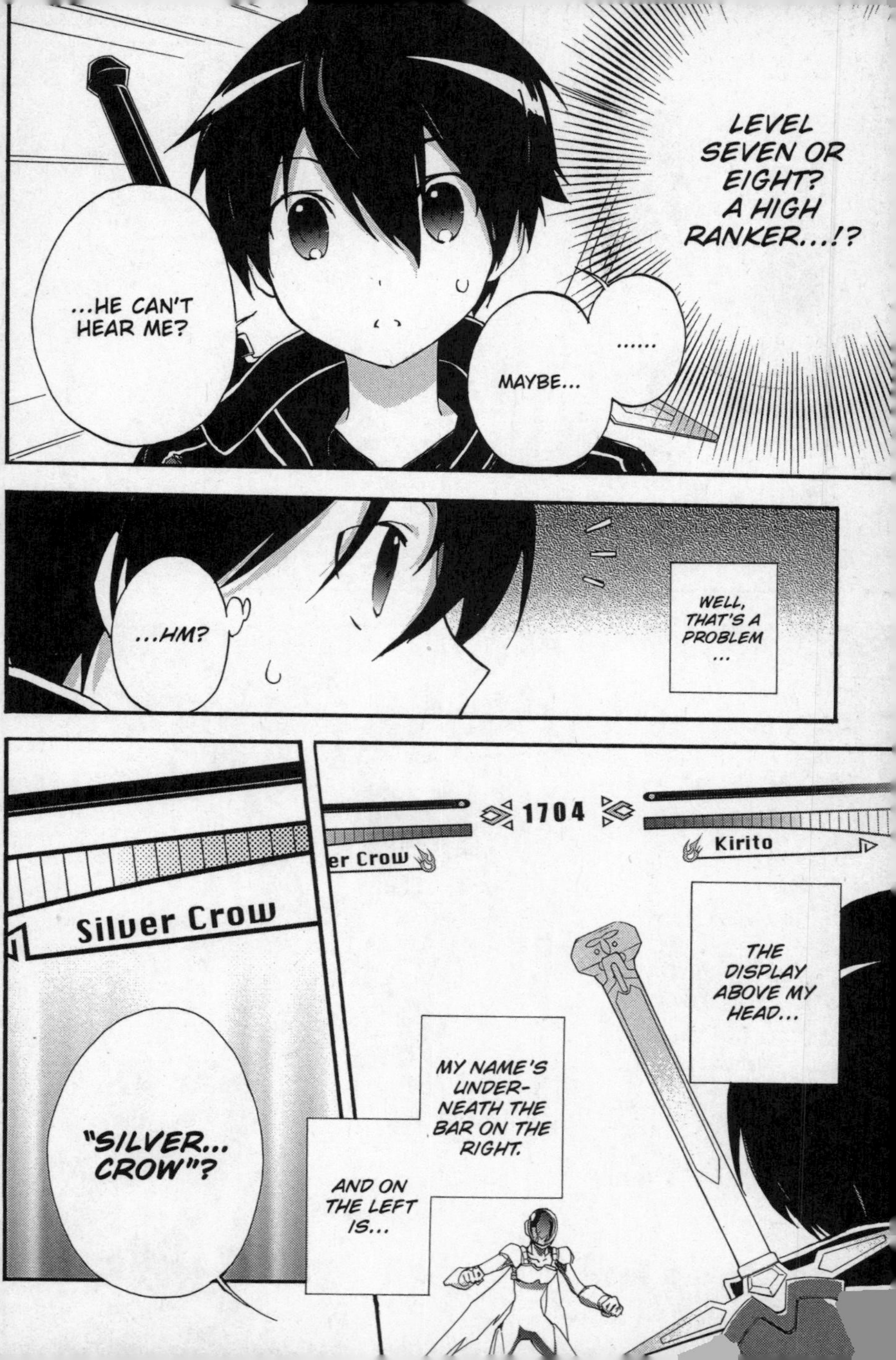
LEVEL SEVEN OR EIGHT? A HIGH RANKER...!?
......
MAYBE...
...HE CAN'T HEAR ME?
WELL, THAT'S A PROBLEM ...
...HM?
1704
Kirito
er Crow
THE DISPLAY ABOVE MY HEAD...
MY NAME'S UNDER-NEATH THE BAR ON THE RIGHT.
AND ON THE LEFT IS...
Silver Crow
"SILVER... CROW"?

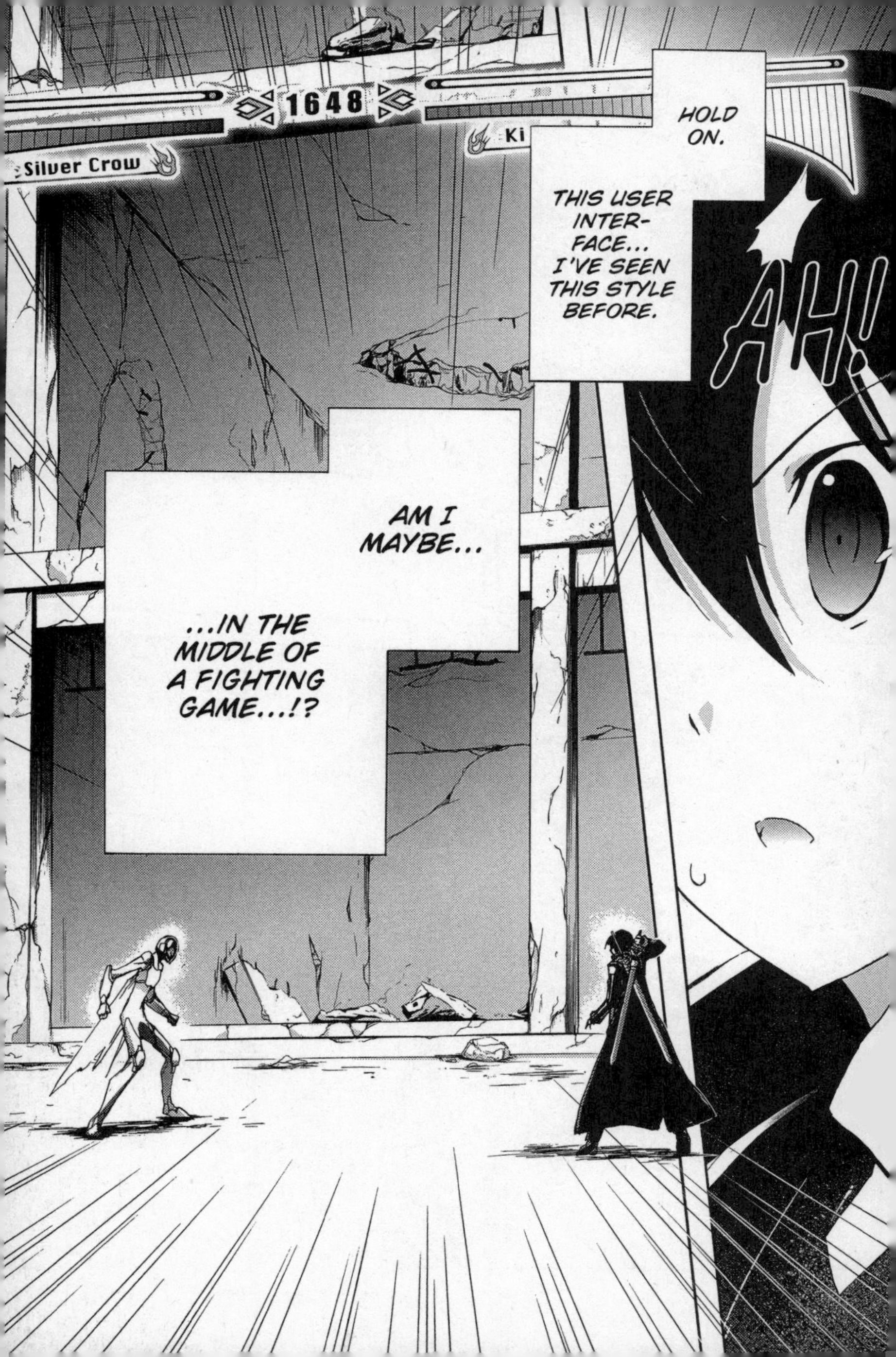
HOLD ON.
THIS USER INTER-FACE... I'VE SEEN THIS STYLE BEFORE.
AH!
1648
Silver Crow
Ki
AM I MAYBE...
...IN THE MIDDLE OF A FIGHTING GAME...!?

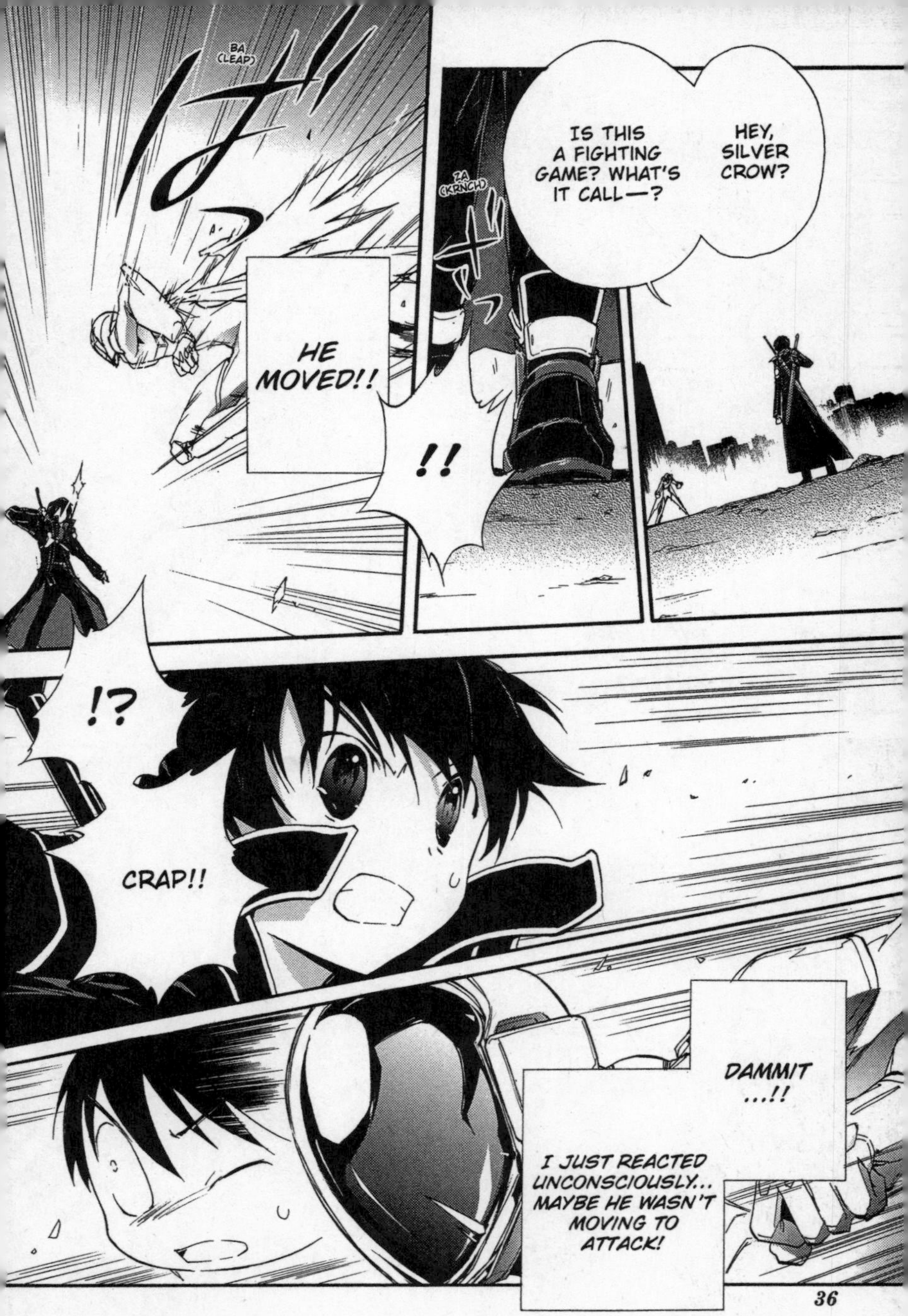
HEY, SILVER CROW?
IS THIS A FIGHTING GAME? WHAT'S IT CALL—?
ZA (KRNCH)
!!
BA (LEAP)
HE MOVED!!
!?
CRAP!!
DAMMIT ...!!
I JUST REACTED UNCONSCIOUSLY... MAYBE HE WASN'T MOVING TO ATTACK!

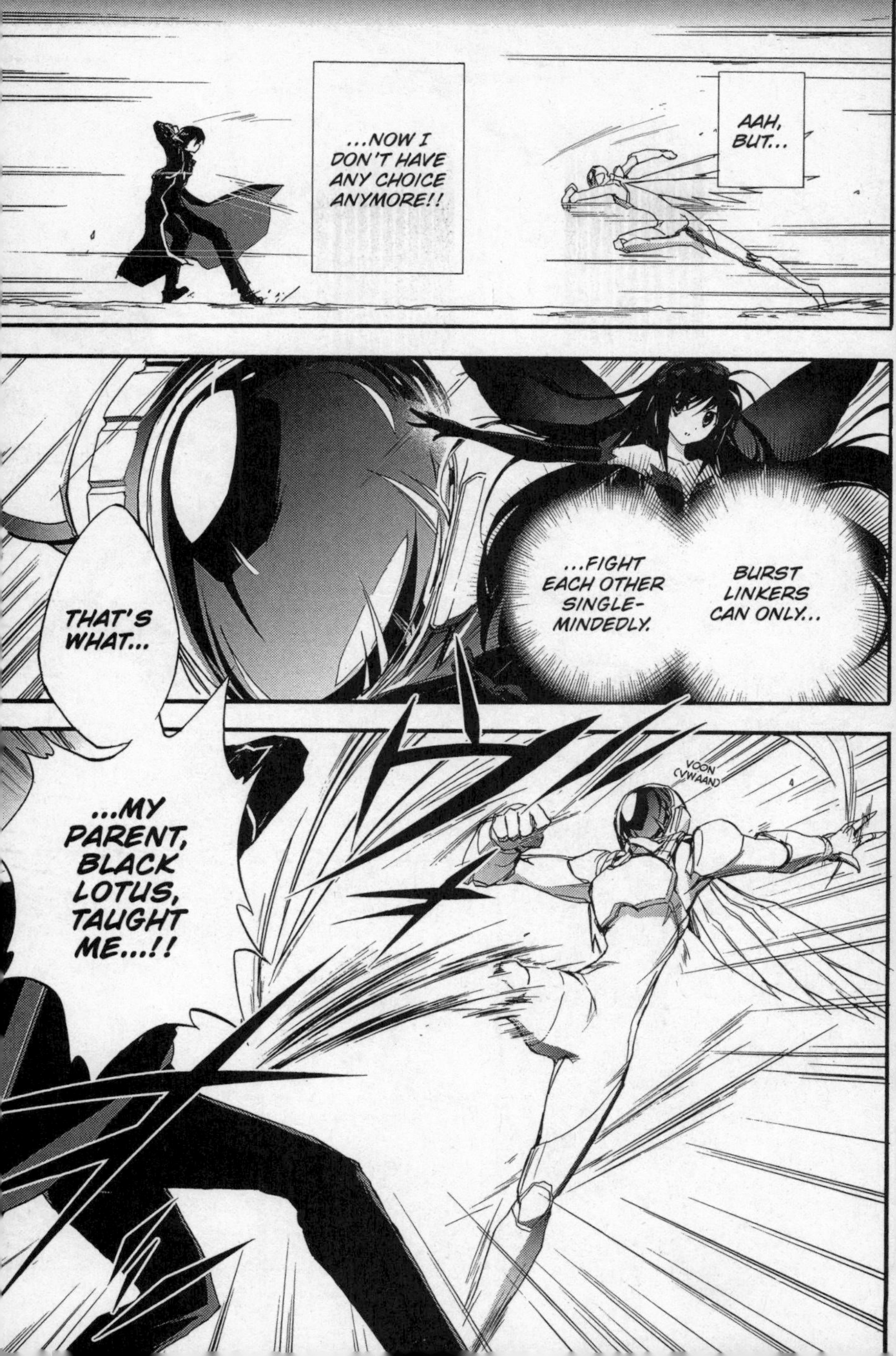
AAH, BUT...
...NOW I DON'T HAVE ANY CHOICE ANYMORE!!
BURST LINKERS CAN ONLY...
...FIGHT EACH OTHER SINGLE-MINDEDLY.
THAT'S WHAT...
VOON (VWAAN)
...MY PARENT, BLACK LOTUS, TAUGHT ME...!!

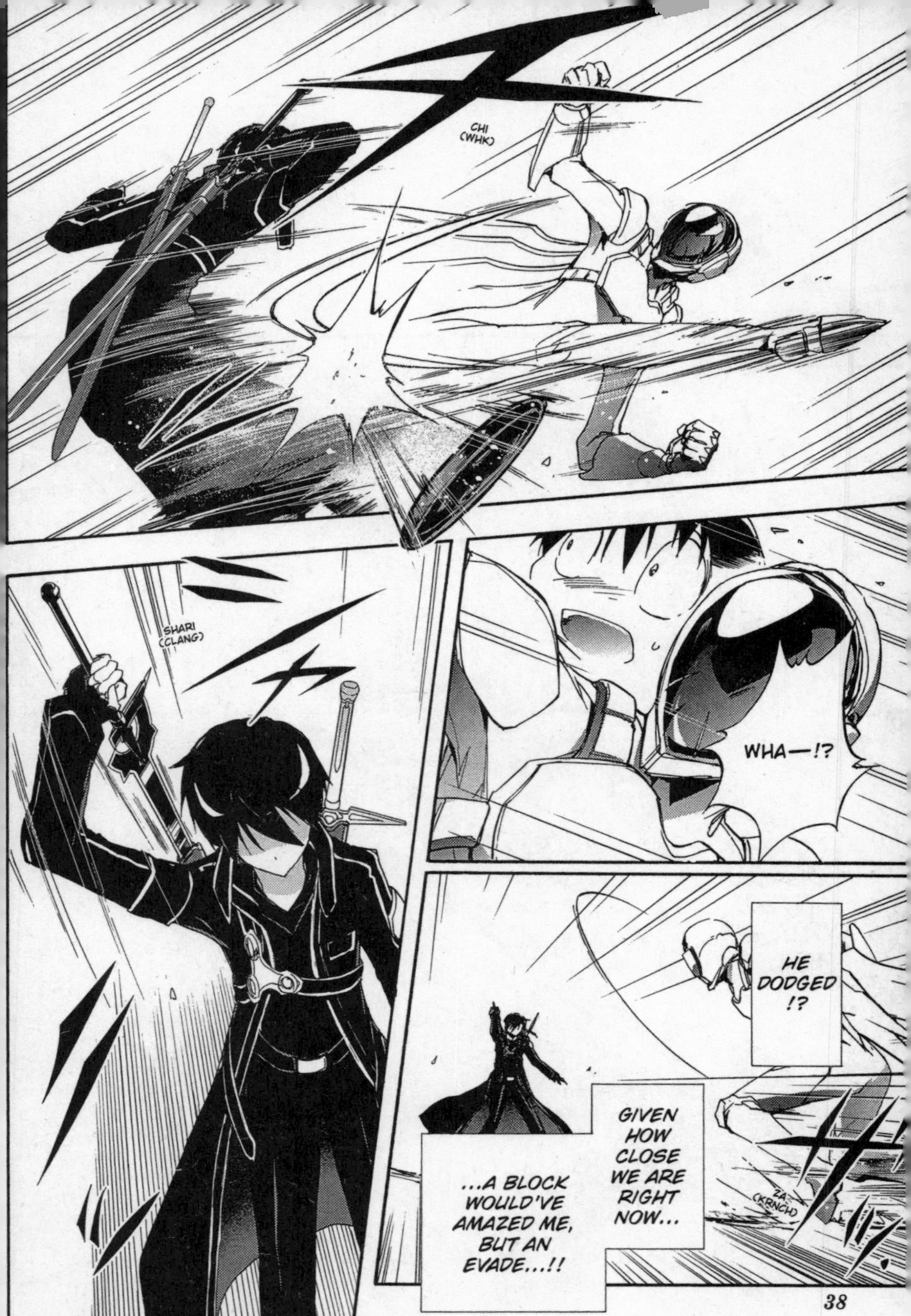
CHI (WHK)
WHA—!?
HE DODGED !?
GIVEN HOW CLOSE WE ARE RIGHT NOW...
...A BLOCK WOULD'VE AMAZED ME, BUT AN EVADE...!!
ZA (KRNCH)
SHARI (CLANG)

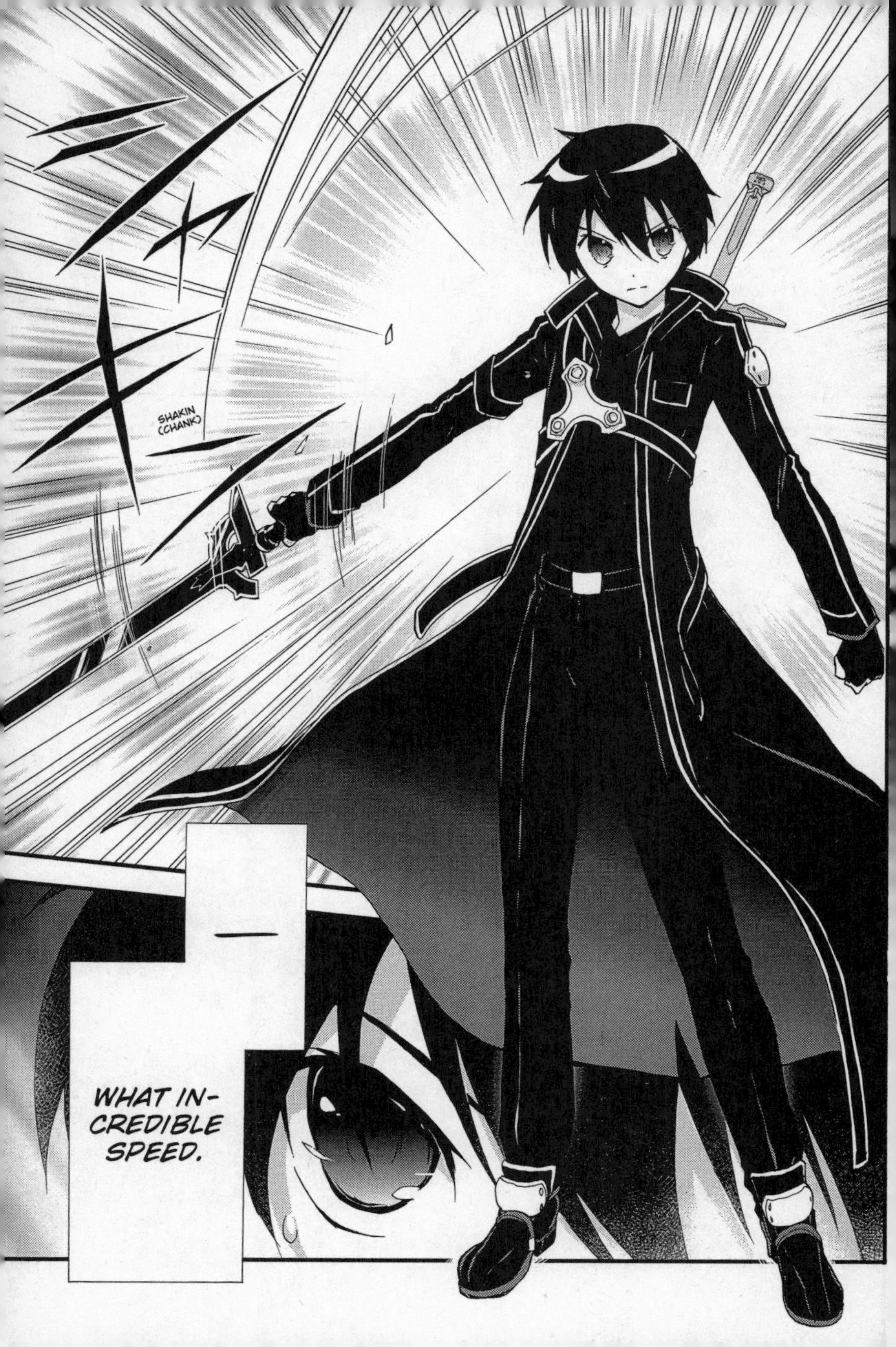
SHAKIN (CHANK)
—
WHAT IN-
CREDIBLE
SPEED.

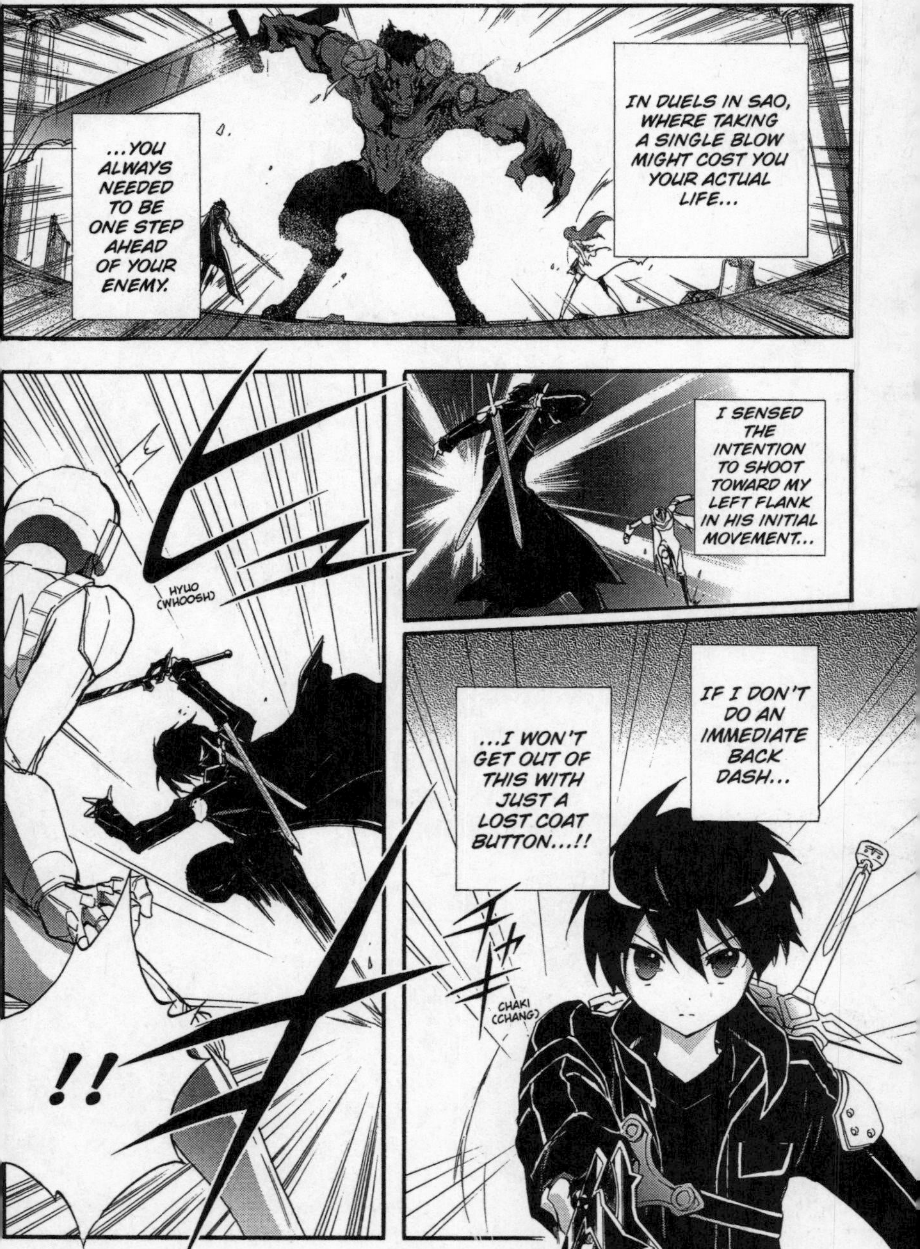
IN DUELS IN SAO, WHERE TAKING A SINGLE BLOW MIGHT COST YOU YOUR ACTUAL LIFE...
...YOU ALWAYS NEEDED TO BE ONE STEP AHEAD OF YOUR ENEMY.
I SENSED THE INTENTION TO SHOOT TOWARD MY LEFT FLANK IN HIS INITIAL MOVEMENT...
IF I DON'T DO AN IMMEDIATE BACK DASH...
...I WON'T GET OUT OF THIS WITH JUST A LOST COAT BUTTON...!!
CHAKI (CHANG)
HYUO (WHOOSH)
!!

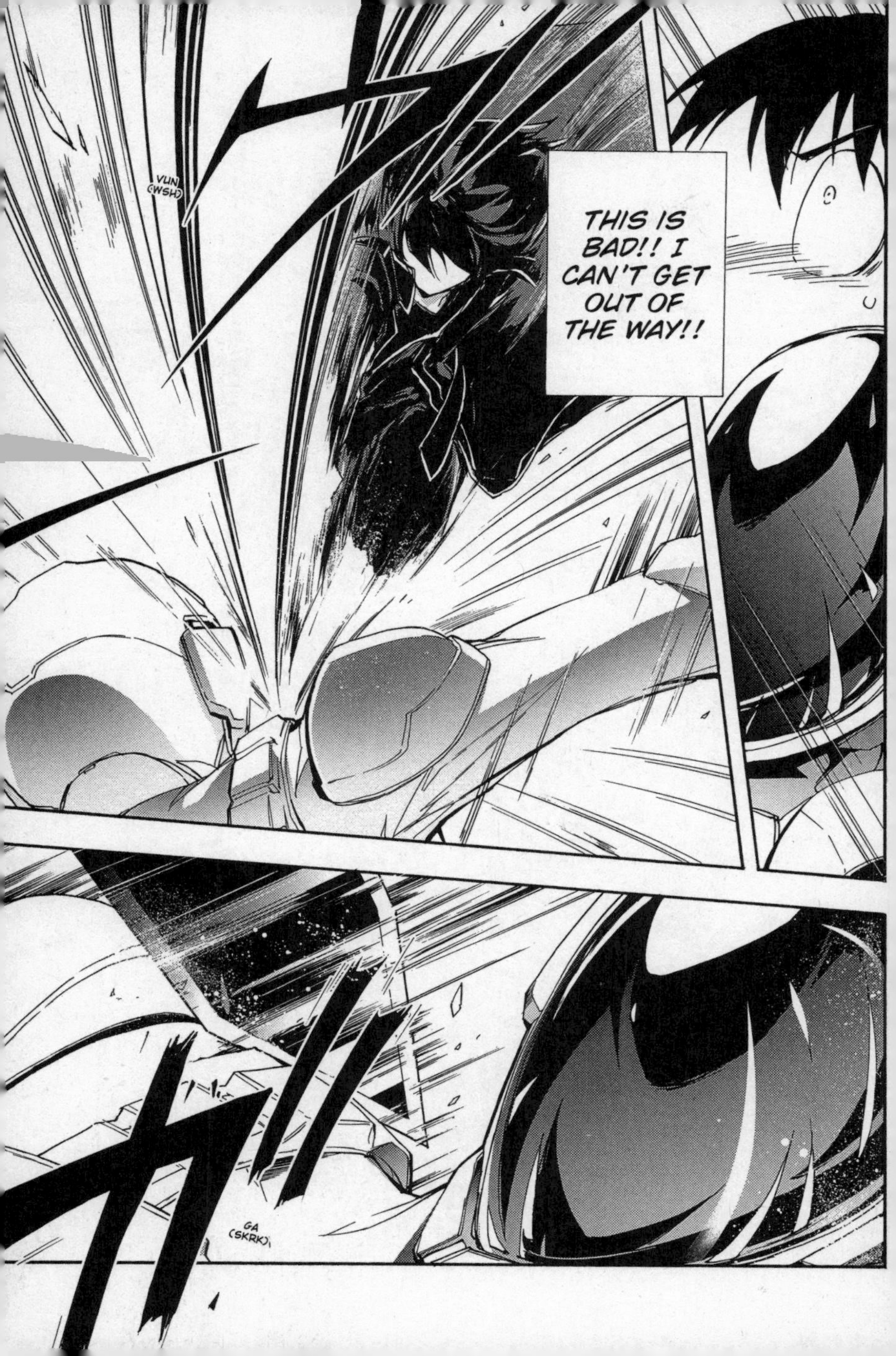
THIS IS BAD!! I CAN'T GET OUT OF THE WAY!!
VUN (WSH)
GA (SKRK)

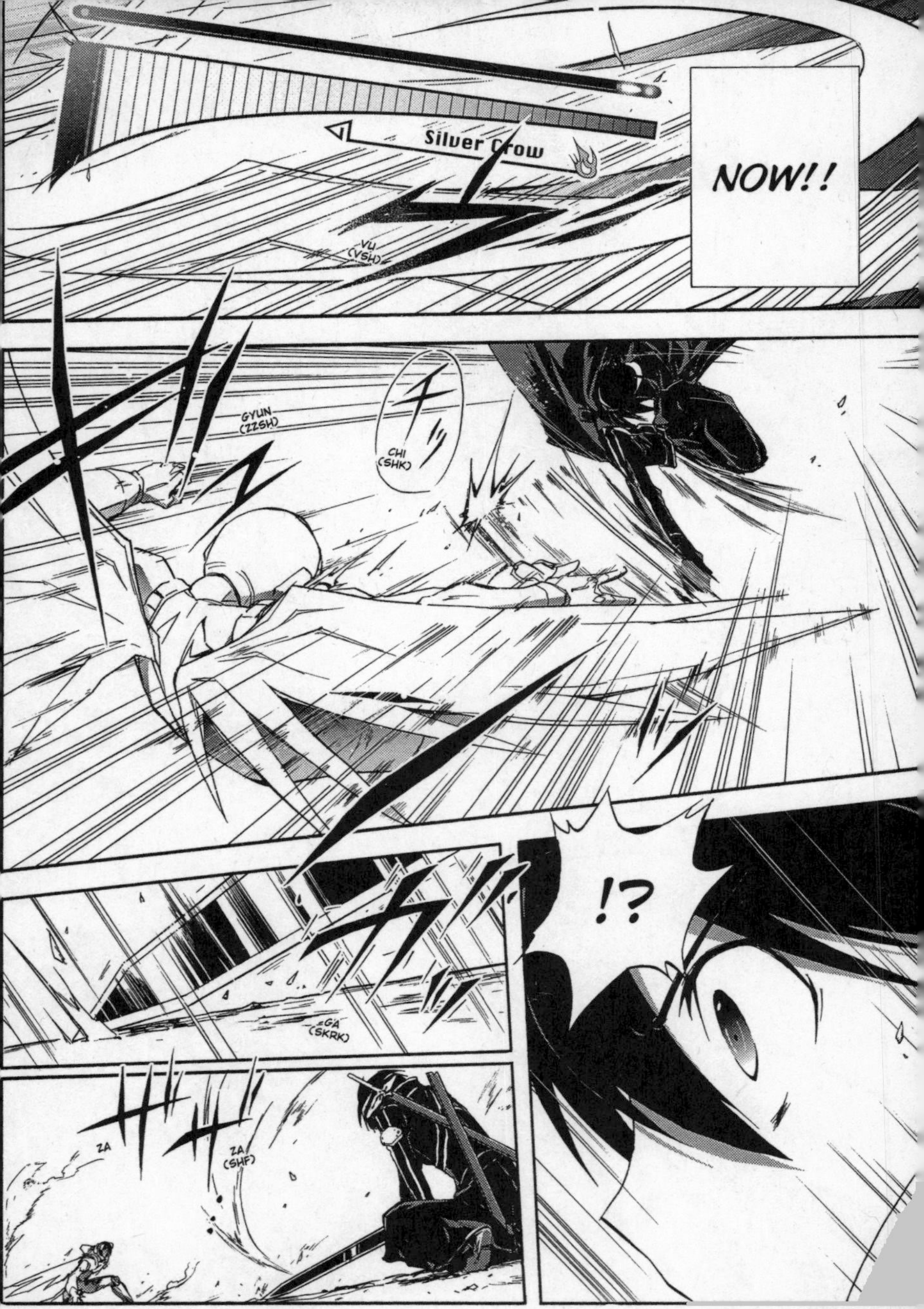
NOW!!
Silver Crow
VU (VSH)
CHI (SHK)
GYUN (ZZSH)
!?
GA (SKRK)
ZA (SHF)
ZA

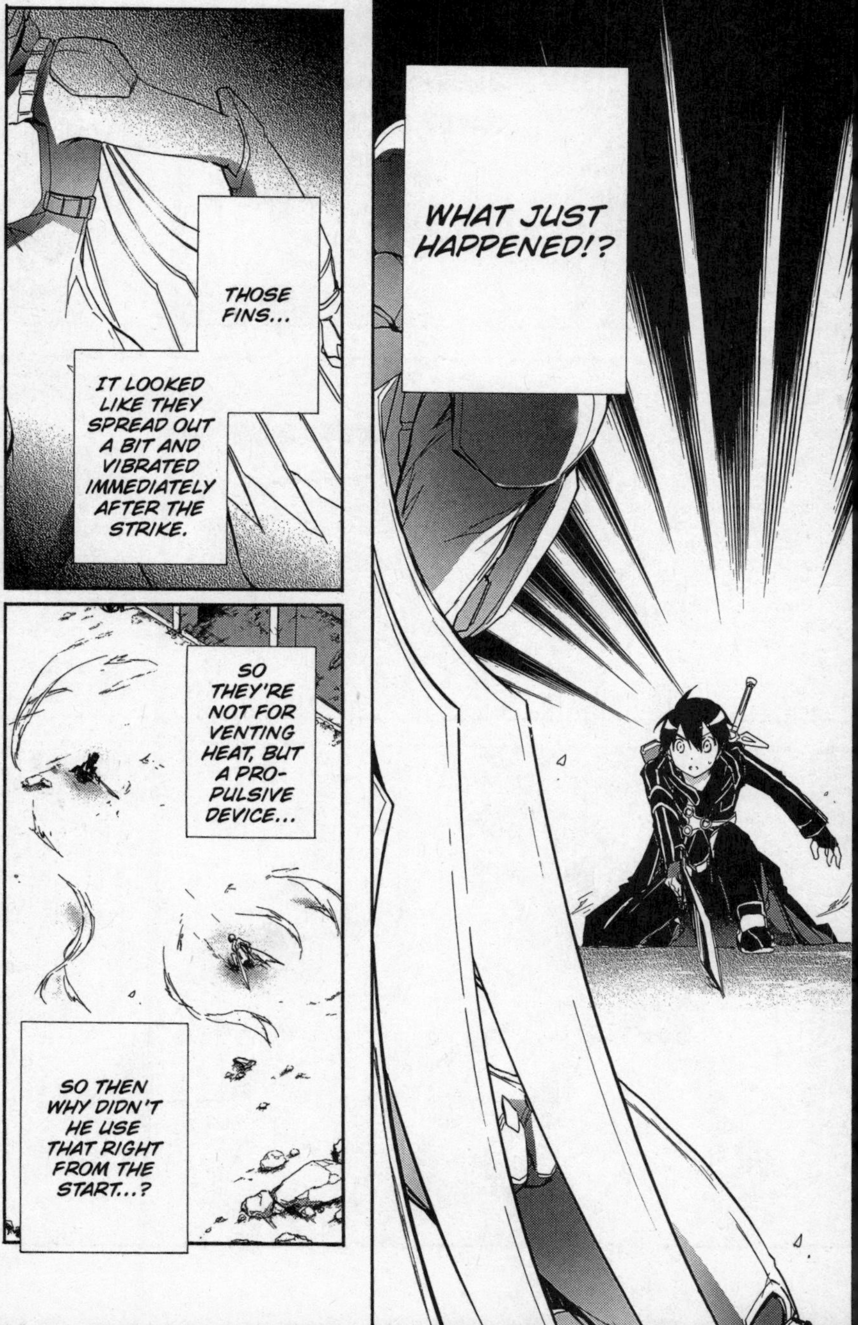
WHAT JUST HAPPENED!?
THOSE FINS...
IT LOOKED LIKE THEY SPREAD OUT A BIT AND VIBRATED IMMEDIATELY AFTER THE STRIKE.
SO THEY'RE NOT FOR VENTING HEAT, BUT A PRO-PULSIVE DEVICE...
SO THEN WHY DIDN'T HE USE THAT RIGHT FROM THE START...?

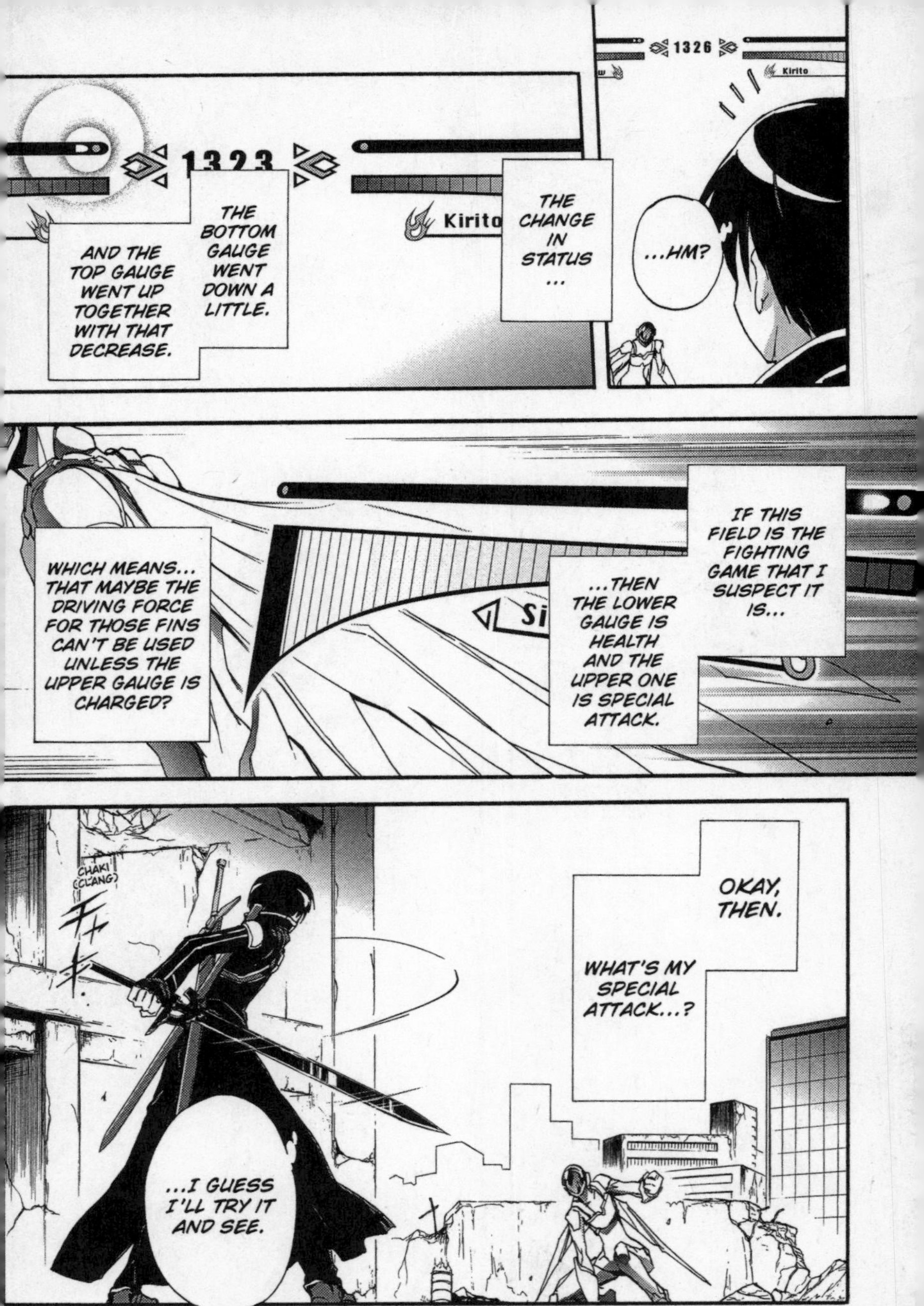
1326
Kirito
...HM?
THE CHANGE IN STATUS ...
1323
Kirito
THE BOTTOM GAUGE WENT DOWN A LITTLE.
AND THE TOP GAUGE WENT UP TOGETHER WITH THAT DECREASE.
IF THIS FIELD IS THE FIGHTING GAME THAT I SUSPECT IT IS...
...THEN THE LOWER GAUGE IS HEALTH AND THE UPPER ONE IS SPECIAL ATTACK.
WHICH MEANS... THAT MAYBE THE DRIVING FORCE FOR THOSE FINS CAN'T BE USED UNLESS THE UPPER GAUGE IS CHARGED?
OKAY, THEN.
WHAT'S MY SPECIAL ATTACK...?
CHAKI (CLANG)
...I GUESS I'LL TRY IT AND SEE.

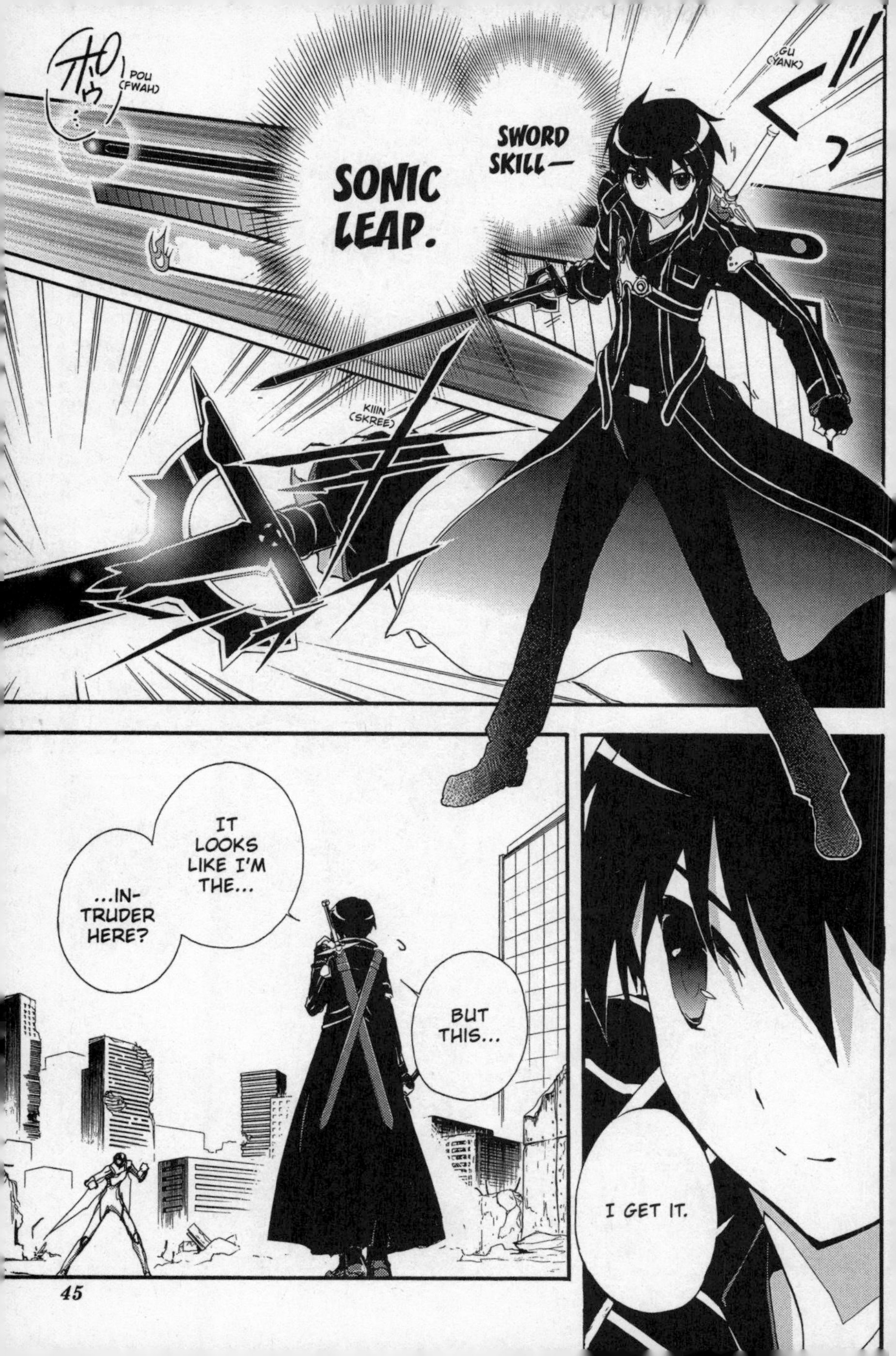
GU (YANK)
SWORD SKILL—
SONIC LEAP.
POU (FWAH)
KIIN (SKREE)
I GET IT.
IT LOOKS LIKE I'M THE...
...IN-TRUDER HERE?
BUT THIS...

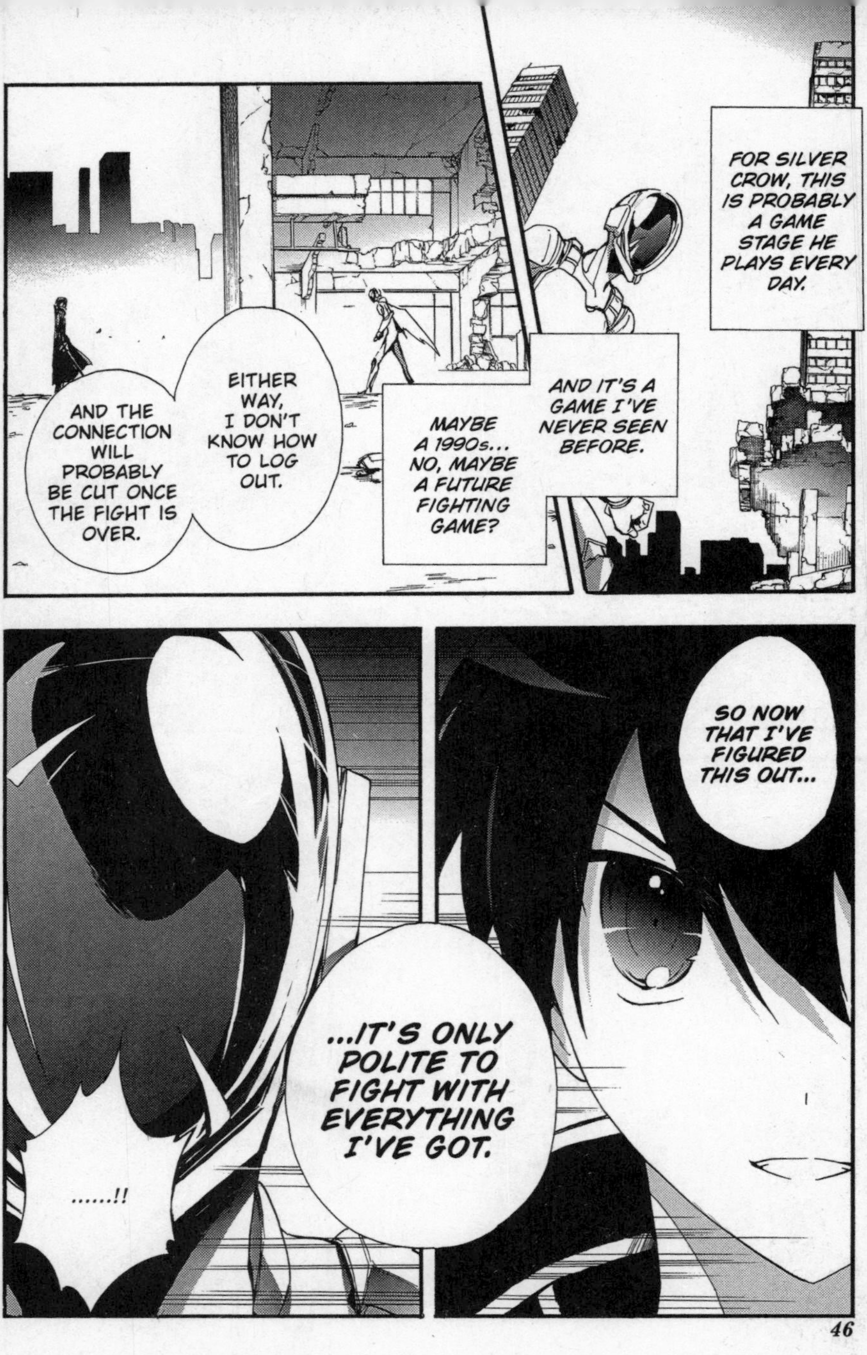
FOR SILVER CROW, THIS IS PROBABLY A GAME STAGE HE PLAYS EVERY DAY.
AND IT'S A GAME I'VE NEVER SEEN BEFORE.
MAYBE A 1990s... NO, MAYBE A FUTURE FIGHTING GAME?
EITHER WAY, I DON'T KNOW HOW TO LOG OUT.
AND THE CONNECTION WILL PROBABLY BE CUT ONCE THE FIGHT IS OVER.
SO NOW THAT I'VE FIGURED THIS OUT...
...IT'S ONLY POLITE TO FIGHT WITH EVERYTHING I'VE GOT.
......!!

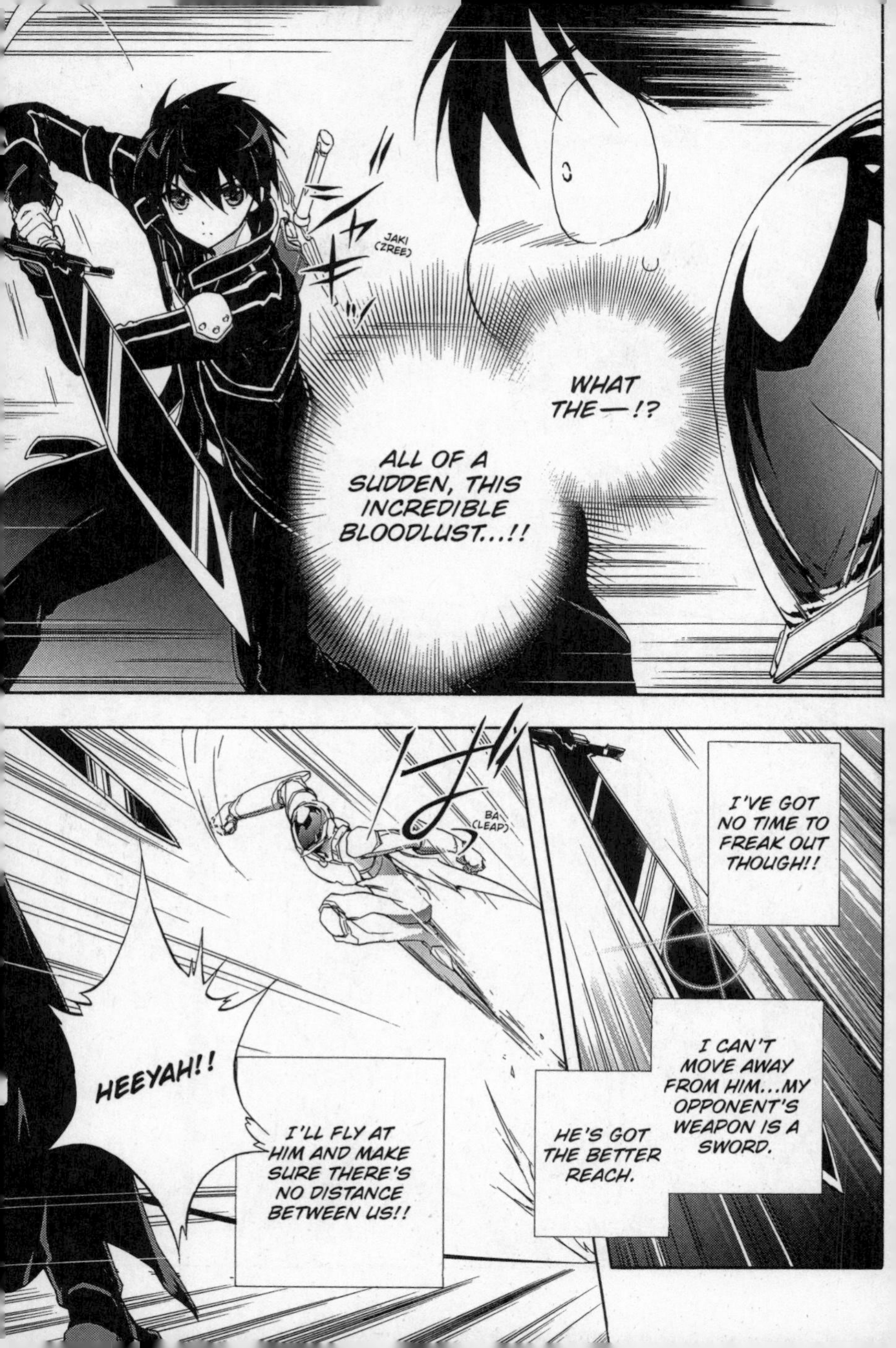

JAKI (ZREE)
WHAT THE—!?
ALL OF A SUDDEN, THIS INCREDIBLE BLOODLUST...!!
I'VE GOT NO TIME TO FREAK OUT THOUGH!!
BA (LEAP)
I CAN'T MOVE AWAY FROM HIM...MY OPPONENT'S WEAPON IS A SWORD.
HE'S GOT THE BETTER REACH.
I'LL FLY AT HIM AND MAKE SURE THERE'S NO DISTANCE BETWEEN US!!
HEEYAH!!

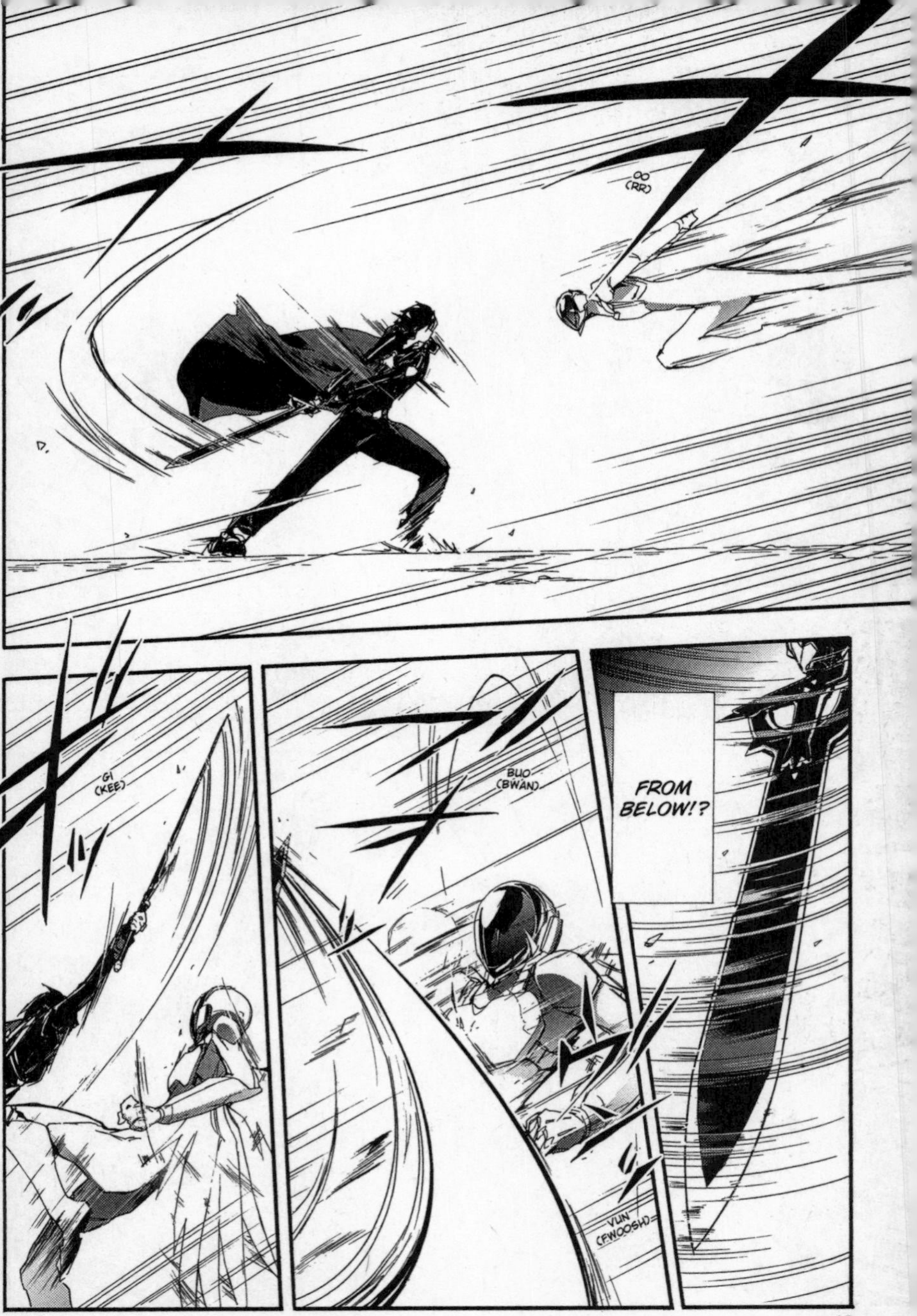
OO
(RR)
FROM BELOW!?
VUN
(FWOOSH)
BUO
(BWAN)
GI
(KEE)

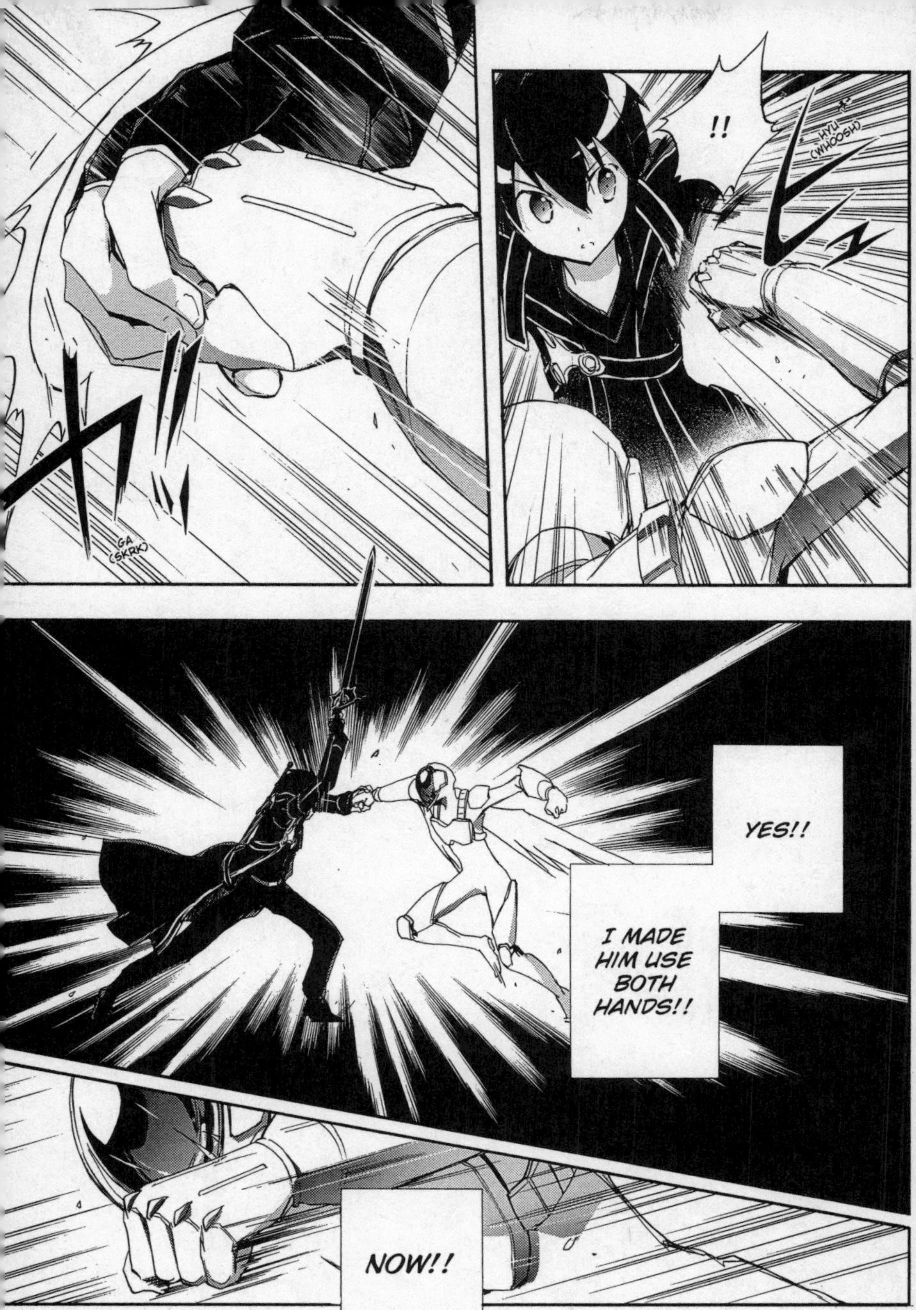
!!
HYU (WHOOSH)
GA (SKRK)
YES!!
I MADE HIM USE BOTH HANDS!!
NOW!!

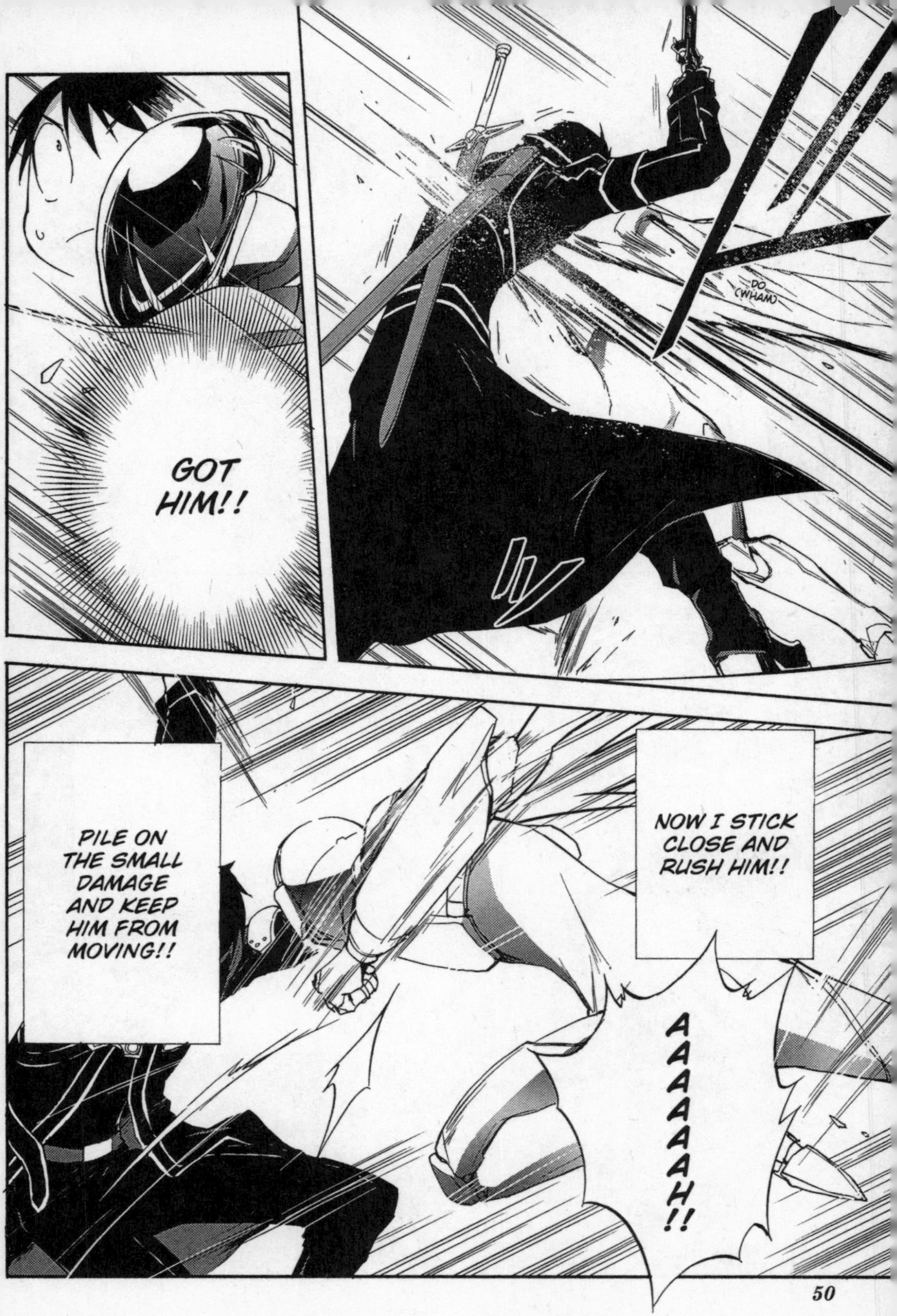
DO (WHAM)
GOT HIM!!
NOW I STICK CLOSE AND RUSH HIM!!
PILE ON THE SMALL DAMAGE AND KEEP HIM FROM MOVING!!
AAAAAAAH!!

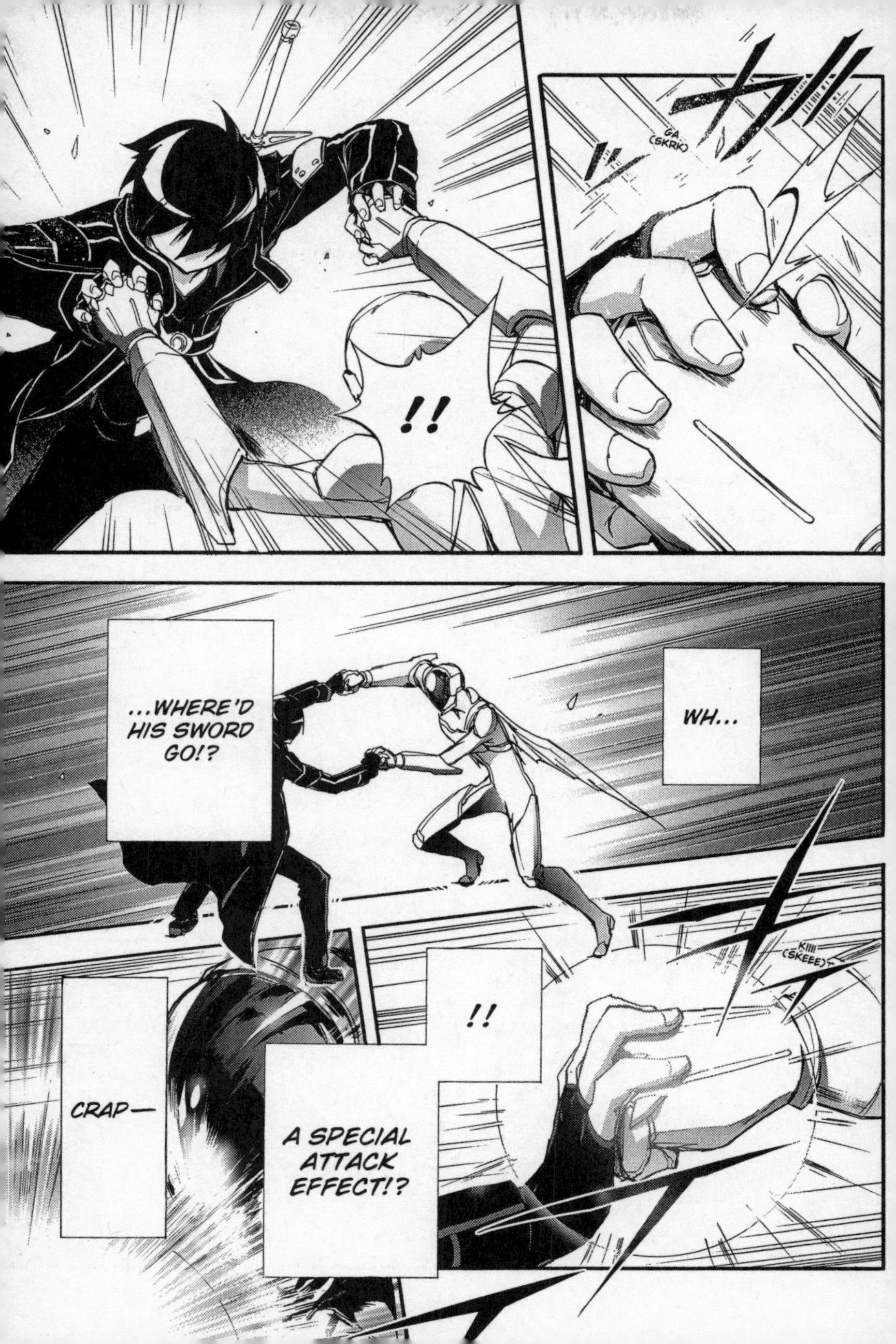

GA (SKRK)
!!
WH...
...WHERE'D HIS SWORD GO!?
KIIII (SKEEE)
!!
A SPECIAL ATTACK EFFECT!?
CRAP—

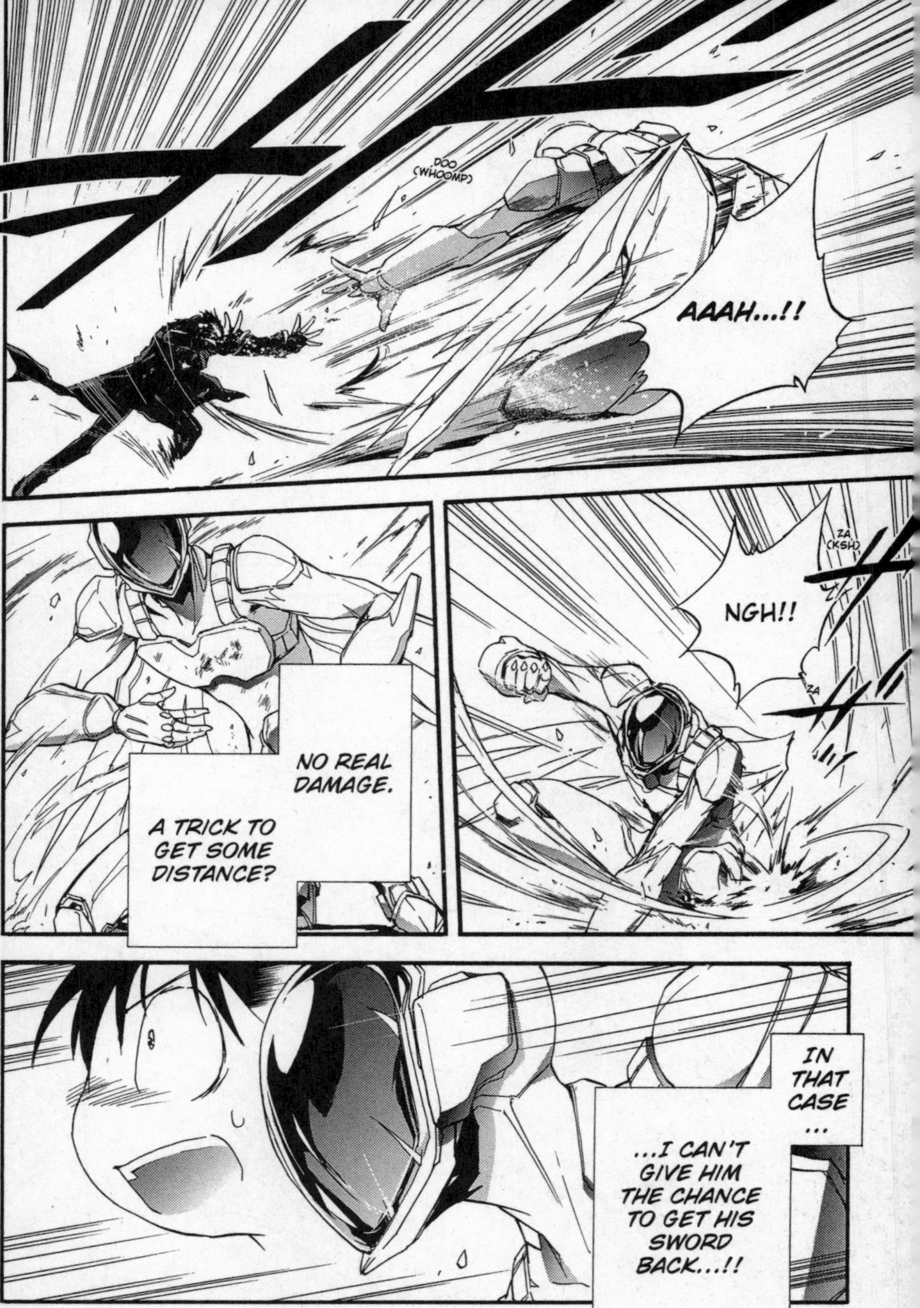
DOO (WHOOMP)
AAAH...!!
ZA (KSH)
NGH!!
ZA
NO REAL DAMAGE.
A TRICK TO GET SOME DISTANCE?
IN THAT CASE...
...I CAN'T GIVE HIM THE CHANCE TO GET HIS SWORD BACK...!!

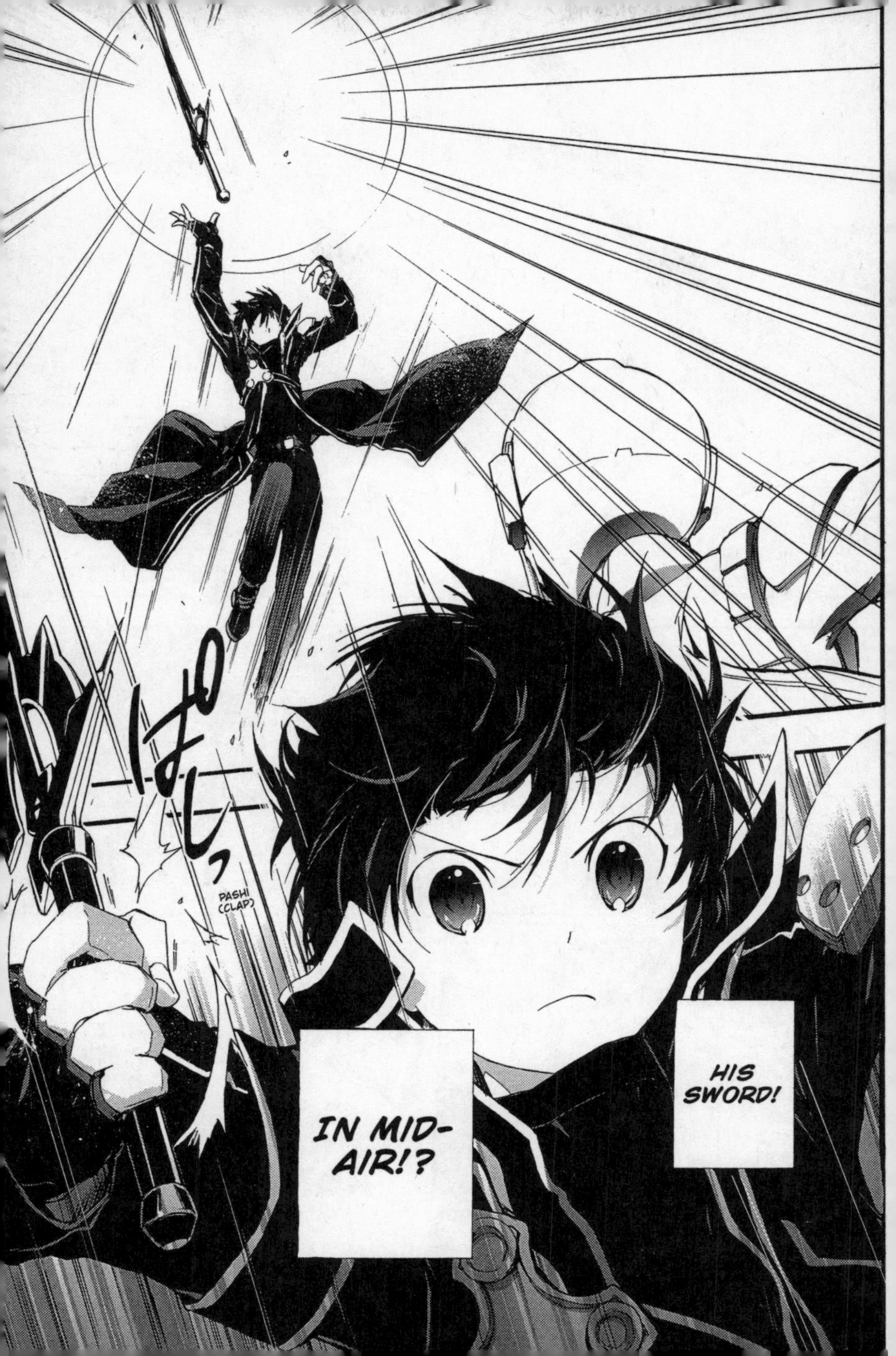
ぱしっ
PASHI (CLAP)
HIS SWORD!
IN MID-AIR!?

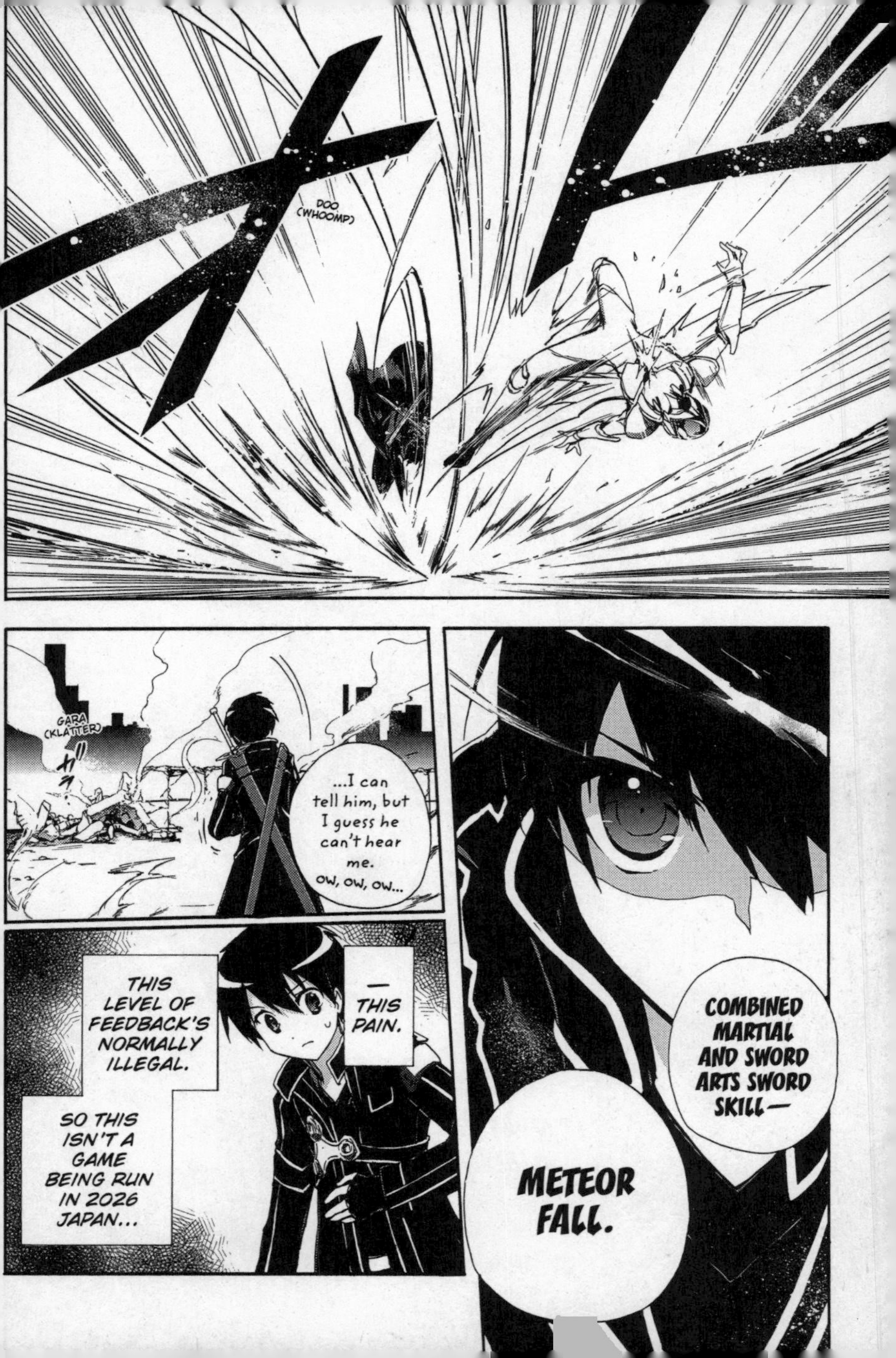
DOO (WHOOMP)
COMBINED MARTIAL AND SWORD ARTS SWORD SKILL—
METEOR FALL.
GARA (KLATTER)
...I can tell him, but I guess he can't hear me. OW, OW, OW...
— THIS PAIN.
THIS LEVEL OF FEEDBACK'S NORMALLY ILLEGAL.
SO THIS ISN'T A GAME BEING RUN IN 2026 JAPAN...

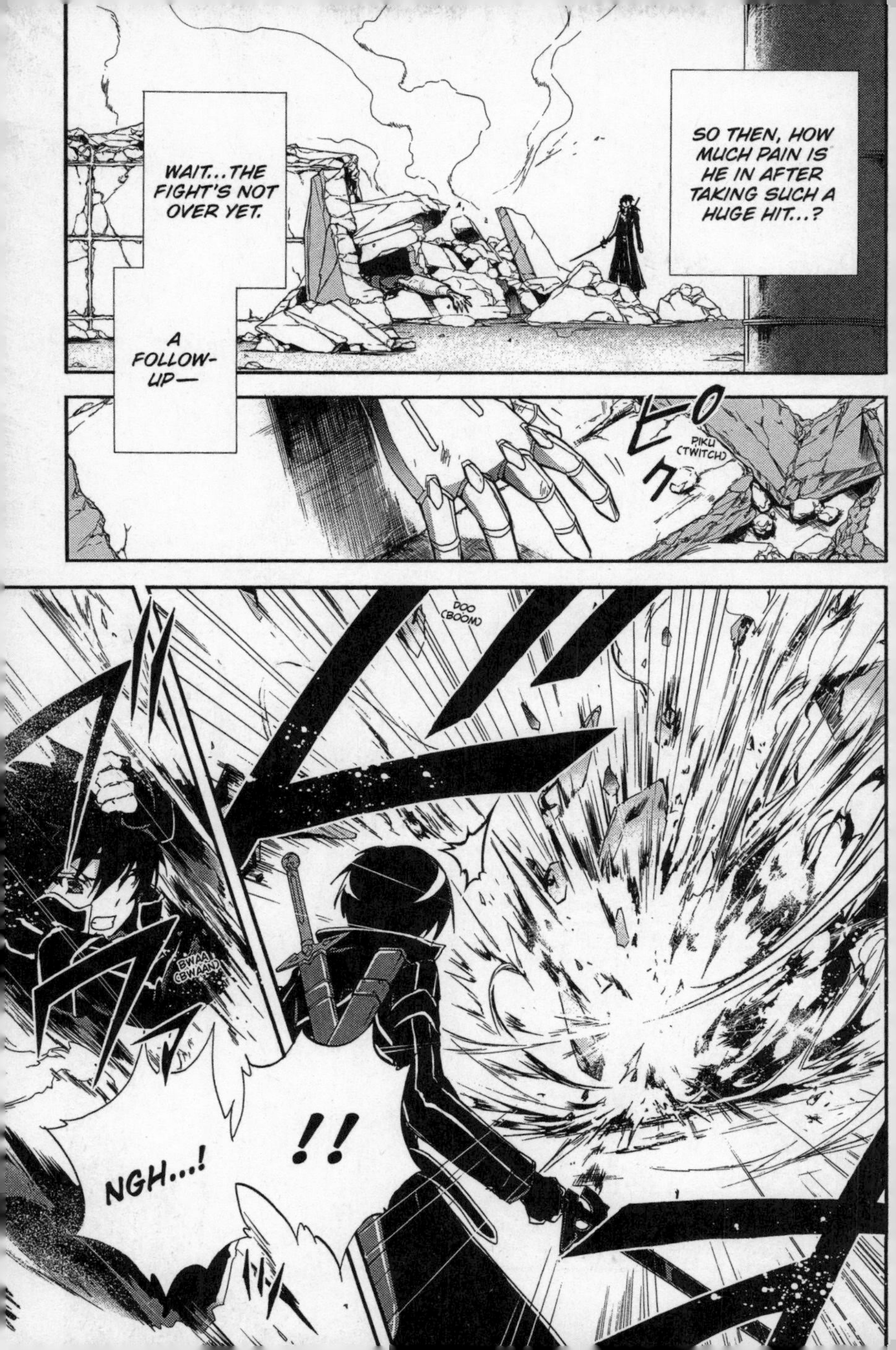
SO THEN, HOW MUCH PAIN IS HE IN AFTER TAKING SUCH A HUGE HIT...?
WAIT...THE FIGHT'S NOT OVER YET.
A FOLLOW-UP—
PIKU (TWITCH)
DOO (BOOM)
!!
BWAA (BWAAN)
NGH...!

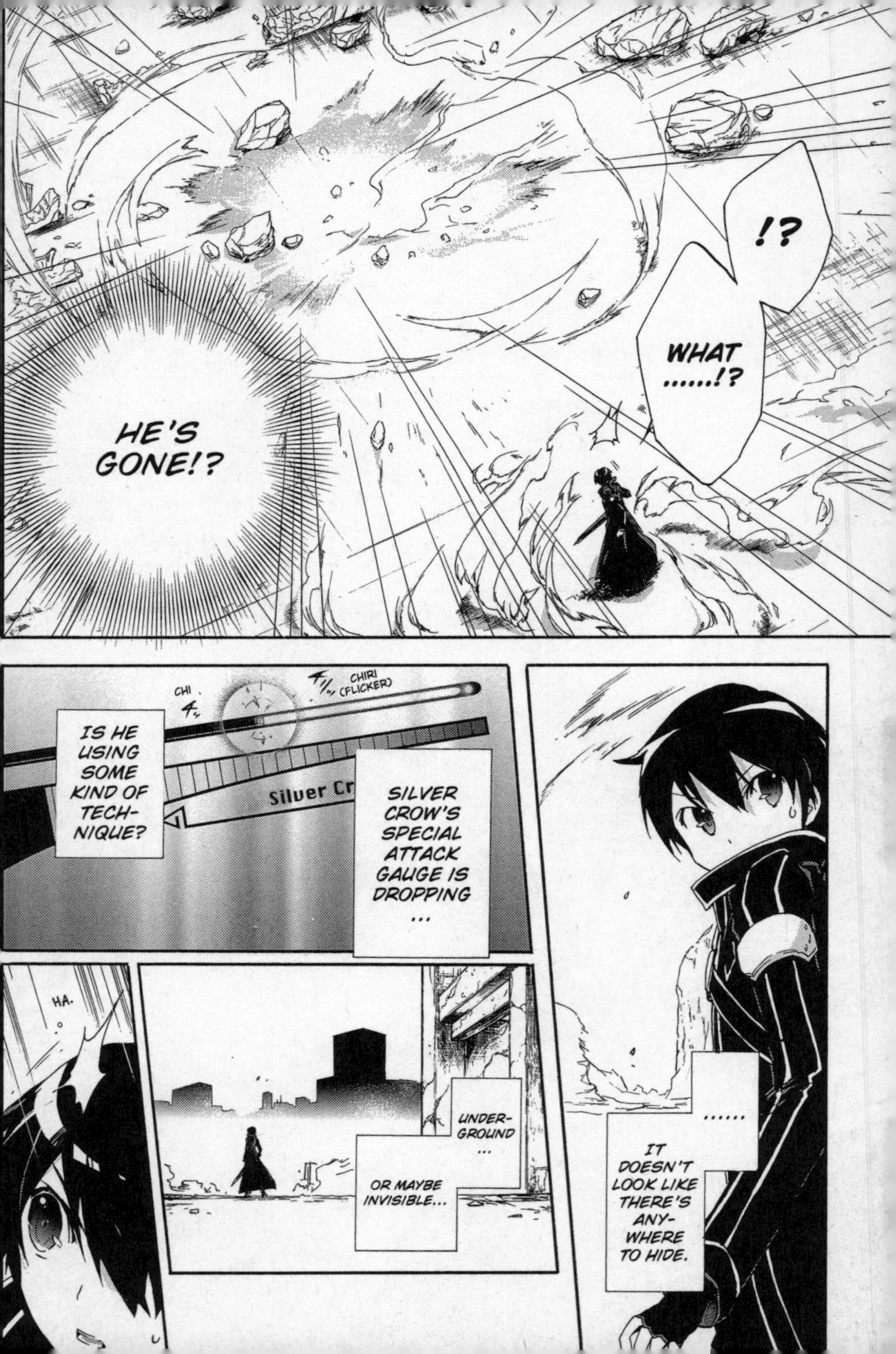
!?
WHAT ......!?
HE'S GONE!?
......
IT DOESN'T LOOK LIKE THERE'S ANY-WHERE TO HIDE.
CHIRI (FLICKER)
CHI
Silver Cr
SILVER CROW'S SPECIAL ATTACK GAUGE IS DROPPING ...
IS HE USING SOME KIND OF TECH-NIQUE?
UNDER-GROUND ...
OR MAYBE INVISIBLE...
HA.

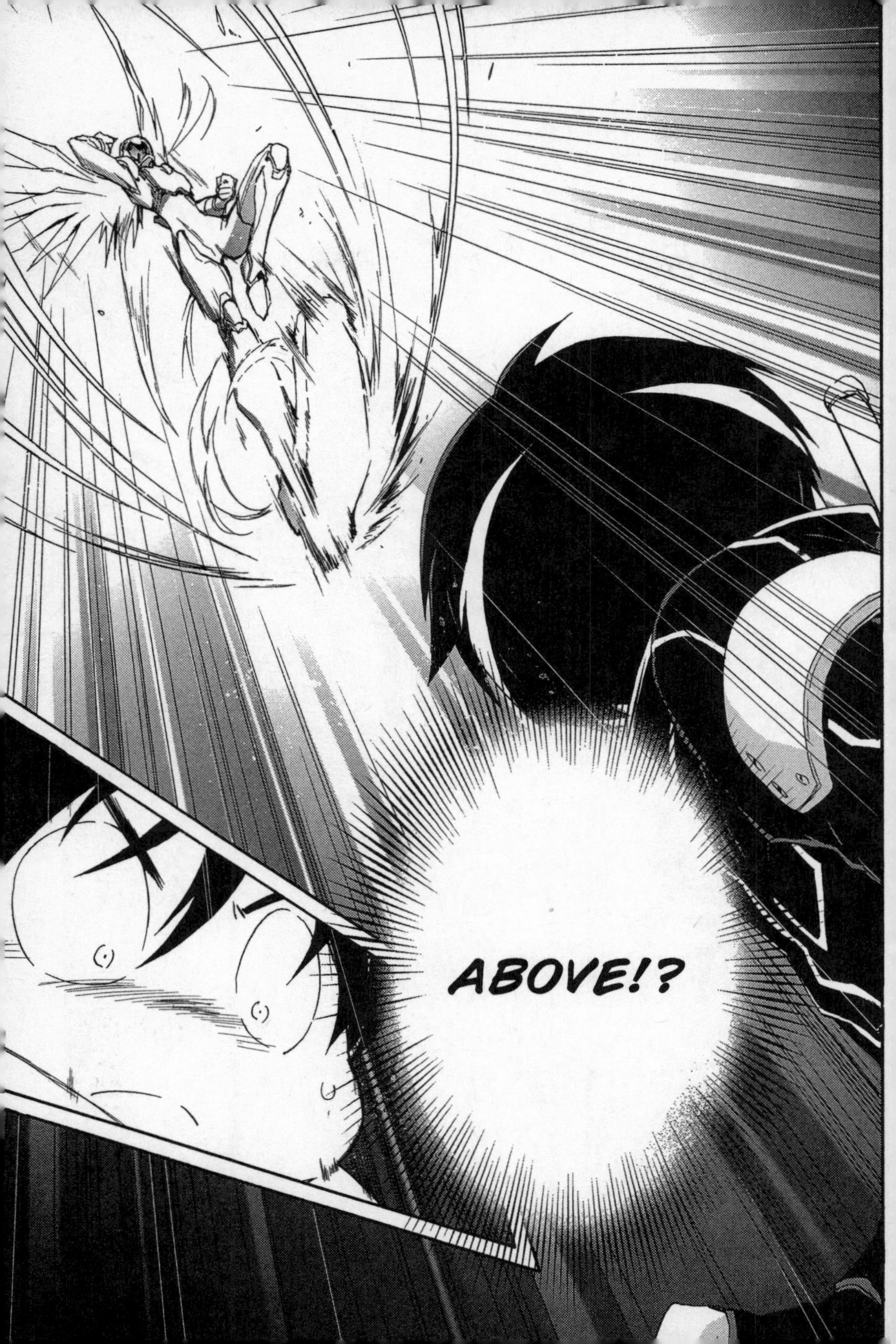
ABOVE!?

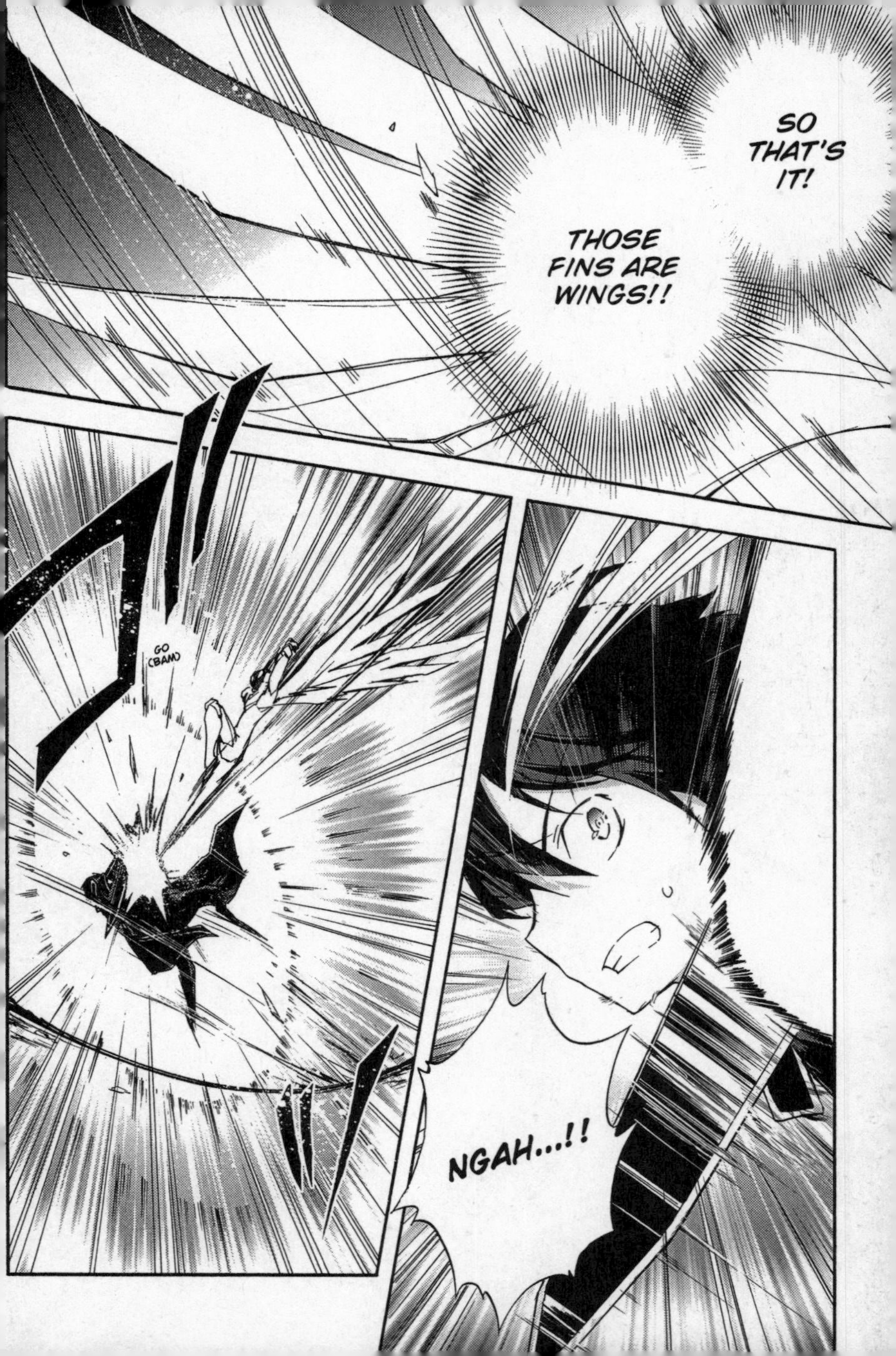
SO THAT'S IT!
THOSE FINS ARE WINGS!!
NGAH...!!
GO (BAM)

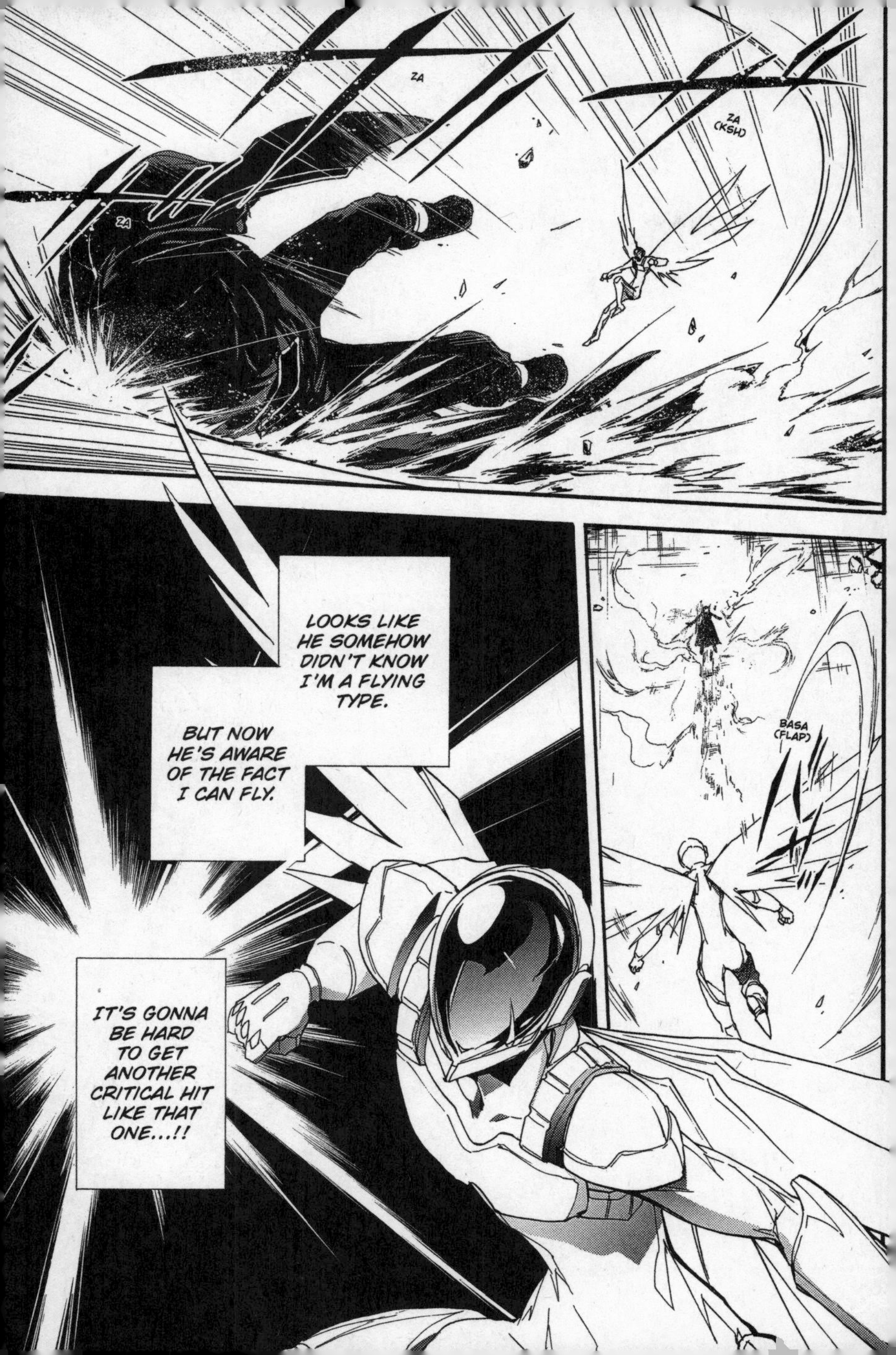
ZA (KSH)
ZA
ZA
BASA (FLAP)
LOOKS LIKE HE SOMEHOW DIDN'T KNOW I'M A FLYING TYPE.
BUT NOW HE'S AWARE OF THE FACT I CAN FLY.
IT'S GONNA BE HARD TO GET ANOTHER CRITICAL HIT LIKE THAT ONE...!!

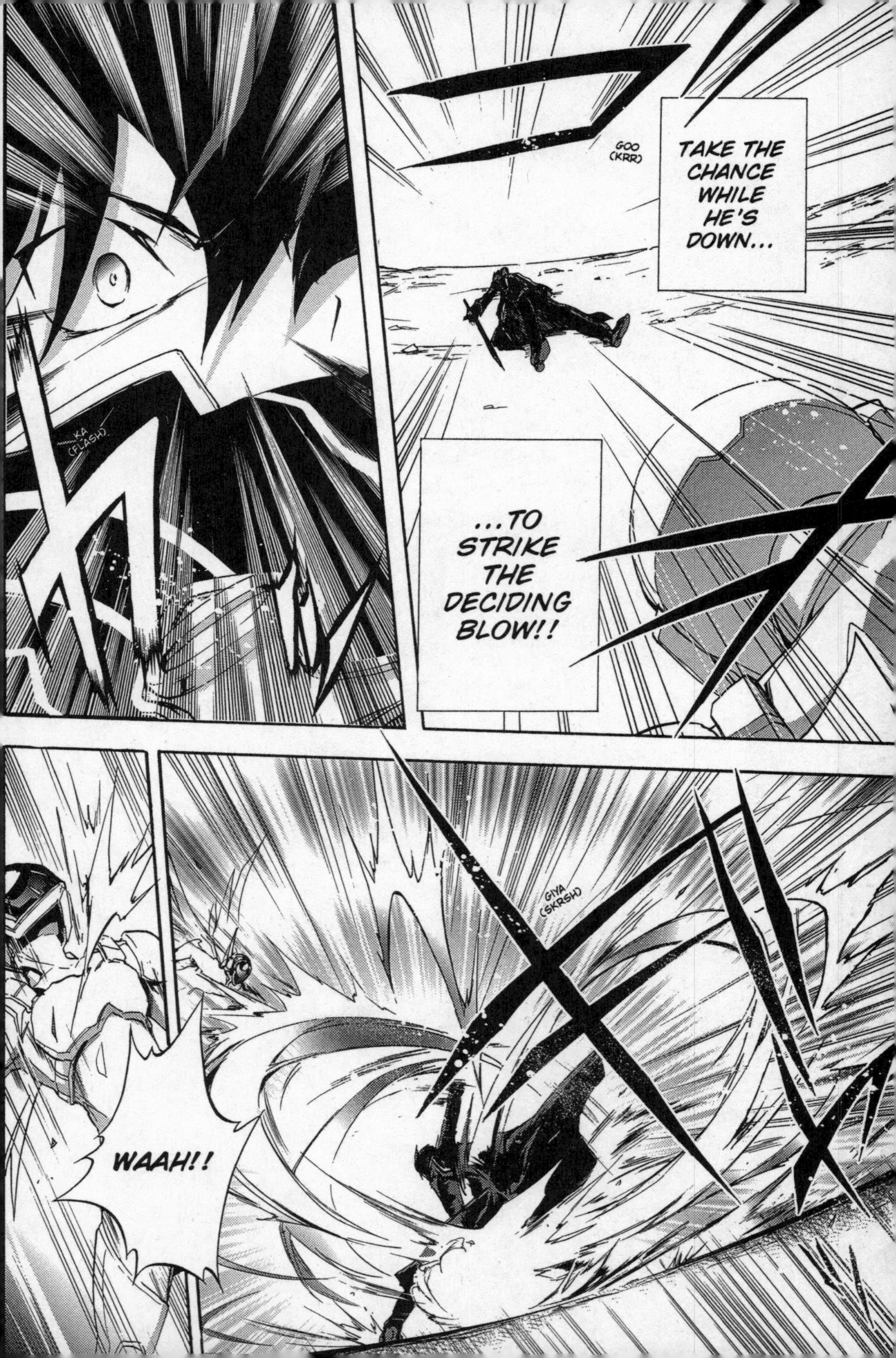
GOO (KRR)
TAKE THE CHANCE WHILE HE'S DOWN...
...TO STRIKE THE DECIDING BLOW!!
KA (FLASH)
GIYA (SKRSH)
WAAH!!

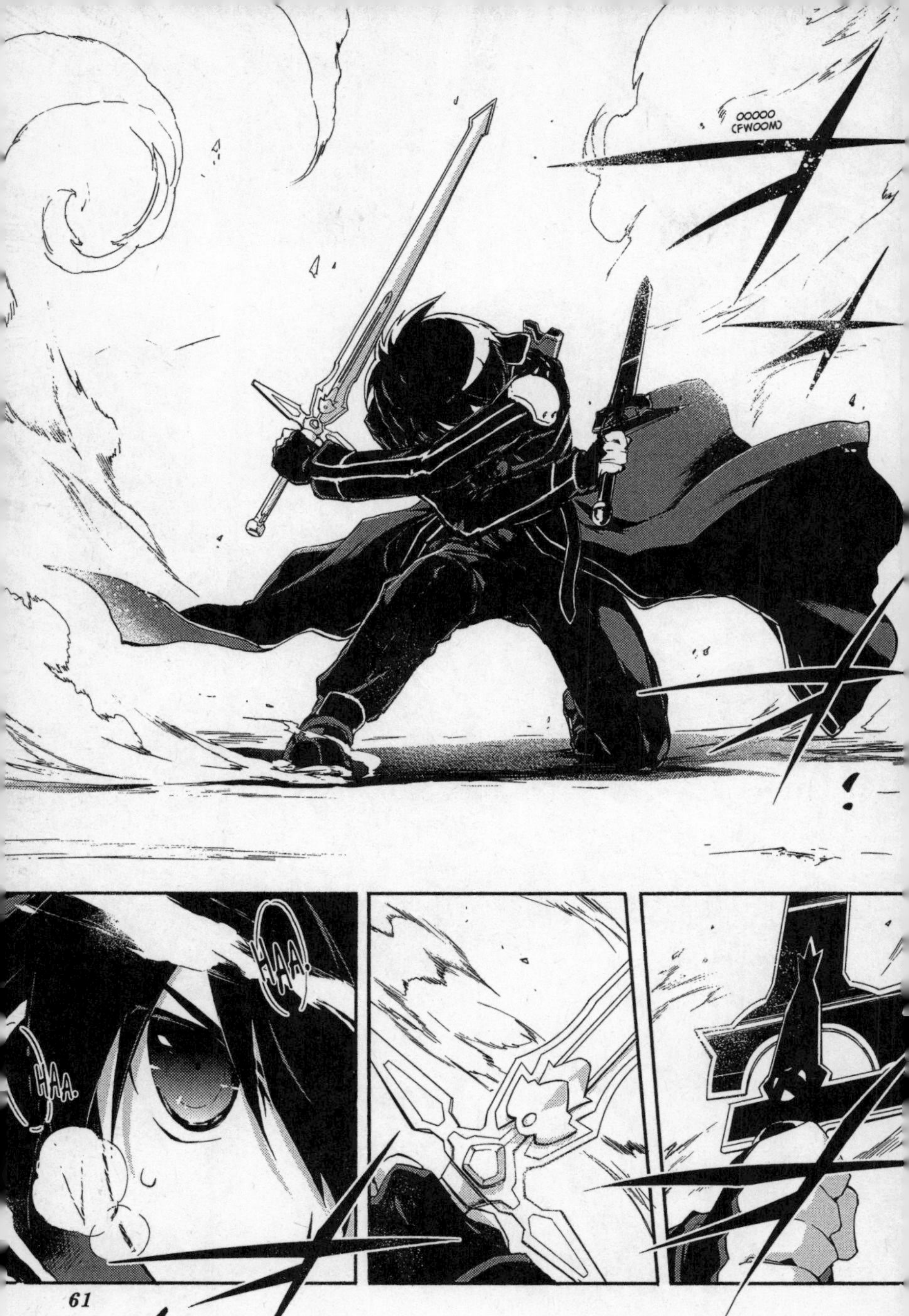
OOOOO
(FWOOM)
HAA!
HAA.

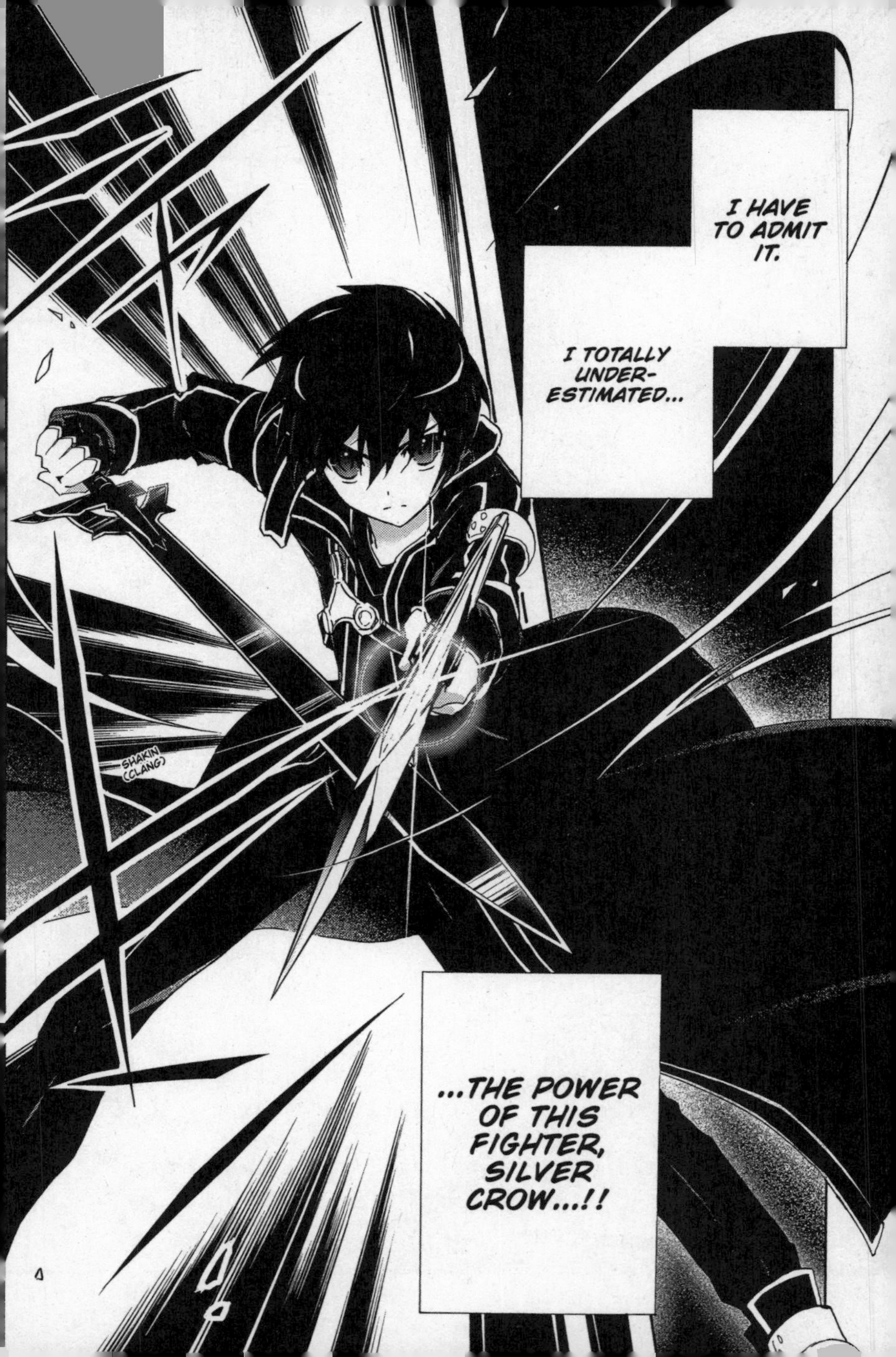
I HAVE TO ADMIT IT.
I TOTALLY UNDER-ESTIMATED...
SHAKIN (CLANG)
...THE POWER OF THIS FIGHTER, SILVER CROW...!!

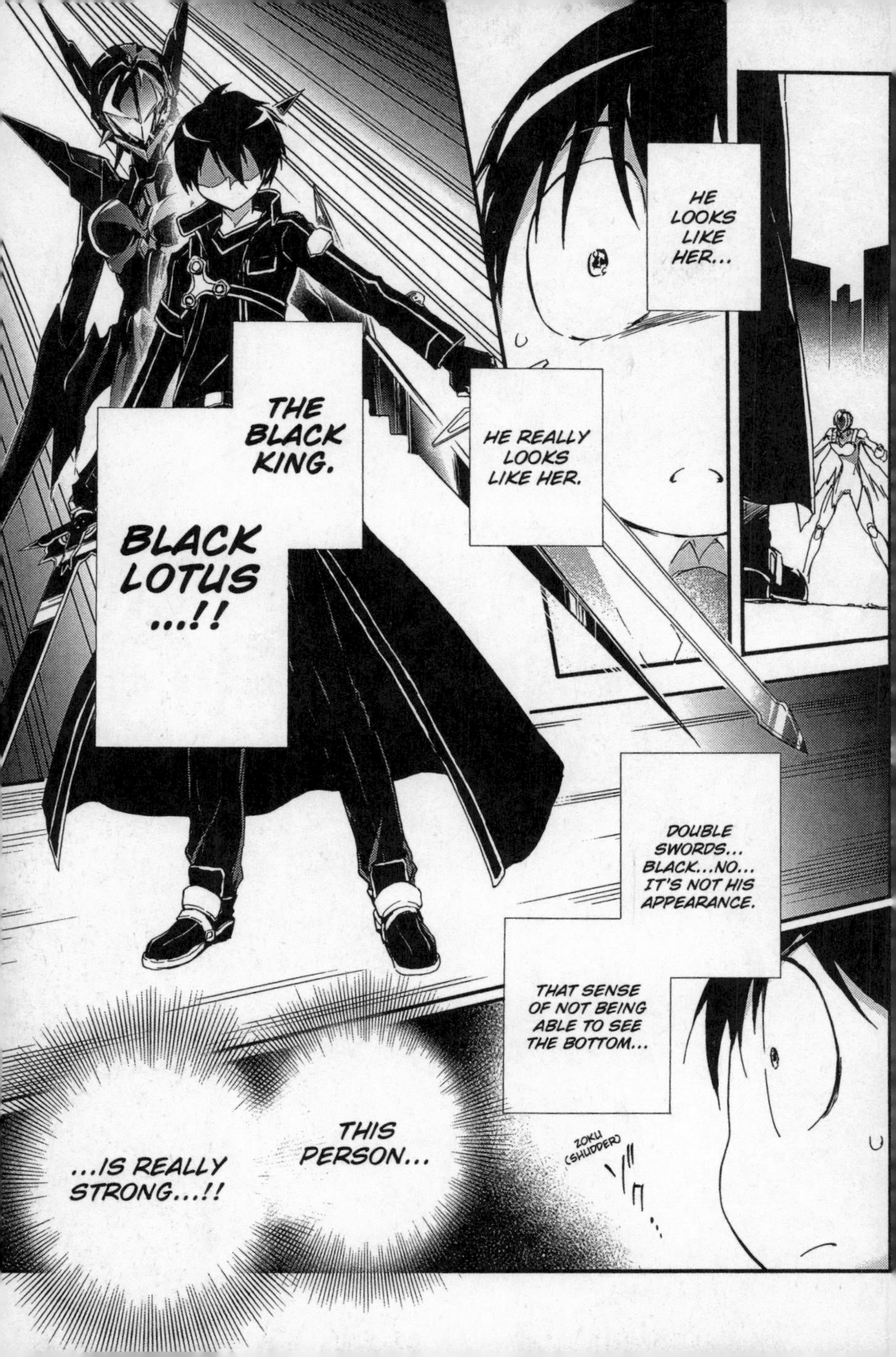
HE LOOKS LIKE HER...
HE REALLY LOOKS LIKE HER.
THE BLACK KING.
BLACK LOTUS ...!!
DOUBLE SWORDS... BLACK...NO... IT'S NOT HIS APPEARANCE.
THAT SENSE OF NOT BEING ABLE TO SEE THE BOTTOM...
ZOKU (SHUDDER)
THIS PERSON...
...IS REALLY STRONG...!!

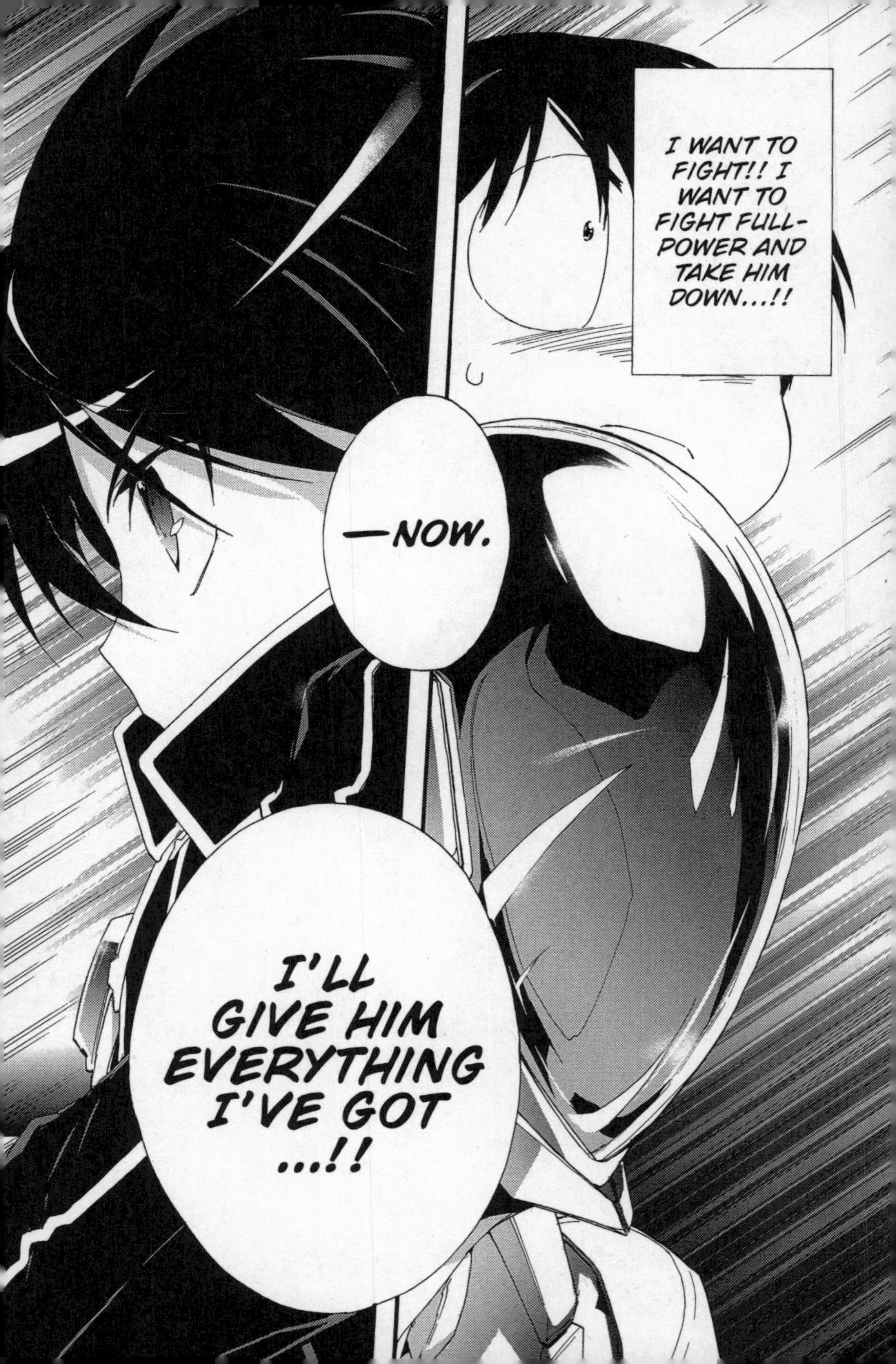
I WANT TO FIGHT!! I WANT TO FIGHT FULL-POWER AND TAKE HIM DOWN...!!
—NOW.
I'LL GIVE HIM EVERYTHING I'VE GOT ...!!

▶▶▶*ACCEL·WORLD*

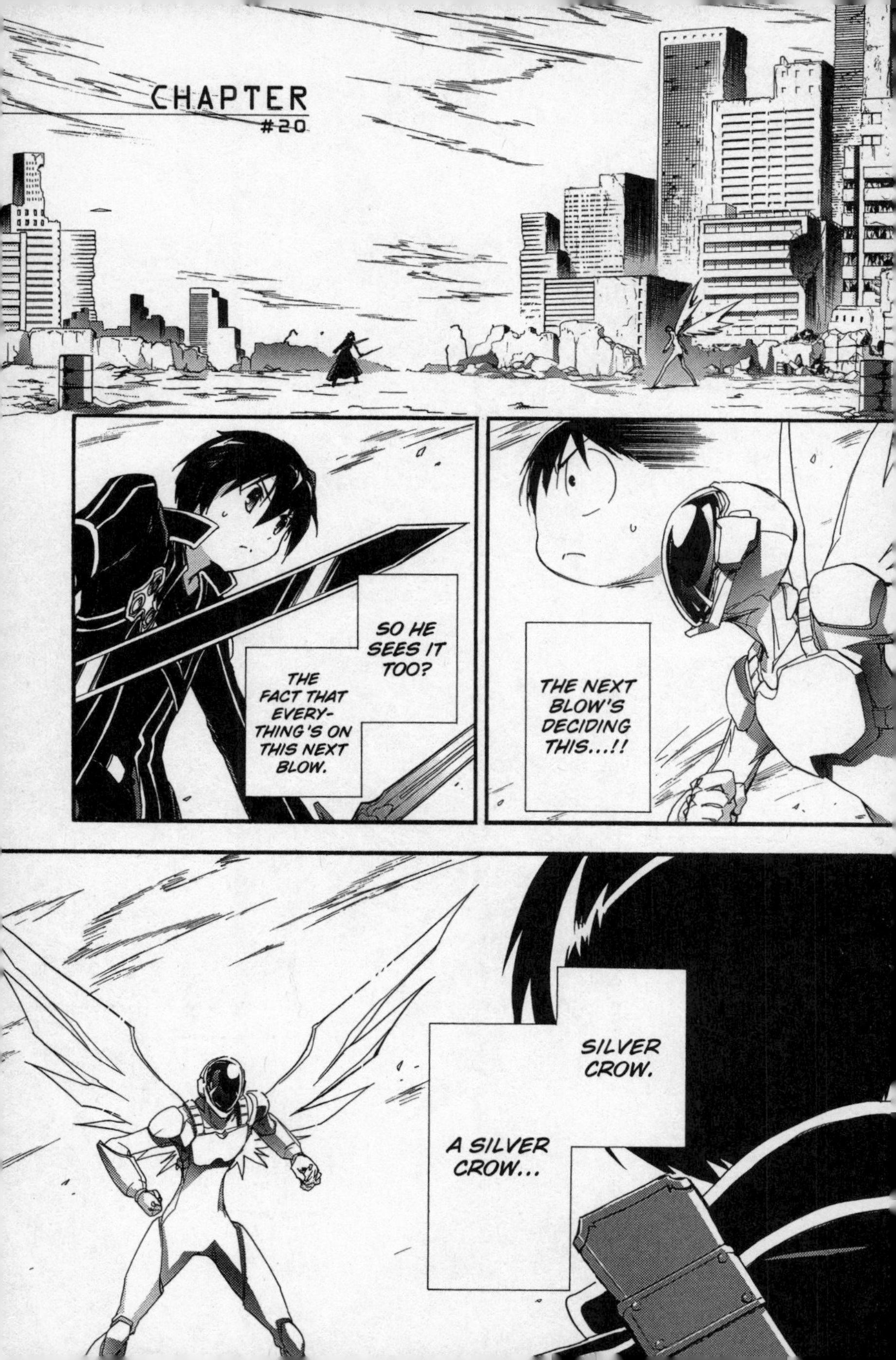
CHAPTER
#20
THE NEXT BLOW'S DECIDING THIS...!!
SO HE SEES IT TOO?
THE FACT THAT EVERY-THING'S ON THIS NEXT BLOW.
SILVER CROW.
A SILVER CROW...

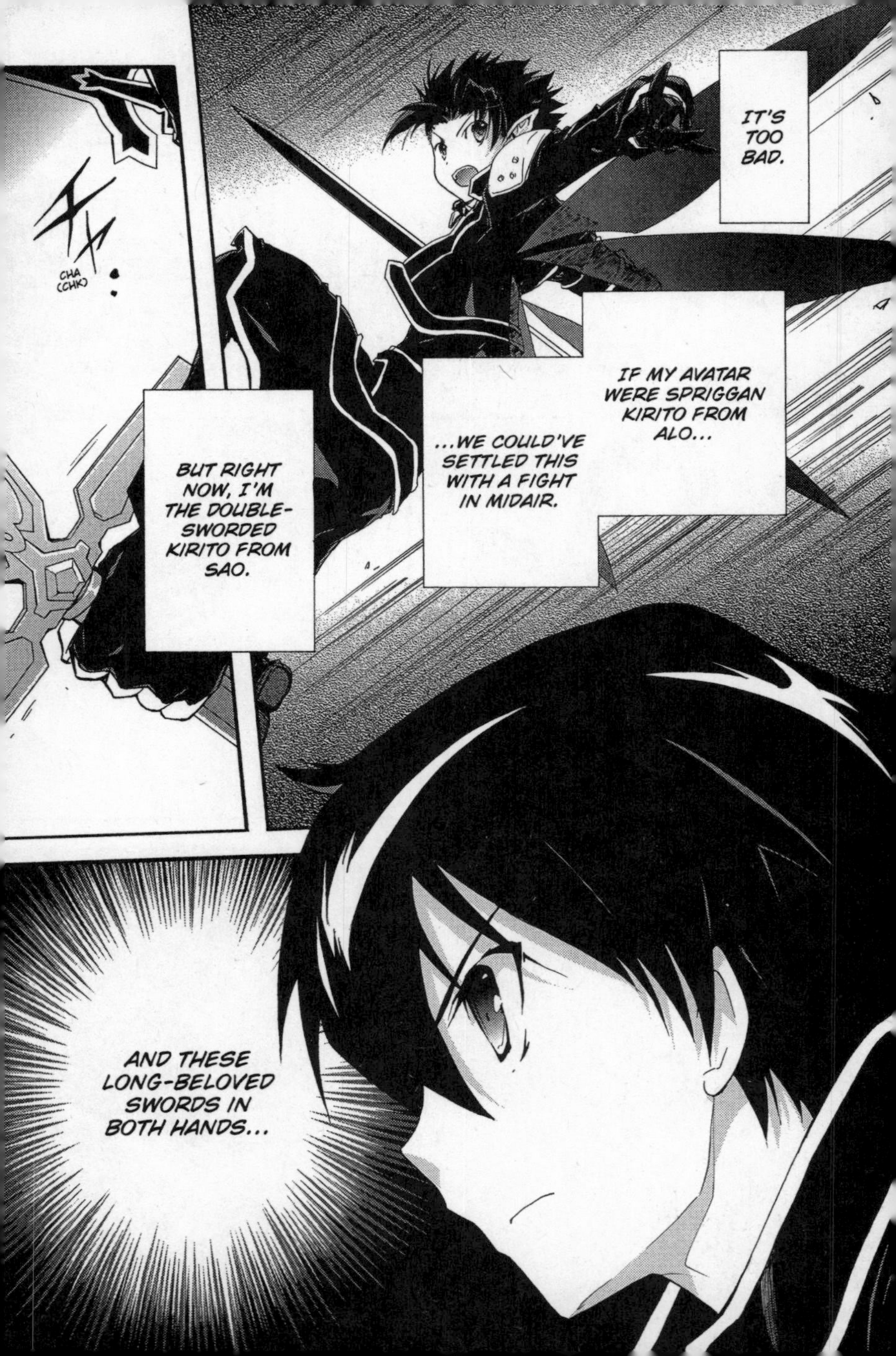
IT'S TOO BAD.
IF MY AVATAR WERE SPRIGGAN KIRITO FROM ALO...
...WE COULD'VE SETTLED THIS WITH A FIGHT IN MIDAIR.
BUT RIGHT NOW, I'M THE DOUBLE-SWORDED KIRITO FROM SAO.
CHA (CHK)
AND THESE LONG-BELOVED SWORDS IN BOTH HANDS...

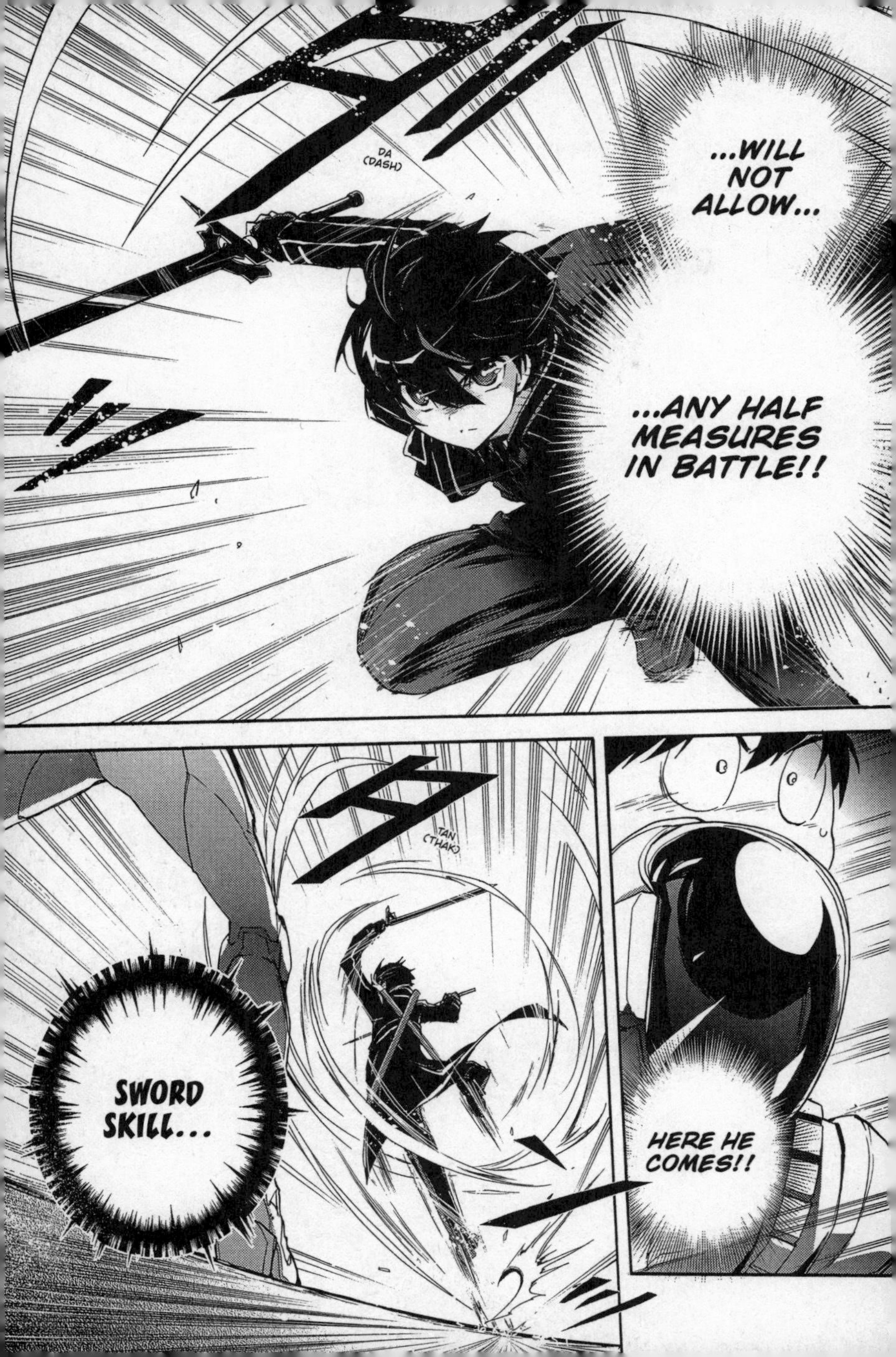
...WILL NOT ALLOW...
DA (DASH)
...ANY HALF MEASURES IN BATTLE!!
HERE HE COMES!!
TAN (THAK)
SWORD SKILL...

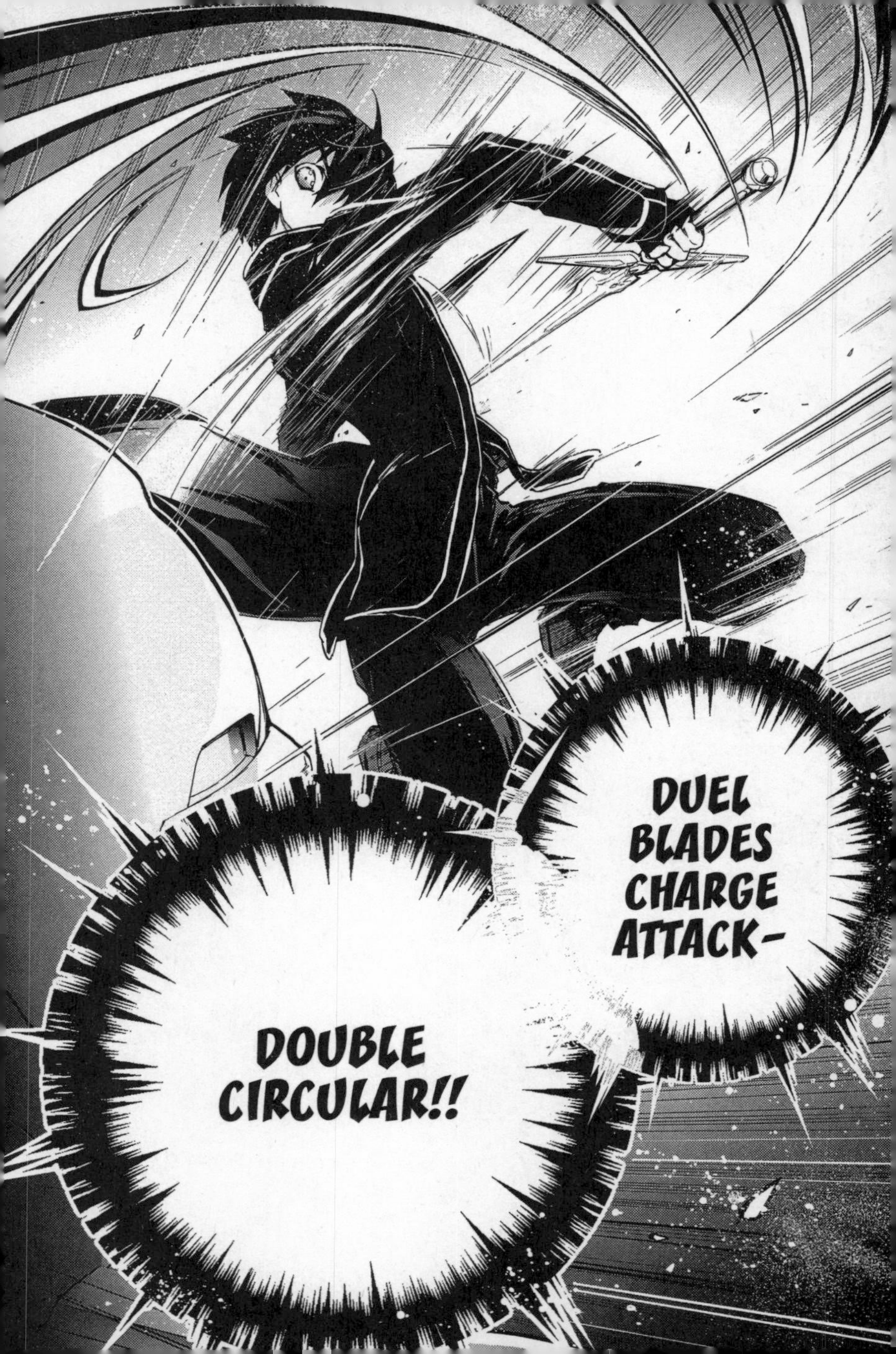
DUEL BLADES CHARGE ATTACK-
DOUBLE CIRCULAR!!

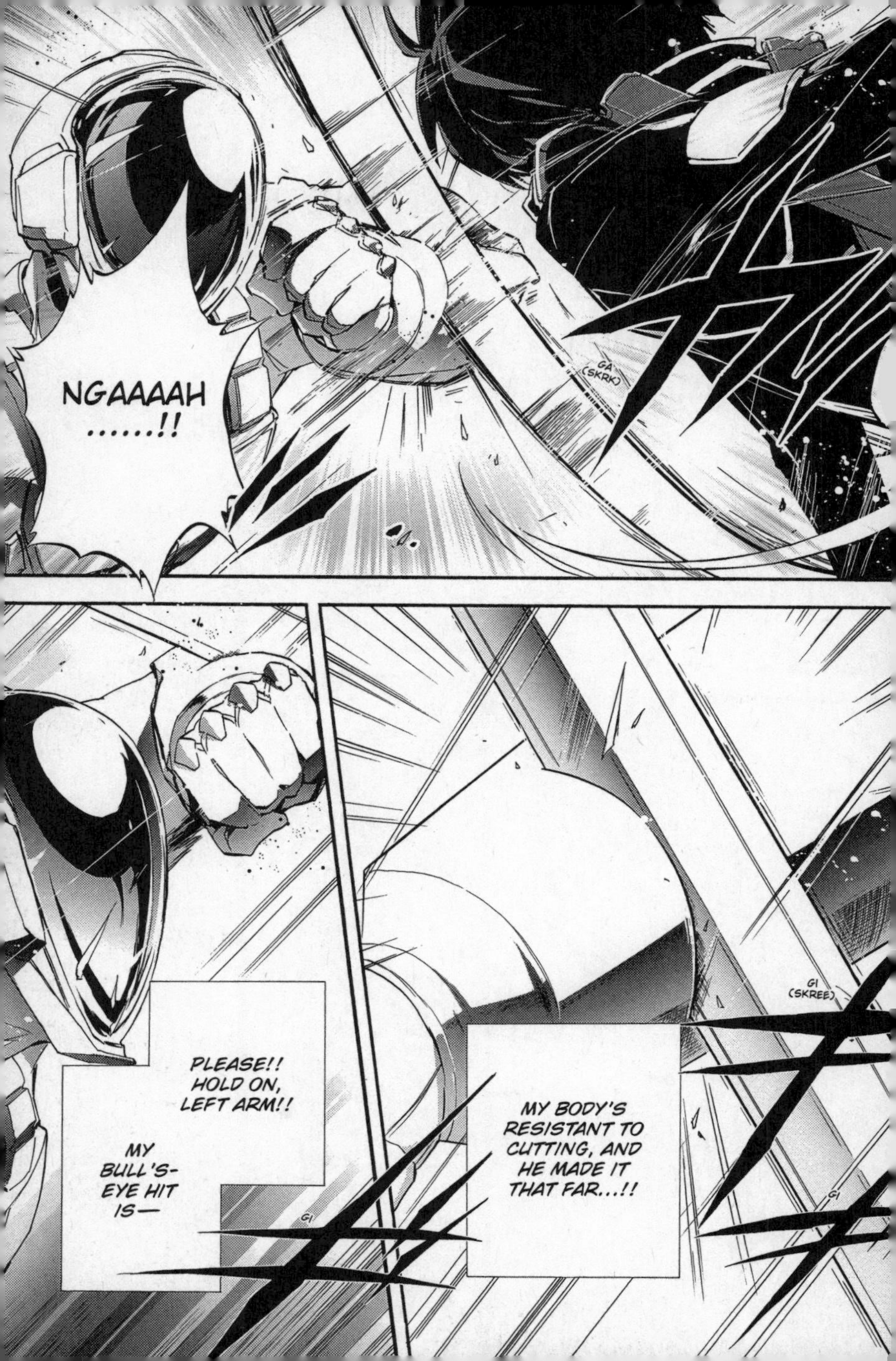
GA (SKRK)
NGAAAAH ......!!
GI (SKREE)
MY BODY'S RESISTANT TO CUTTING, AND HE MADE IT THAT FAR...!!
GI
PLEASE!! HOLD ON, LEFT ARM!!
MY BULL'S-EYE HIT IS—
GI

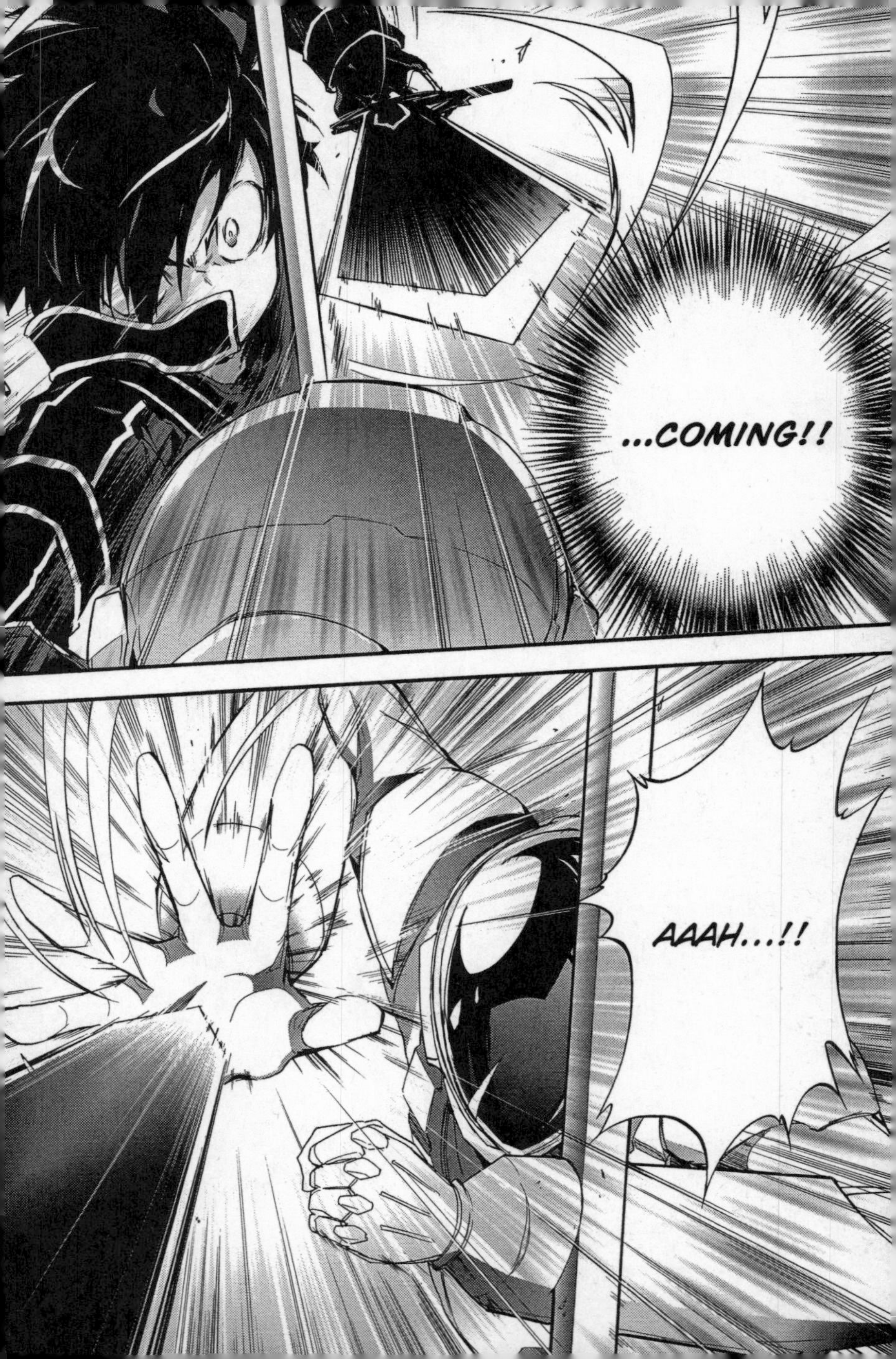
...COMING!!
AAAH...!!

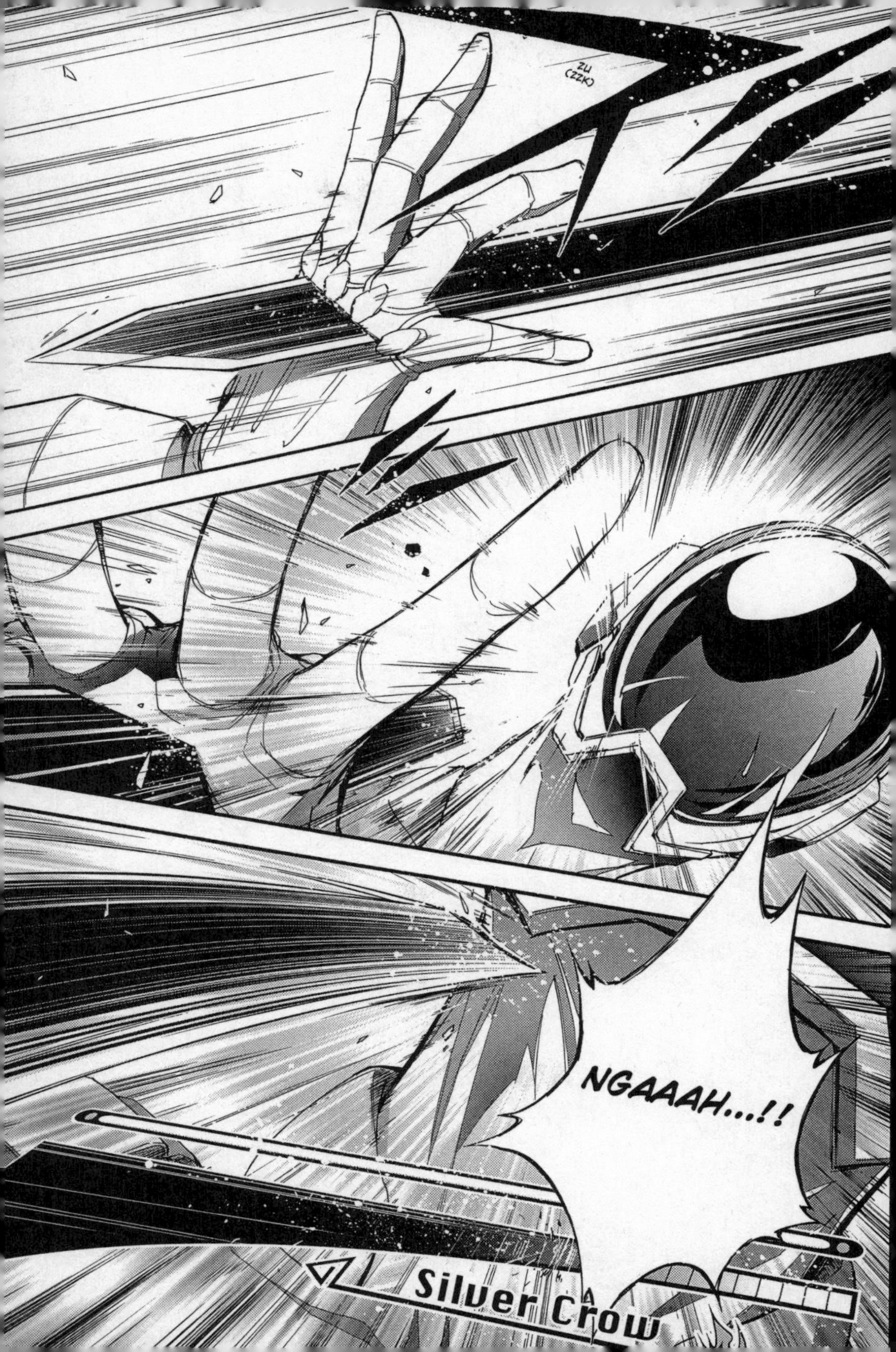
ZU
(ZZK)
NGAAAH...!!
Silver Crow

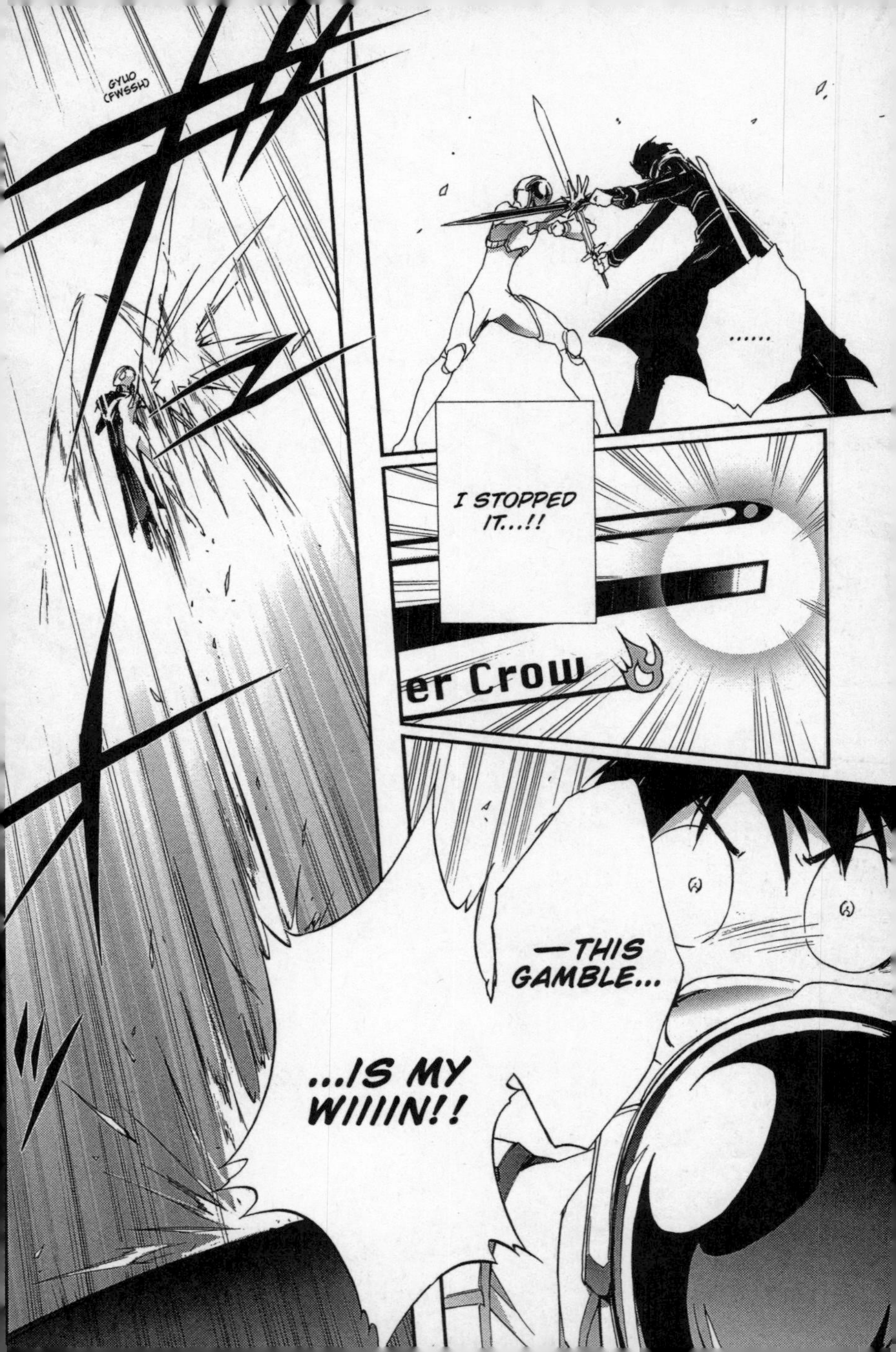
......
I STOPPED IT...!!
er Crow
GYUO
(FWSSH)
—THIS GAMBLE...
...IS MY WIIIIN!!

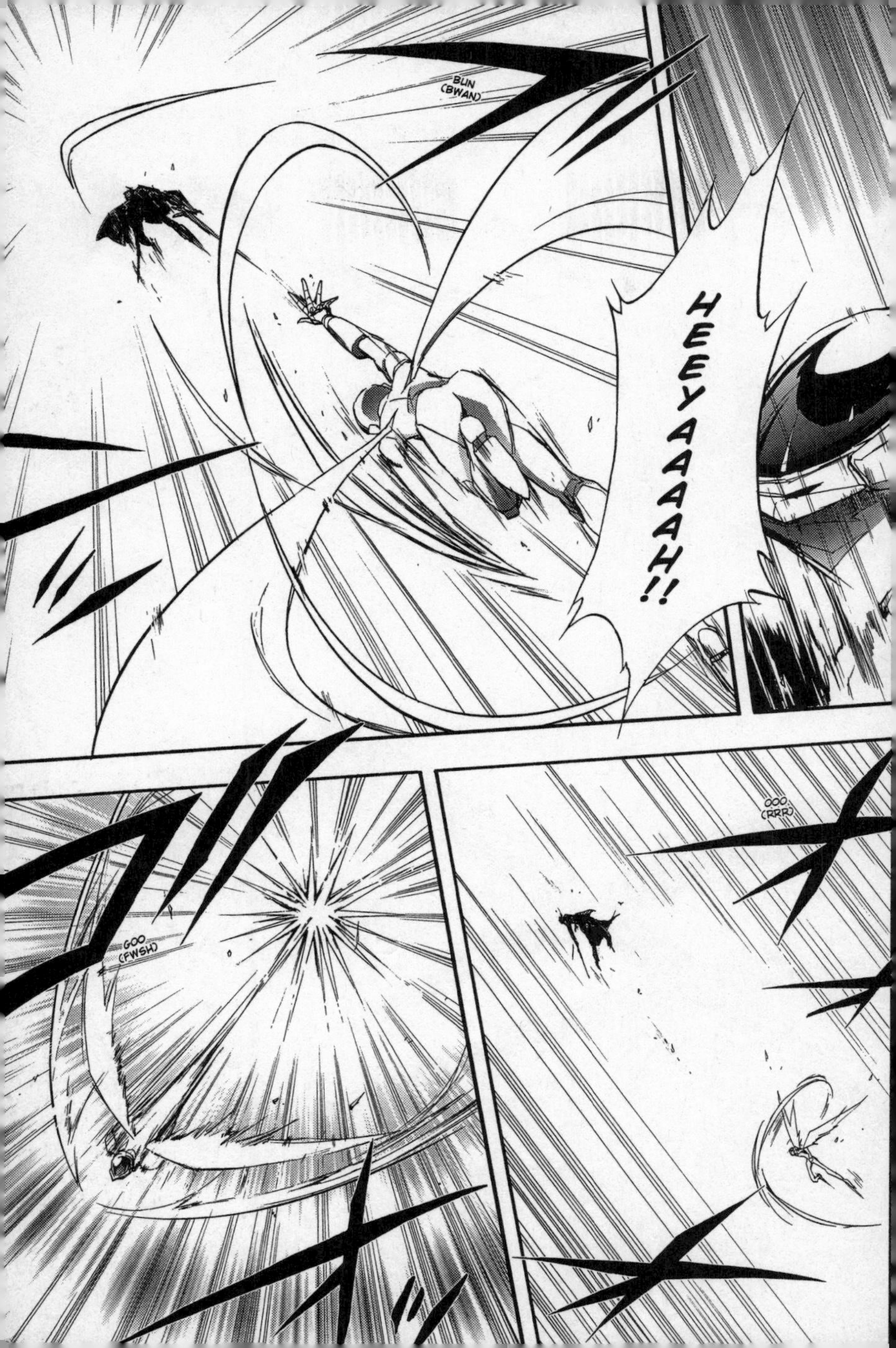
BUN (BWAN)
HEEYAAAAH!!
OOO (RRR)
GOO (FWSH)

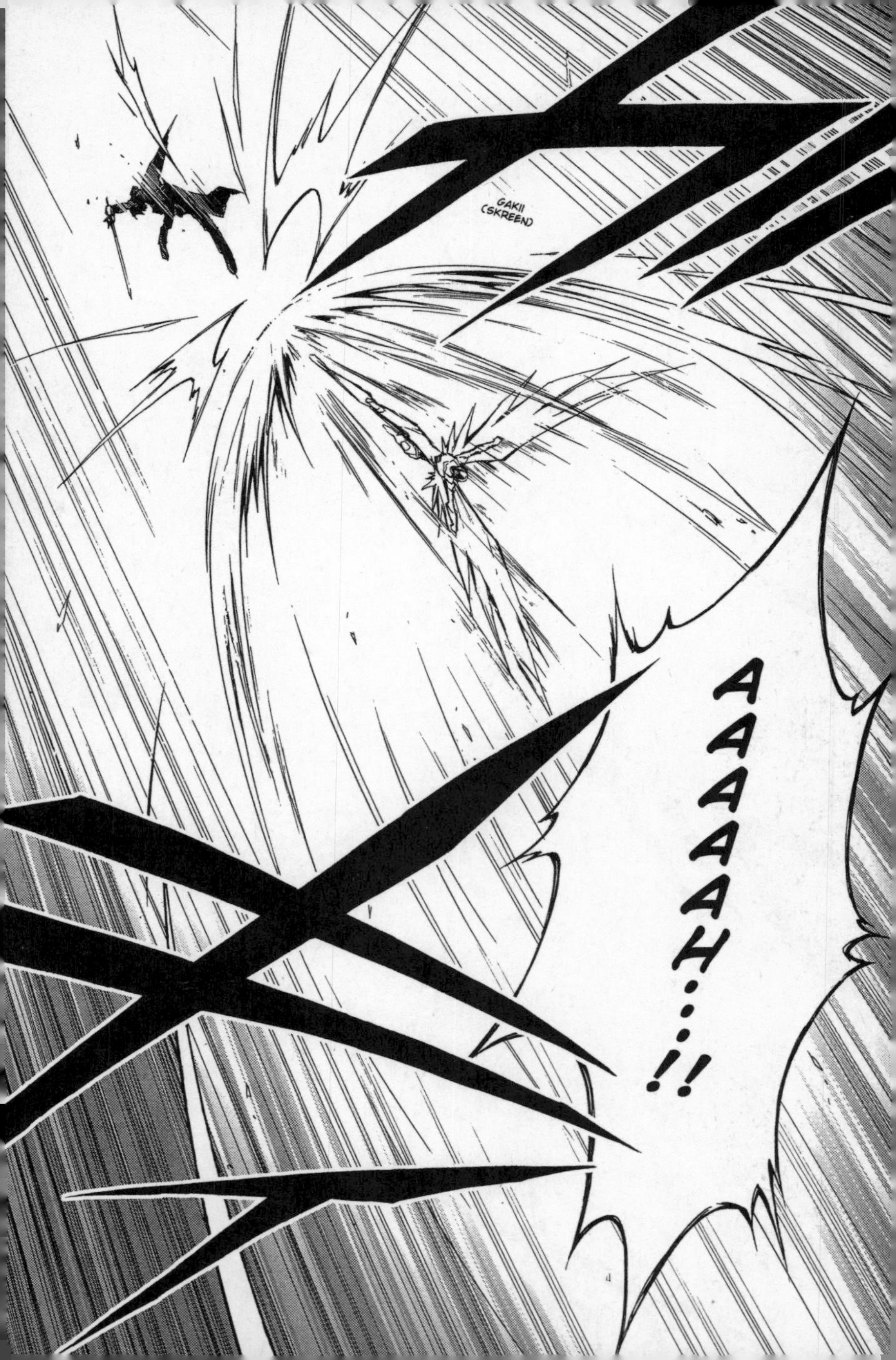
GAKII
(SKREEN)
AAAAAH...!!

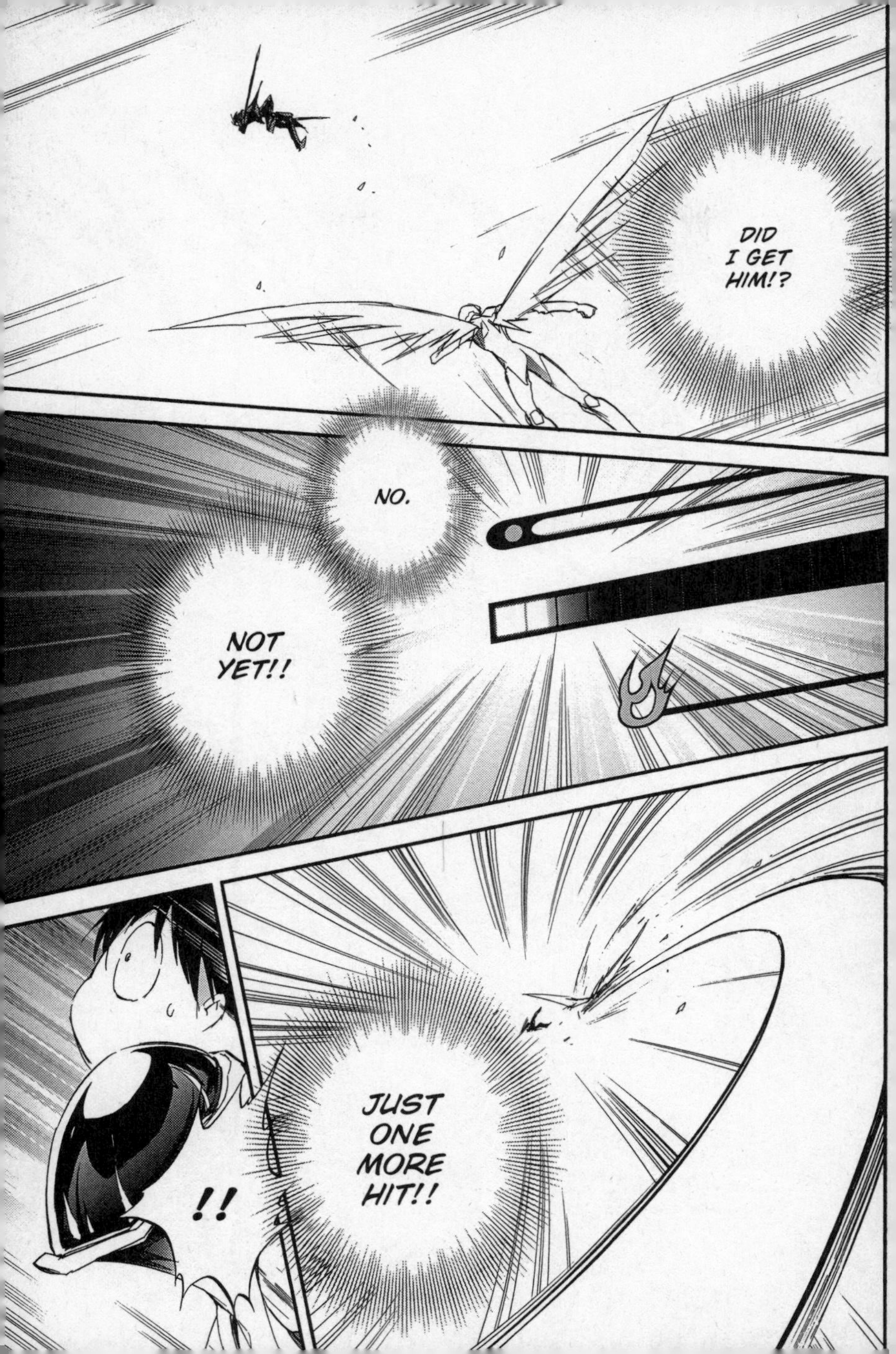
DID I GET HIM!?
NO.
NOT YET!!
JUST ONE MORE HIT!!
!!

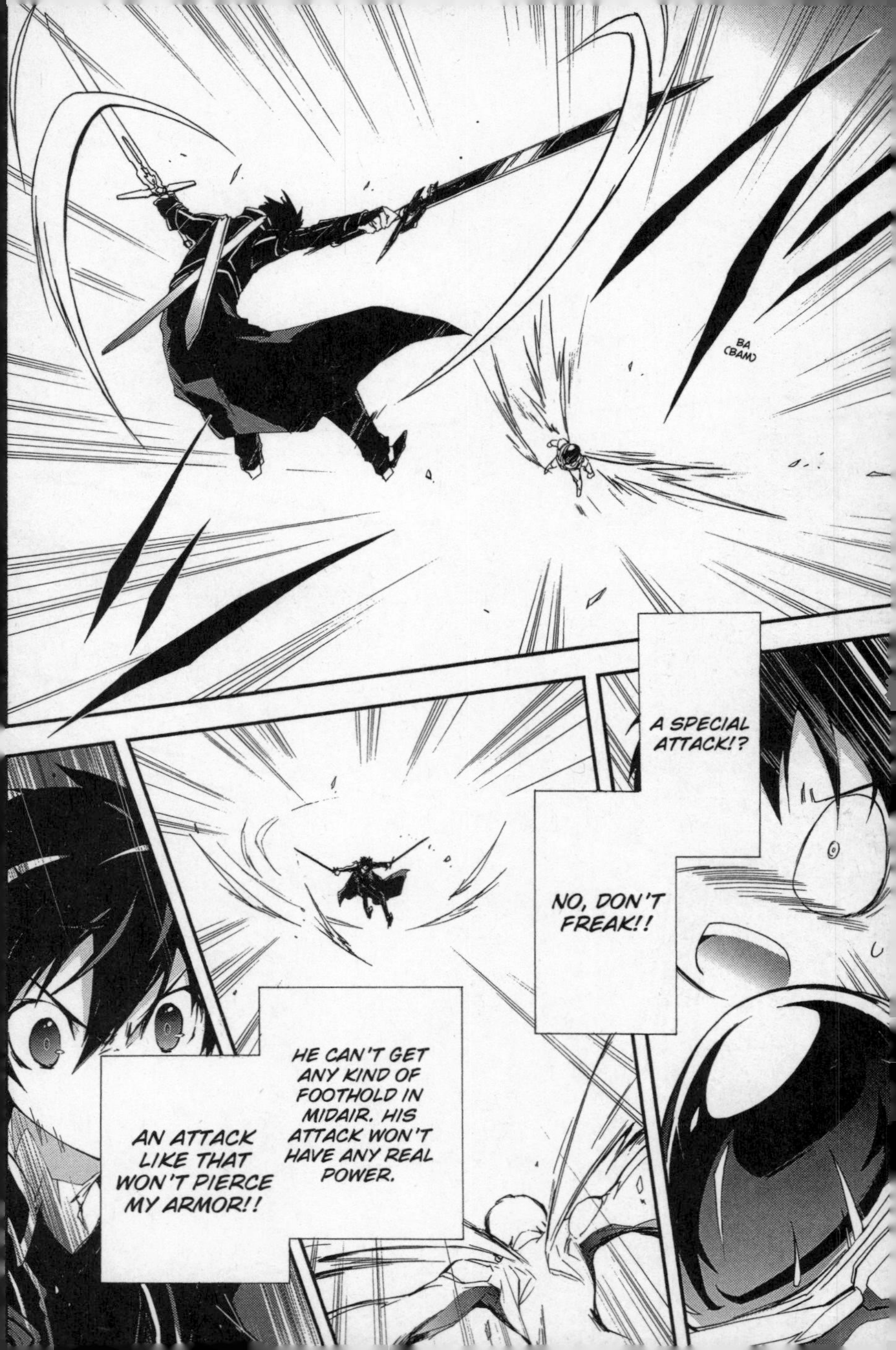
BA (BAM)
A SPECIAL ATTACK!?
NO, DON'T FREAK!!
HE CAN'T GET ANY KIND OF FOOTHOLD IN MIDAIR. HIS ATTACK WON'T HAVE ANY REAL POWER.
AN ATTACK LIKE THAT WON'T PIERCE MY ARMOR!!

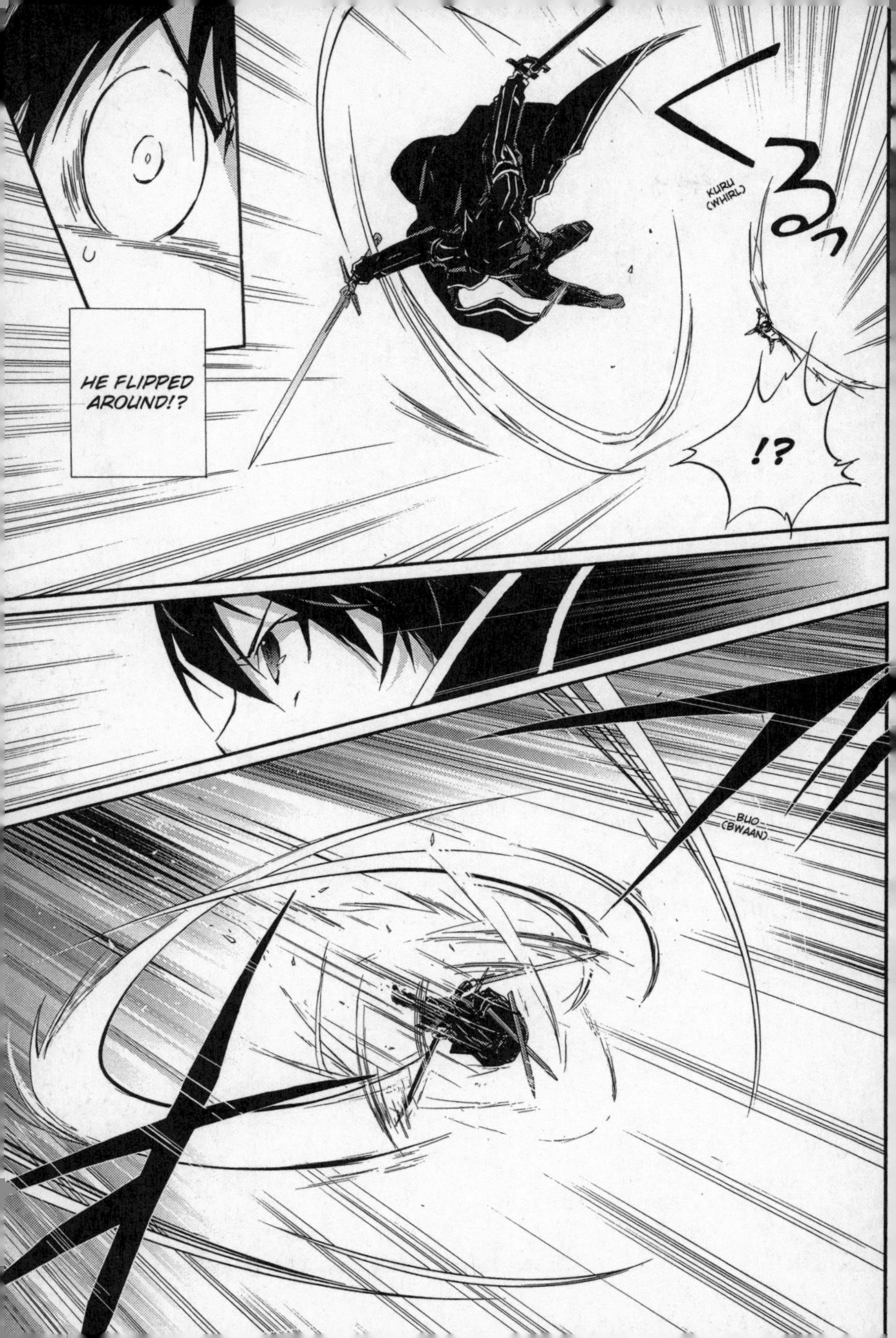
KURU
(WHIRL)
!?
HE FLIPPED AROUND!?
BUO
(BWAAN)

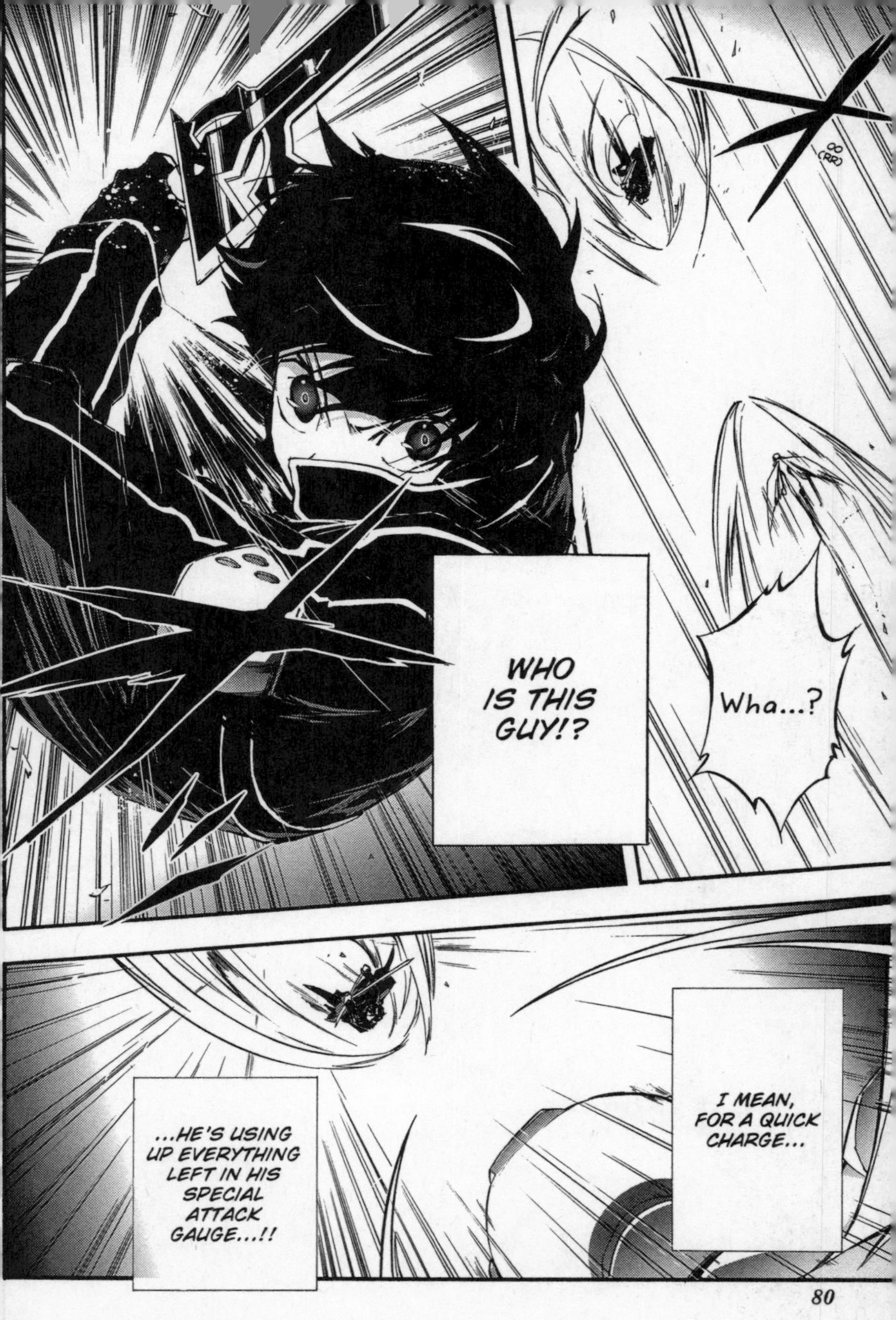
(RR)
Wha...?
WHO IS THIS GUY!?
I MEAN, FOR A QUICK CHARGE...
...HE'S USING UP EVERYTHING LEFT IN HIS SPECIAL ATTACK GAUGE...!!

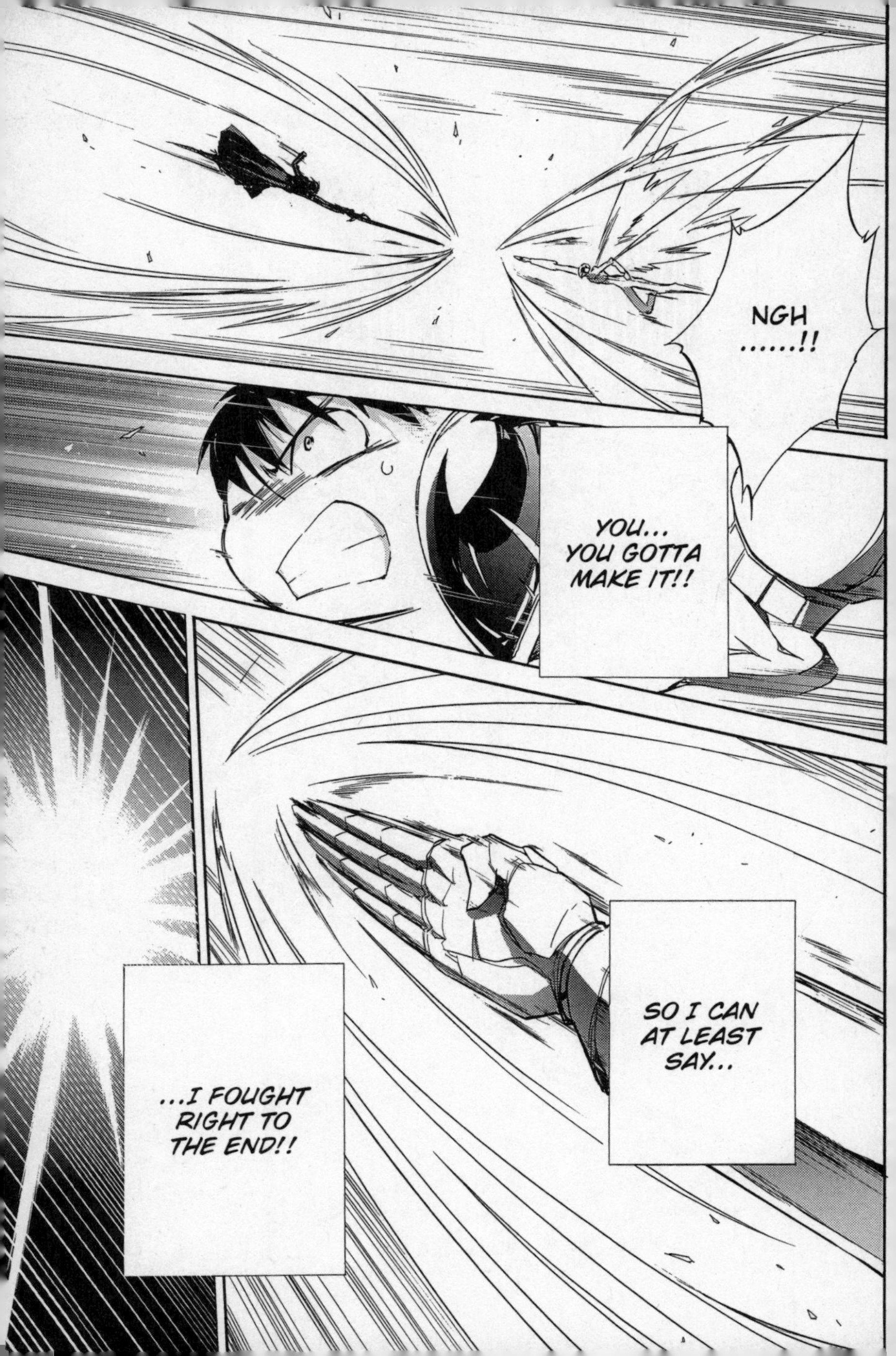
NGH ......!!
YOU... YOU GOTTA MAKE IT!!
SO I CAN AT LEAST SAY...
...I FOUGHT RIGHT TO THE END!!

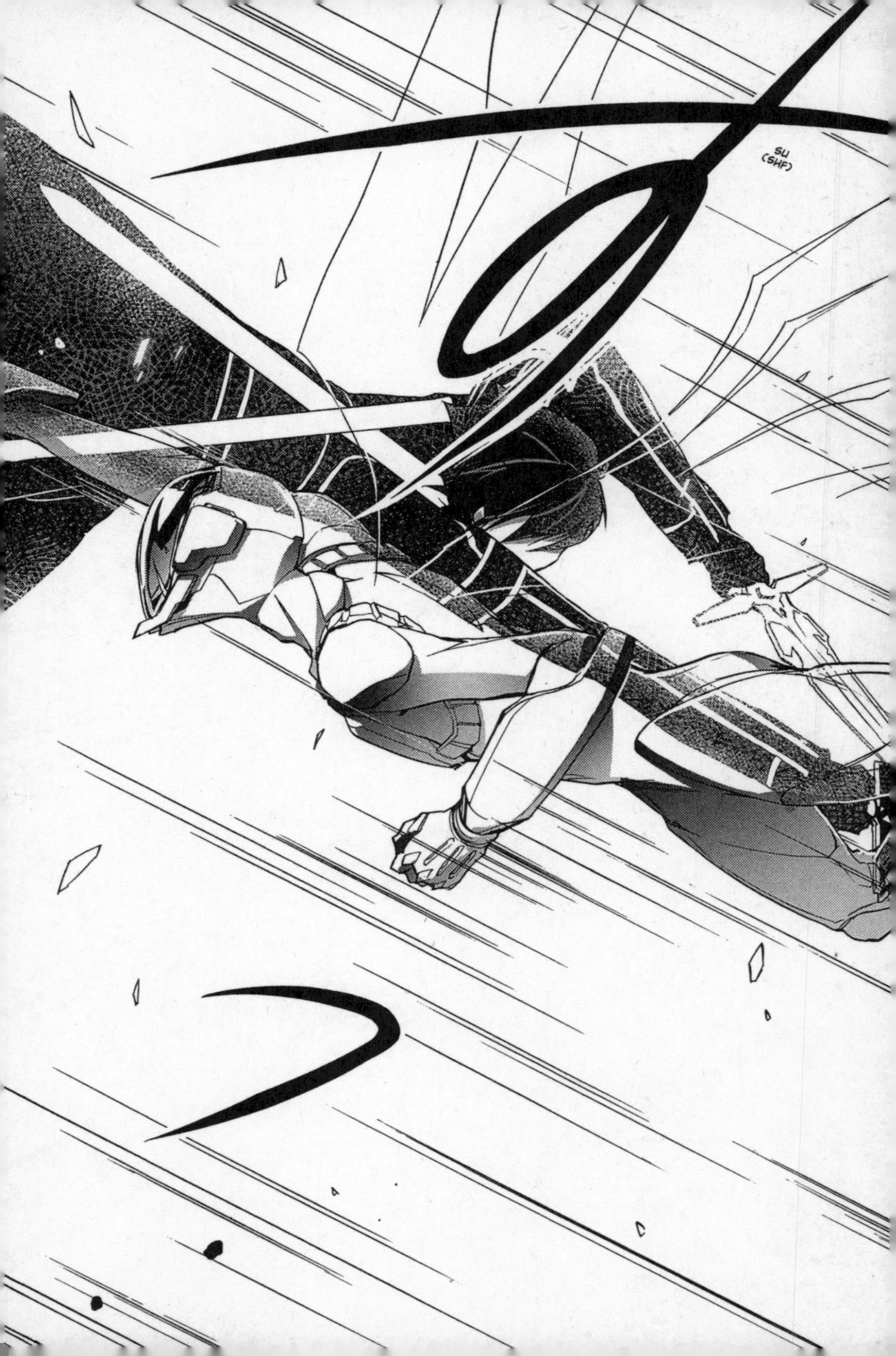
SU
(SHF)

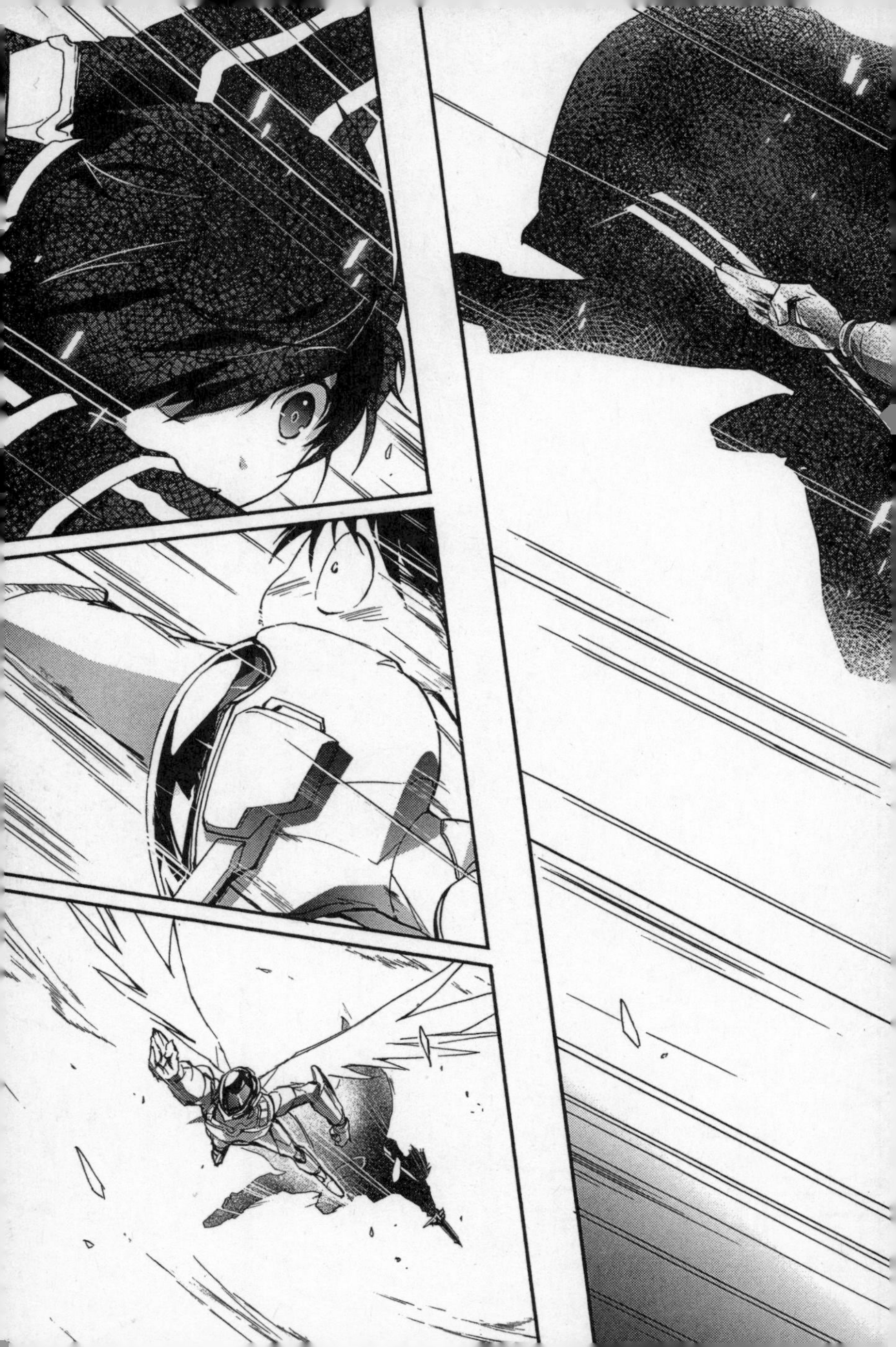

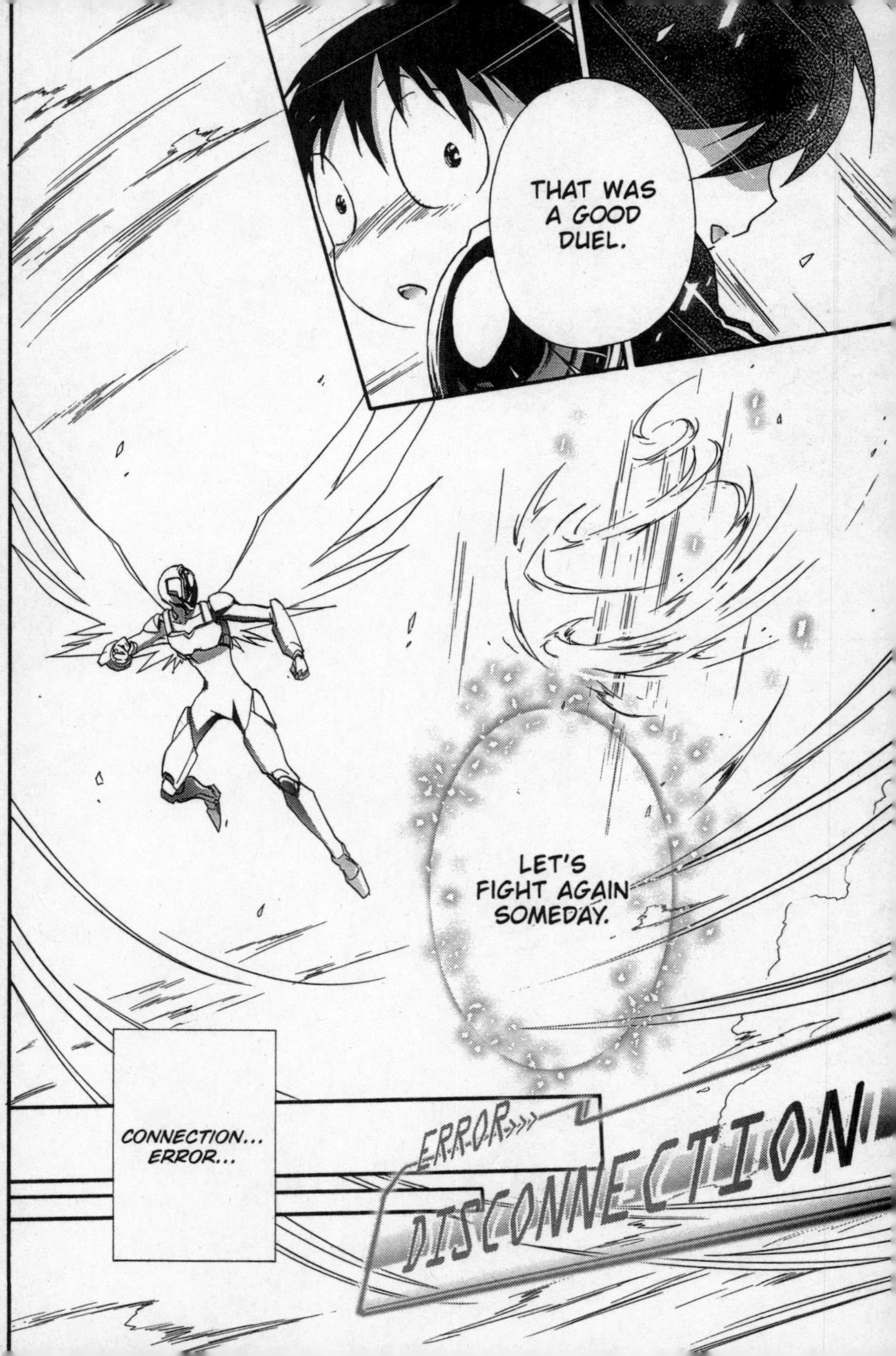
THAT WAS A GOOD DUEL.
LET'S FIGHT AGAIN SOMEDAY.
CONNECTION... ERROR...
ERROR
DISCONNECTION

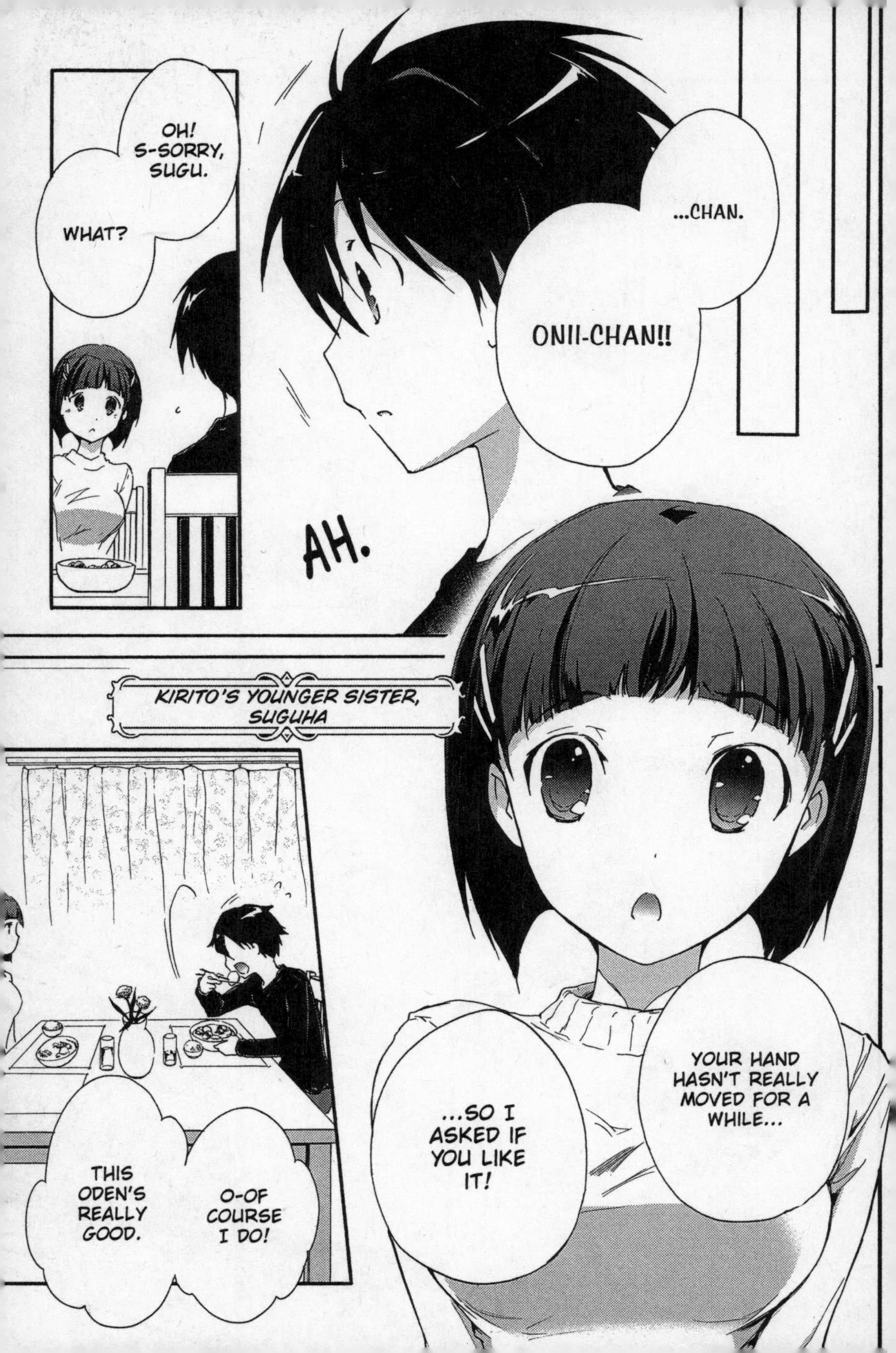
...CHAN.
ONII-CHAN!!
AH.
OH! S-SORRY, SUGU.
WHAT?
YOUR HAND HASN'T REALLY MOVED FOR A WHILE...
...SO I ASKED IF YOU LIKE IT!
KIRITO'S YOUNGER SISTER, SUGUHA
O-OF COURSE I DO!
THIS ODEN'S REALLY GOOD.

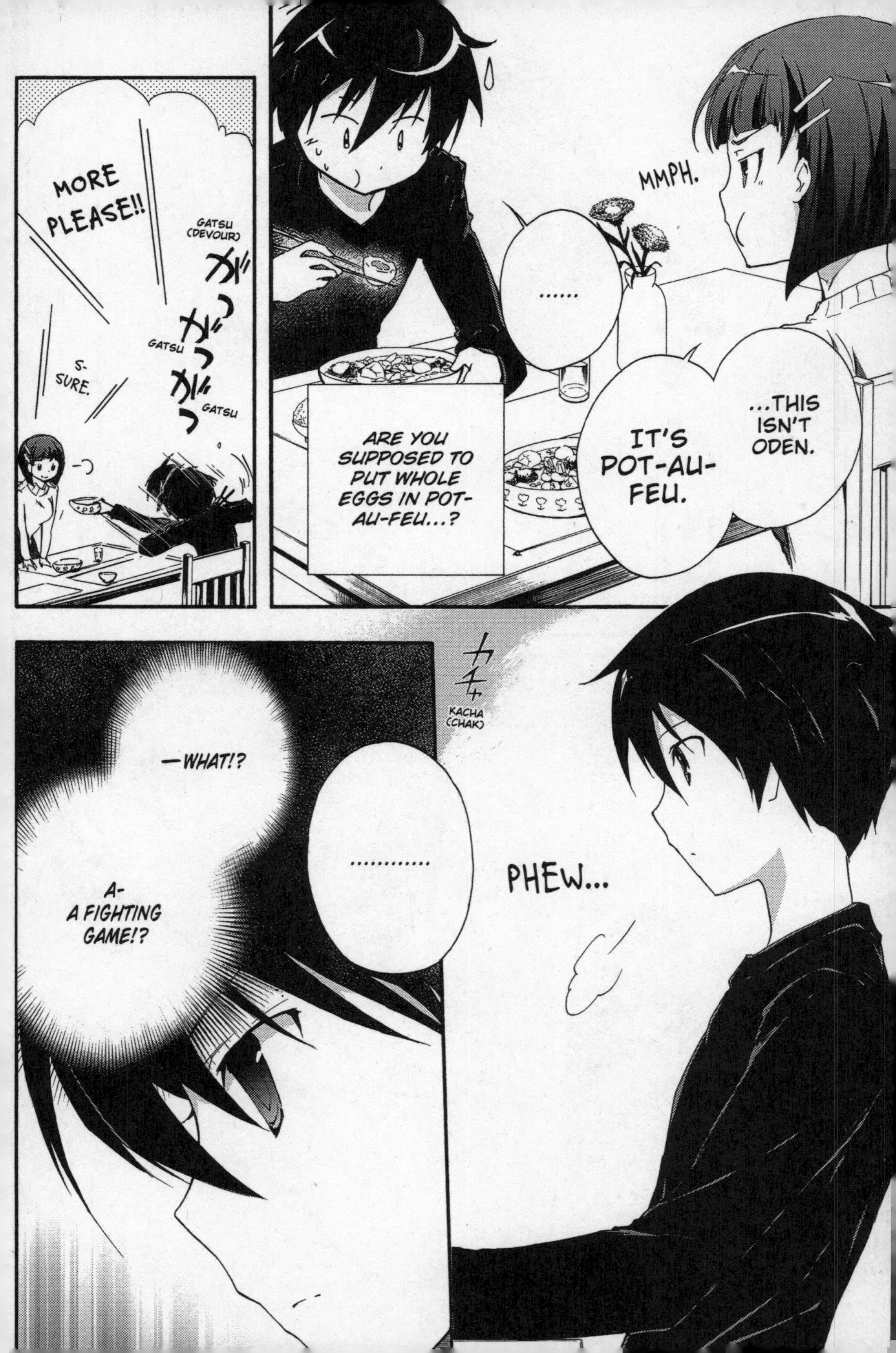
MMPH.
...THIS ISN'T ODEN.
IT'S POT-AU-FEU.
......
ARE YOU SUPPOSED TO PUT WHOLE EGGS IN POT-AU-FEU...?
MORE PLEASE!!
がっ
GATSU (DEVOUR)
がっ
GATSU
がっ
GATSU
S-SURE.
カチャ
KACHA (CHAK)
PHEW...
....
—WHAT!?
A-
A FIGHTING GAME!?

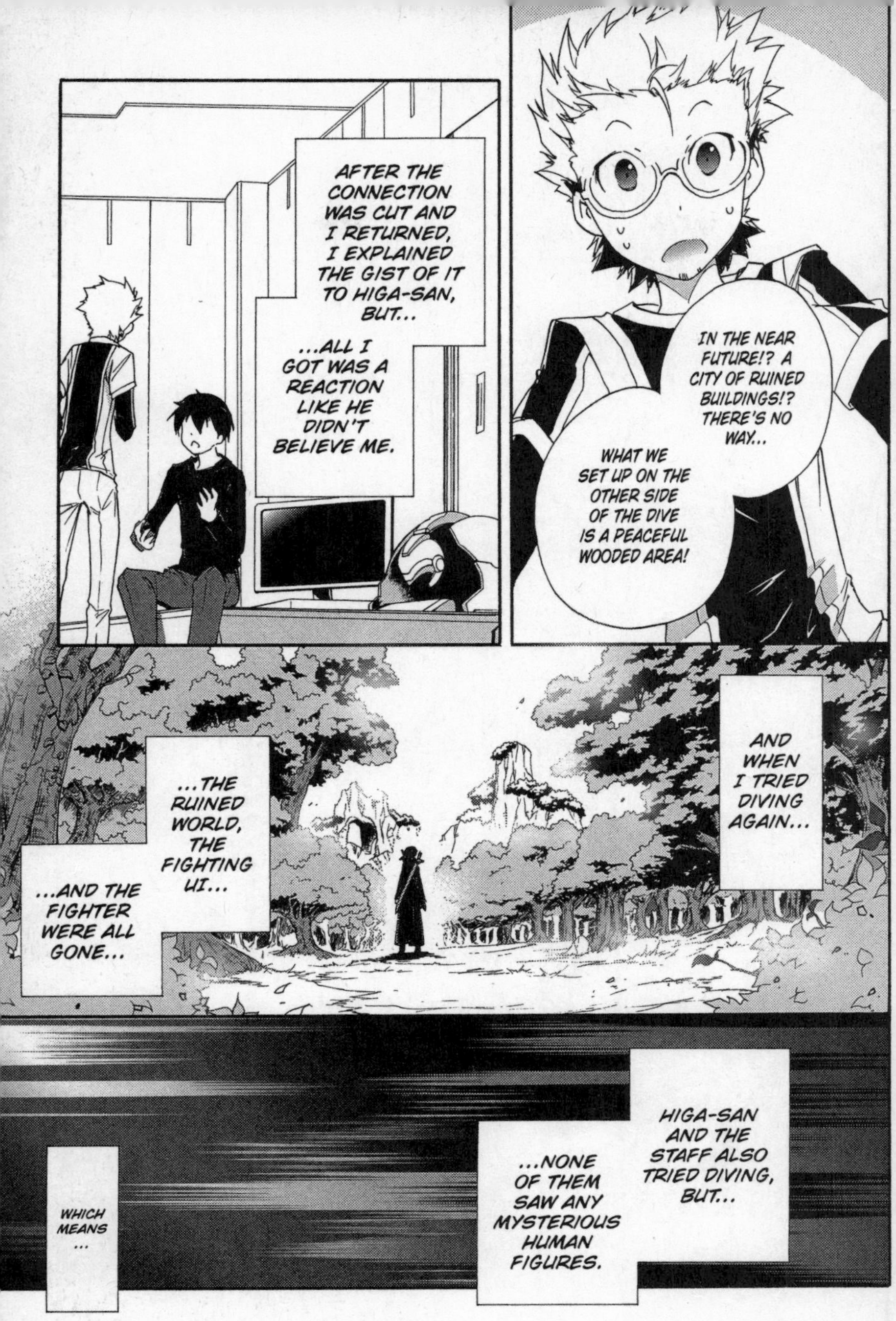
IN THE NEAR FUTURE!? A CITY OF RUINED BUILDINGS!? THERE'S NO WAY...
WHAT WE SET UP ON THE OTHER SIDE OF THE DIVE IS A PEACEFUL WOODED AREA!
AFTER THE CONNECTION WAS CUT AND I RETURNED, I EXPLAINED THE GIST OF IT TO HIGA-SAN, BUT...
...ALL I GOT WAS A REACTION LIKE HE DIDN'T BELIEVE ME.
AND WHEN I TRIED DIVING AGAIN...
...THE RUINED WORLD, THE FIGHTING UI...
...AND THE FIGHTER WERE ALL GONE...
HIGA-SAN AND THE STAFF ALSO TRIED DIVING, BUT...
...NONE OF THEM SAW ANY MYSTERIOUS HUMAN FIGURES.
WHICH MEANS ...

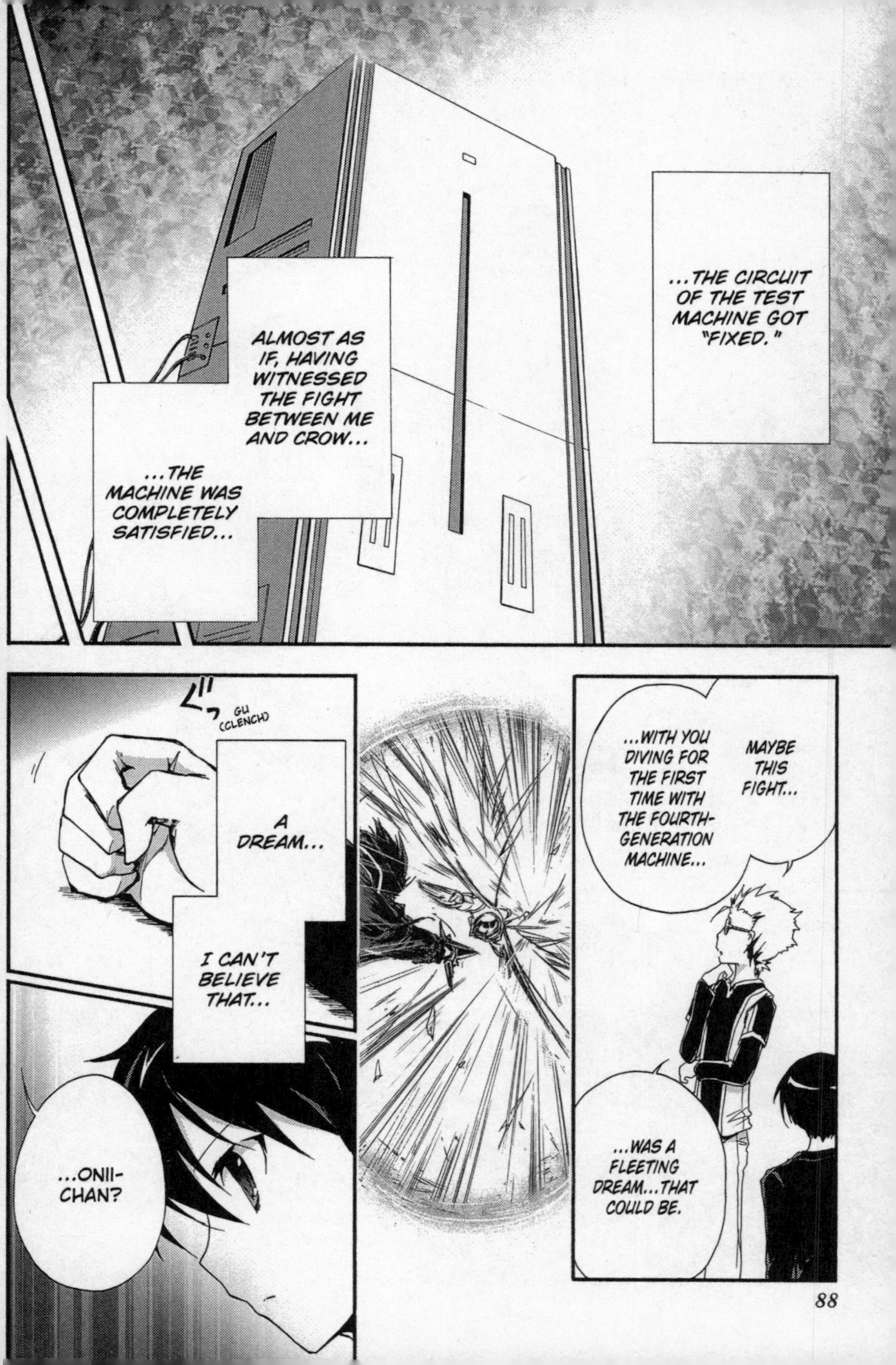
...THE CIRCUIT OF THE TEST MACHINE GOT "FIXED."
ALMOST AS IF, HAVING WITNESSED THE FIGHT BETWEEN ME AND CROW...
...THE MACHINE WAS COMPLETELY SATISFIED...
MAYBE THIS FIGHT...
...WITH YOU DIVING FOR THE FIRST TIME WITH THE FOURTH-GENERATION MACHINE...
...WAS A FLEETING DREAM...THAT COULD BE.
GU (CLENCH)
A DREAM...
I CAN'T BELIEVE THAT...
...ONII-CHAN?

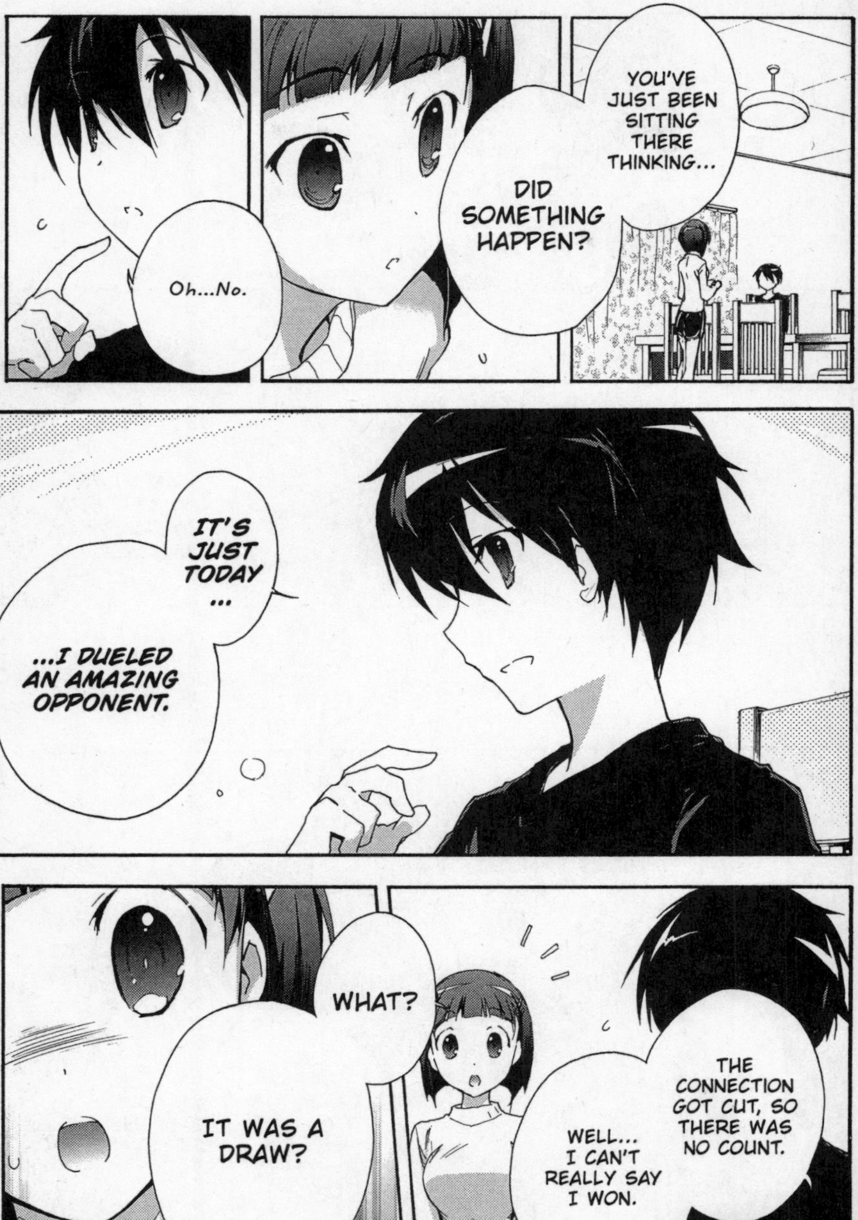
YOU'VE JUST BEEN SITTING THERE THINKING...
DID SOMETHING HAPPEN?
Oh...No.
IT'S JUST TODAY...
...I DUELED AN AMAZING OPPONENT.
THE CONNECTION GOT CUT, SO THERE WAS NO COUNT.
WELL... I CAN'T REALLY SAY I WON.
WHAT?
IT WAS A DRAW?

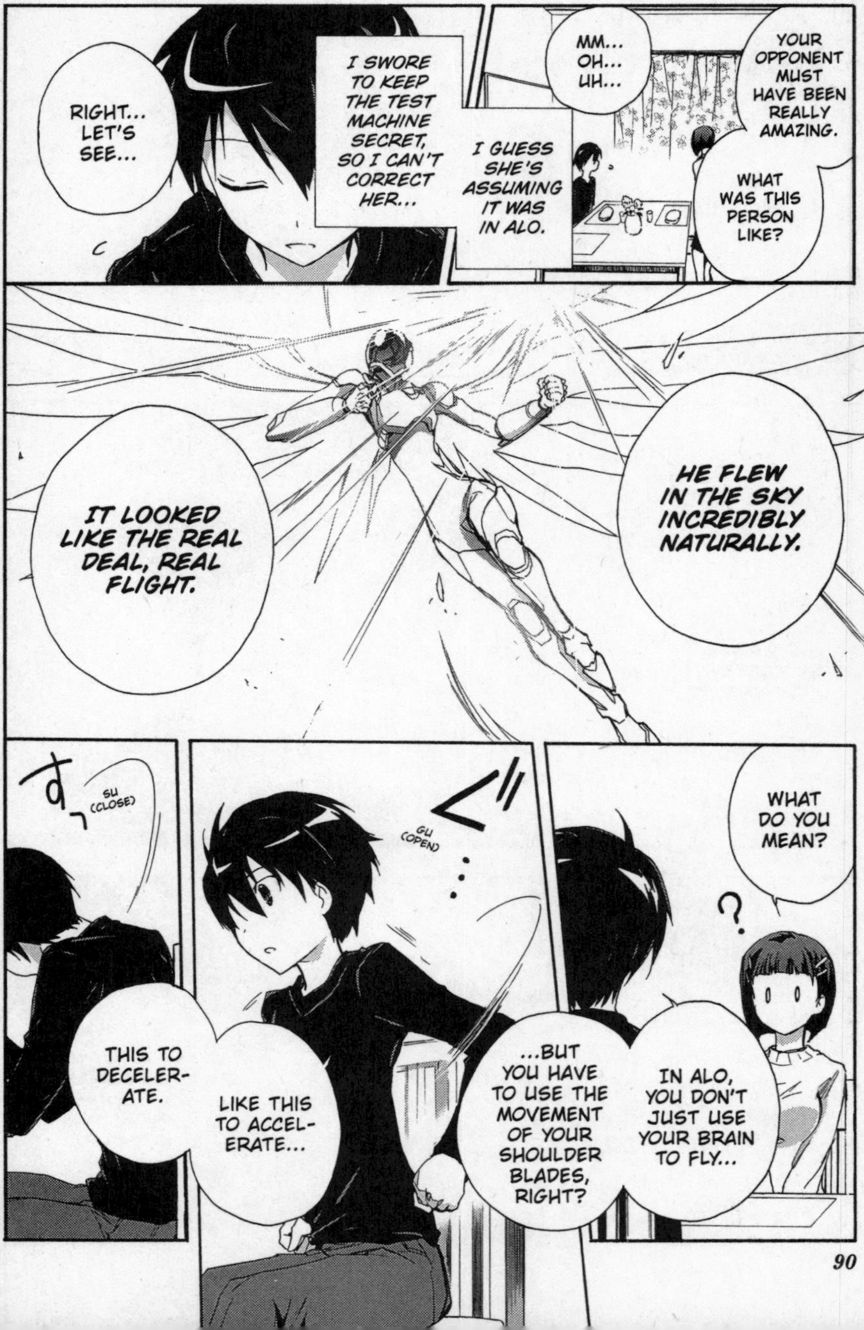
YOUR OPPONENT MUST HAVE BEEN REALLY AMAZING.
WHAT WAS THIS PERSON LIKE?
MM... OH... UH...
I GUESS SHE'S ASSUMING IT WAS IN ALO.
I SWORE TO KEEP THE TEST MACHINE SECRET, SO I CAN'T CORRECT HER...
RIGHT... LET'S SEE...
HE FLEW IN THE SKY INCREDIBLY NATURALLY.
IT LOOKED LIKE THE REAL DEAL, REAL FLIGHT.
WHAT DO YOU MEAN?
IN ALO, YOU DON'T JUST USE YOUR BRAIN TO FLY...
...BUT YOU HAVE TO USE THE MOVEMENT OF YOUR SHOULDER BLADES, RIGHT?
GU (OPEN)
LIKE THIS TO ACCEL-ERATE...
す
SU (CLOSE)
THIS TO DECELER-ATE.

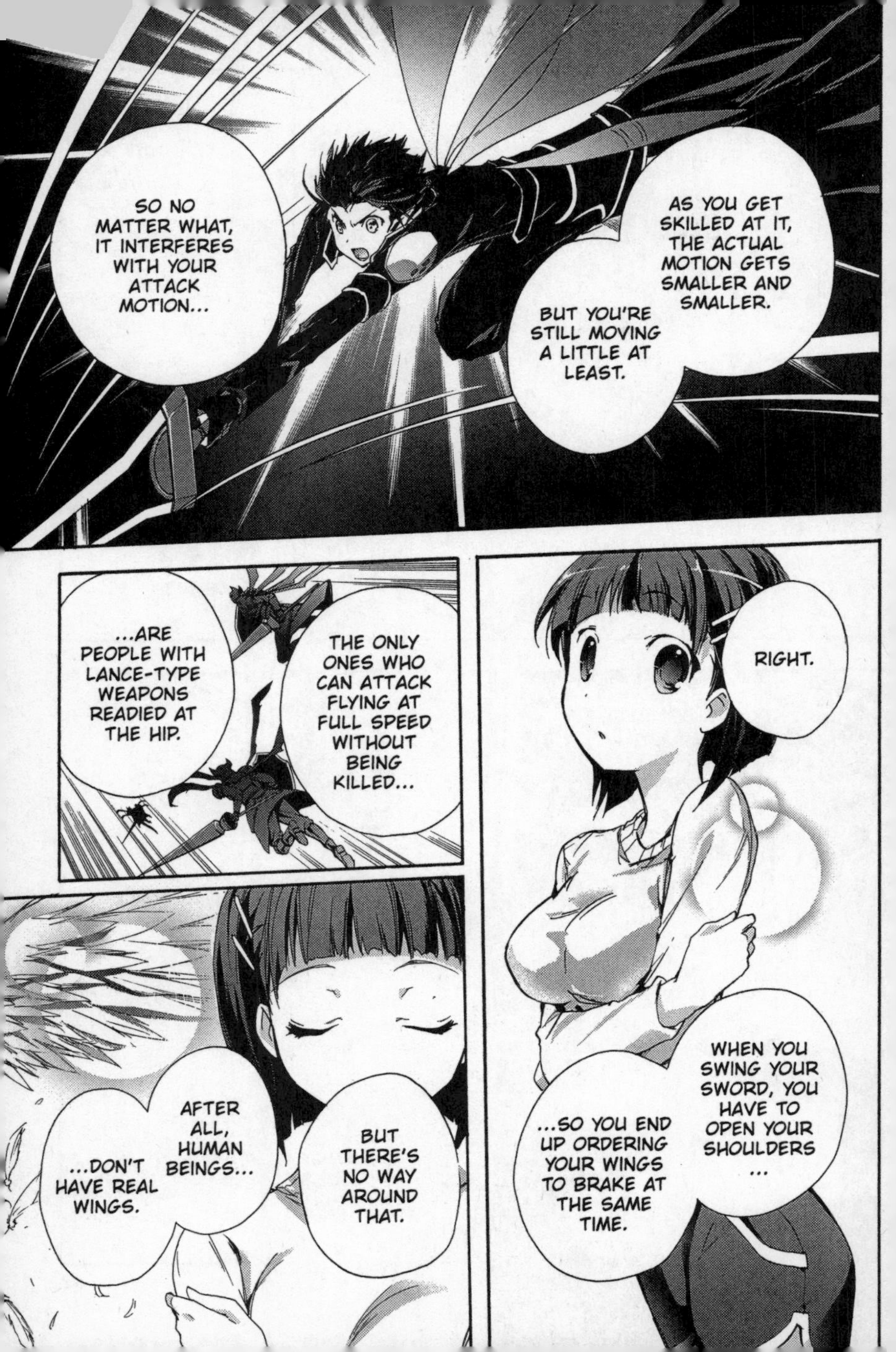
AS YOU GET SKILLED AT IT, THE ACTUAL MOTION GETS SMALLER AND SMALLER.
BUT YOU'RE STILL MOVING A LITTLE AT LEAST.
SO NO MATTER WHAT, IT INTERFERES WITH YOUR ATTACK MOTION...
RIGHT.
WHEN YOU SWING YOUR SWORD, YOU HAVE TO OPEN YOUR SHOULDERS...
...SO YOU END UP ORDERING YOUR WINGS TO BRAKE AT THE SAME TIME.
THE ONLY ONES WHO CAN ATTACK FLYING AT FULL SPEED WITHOUT BEING KILLED...
...ARE PEOPLE WITH LANCE-TYPE WEAPONS READIED AT THE HIP.
BUT THERE'S NO WAY AROUND THAT.
AFTER ALL, HUMAN BEINGS...
...DON'T HAVE REAL WINGS.

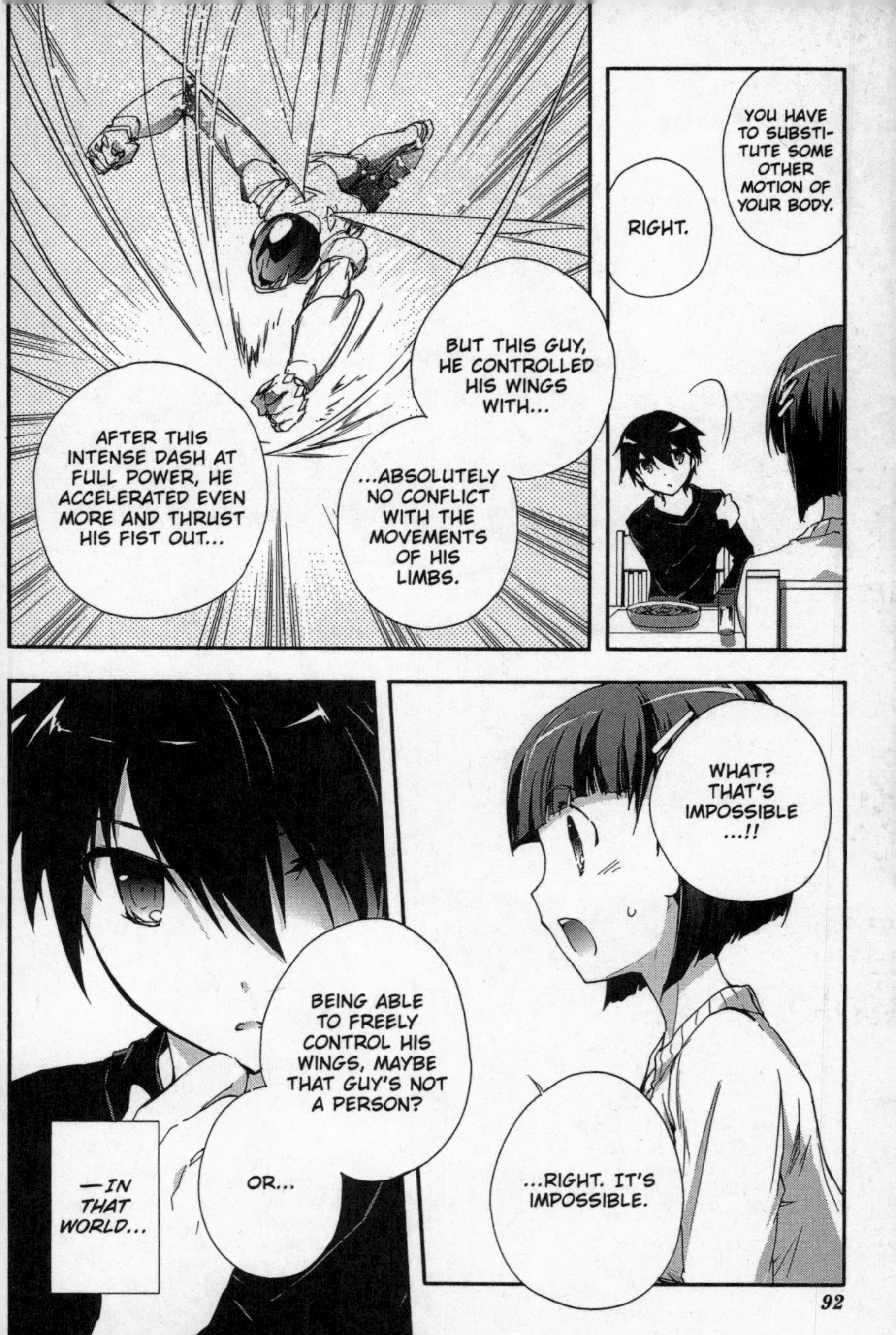

YOU HAVE TO SUBSTITUTE SOME OTHER MOTION OF YOUR BODY.
RIGHT.
BUT THIS GUY, HE CONTROLLED HIS WINGS WITH...
...ABSOLUTELY NO CONFLICT WITH THE MOVEMENTS OF HIS LIMBS.
AFTER THIS INTENSE DASH AT FULL POWER, HE ACCELERATED EVEN MORE AND THRUST HIS FIST OUT...
WHAT? THAT'S IMPOSSIBLE ...!!
...RIGHT. IT'S IMPOSSIBLE.
BEING ABLE TO FREELY CONTROL HIS WINGS, MAYBE THAT GUY'S NOT A PERSON?
OR...
—IN THAT WORLD...

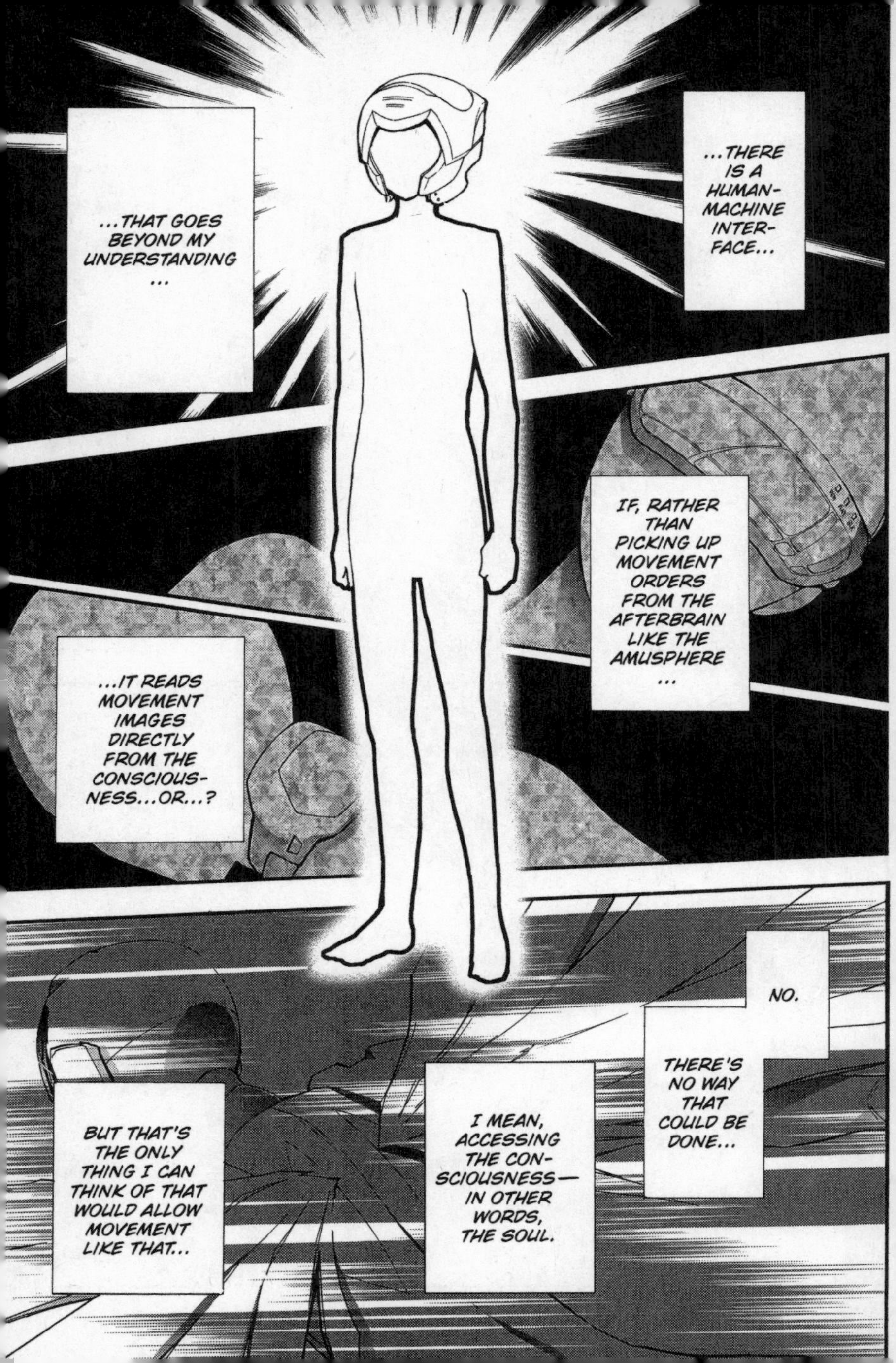
...THERE IS A HUMAN-MACHINE INTERFACE...
...THAT GOES BEYOND MY UNDERSTANDING...
IF, RATHER THAN PICKING UP MOVEMENT ORDERS FROM THE AFTERBRAIN LIKE THE AMUSPHERE...
...IT READS MOVEMENT IMAGES DIRECTLY FROM THE CONSCIOUSNESS...OR...?
NO.
THERE'S NO WAY THAT COULD BE DONE...
I MEAN, ACCESSING THE CONSCIOUSNESS—IN OTHER WORDS, THE SOUL.
BUT THAT'S THE ONLY THING I CAN THINK OF THAT WOULD ALLOW MOVEMENT LIKE THAT...

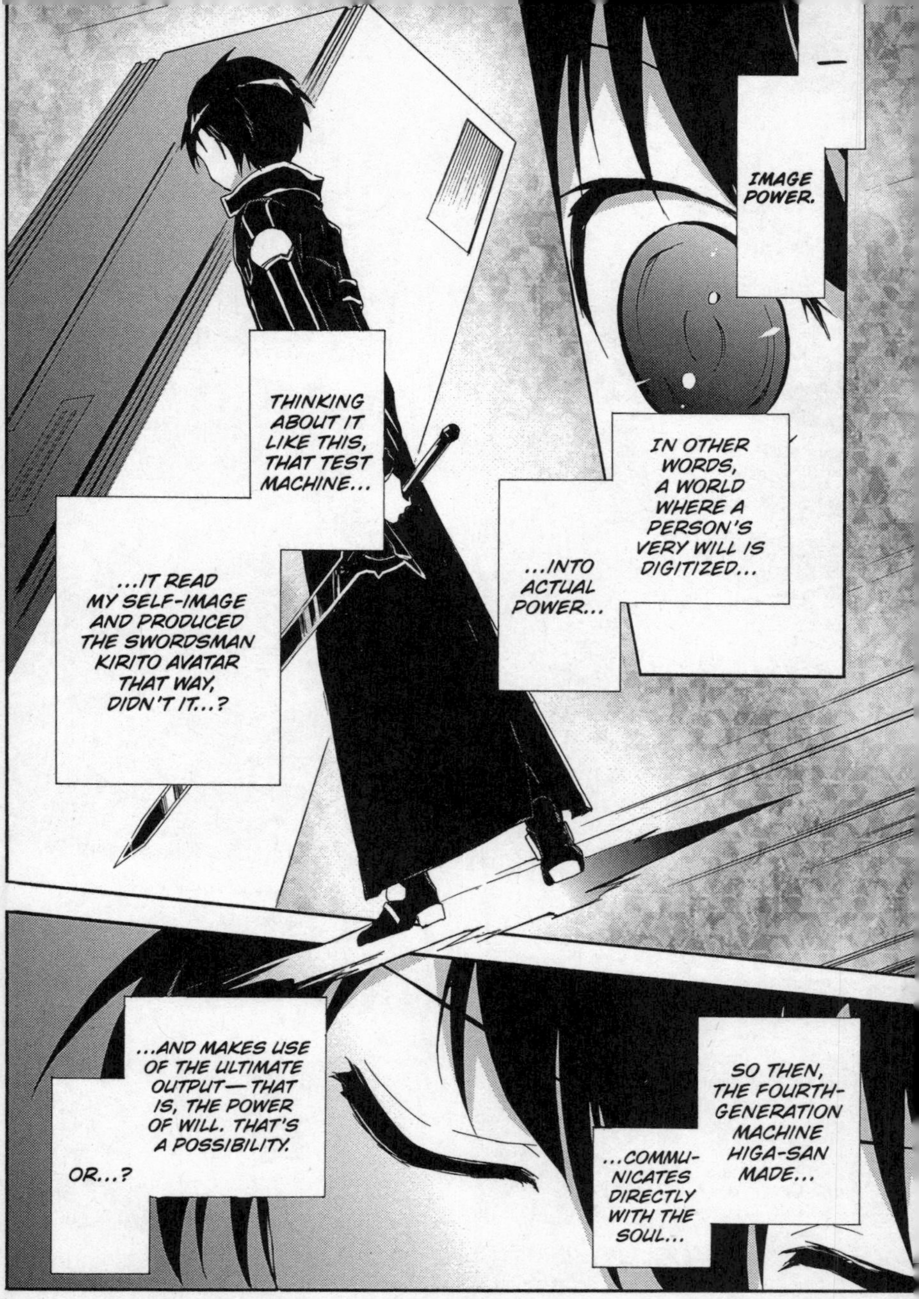
IMAGE POWER.
IN OTHER WORDS, A WORLD WHERE A PERSON'S VERY WILL IS DIGITIZED...
...INTO ACTUAL POWER...
THINKING ABOUT IT LIKE THIS, THAT TEST MACHINE...
...IT READ MY SELF-IMAGE AND PRODUCED THE SWORDSMAN KIRITO AVATAR THAT WAY, DIDN'T IT...?
SO THEN, THE FOURTH-GENERATION MACHINE HIGA-SAN MADE...
...COMMUNICATES DIRECTLY WITH THE SOUL...
...AND MAKES USE OF THE ULTIMATE OUTPUT—THAT IS, THE POWER OF WILL. THAT'S A POSSIBILITY.
OR...?

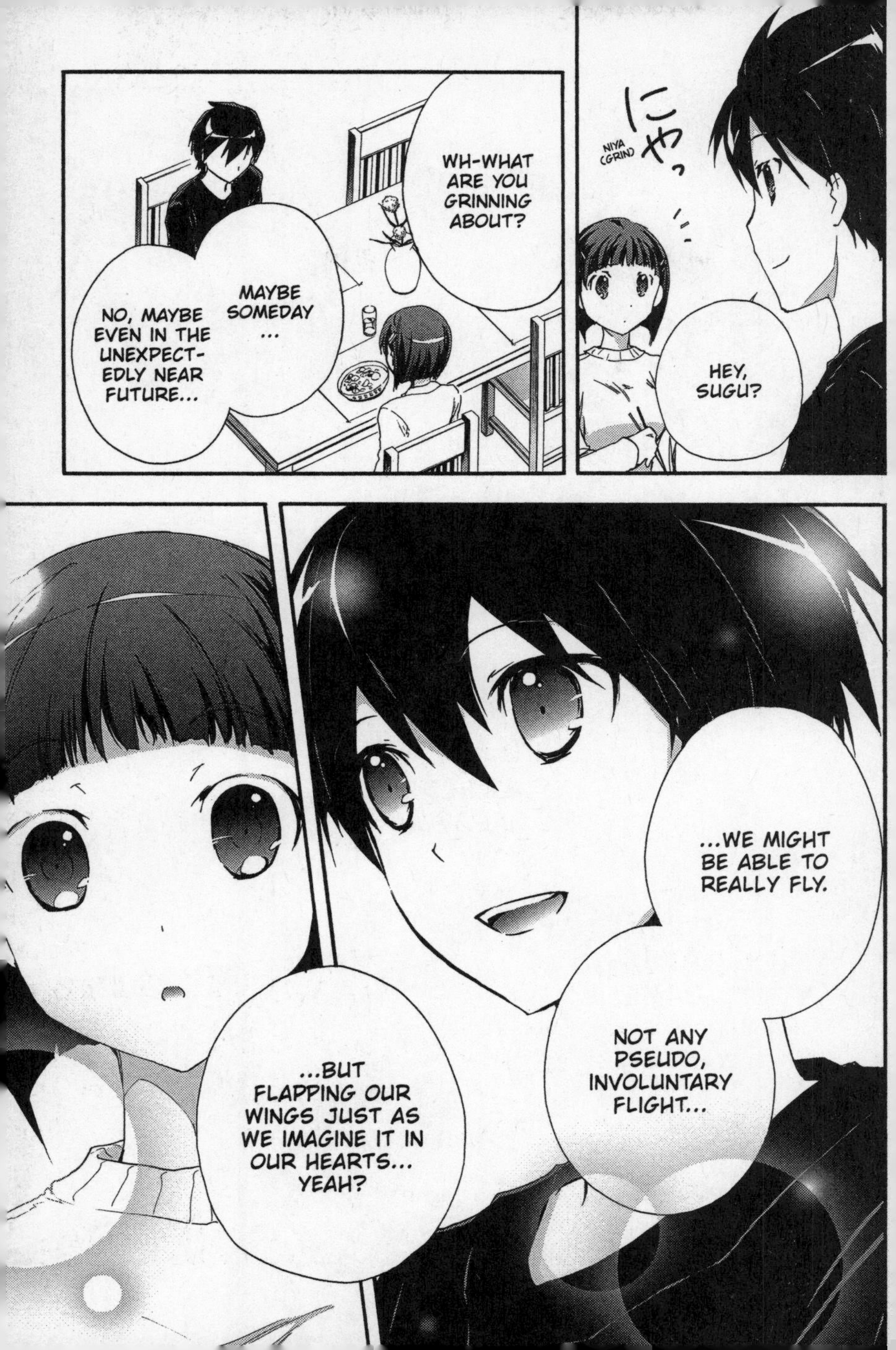

にやっ
NIYA (GRIN)
HEY, SUGU?
WH-WHAT ARE YOU GRINNING ABOUT?
MAYBE SOMEDAY ...
NO, MAYBE EVEN IN THE UNEXPECTEDLY NEAR FUTURE...
...WE MIGHT BE ABLE TO REALLY FLY.
NOT ANY PSEUDO, INVOLUNTARY FLIGHT...
...BUT FLAPPING OUR WINGS JUST AS WE IMAGINE IT IN OUR HEARTS... YEAH?

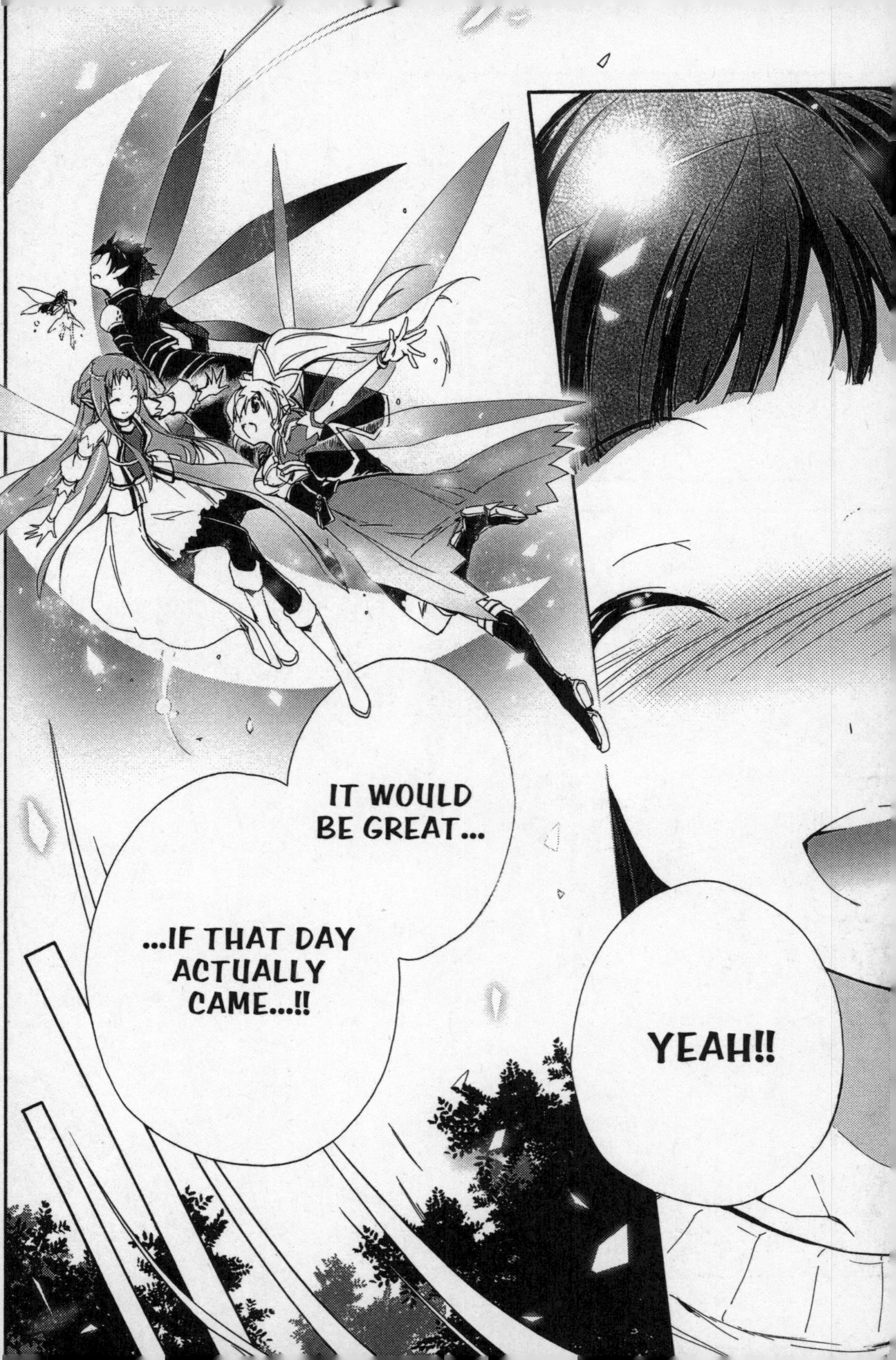
IT WOULD BE GREAT...
...IF THAT DAY ACTUALLY CAME...!!
YEAH!!

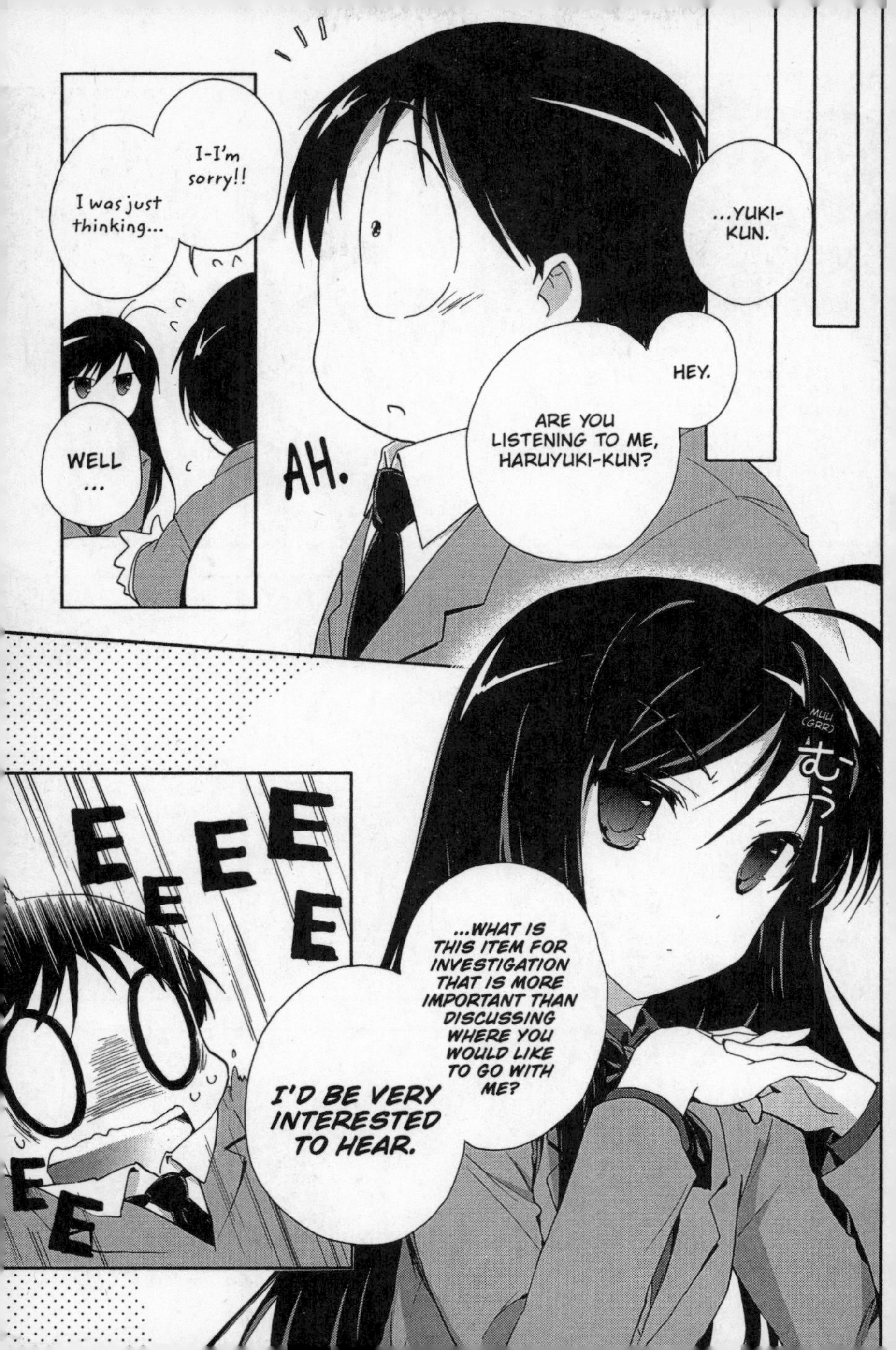
...YUKI-KUN.
HEY.
ARE YOU LISTENING TO ME, HARUYUKI-KUN?
AH.
I-I'm sorry!!
I was just thinking...
WELL ...
MUU (GRR)
むぅー
...WHAT IS THIS ITEM FOR INVESTIGATION THAT IS MORE IMPORTANT THAN DISCUSSING WHERE YOU WOULD LIKE TO GO WITH ME?
I'D BE VERY INTERESTED TO HEAR.
EEEEE
EE

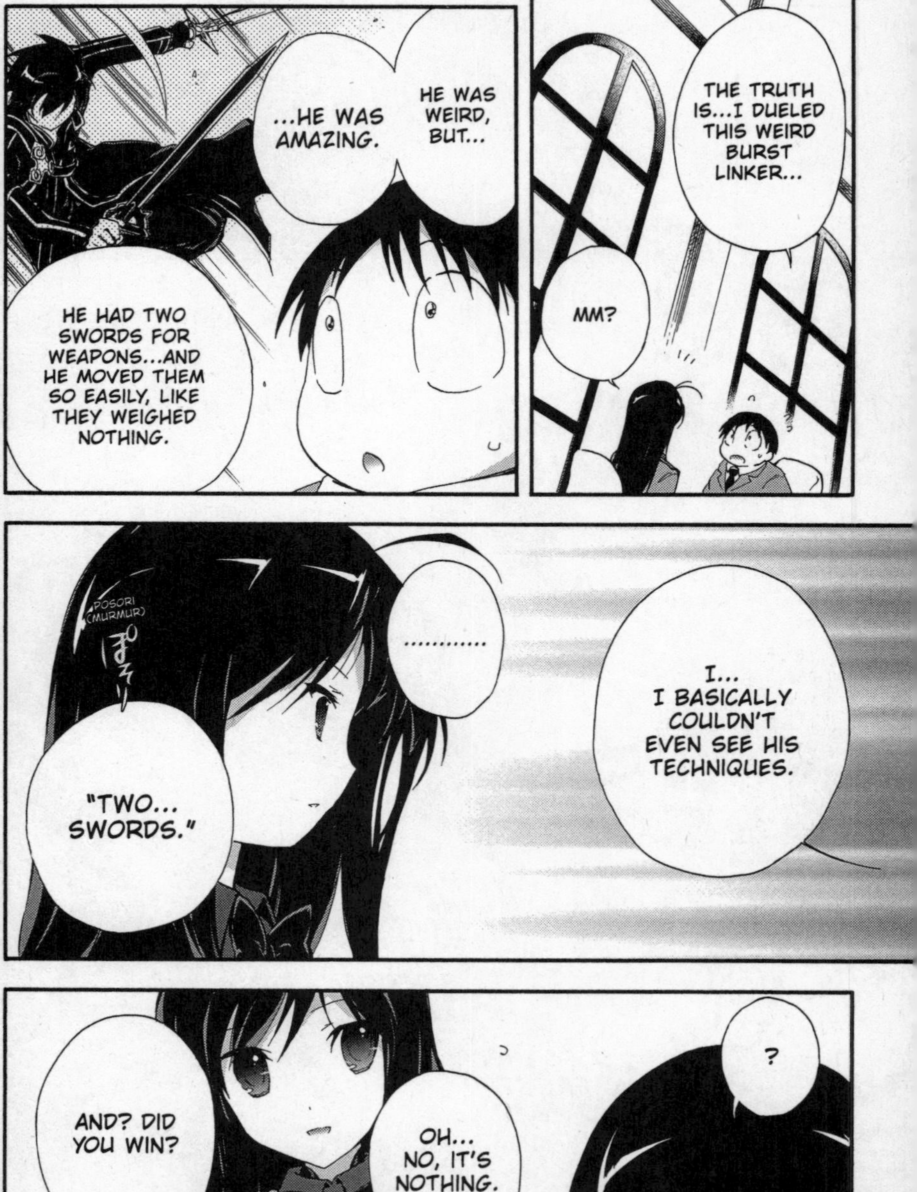
THE TRUTH IS...I DUELED THIS WEIRD BURST LINKER...
MM?
HE WAS WEIRD, BUT...
...HE WAS AMAZING.
HE HAD TWO SWORDS FOR WEAPONS...AND HE MOVED THEM SO EASILY, LIKE THEY WEIGHED NOTHING.
I... I BASICALLY COULDN'T EVEN SEE HIS TECHNIQUES.
....
POSORI (MURMUR)
"TWO... SWORDS."
?
OH... NO, IT'S NOTHING.
AND? DID YOU WIN?

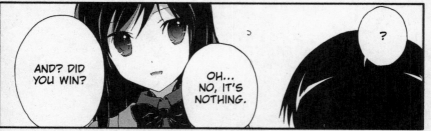

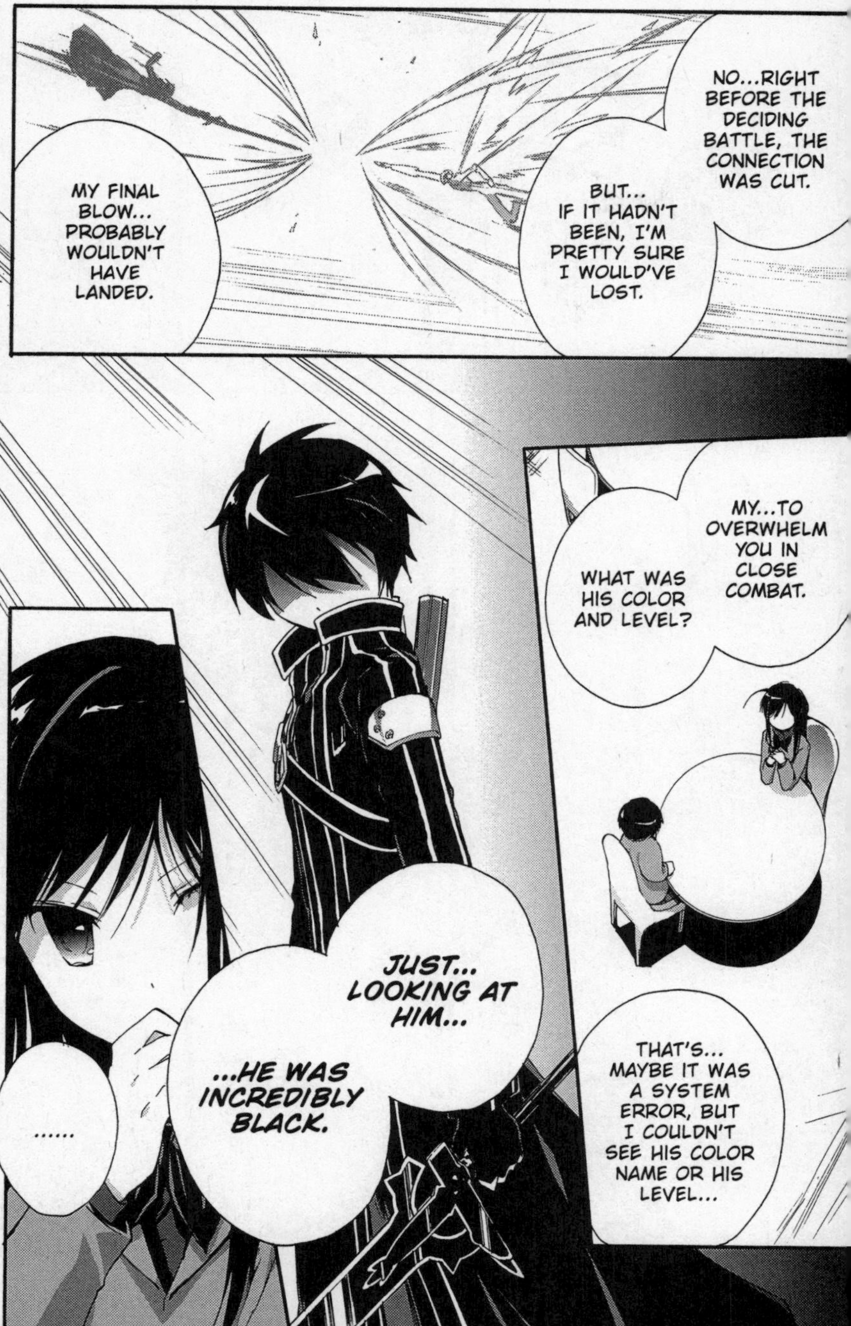
NO...RIGHT BEFORE THE DECIDING BATTLE, THE CONNECTION WAS CUT.
BUT... IF IT HADN'T BEEN, I'M PRETTY SURE I WOULD'VE LOST.
MY FINAL BLOW... PROBABLY WOULDN'T HAVE LANDED.
MY...TO OVERWHELM YOU IN CLOSE COMBAT.
WHAT WAS HIS COLOR AND LEVEL?
THAT'S... MAYBE IT WAS A SYSTEM ERROR, BUT I COULDN'T SEE HIS COLOR NAME OR HIS LEVEL...
JUST... LOOKING AT HIM...
...HE WAS INCREDIBLY BLACK.
......

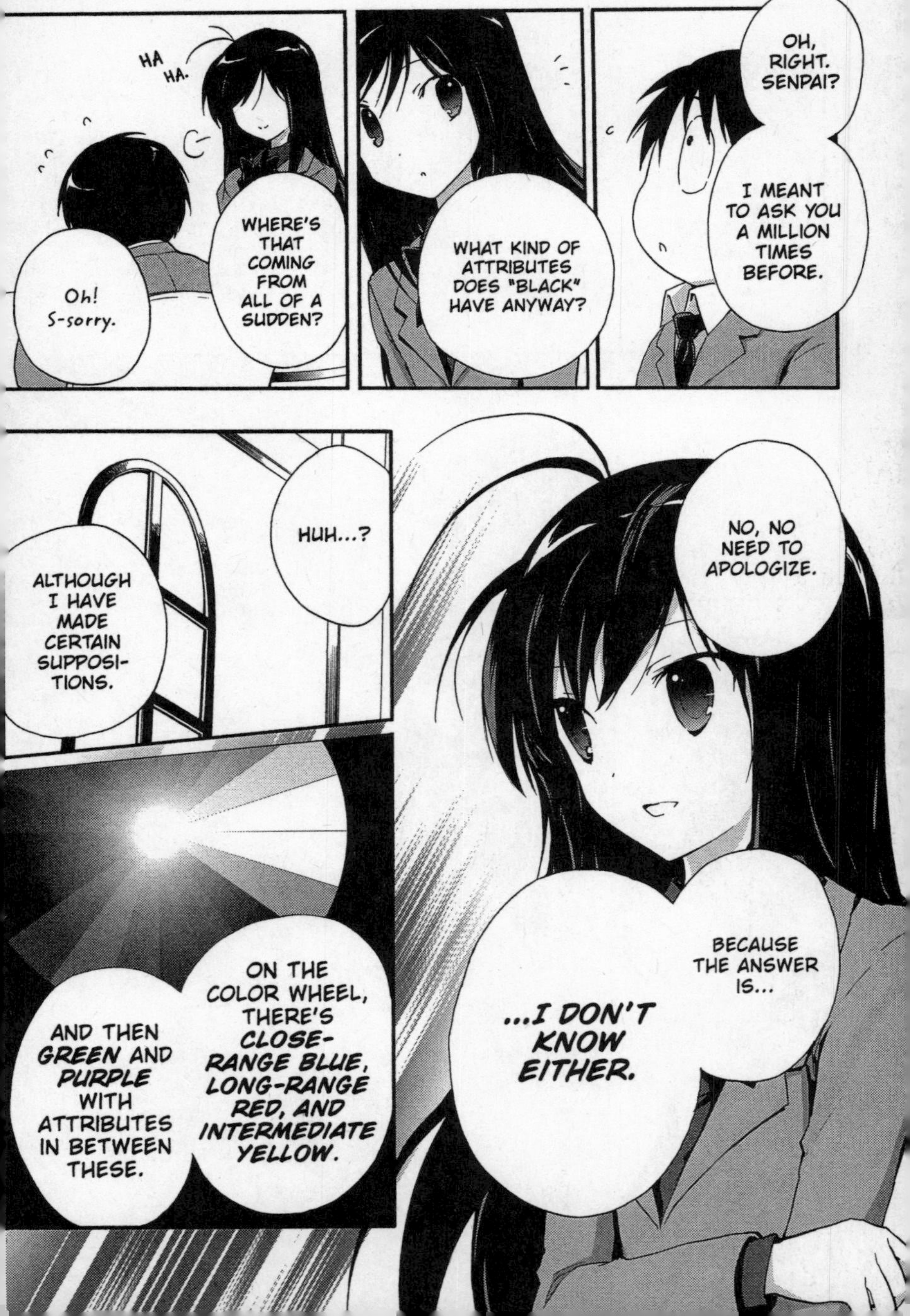
OH, RIGHT. SENPAI?
I MEANT TO ASK YOU A MILLION TIMES BEFORE.
WHAT KIND OF ATTRIBUTES DOES "BLACK" HAVE ANYWAY?
HA HA.
WHERE'S THAT COMING FROM ALL OF A SUDDEN?
Oh! S-sorry.
NO, NO NEED TO APOLOGIZE.
HUH...?
ALTHOUGH I HAVE MADE CERTAIN SUPPOSITIONS.
ON THE COLOR WHEEL, THERE'S CLOSE-RANGE BLUE, LONG-RANGE RED, AND INTERMEDIATE YELLOW.
AND THEN GREEN AND PURPLE WITH ATTRIBUTES IN BETWEEN THESE.
BECAUSE THE ANSWER IS...
...I DON'T KNOW EITHER.

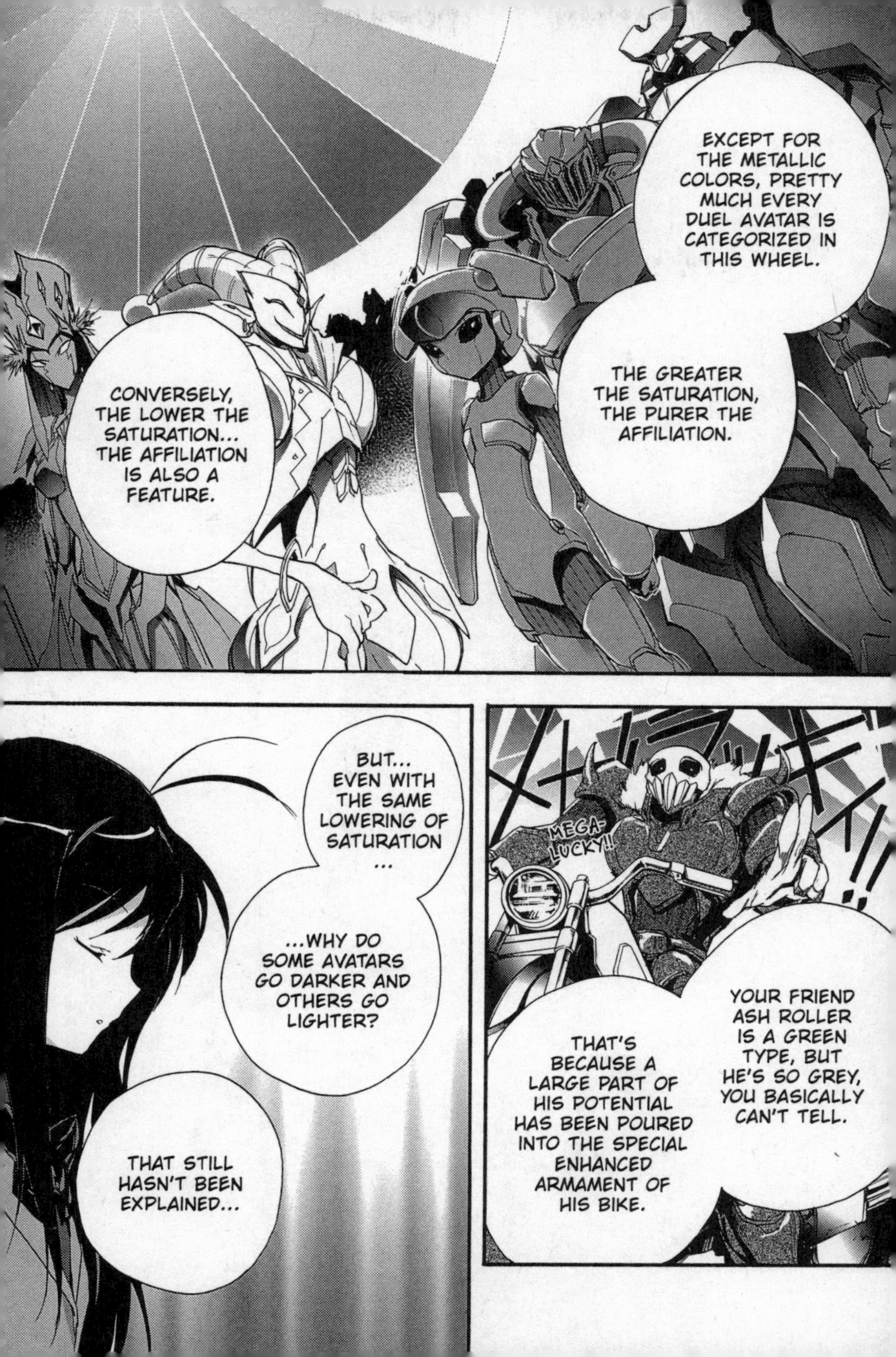
EXCEPT FOR THE METALLIC COLORS, PRETTY MUCH EVERY DUEL AVATAR IS CATEGORIZED IN THIS WHEEL.
THE GREATER THE SATURATION, THE PURER THE AFFILIATION.
CONVERSELY, THE LOWER THE SATURATION... THE AFFILIATION IS ALSO A FEATURE.
MEGA-LUCKY!!
YOUR FRIEND ASH ROLLER IS A GREEN TYPE, BUT HE'S SO GREY, YOU BASICALLY CAN'T TELL.
THAT'S BECAUSE A LARGE PART OF HIS POTENTIAL HAS BEEN POURED INTO THE SPECIAL ENHANCED ARMAMENT OF HIS BIKE.
BUT... EVEN WITH THE SAME LOWERING OF SATURATION...
...WHY DO SOME AVATARS GO DARKER AND OTHERS GO LIGHTER?
THAT STILL HASN'T BEEN EXPLAINED...

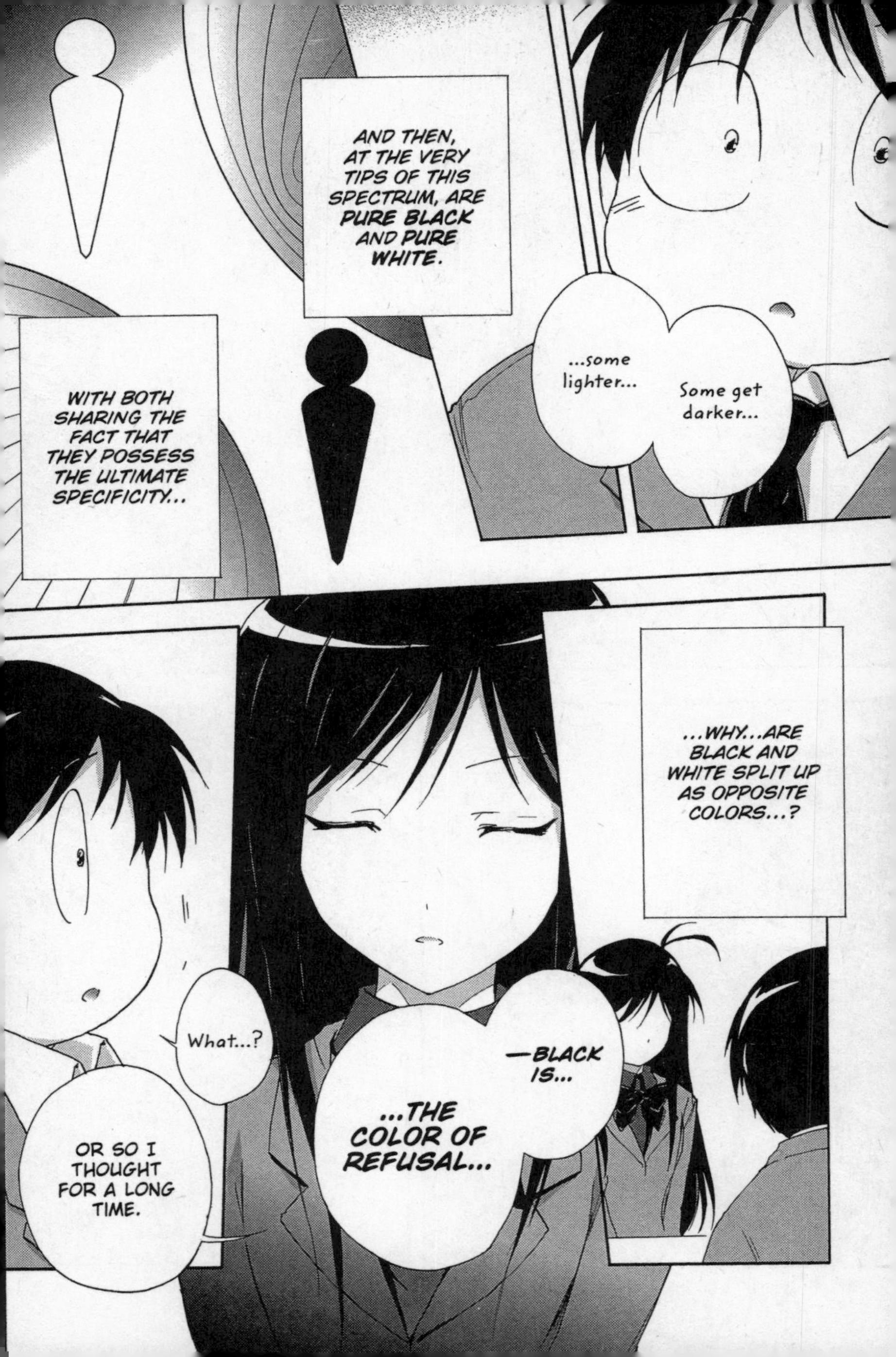

Some get darker...
...some lighter...
AND THEN, AT THE VERY TIPS OF THIS SPECTRUM, ARE PURE BLACK AND PURE WHITE.
WITH BOTH SHARING THE FACT THAT THEY POSSESS THE ULTIMATE SPECIFICITY...
...WHY...ARE BLACK AND WHITE SPLIT UP AS OPPOSITE COLORS...?
—BLACK IS...
...THE COLOR OF REFUSAL...
What...?
OR SO I THOUGHT FOR A LONG TIME.

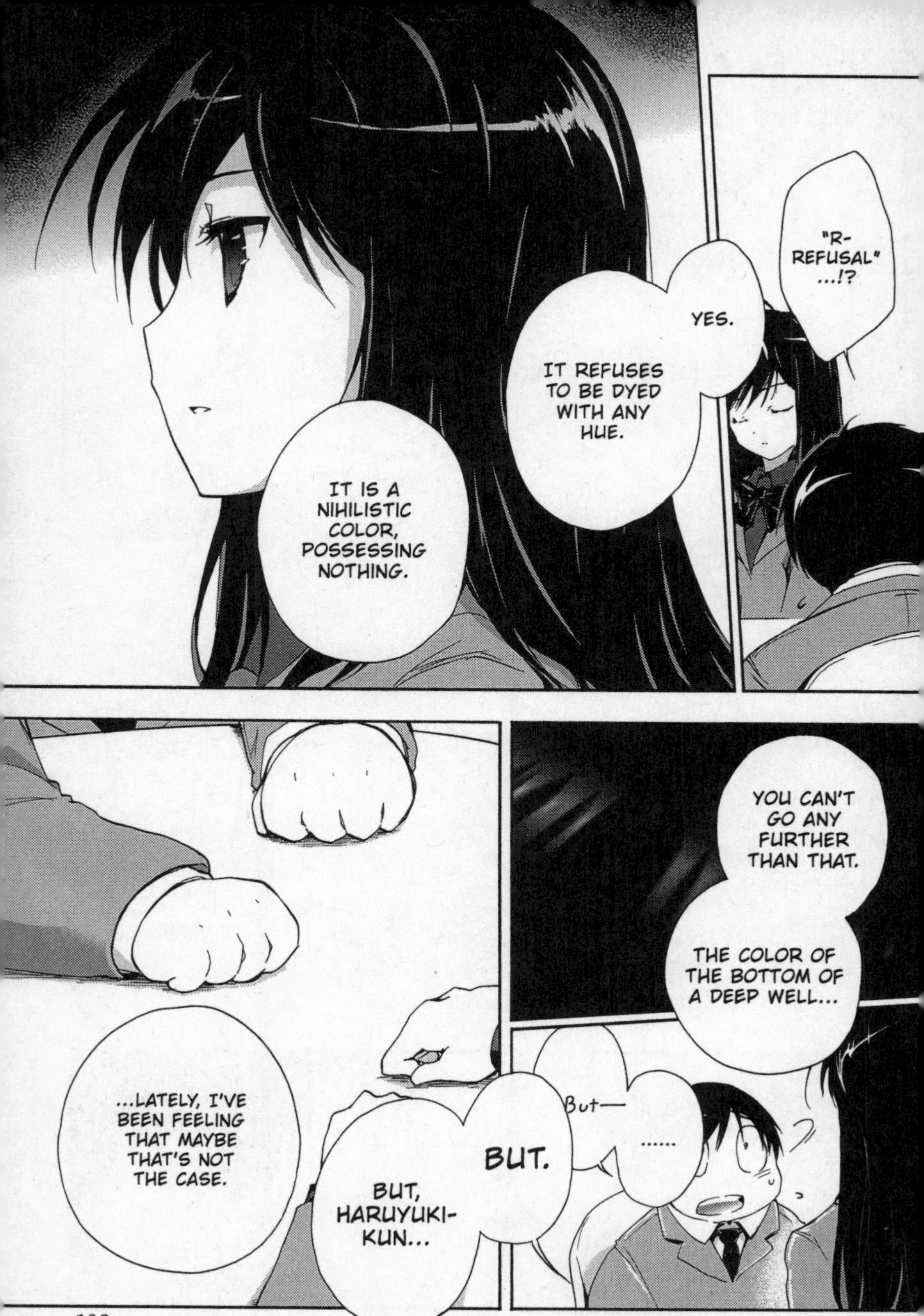
"R-REFUSAL" ...!?
YES.
IT REFUSES TO BE DYED WITH ANY HUE.
IT IS A NIHILISTIC COLOR, POSSESSING NOTHING.
YOU CAN'T GO ANY FURTHER THAN THAT.
THE COLOR OF THE BOTTOM OF A DEEP WELL...
But—
......
BUT.
BUT, HARUYUKI-KUN...
...LATELY, I'VE BEEN FEELING THAT MAYBE THAT'S NOT THE CASE.

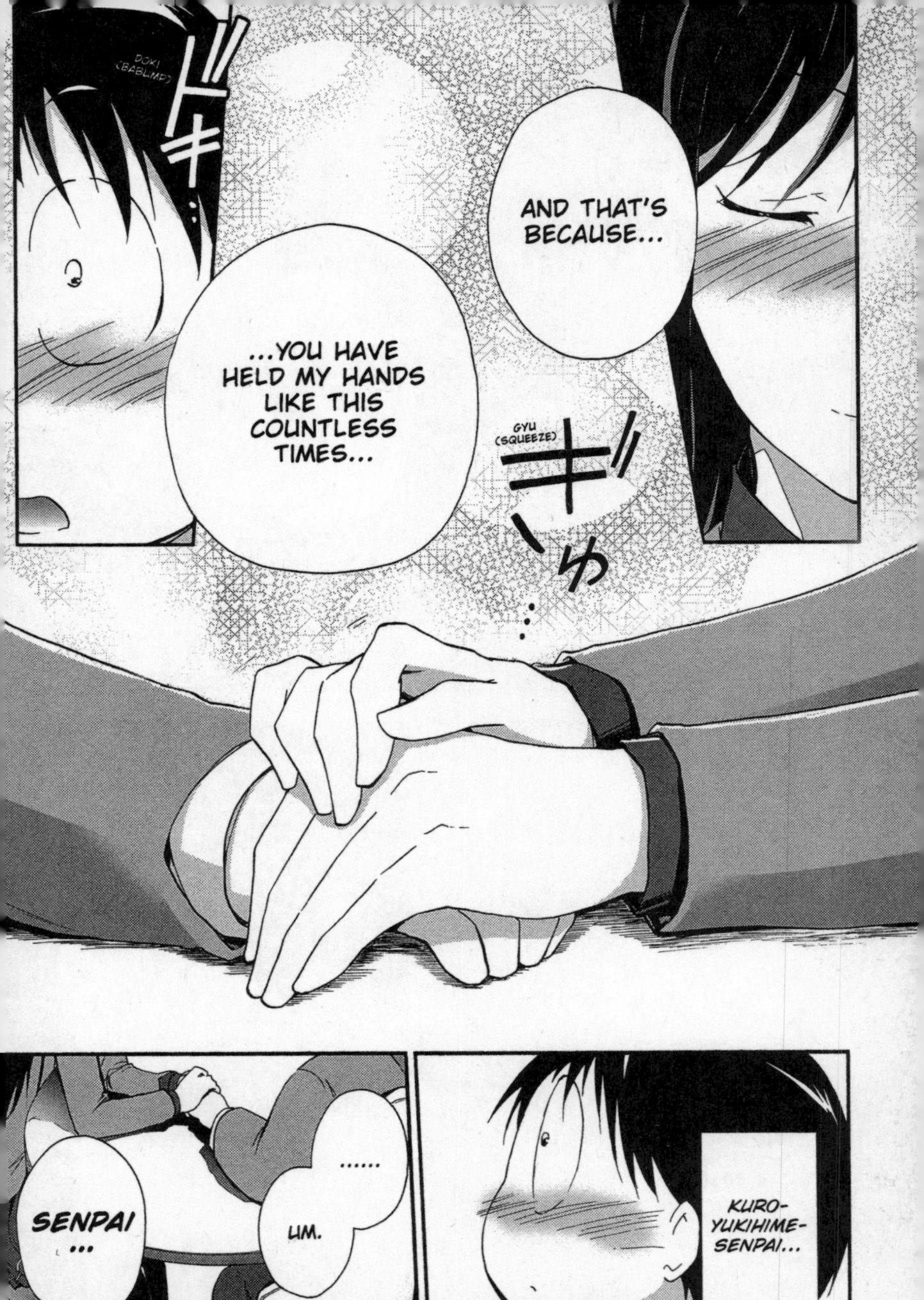
AND THAT'S BECAUSE...
...YOU HAVE HELD MY HANDS LIKE THIS COUNTLESS TIMES...
DOKI (BABUMP)
GYU (SQUEEZE)
KURO-YUKIHIME-SENPAI...
......
UM.
SENPAI ...

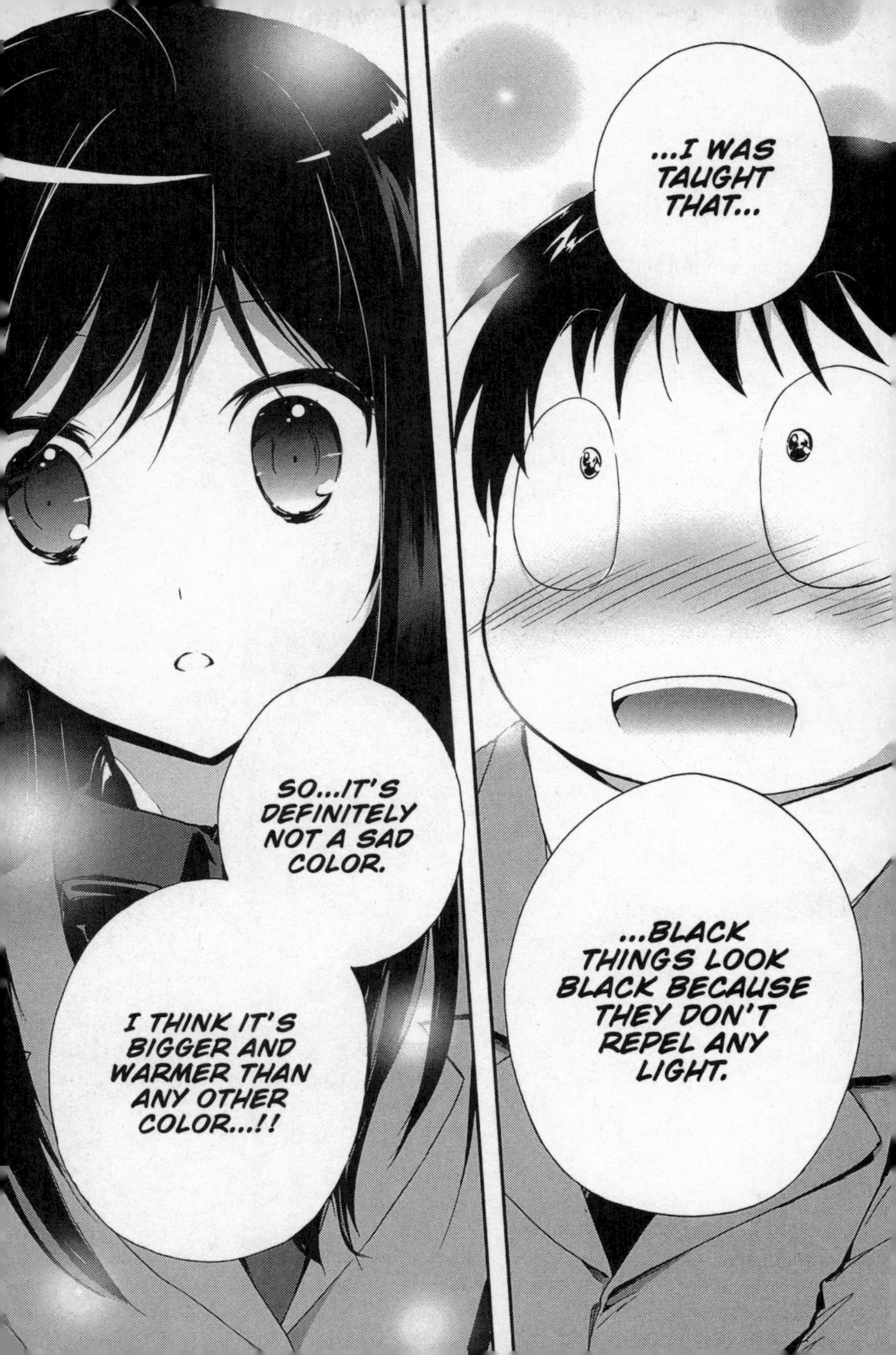
...I WAS TAUGHT THAT...
...BLACK THINGS LOOK BLACK BECAUSE THEY DON'T REPEL ANY LIGHT.
SO...IT'S DEFINITELY NOT A SAD COLOR.
I THINK IT'S BIGGER AND WARMER THAN ANY OTHER COLOR...!!

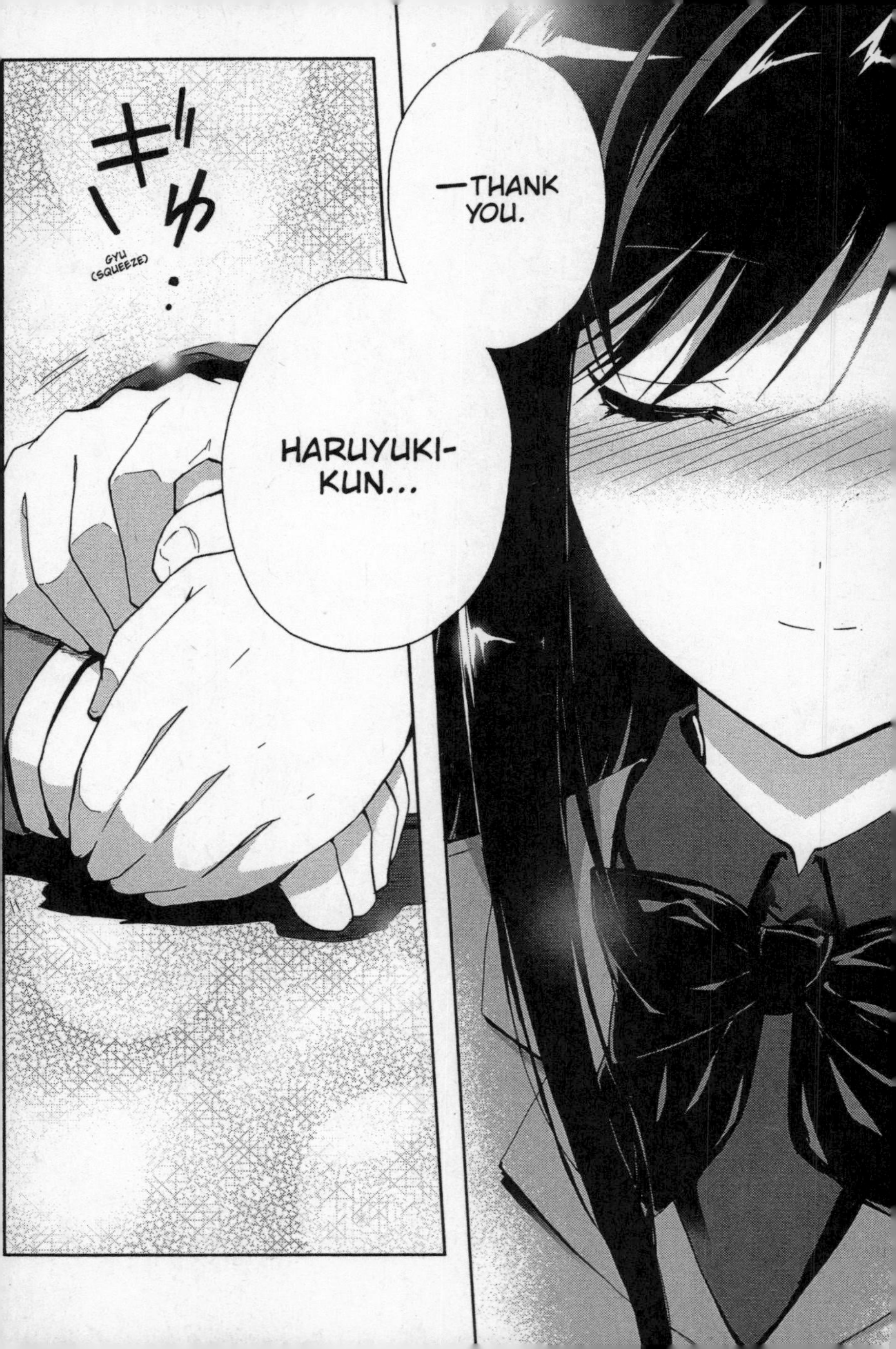
—THANK YOU.
HARUYUKI-KUN...
ぎゅ
GYU (SQUEEZE)

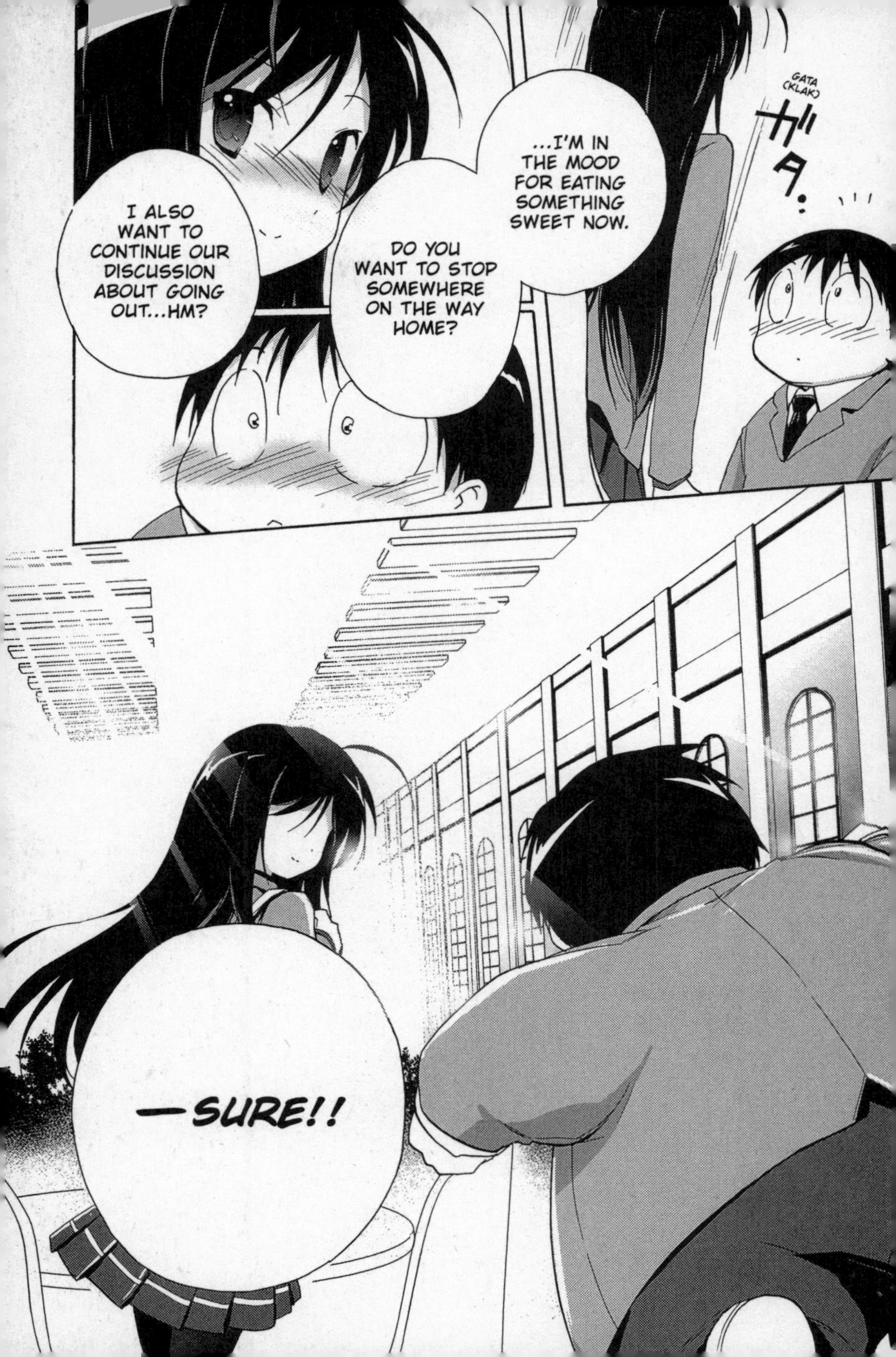
GATA (KLAK)
ガタ
...I'M IN THE MOOD FOR EATING SOMETHING SWEET NOW.
DO YOU WANT TO STOP SOMEWHERE ON THE WAY HOME?
I ALSO WANT TO CONTINUE OUR DISCUSSION ABOUT GOING OUT...HM?
—SURE!!

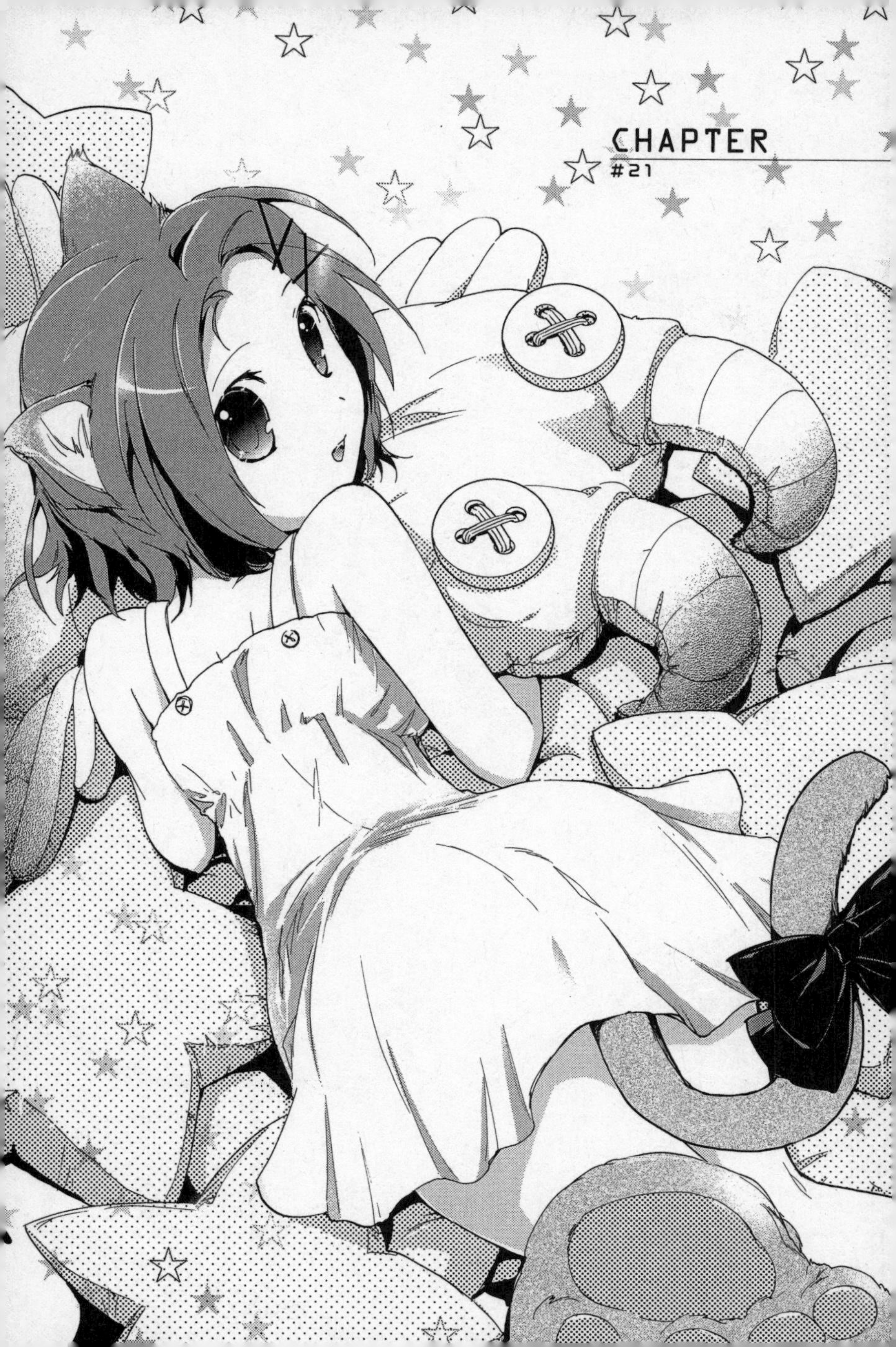
CHAPTER
#21

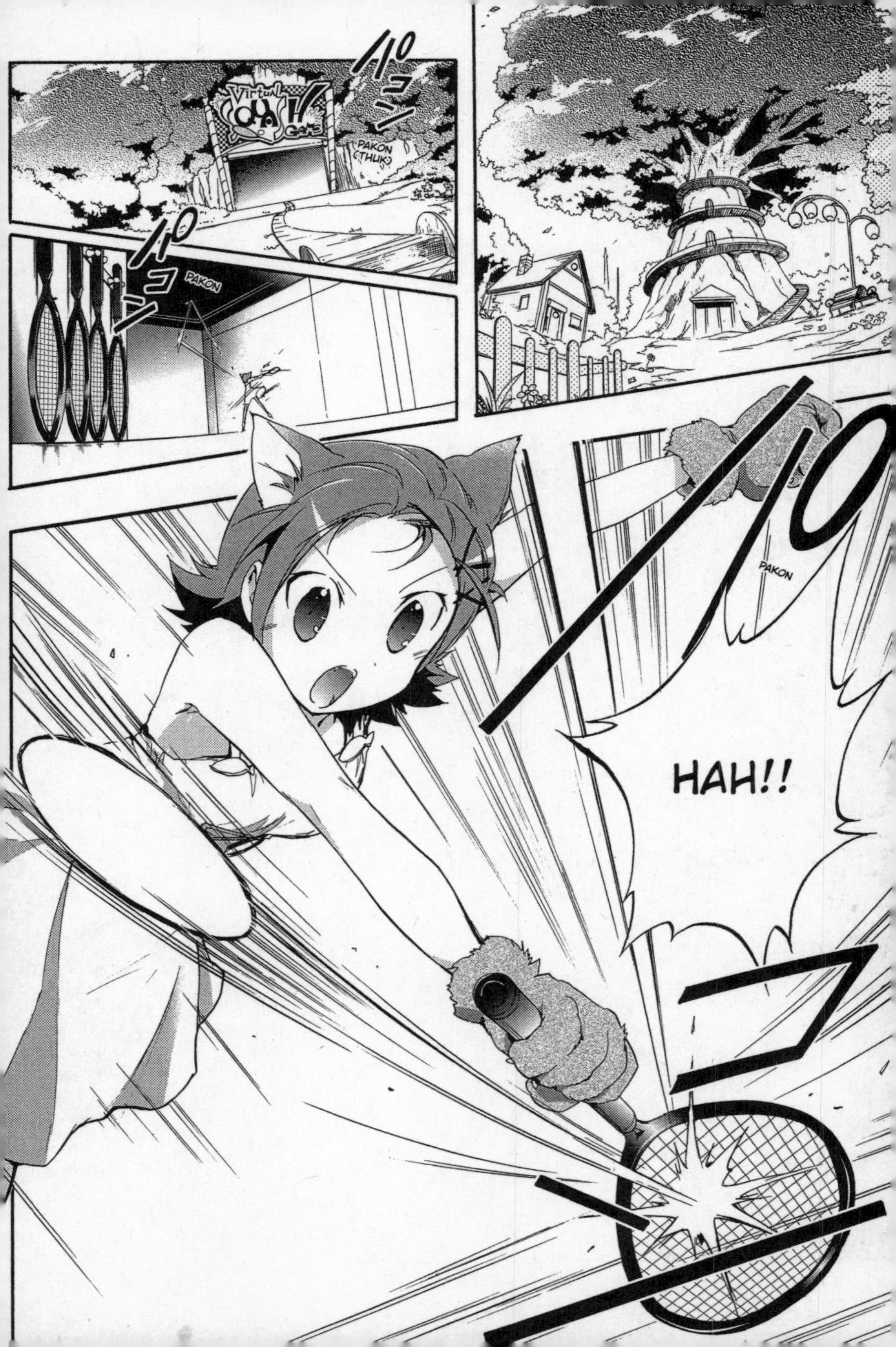

パコン
PAKON (THUK)
パコン
PAKON
パコン
PAKON
HAH!!

!!

BEST RANKING

	SCORE	RANKER
LEVEL	152		UNKNOWN
1st	152	2635924 PTS	HARUYUKI
2nd	149	2487328 PTS	HARUYUKI
3rd	148	2449783 PTS	HARUYUKI
4th	146	2314334 PTS	HARUYUKI
5th	145	2306603 PTS	HARUYUKI
6th	143	2227434 PTS	HARUYUKI
7th	142	2118763 PTS	HARUYUKI
8th	139	2049845 PTS	HARUYUKI
9th	137	1937433 PTS	CHIYURI
10th	136	1916734 PTS	

PI
(BEEP)

NYAH!?

I FINALLY MADE IT INTO THE TOP TE—

YESSSS!!

BYUN
(FWOOSH)

Aaah.

BUBUU
(BZZ)

PON
(PLOK)

111

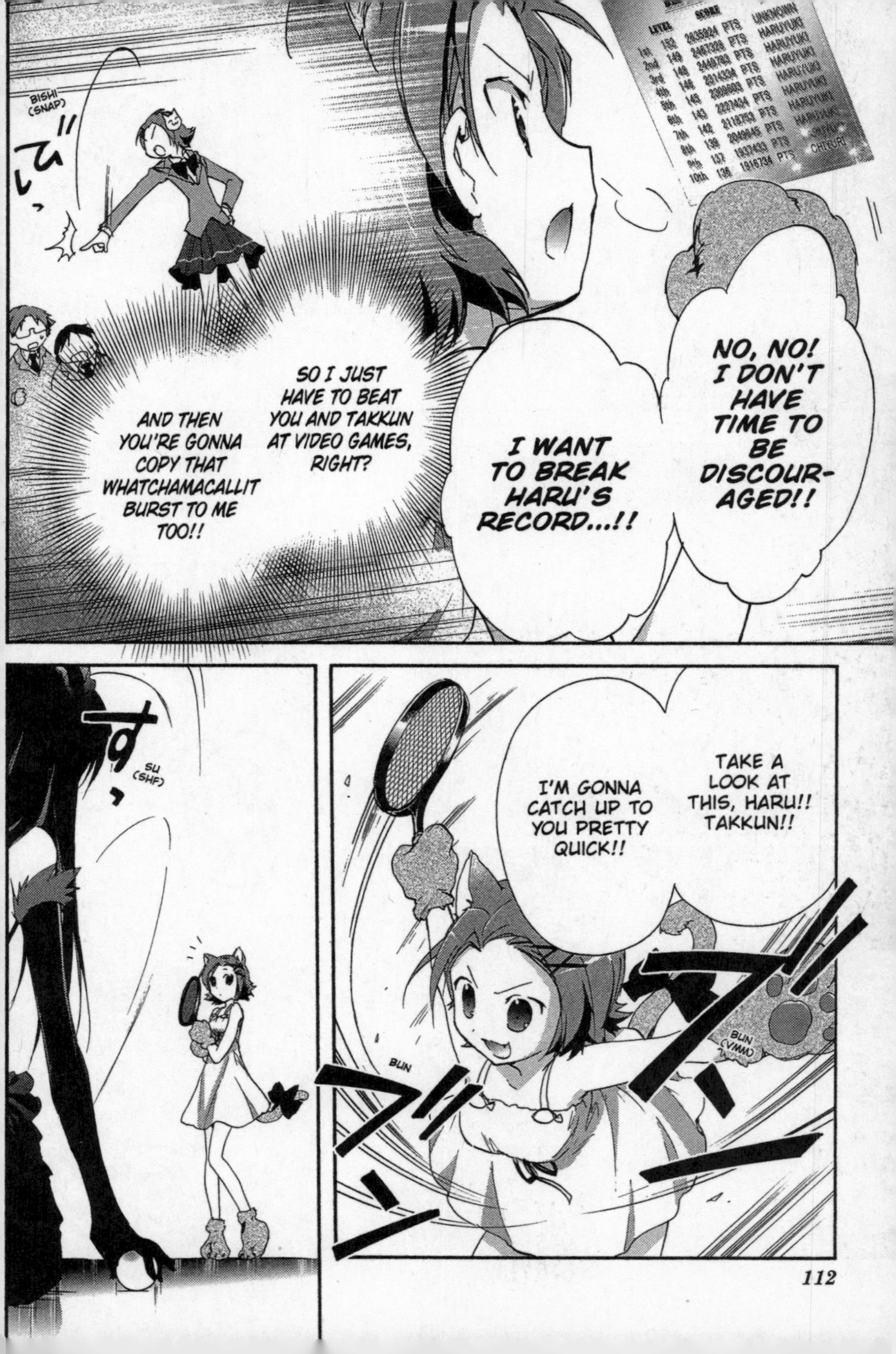
NO, NO! I DON'T HAVE TIME TO BE DISCOURAGED!!
I WANT TO BREAK HARU'S RECORD...!!
SO I JUST HAVE TO BEAT YOU AND TAKKUN AT VIDEO GAMES, RIGHT?
AND THEN YOU'RE GONNA COPY THAT WHATCHAMACALLIT BURST TO ME TOO!!
BISHI (SNAP)
TAKE A LOOK AT THIS, HARU!! TAKKUN!!
I'M GONNA CATCH UP TO YOU PRETTY QUICK!!
BUN (VMM)
BUN
SU (SHF)

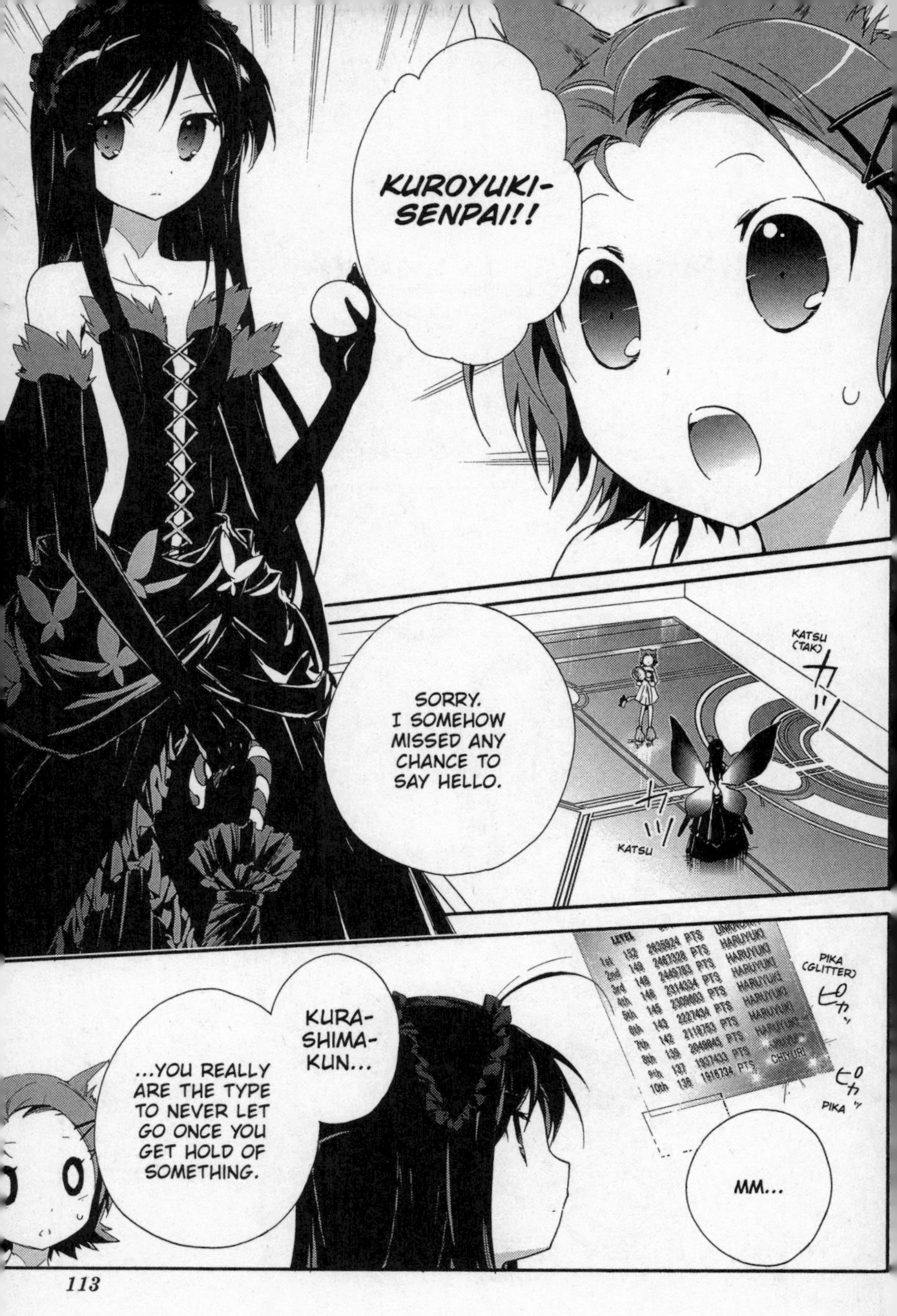
KUROYUKI-SENPAI!!
KATSU (TAK)
KATSU
SORRY. I SOMEHOW MISSED ANY CHANCE TO SAY HELLO.
PIKA (GLITTER)
PIKA
MM...
KURA-SHIMA-KUN...
...YOU REALLY ARE THE TYPE TO NEVER LET GO ONCE YOU GET HOLD OF SOMETHING.

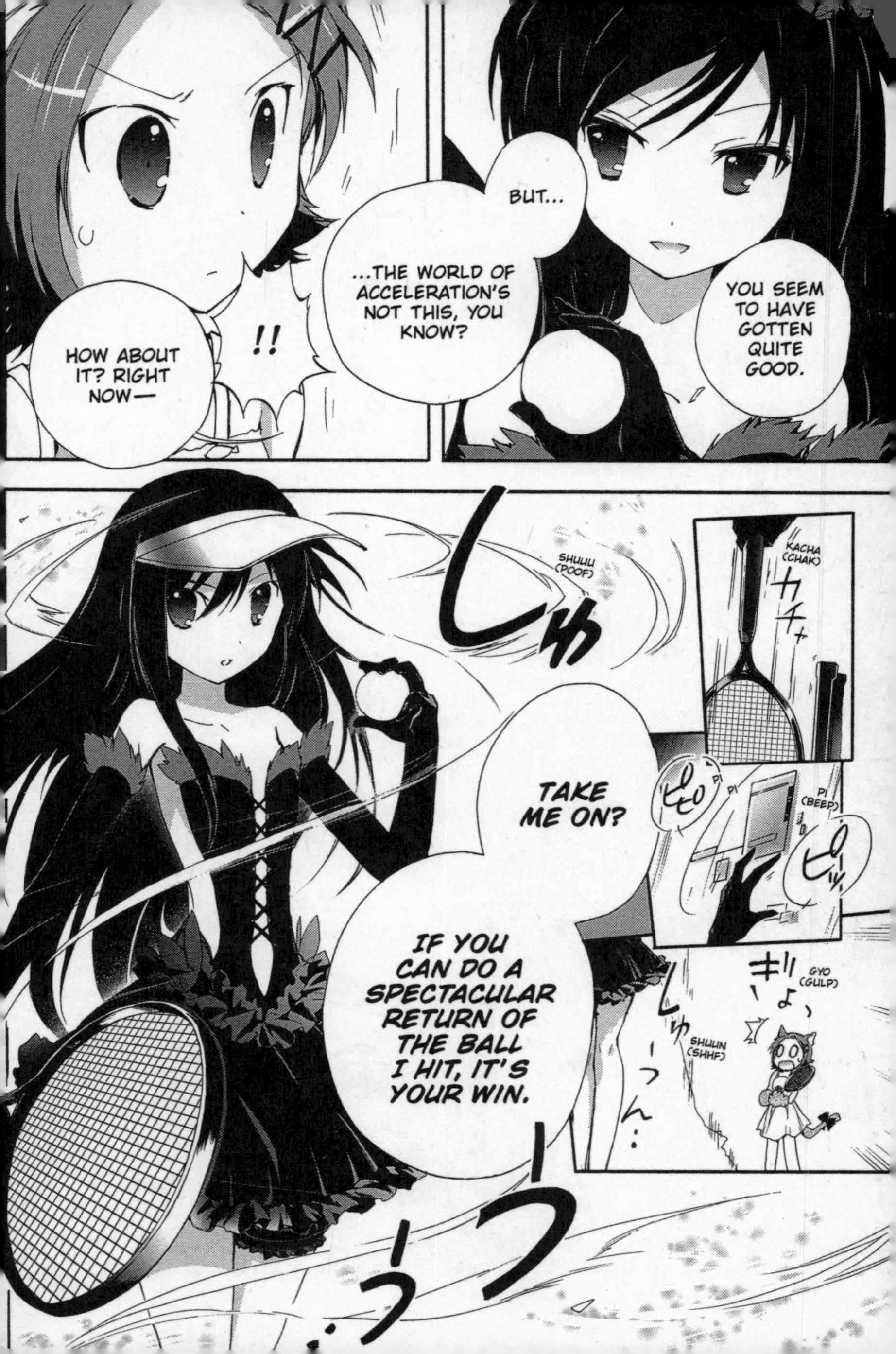

YOU SEEM TO HAVE GOTTEN QUITE GOOD.
BUT...
...THE WORLD OF ACCELERATION'S NOT THIS, YOU KNOW?
!!
HOW ABOUT IT? RIGHT NOW—
KACHA (CHAK)
PI PI
PI (BEEP)
GYO (GULP)
SHUUN (SHHF)
SHUUU (POOF)
TAKE ME ON?
IF YOU CAN DO A SPECTACULAR RETURN OF THE BALL I HIT, IT'S YOUR WIN.

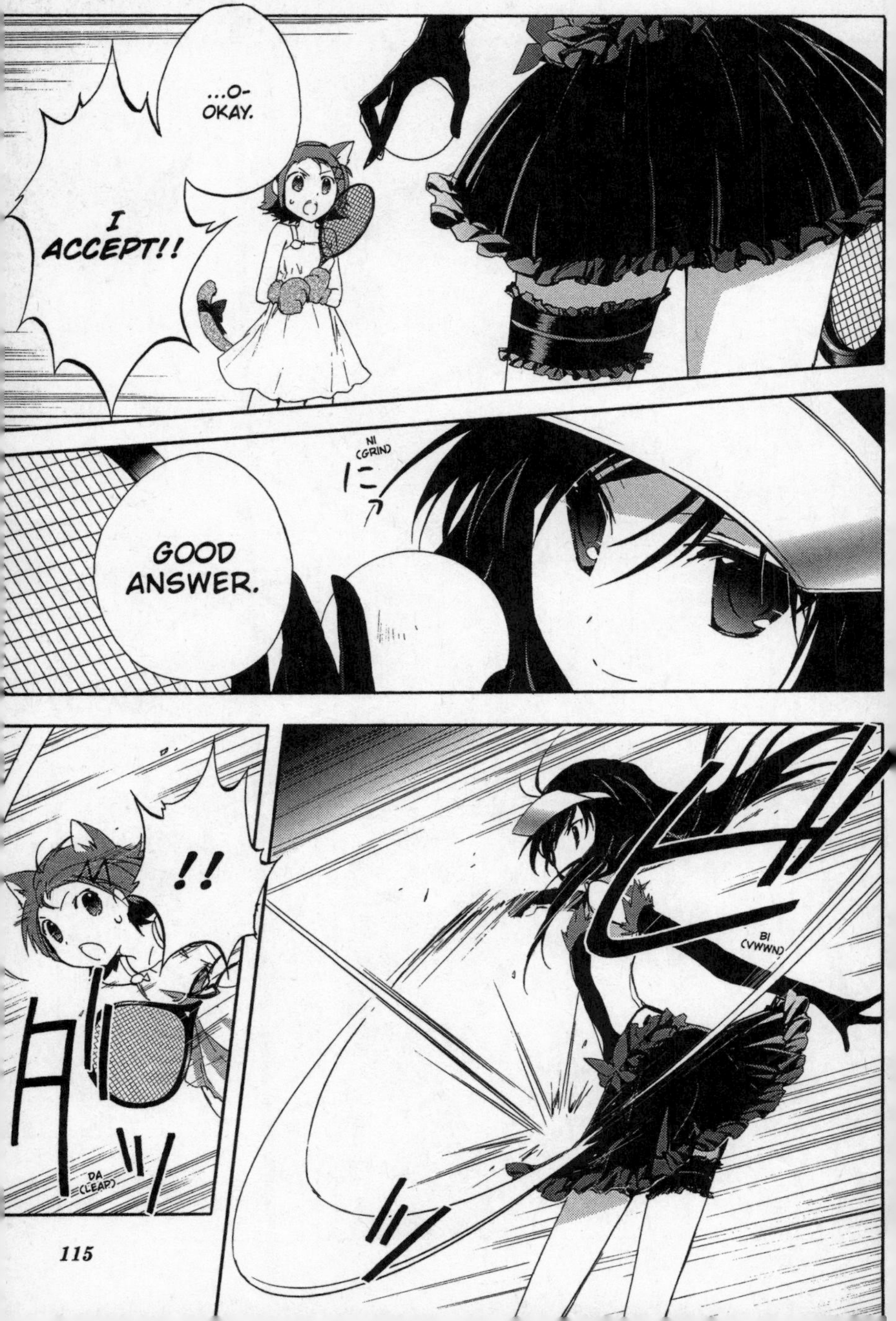

...O-
OKAY.
I ACCEPT!!
NI (GRIND)
GOOD ANSWER.
BI (VWWN)
!!
DA (LEAP)

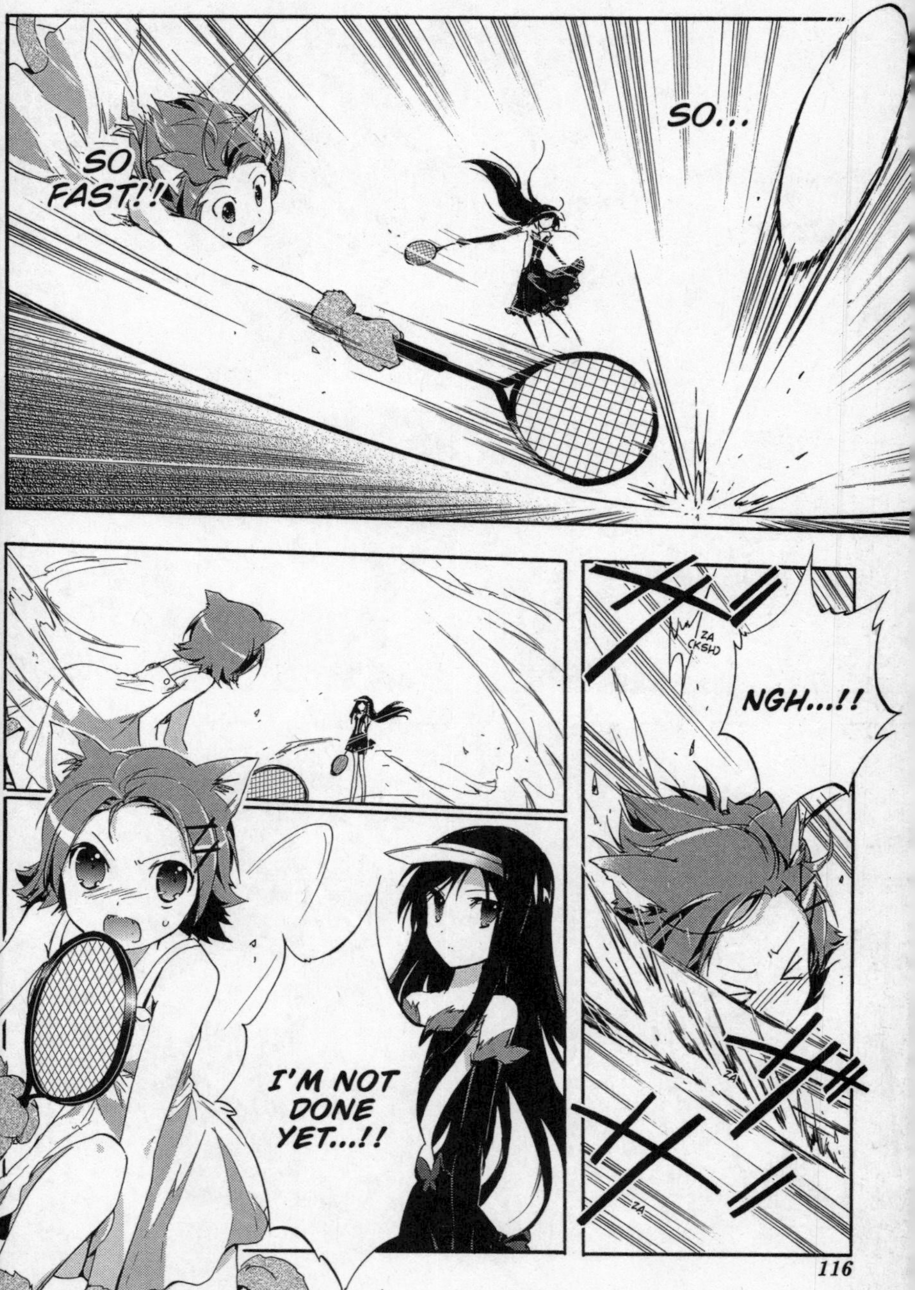
SO...
SO FAST!!
ZA (KSH)
NGH...!!
ZA
ZA
I'M NOT DONE YET...!!

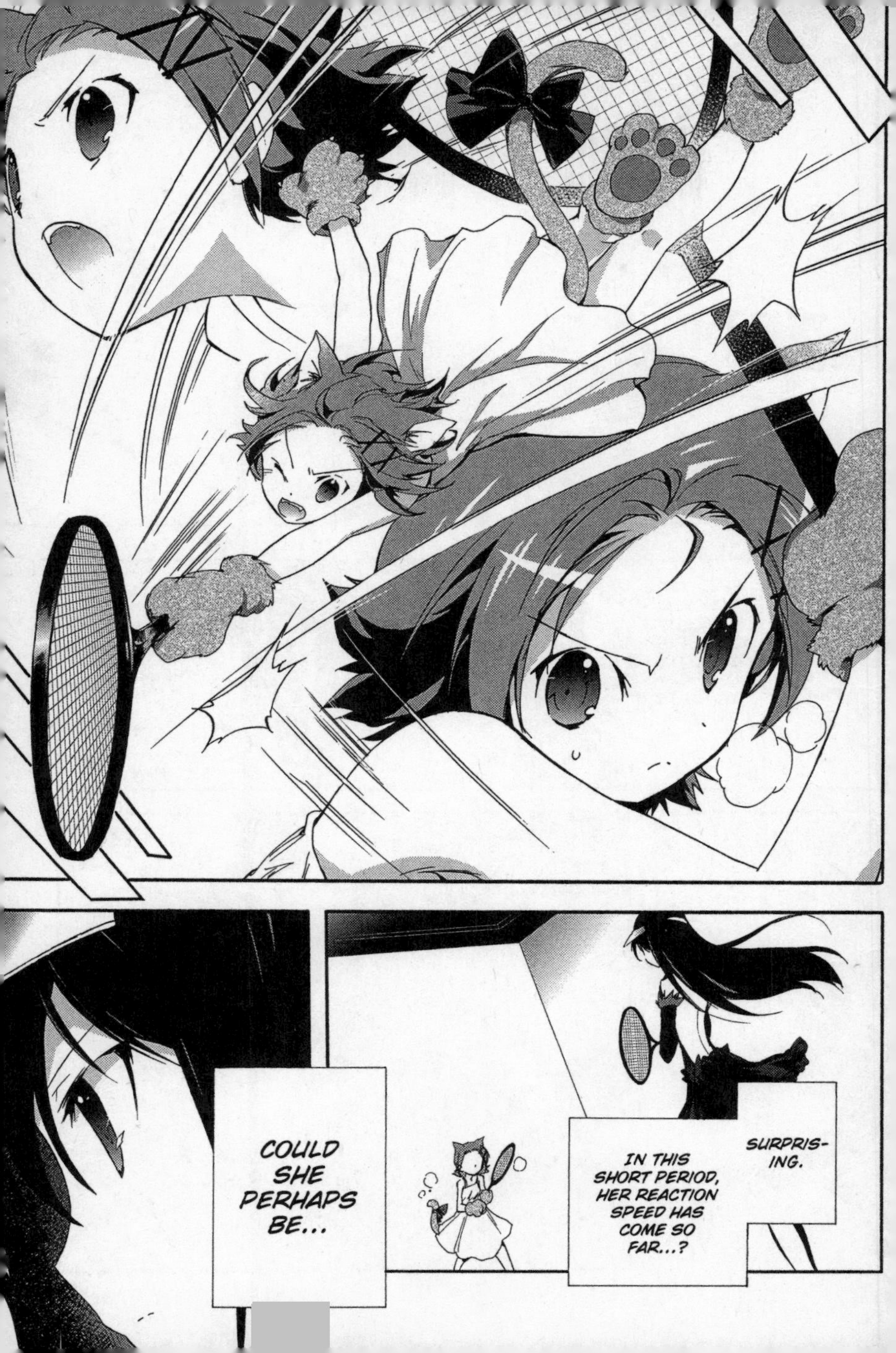
SURPRIS-ING.
IN THIS SHORT PERIOD, HER REACTION SPEED HAS COME SO FAR...?
COULD SHE PERHAPS BE...

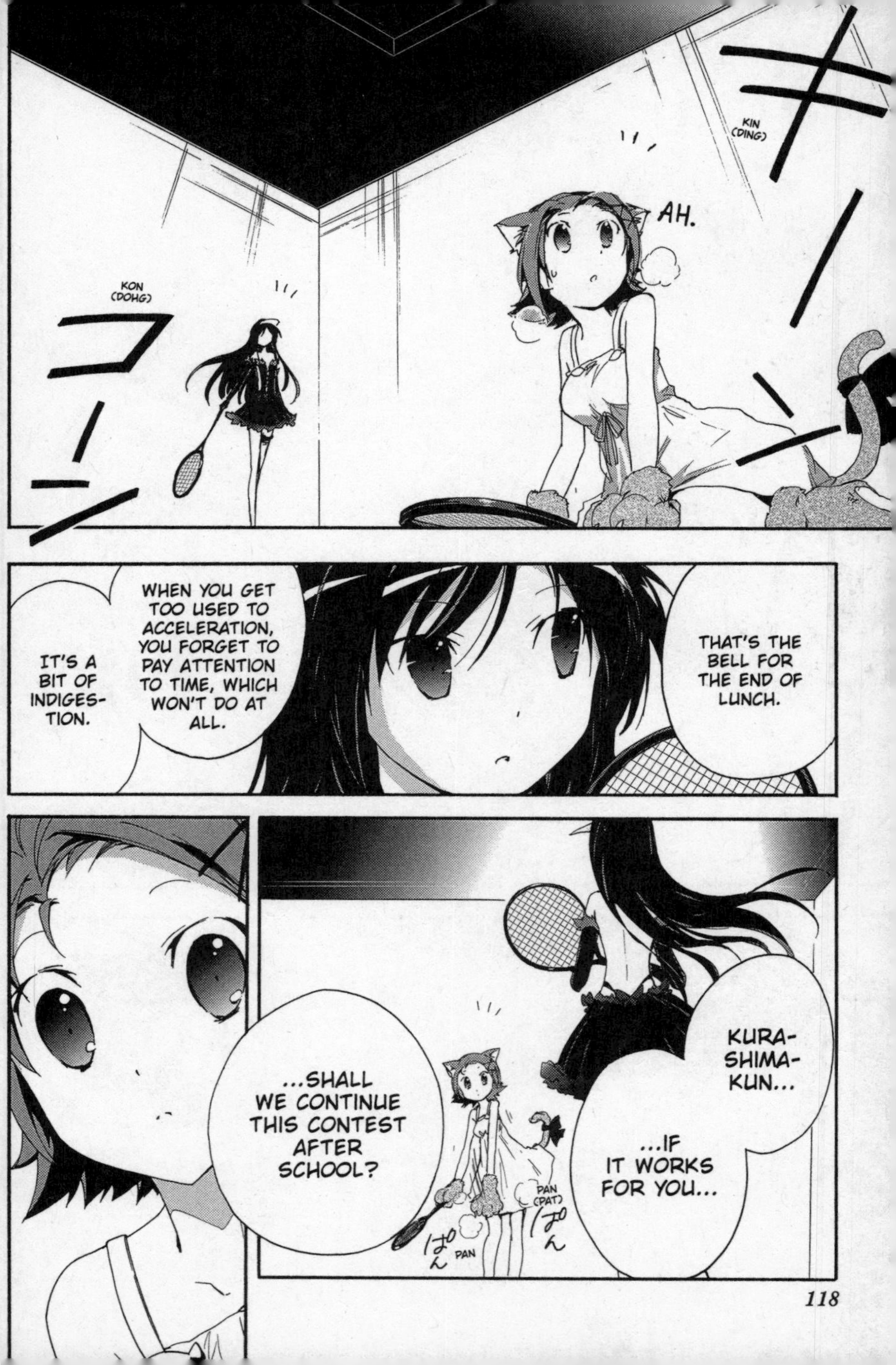
KIN (DING)
AH.
KON (DOHG)
THAT'S THE BELL FOR THE END OF LUNCH.
WHEN YOU GET TOO USED TO ACCELERATION, YOU FORGET TO PAY ATTENTION TO TIME, WHICH WON'T DO AT ALL.
IT'S A BIT OF INDIGES-TION.
KURA-SHIMA-KUN...
...IF IT WORKS FOR YOU...
ぱん PAN (PAT)
...SHALL WE CONTINUE THIS CONTEST AFTER SCHOOL?
ぱん PAN

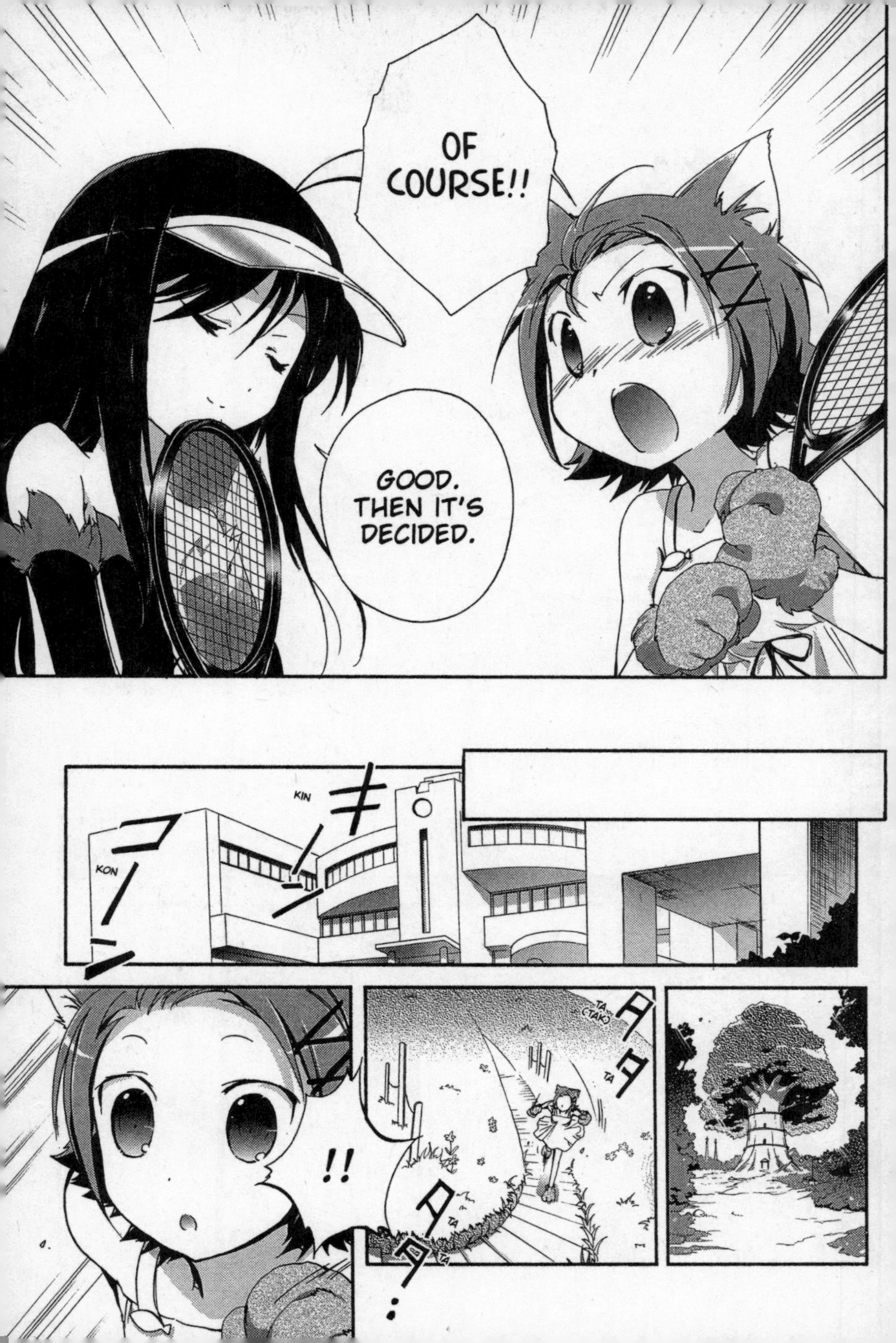

OF COURSE!!
GOOD. THEN IT'S DECIDED.
KIN
KON
TA (TAK)
TA
TA
TA
!!

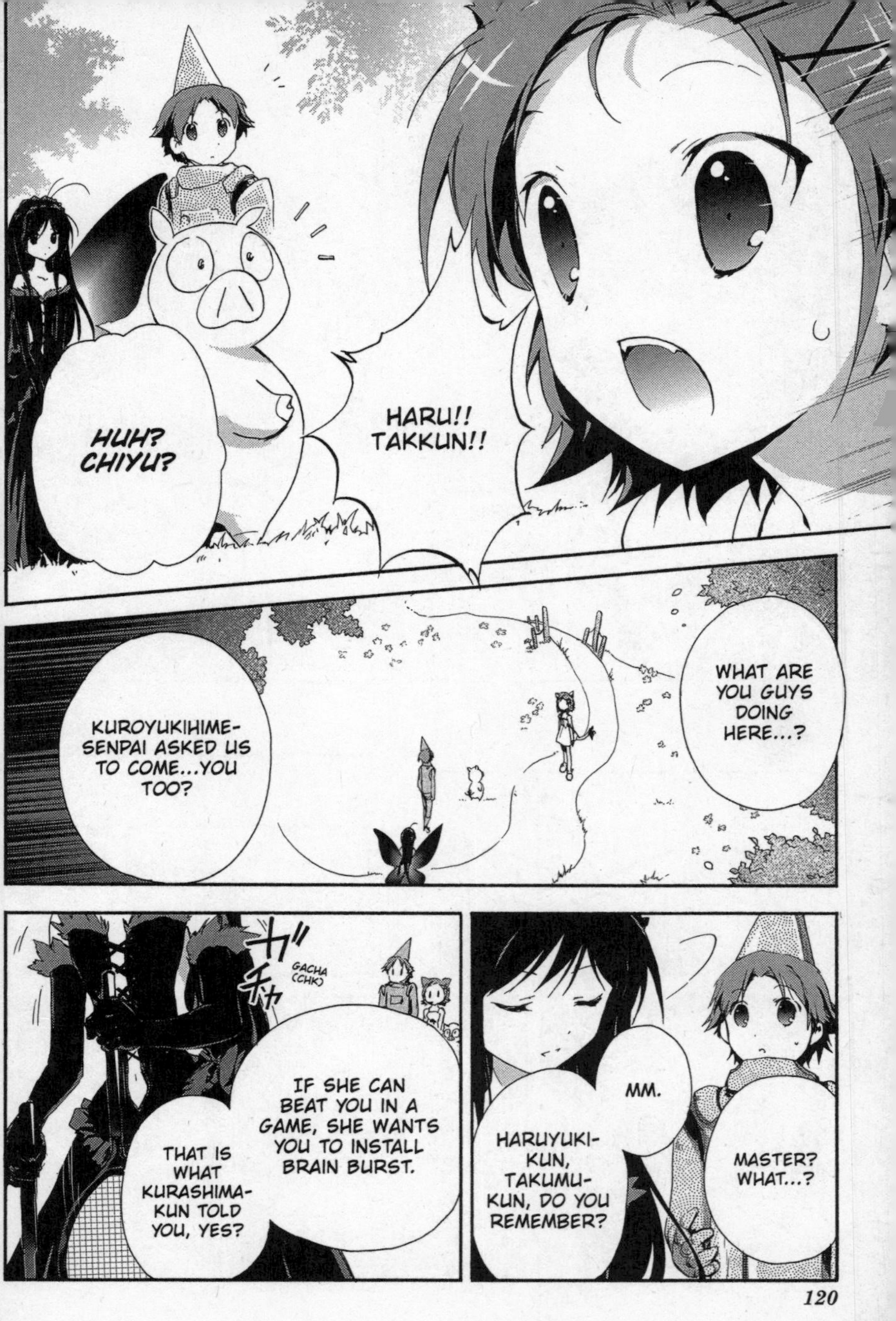
HARU!! TAKKUN!!
HUH? CHIYU?
WHAT ARE YOU GUYS DOING HERE...?
KUROYUKIHIME-SENPAI ASKED US TO COME...YOU TOO?
MASTER? WHAT...?
MM.
HARUYUKI-KUN, TAKUMU-KUN, DO YOU REMEMBER?
ガチャ
GACHA (CHK)
IF SHE CAN BEAT YOU IN A GAME, SHE WANTS YOU TO INSTALL BRAIN BURST.
THAT IS WHAT KURASHIMA-KUN TOLD YOU, YES?

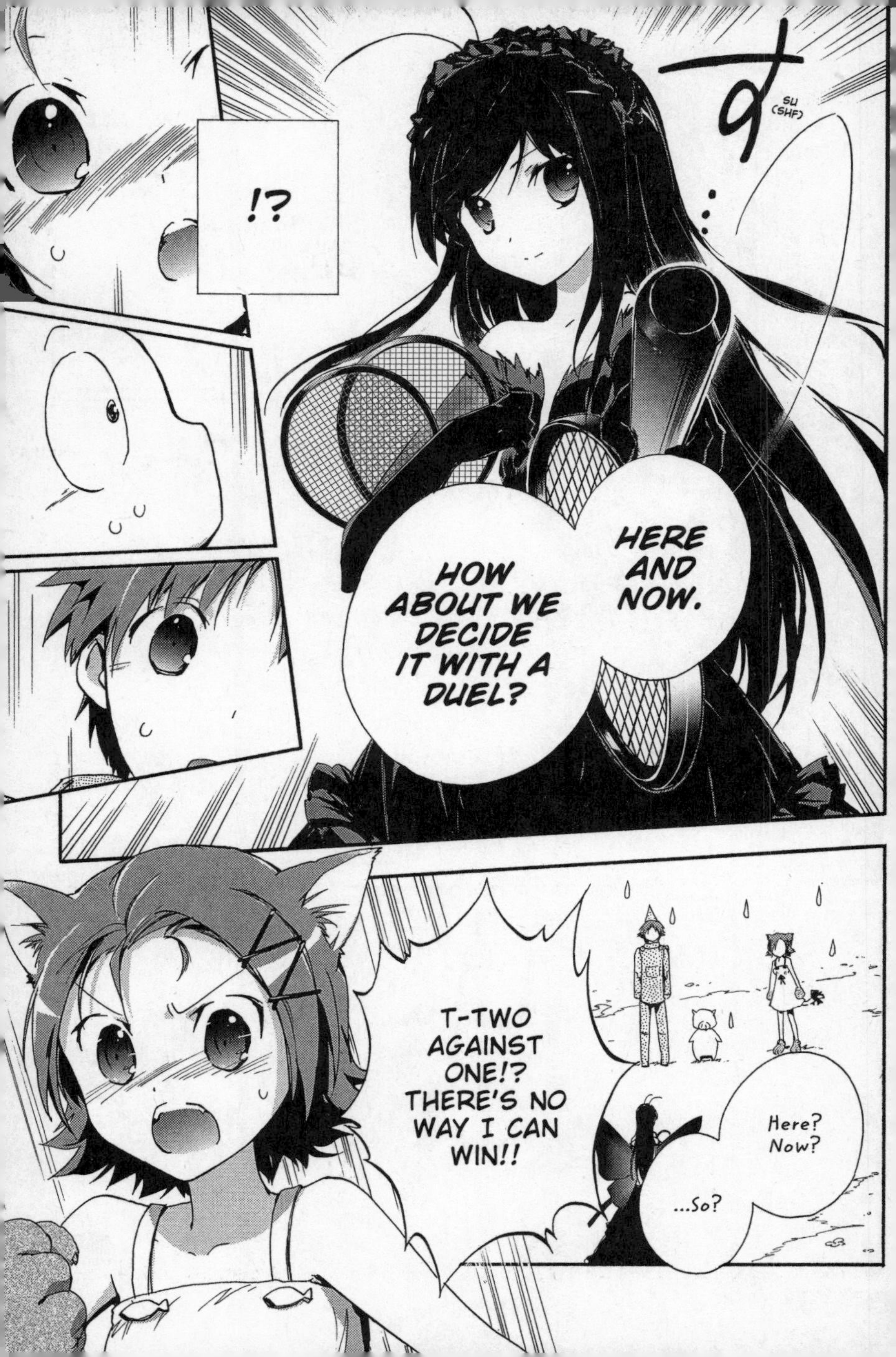
す
SU (SHF)
HOW ABOUT WE DECIDE IT WITH A DUEL? HERE AND NOW.
!?
Here? Now?
...So?
T-TWO AGAINST ONE!? THERE'S NO WAY I CAN WIN!!

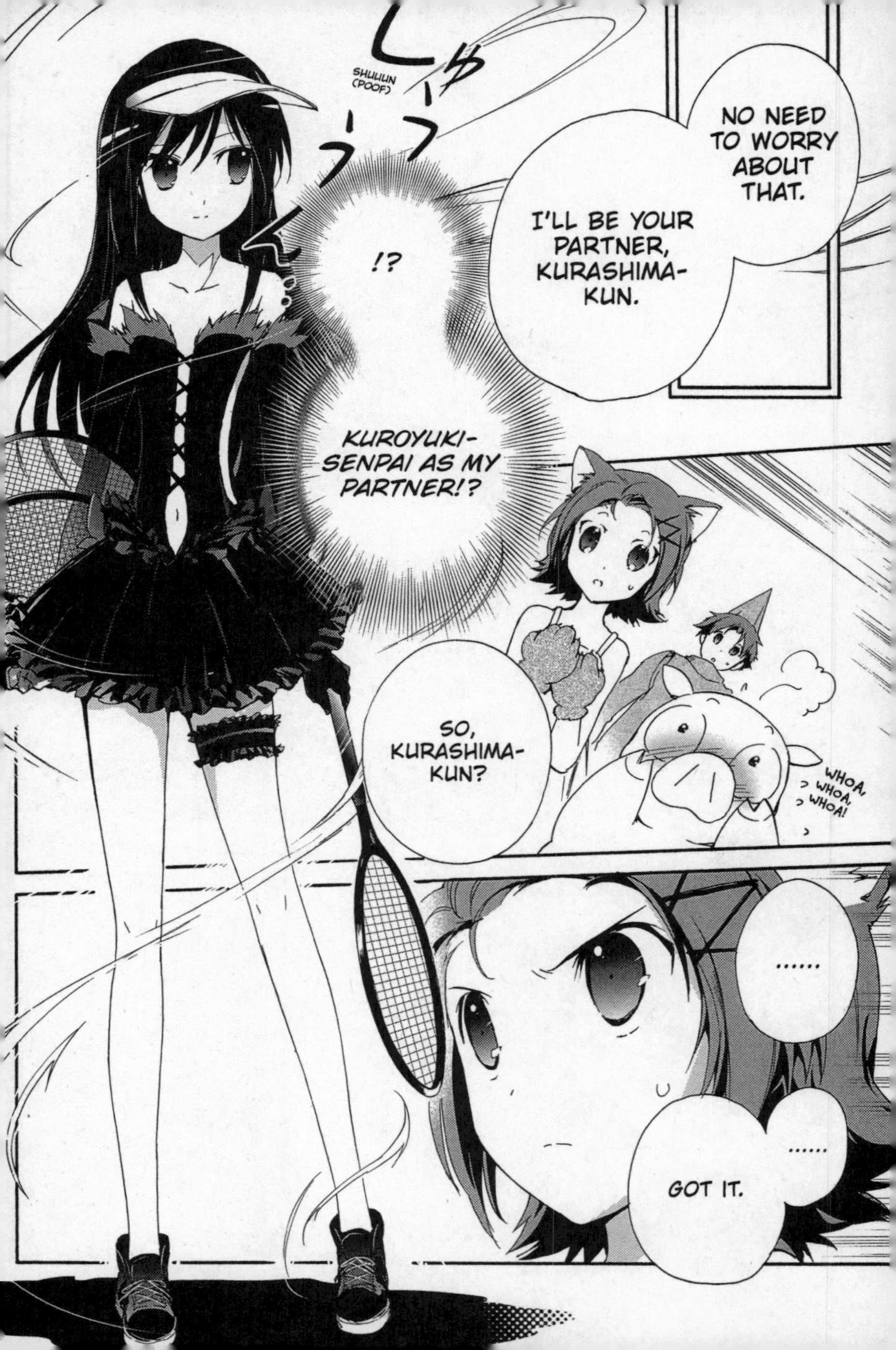
NO NEED TO WORRY ABOUT THAT.
I'LL BE YOUR PARTNER, KURASHIMA-KUN.
SHUUUN (POOF)
!?
KUROYUKI-SENPAI AS MY PARTNER!?
SO, KURASHIMA-KUN?
WHOA, WHOA, WHOA!
......
...... GOT IT.

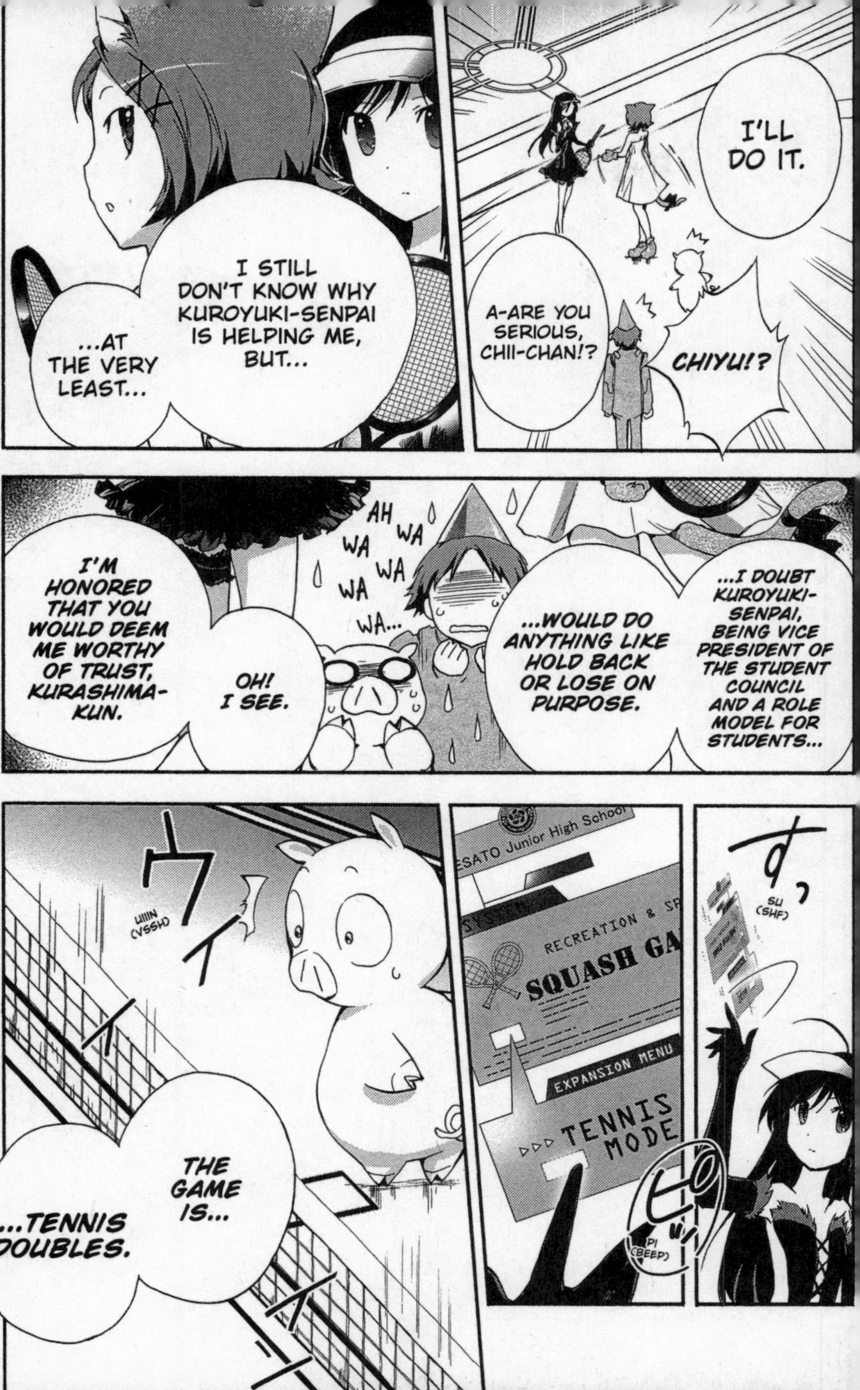
I'LL DO IT.
CHIYU!?
A-ARE YOU SERIOUS, CHII-CHAN!?
I STILL DON'T KNOW WHY KUROYUKI-SENPAI IS HELPING ME, BUT...
...AT THE VERY LEAST...
...I DOUBT KUROYUKI-SENPAI, BEING VICE PRESIDENT OF THE STUDENT COUNCIL AND A ROLE MODEL FOR STUDENTS...
...WOULD DO ANYTHING LIKE HOLD BACK OR LOSE ON PURPOSE.
AH WA WA WA WA WA...
OH! I SEE.
I'M HONORED THAT YOU WOULD DEEM ME WORTHY OF TRUST, KURASHIMA-KUN.
すっ
SU (SHF)
ESATO Junior High School
RECREATION & SP
SQUASH GA
EXPANSION MENU
TENNIS MODE
PI (BEEP)
UIIIN (VSSH)
THE GAME IS...
...TENNIS DOUBLES.

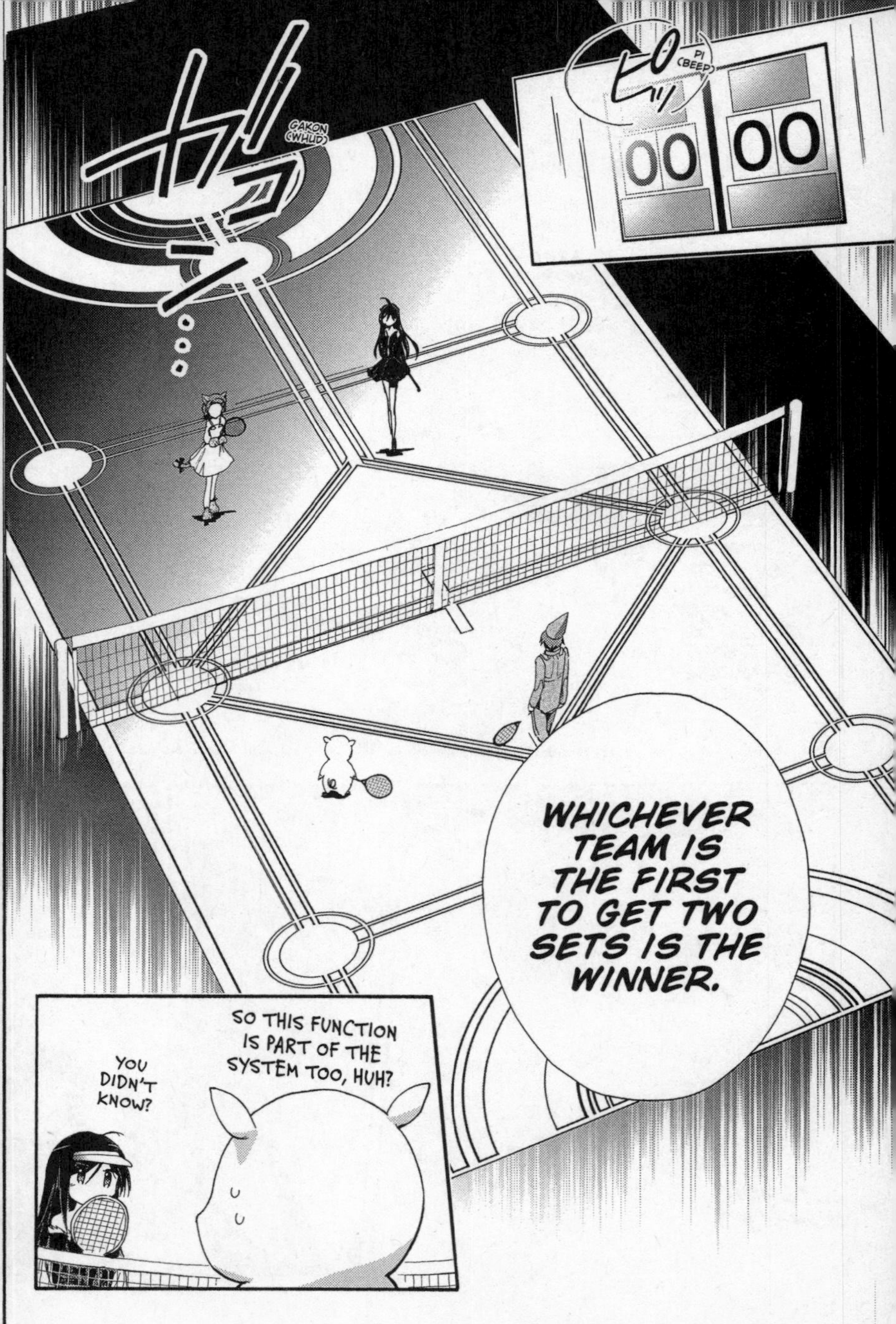
PI (BEEP)
GAKON (WHUD)
00 00
WHICHEVER TEAM IS THE FIRST TO GET TWO SETS IS THE WINNER.
SO THIS FUNCTION IS PART OF THE SYSTEM TOO, HUH?
YOU DIDN'T KNOW?

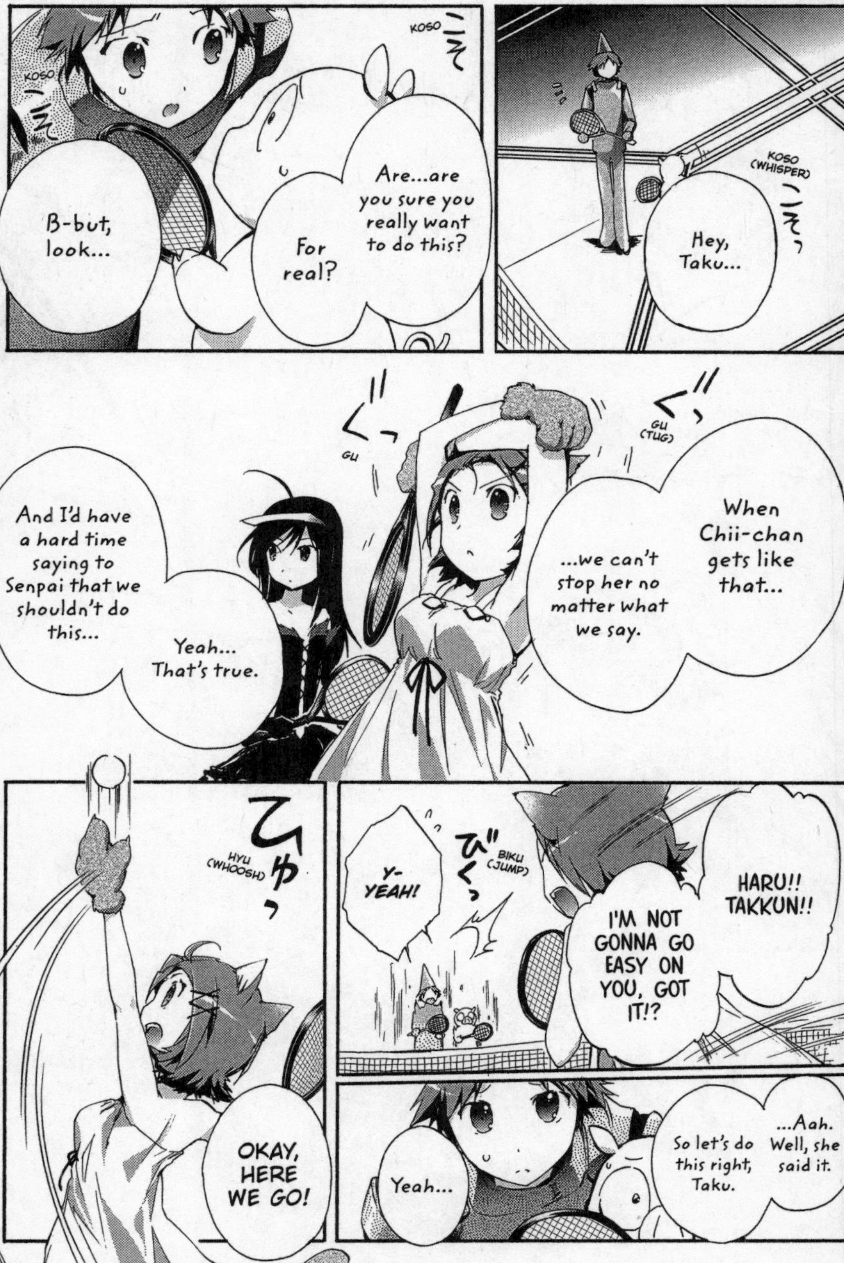
KOSO (WHISPER)
Hey, Taku...
KOSO
Are...are you sure you really want to do this?
For real?
KOSO
B-but, look...
GU (TUG)
When Chii-chan gets like that...
...we can't stop her no matter what we say.
GU
And I'd have a hard time saying to Senpai that we shouldn't do this...
Yeah... That's true.
HARU!! TAKKUN!!
I'M NOT GONNA GO EASY ON YOU, GOT IT!?
BIKU (JUMP)
Y-YEAH!
...Aah. Well, she said it.
So let's do this right, Taku.
Yeah...
HYU (WHOOSH)
OKAY, HERE WE GO!

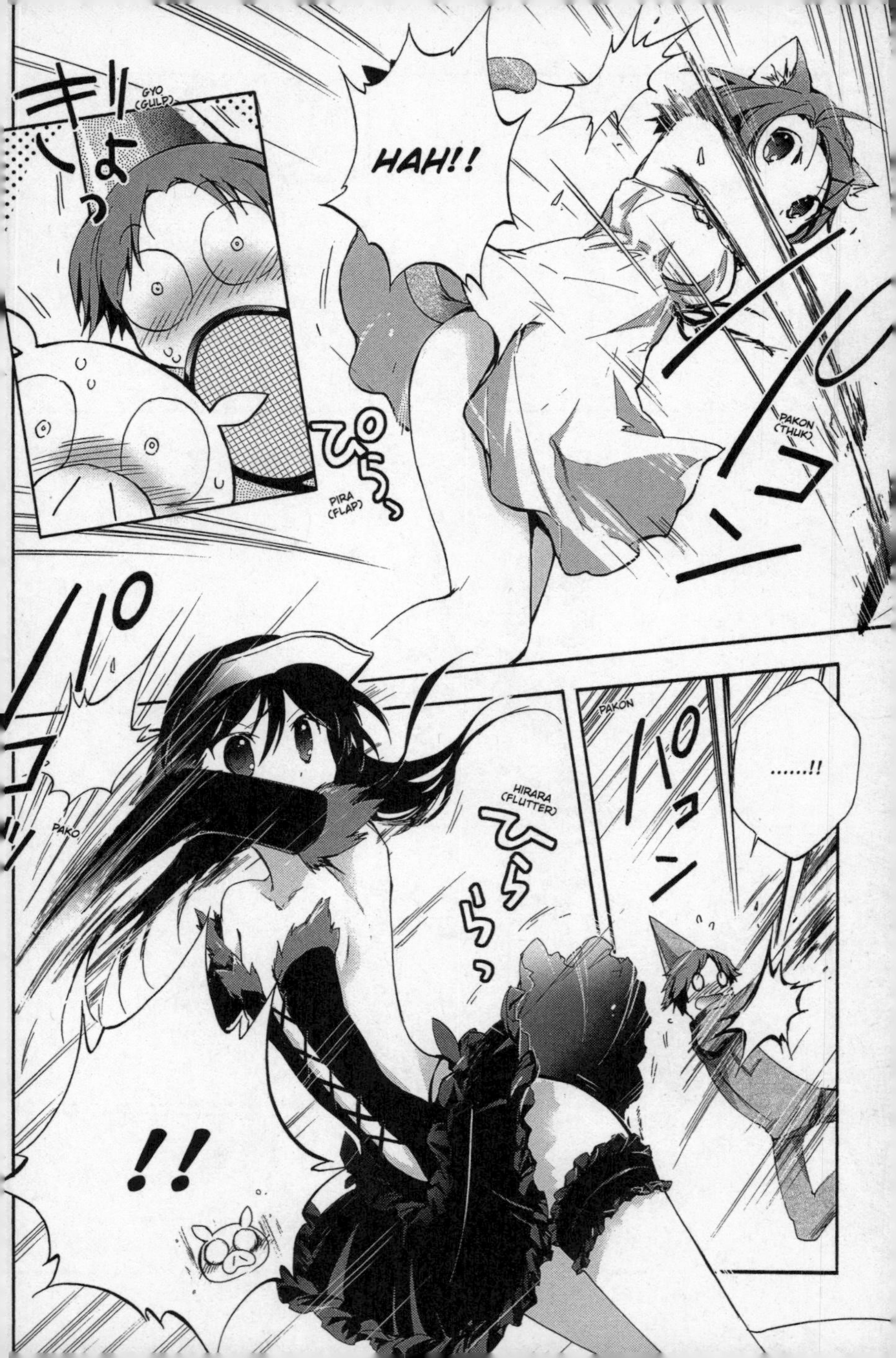
HAH!!
パコーン
PAKON (THUK)
ぴらっ
PIRA (FLAP)
ぎょっ
GYO (GULP)
パコン
PAKON
......!!
ひららっ
HIRARA (FLUTTER)
パコッ
PAKO
!!

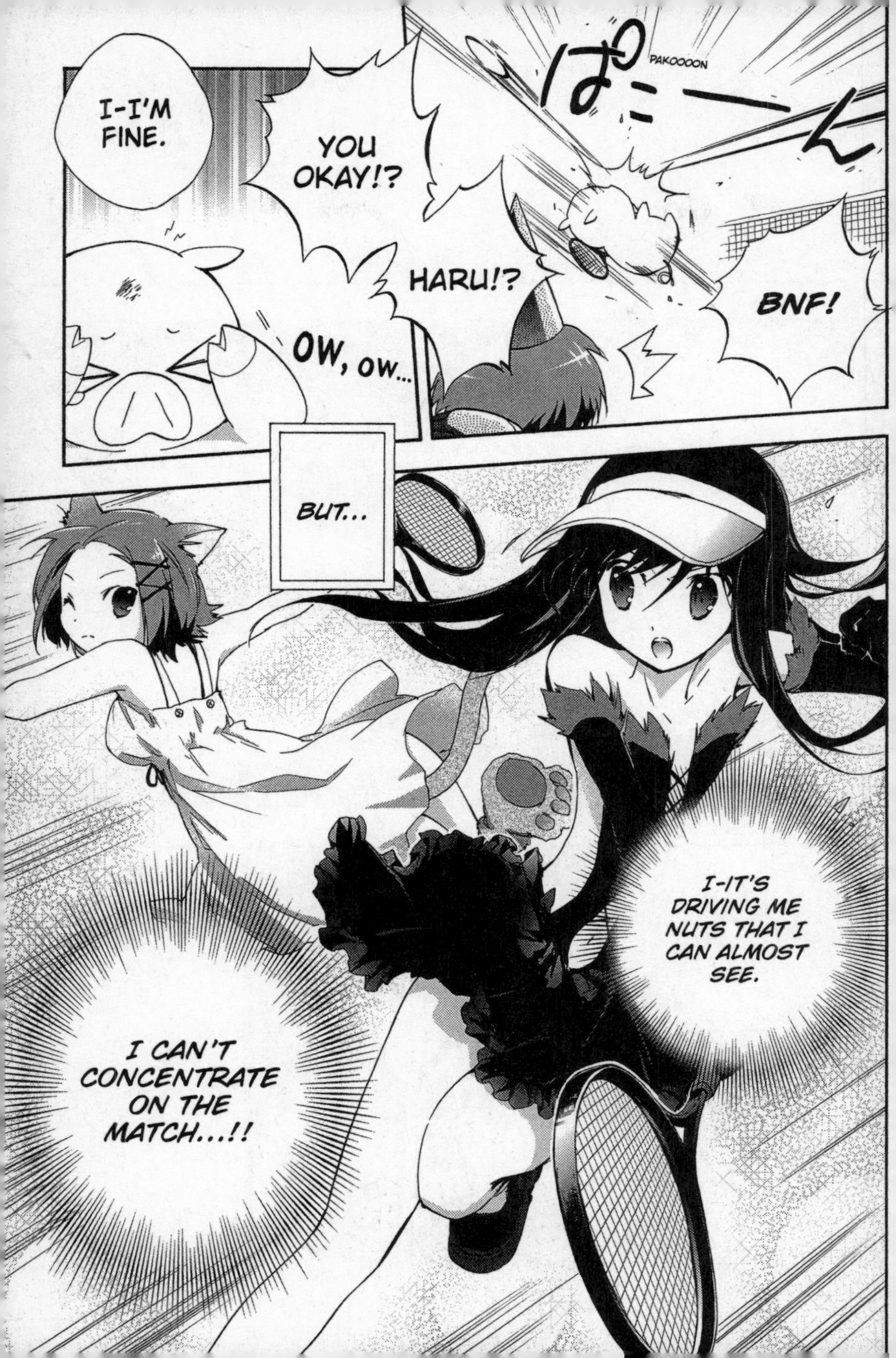

ぱこーん
PAKOOOON
BNF!
HARU!?
YOU OKAY!?
OW, OW...
I-I'M FINE.
BUT...
I-IT'S DRIVING ME NUTS THAT I CAN ALMOST SEE.
I CAN'T CONCENTRATE ON THE MATCH...!!

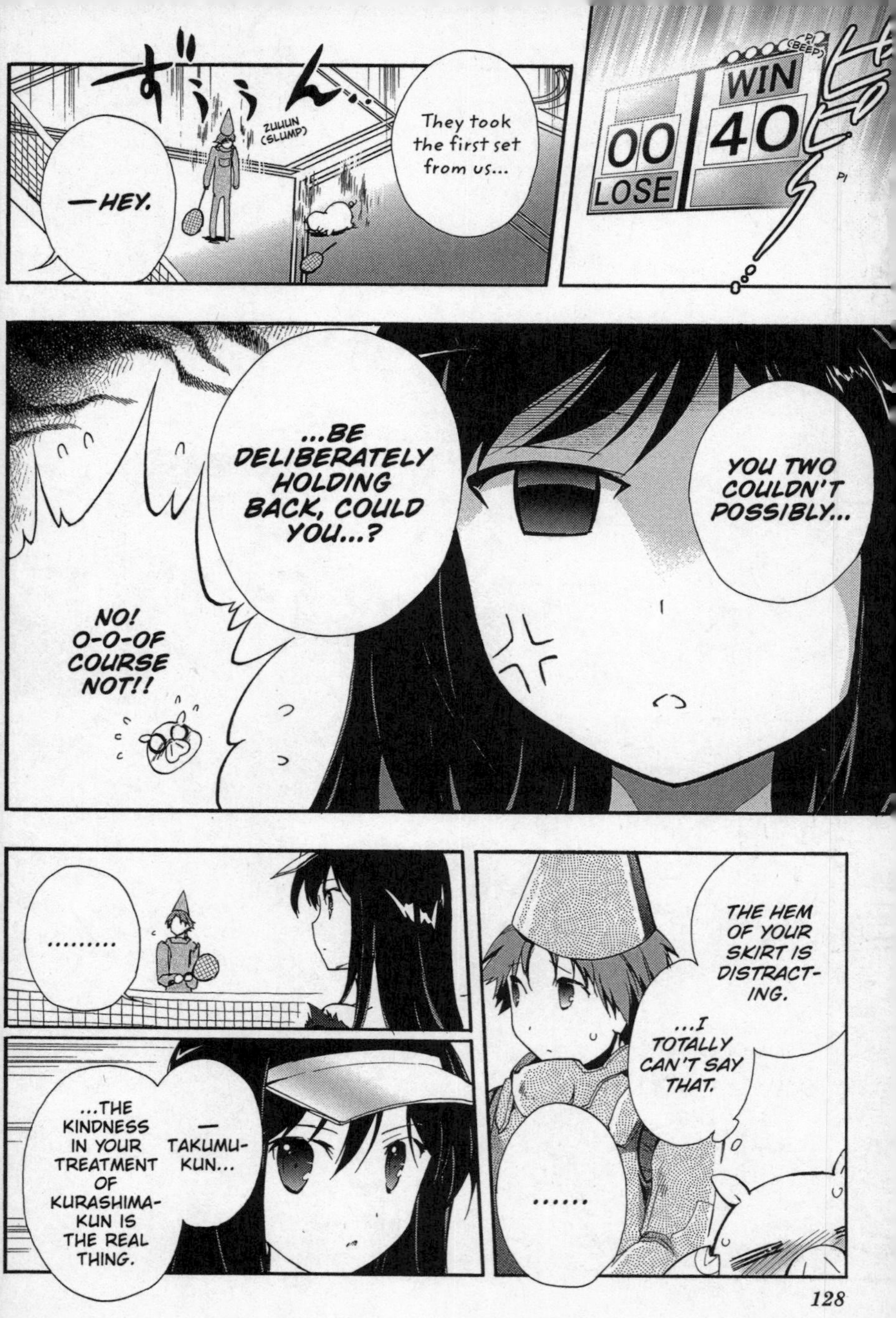
PI (BEEP)
WIN
40
00
LOSE
PI
They took the first set from us...
ZUUUN (SLUMP)
—HEY.
YOU TWO COULDN'T POSSIBLY...
...BE DELIBERATELY HOLDING BACK, COULD YOU...?
NO! O-O-OF COURSE NOT!!
THE HEM OF YOUR SKIRT IS DISTRACT-ING.
...I TOTALLY CAN'T SAY THAT.
......
....
—TAKUMU-KUN...
...THE KINDNESS IN YOUR TREATMENT OF KURASHIMA-KUN IS THE REAL THING.

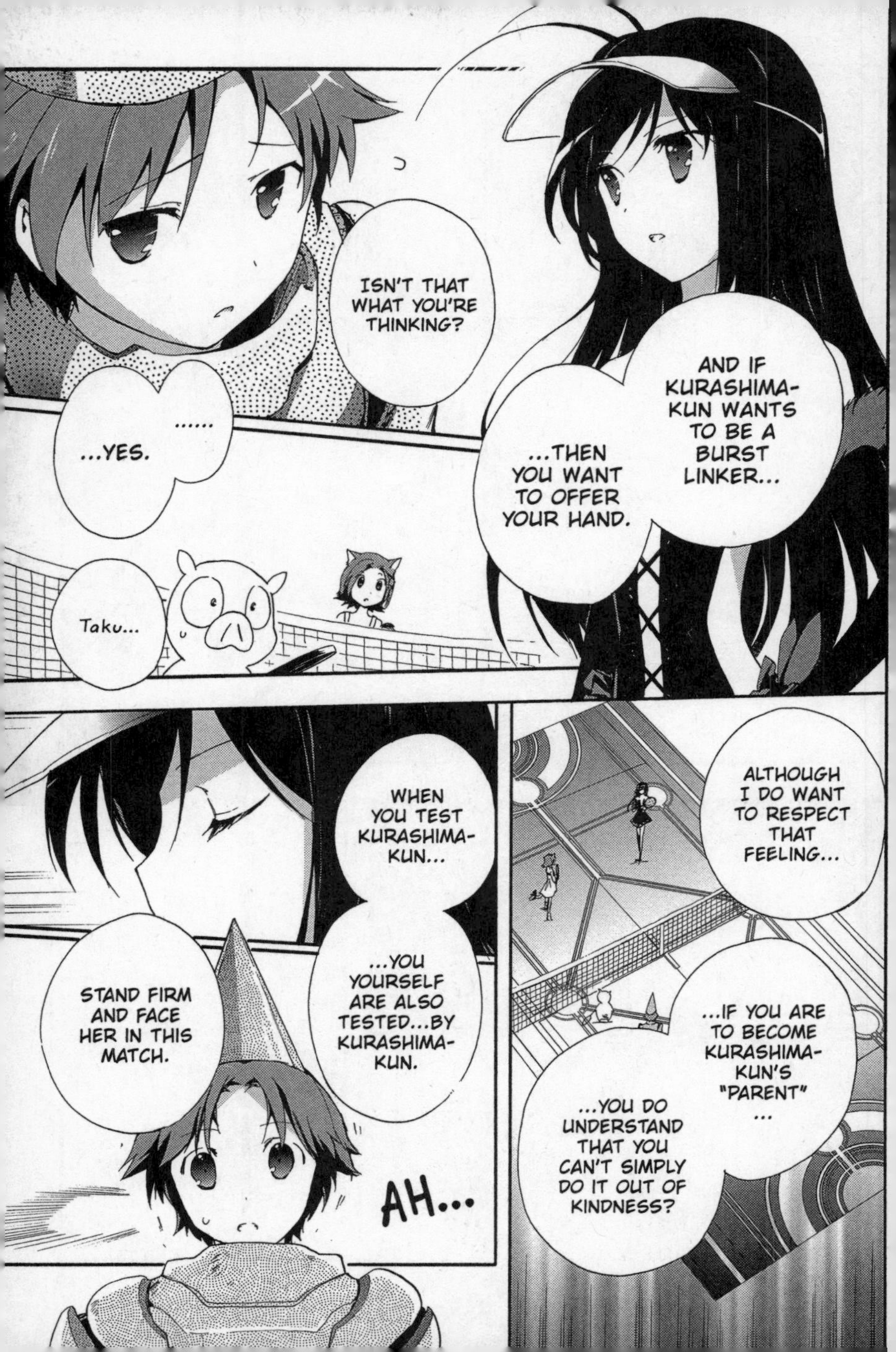
AND IF KURASHIMA-KUN WANTS TO BE A BURST LINKER...
...THEN YOU WANT TO OFFER YOUR HAND.
ISN'T THAT WHAT YOU'RE THINKING?
......
...YES.
Taku...
ALTHOUGH I DO WANT TO RESPECT THAT FEELING...
...IF YOU ARE TO BECOME KURASHIMA-KUN'S "PARENT" ...
...YOU DO UNDERSTAND THAT YOU CAN'T SIMPLY DO IT OUT OF KINDNESS?
WHEN YOU TEST KURASHIMA-KUN...
...YOU YOURSELF ARE ALSO TESTED...BY KURASHIMA-KUN.
STAND FIRM AND FACE HER IN THIS MATCH.
AH...

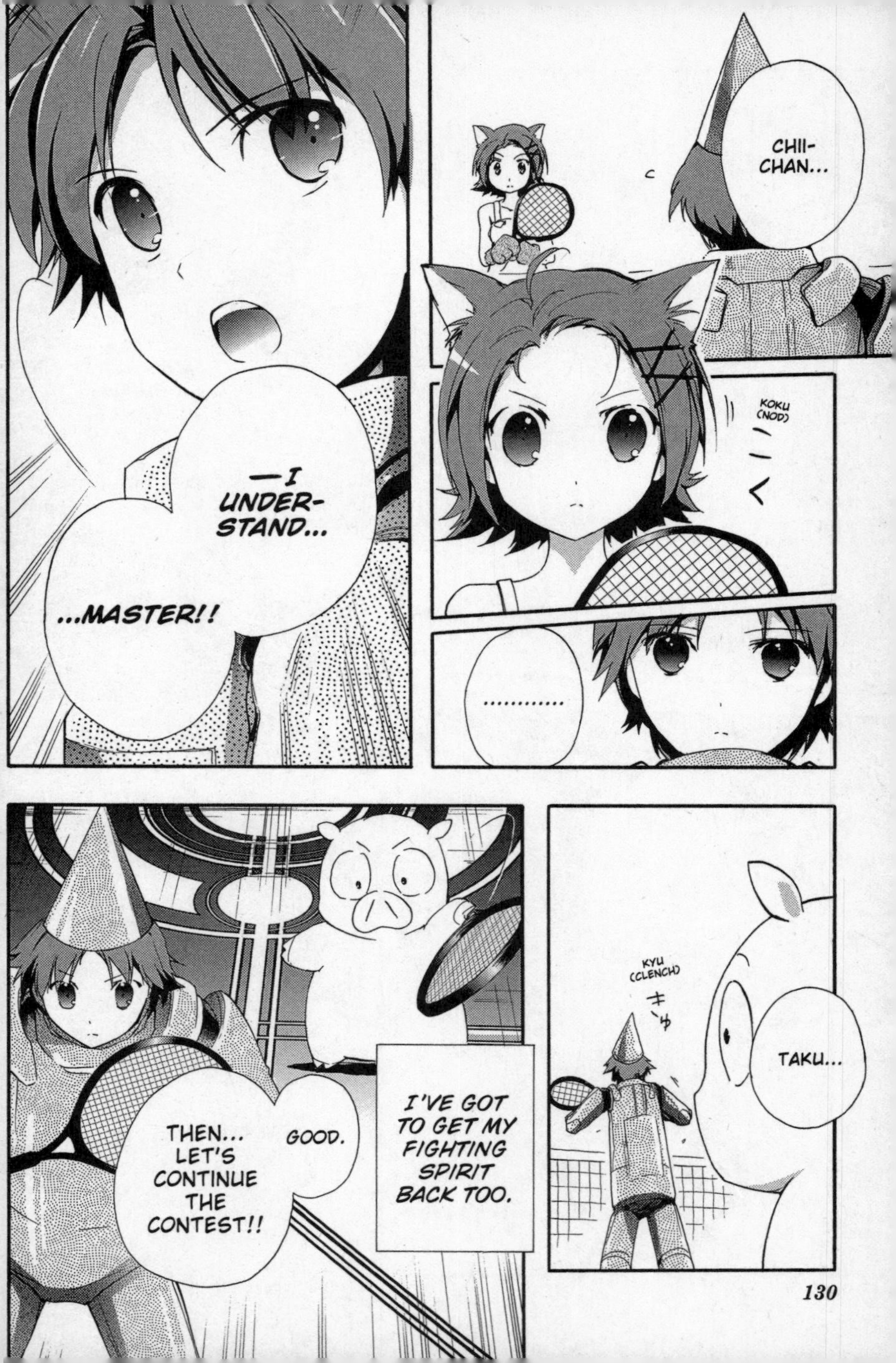
CHII-CHAN...
KOKU (NOD)
....
—I UNDERSTAND...
...MASTER!!
KYU (CLENCH)
TAKU...
I'VE GOT TO GET MY FIGHTING SPIRIT BACK TOO.
GOOD.
THEN... LET'S CONTINUE THE CONTEST!!

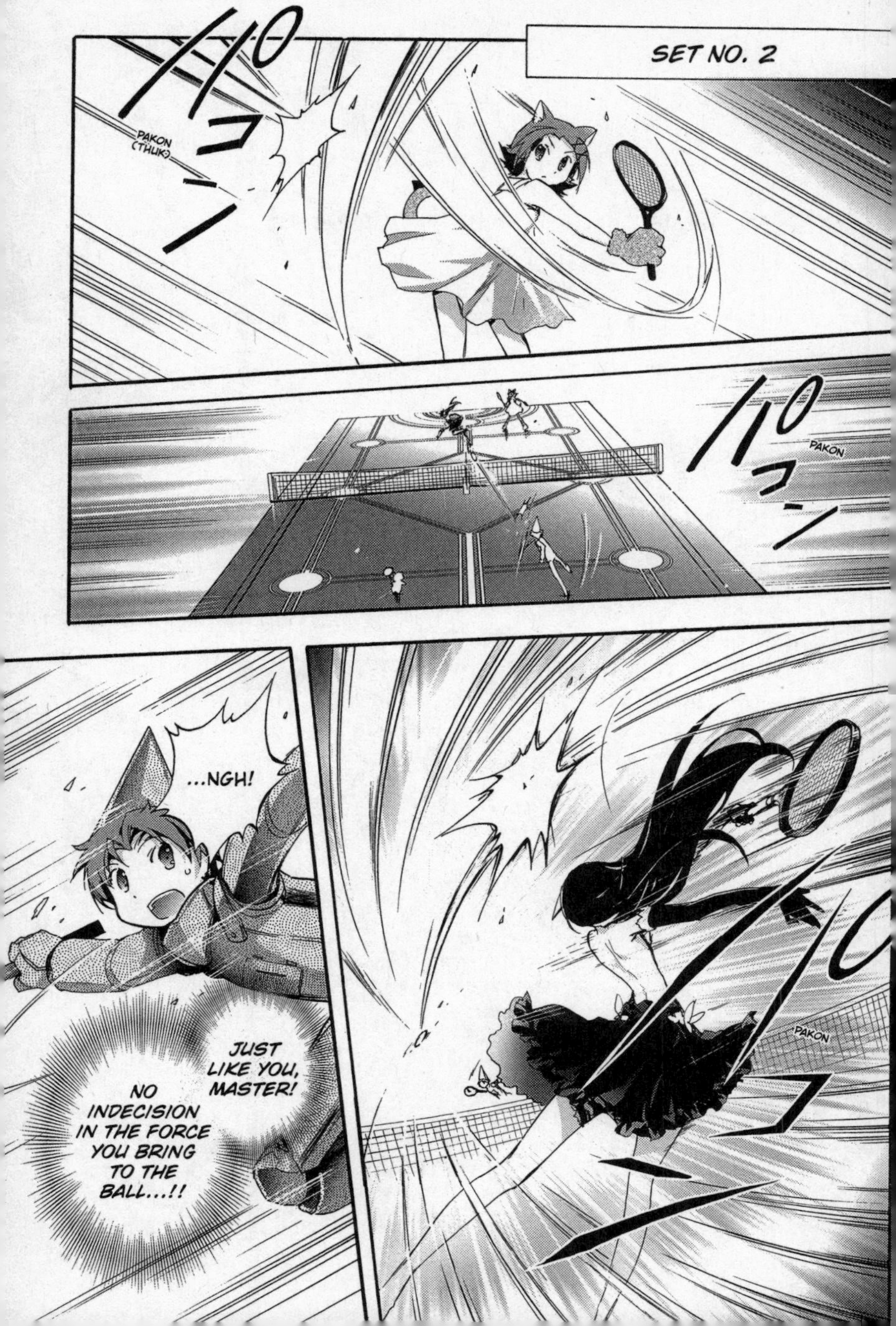
SET NO. 2
PAKON (THUK)
PAKON
PAKON
...NGH!
NO INDECISION IN THE FORCE YOU BRING TO THE BALL...!!
JUST LIKE YOU, MASTER!

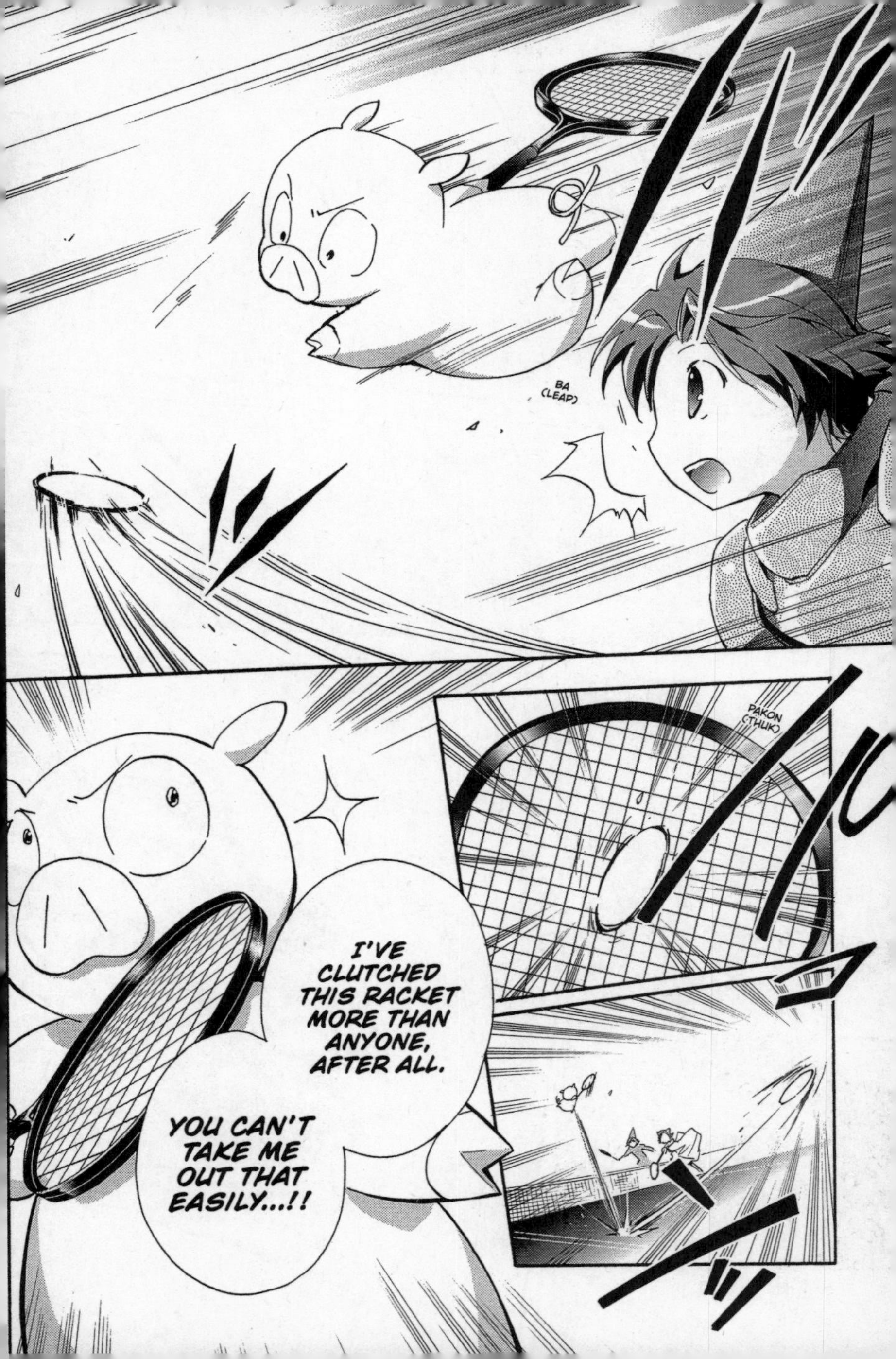
BA (LEAP)
PAKON (THUK)
I'VE CLUTCHED THIS RACKET MORE THAN ANYONE, AFTER ALL.
YOU CAN'T TAKE ME OUT THAT EASILY...!!

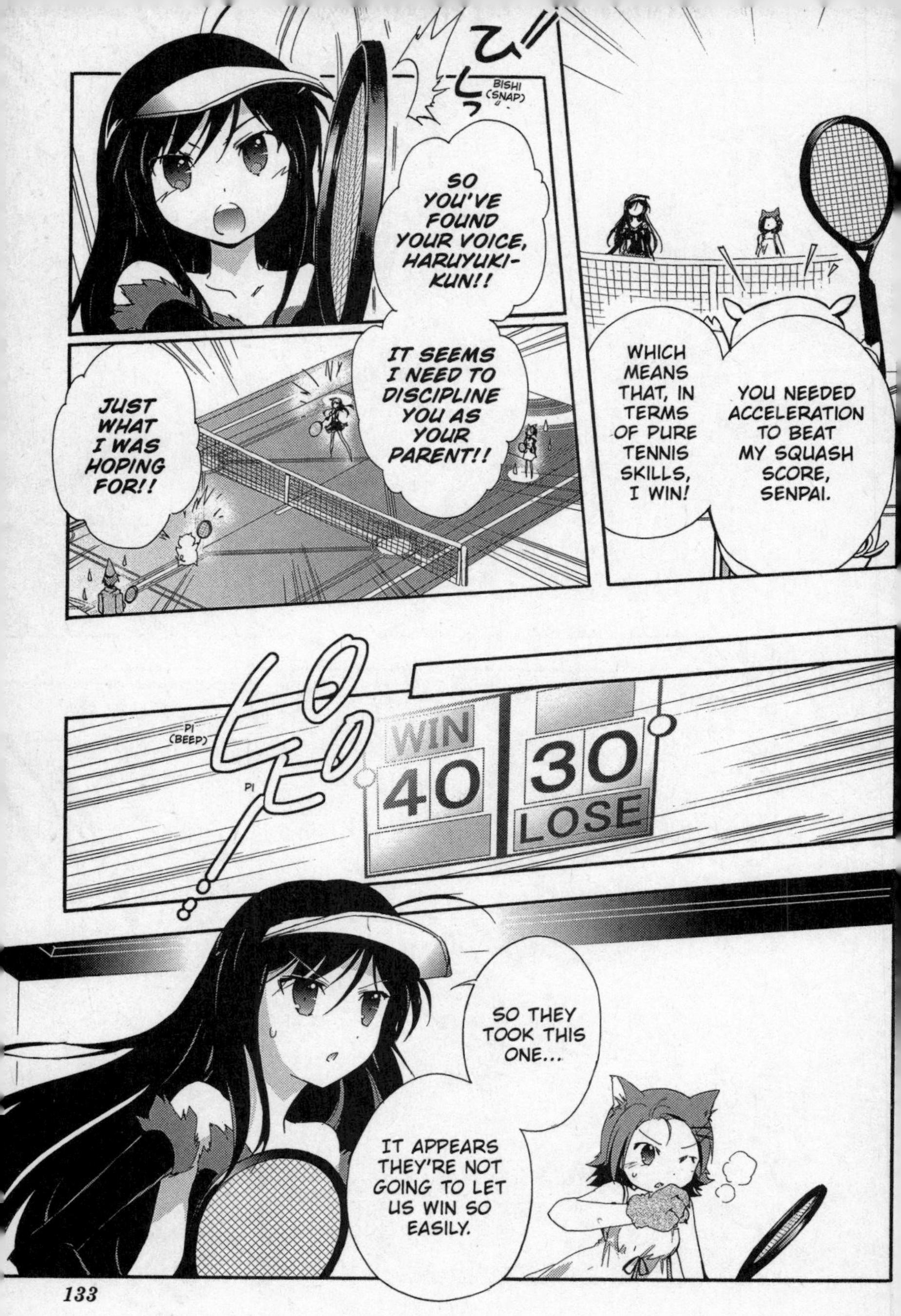

YOU NEEDED ACCELERATION TO BEAT MY SQUASH SCORE, SENPAI.
WHICH MEANS THAT, IN TERMS OF PURE TENNIS SKILLS, I WIN!
BISHI (SNAP)
SO YOU'VE FOUND YOUR VOICE, HARUYUKI-KUN!!
IT SEEMS I NEED TO DISCIPLINE YOU AS YOUR PARENT!!
JUST WHAT I WAS HOPING FOR!!
PI (BEEP)
PI
WIN
40
30
LOSE
SO THEY TOOK THIS ONE...
IT APPEARS THEY'RE NOT GOING TO LET US WIN SO EASILY.

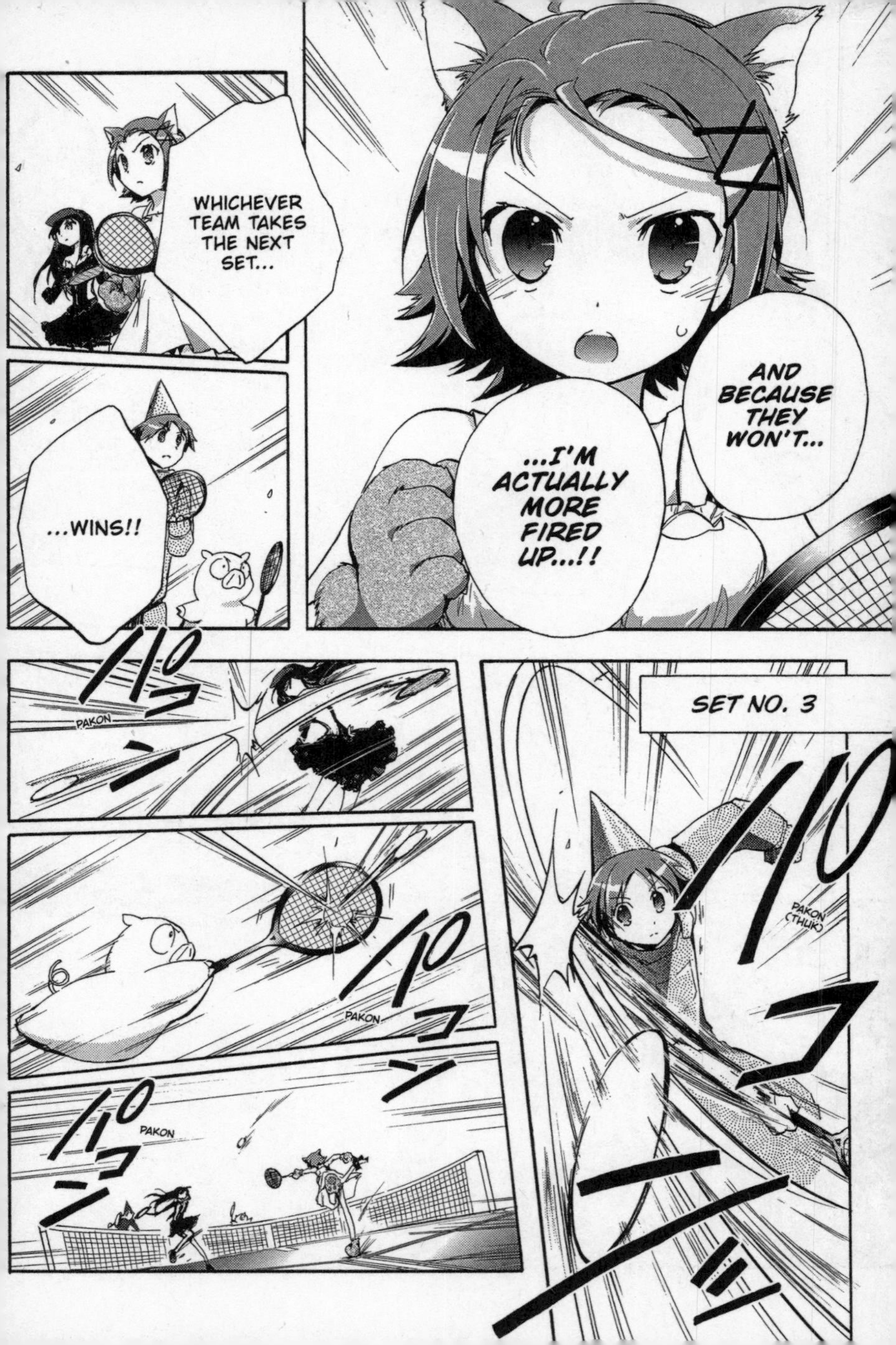
AND BECAUSE THEY WON'T...
...I'M ACTUALLY MORE FIRED UP...!!
WHICHEVER TEAM TAKES THE NEXT SET...
...WINS!!
SET NO. 3
PAKON (THUK)
PAKON
PAKON
PAKON

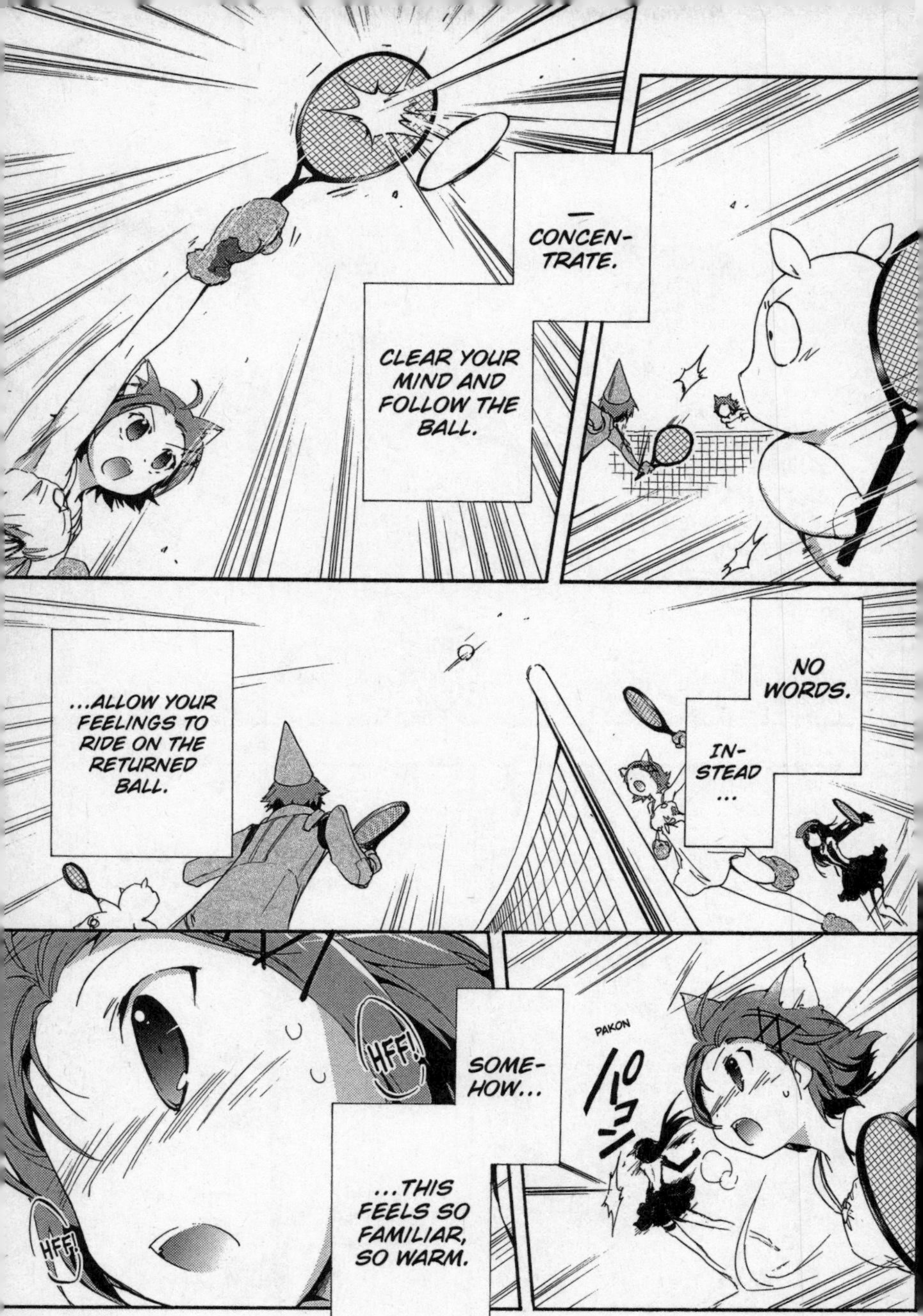
—CONCEN-TRATE.
CLEAR YOUR MIND AND FOLLOW THE BALL.
NO WORDS.
IN-STEAD...
...ALLOW YOUR FEELINGS TO RIDE ON THE RETURNED BALL.
PAKON
SOME-HOW...
...THIS FEELS SO FAMILIAR, SO WARM.
HFF!
HFF!

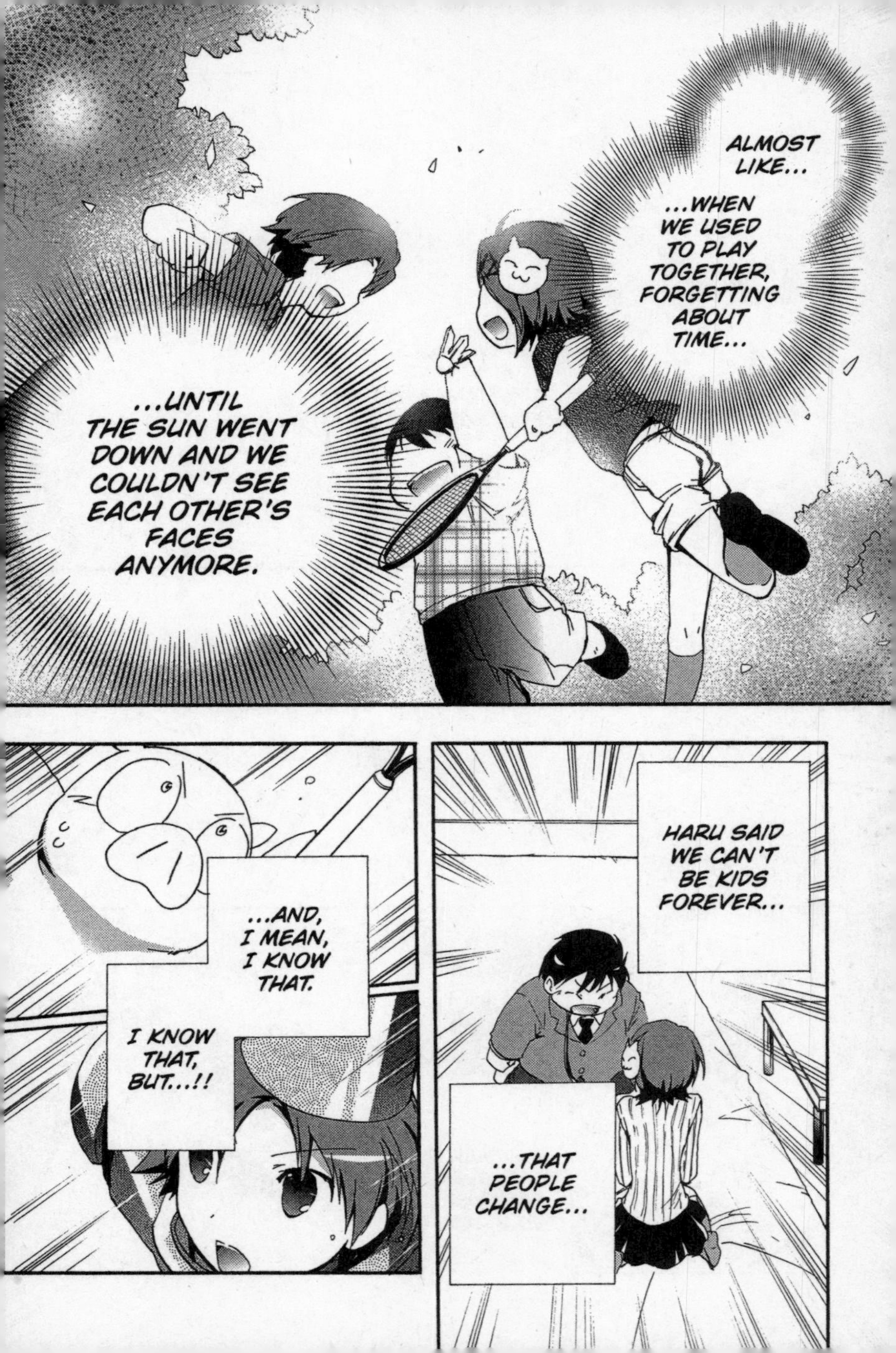
ALMOST LIKE...
...WHEN WE USED TO PLAY TOGETHER, FORGETTING ABOUT TIME...
...UNTIL THE SUN WENT DOWN AND WE COULDN'T SEE EACH OTHER'S FACES ANYMORE.
HARU SAID WE CAN'T BE KIDS FOREVER...
...THAT PEOPLE CHANGE...
...AND, I MEAN, I KNOW THAT.
I KNOW THAT, BUT...!!

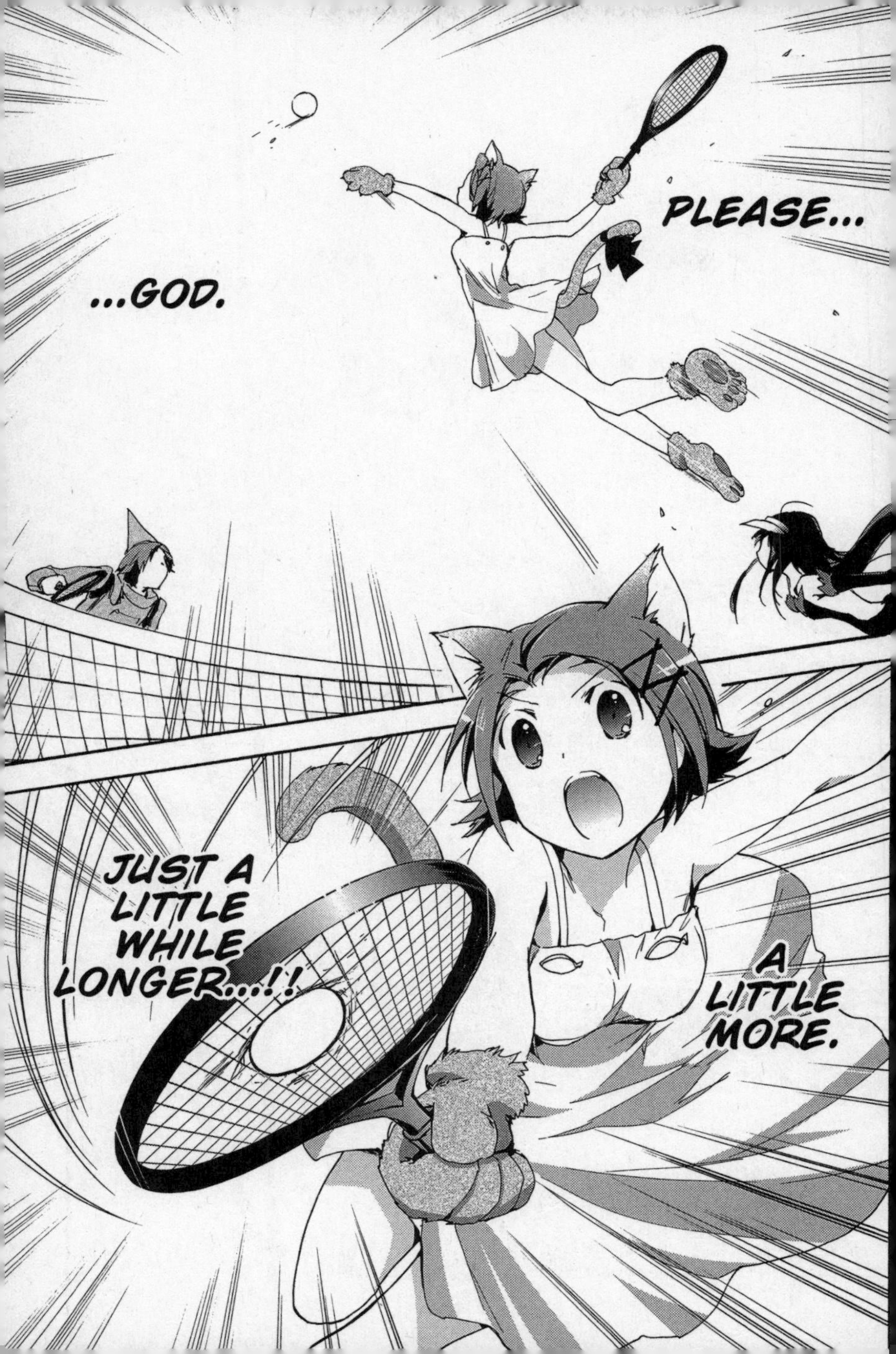
PLEASE...
...GOD.
A LITTLE MORE.
JUST A LITTLE WHILE LONGER...!!

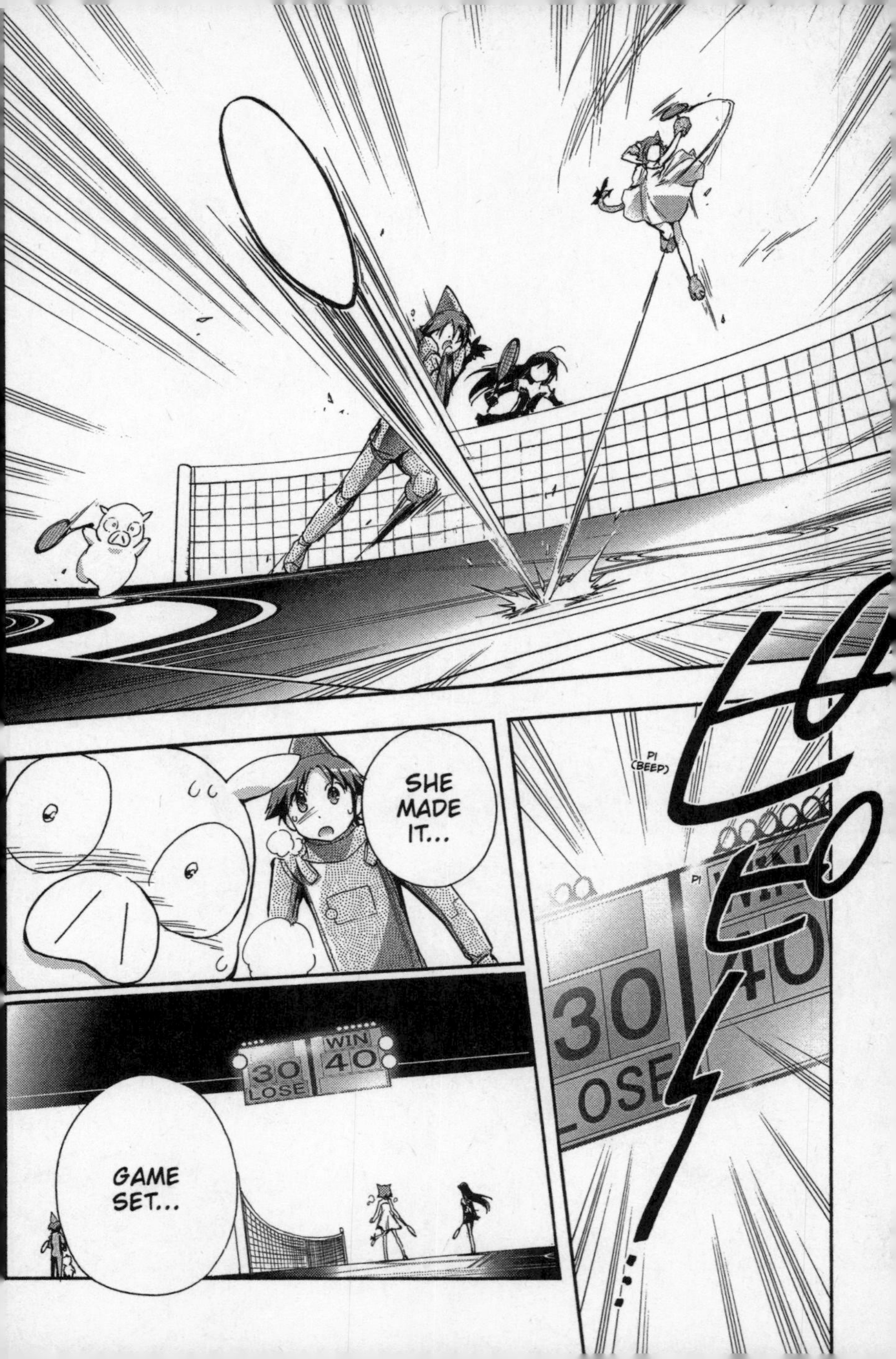
PI
(BEEP)
PI
30
40
LOSE
SHE MADE IT...
WIN
40
30
LOSE
GAME SET...

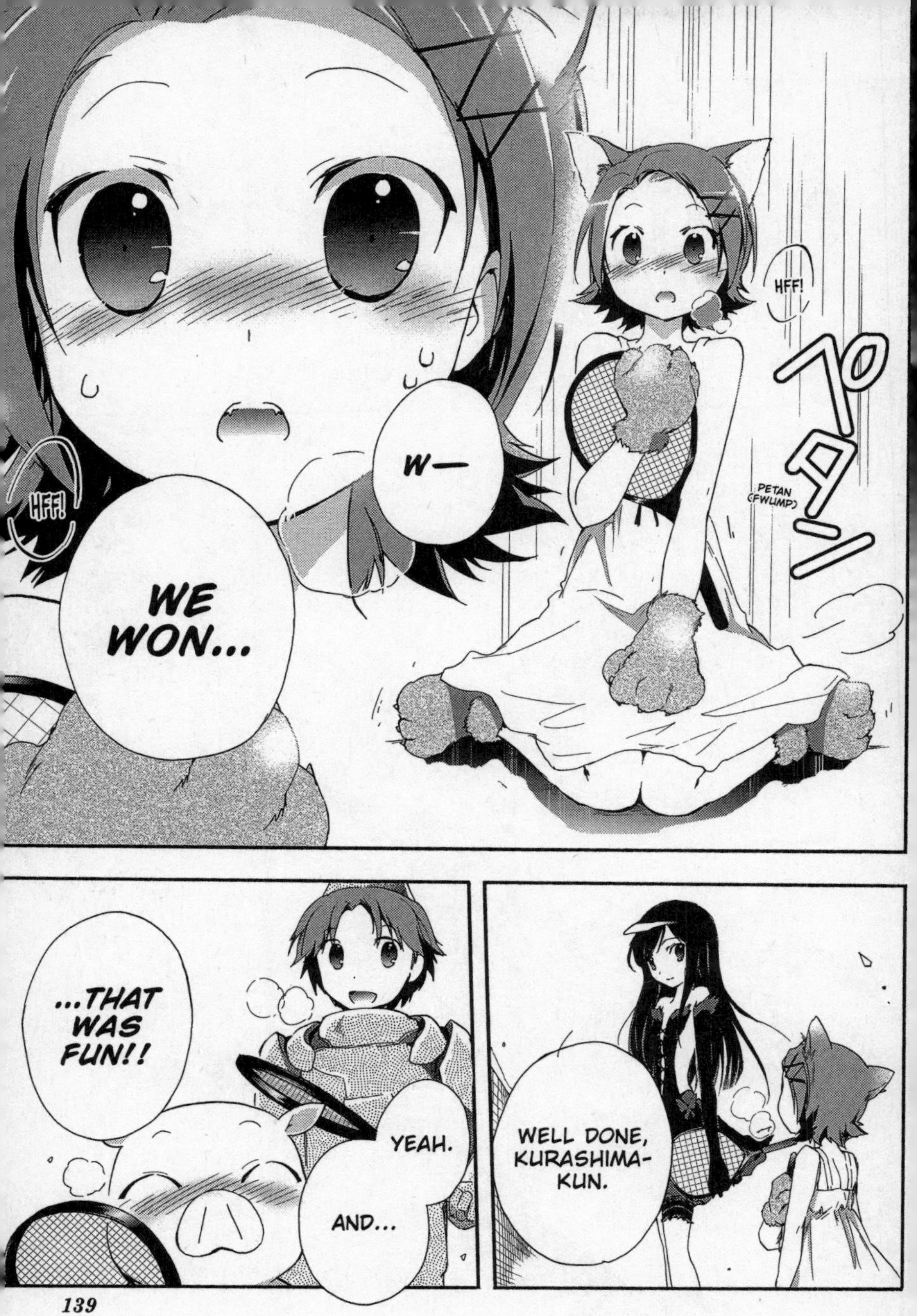
HFF!
ペタン
PETAN (FWUMP)
W—
HFF!
WE WON...
WELL DONE, KURASHIMA-KUN.
...THAT WAS FUN!!
YEAH.
AND...

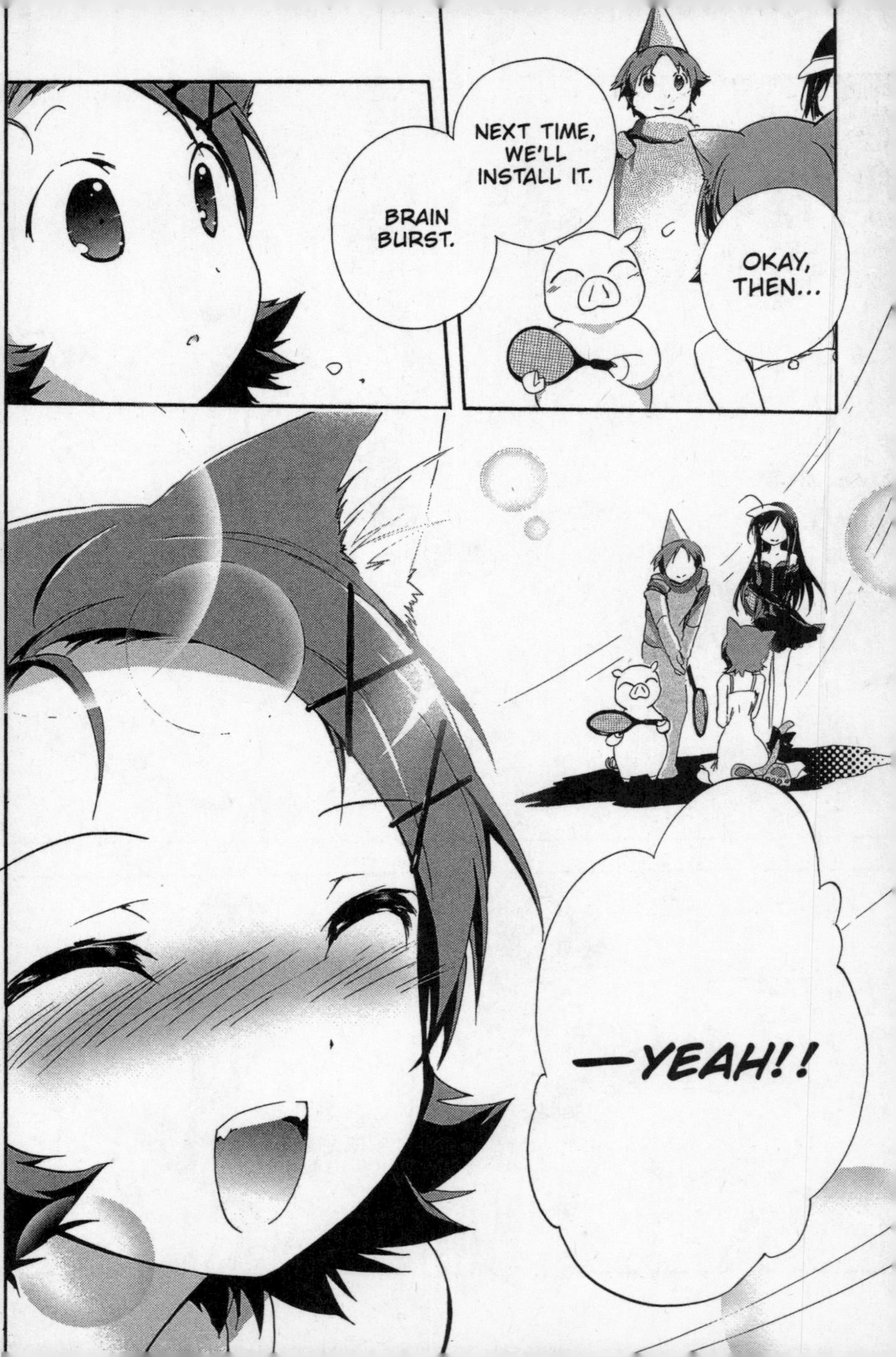
OKAY, THEN...
NEXT TIME, WE'LL INSTALL IT.
BRAIN BURST.
—YEAH!!

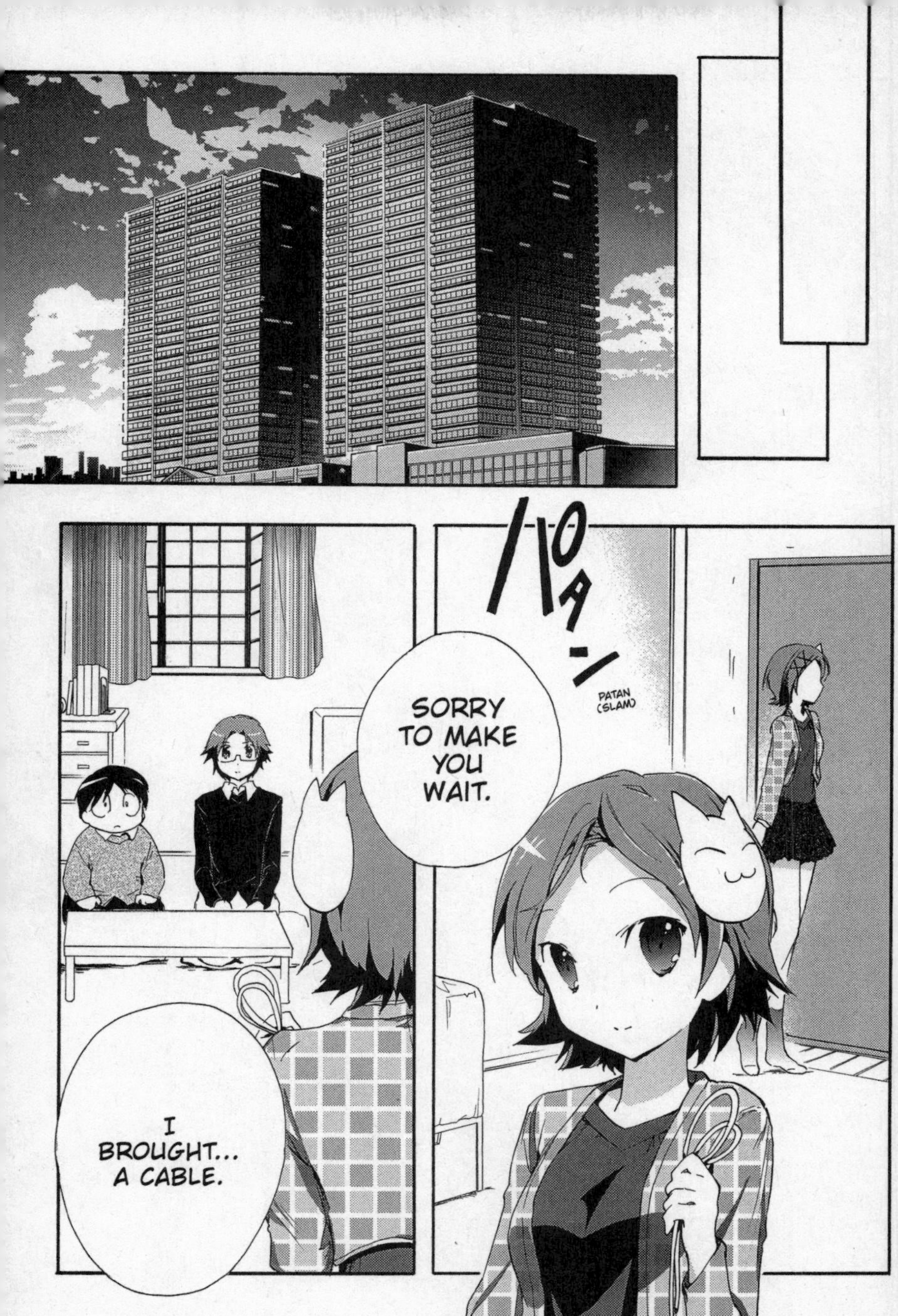
パタン
PATAN (SLAM)
SORRY TO MAKE YOU WAIT.
I BROUGHT... A CABLE.

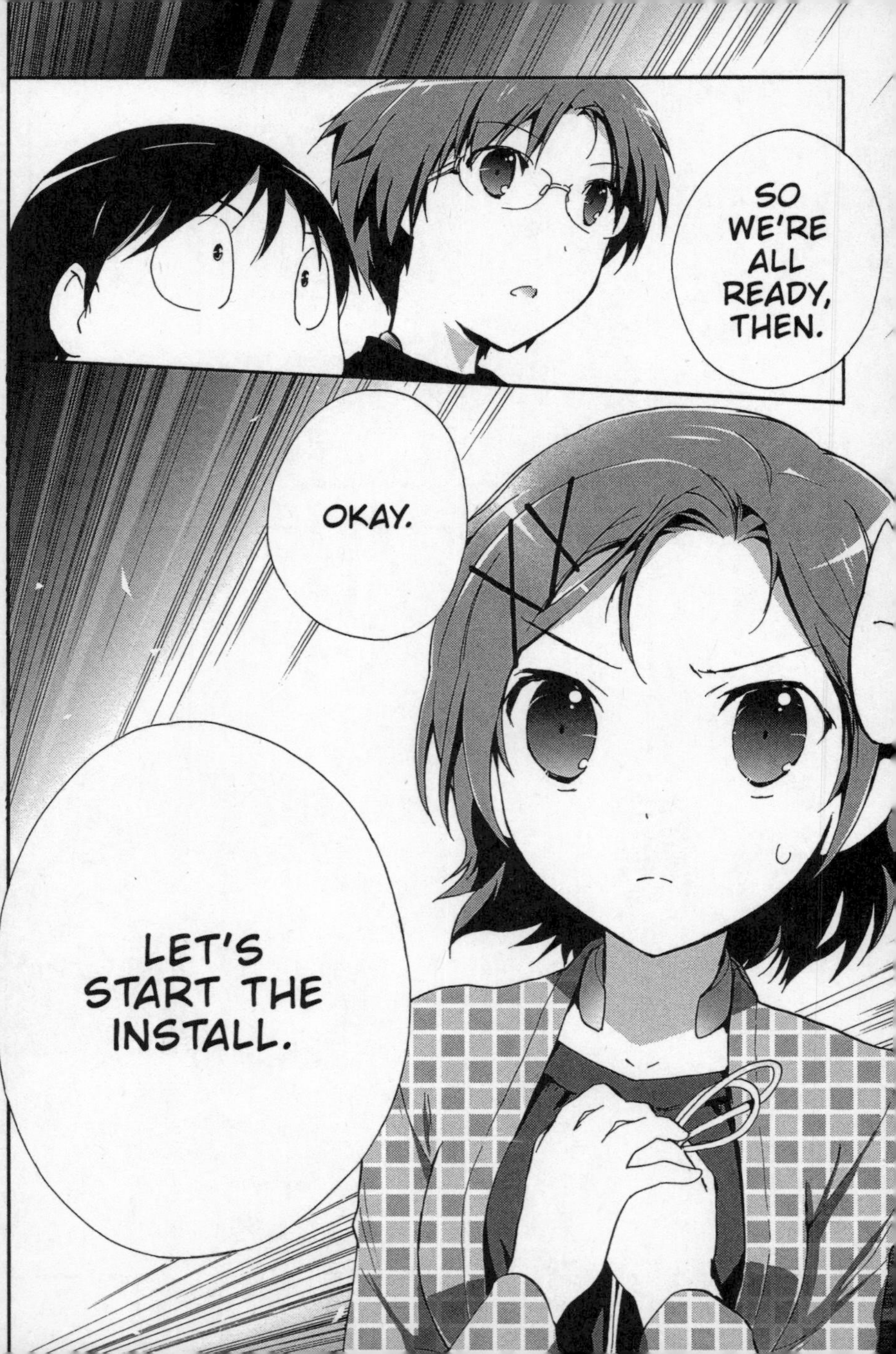
SO WE'RE ALL READY, THEN.
OKAY.
LET'S START THE INSTALL.

▶▶▶ *ACCEL·WORLD*

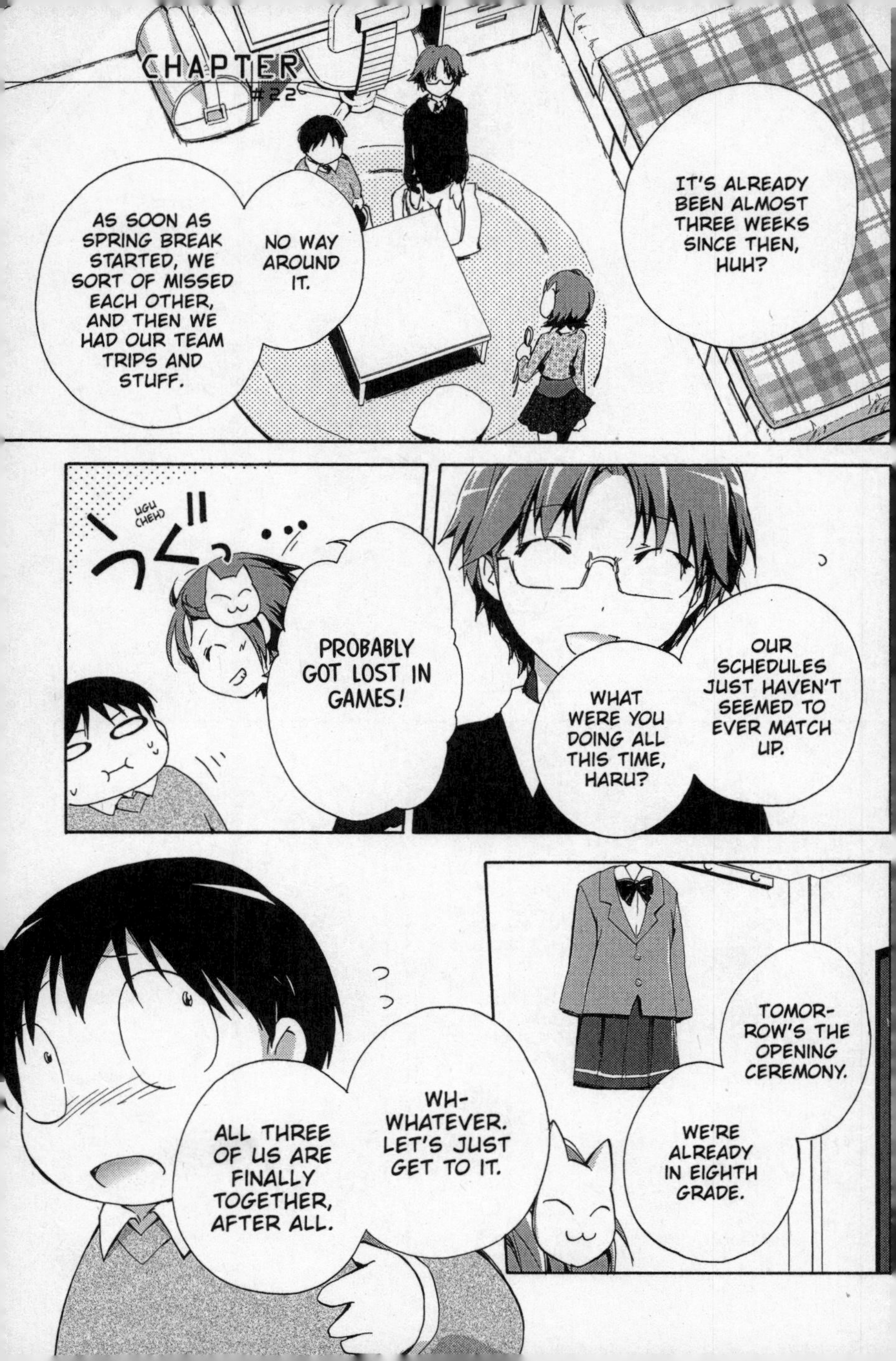
CHAPTER #22
IT'S ALREADY BEEN ALMOST THREE WEEKS SINCE THEN, HUH?
NO WAY AROUND IT.
AS SOON AS SPRING BREAK STARTED, WE SORT OF MISSED EACH OTHER, AND THEN WE HAD OUR TEAM TRIPS AND STUFF.
OUR SCHEDULES JUST HAVEN'T SEEMED TO EVER MATCH UP.
WHAT WERE YOU DOING ALL THIS TIME, HARU?
PROBABLY GOT LOST IN GAMES!
UGU (HEH)
TOMORROW'S THE OPENING CEREMONY.
WE'RE ALREADY IN EIGHTH GRADE.
WH-WHATEVER. LET'S JUST GET TO IT.
ALL THREE OF US ARE FINALLY TOGETHER, AFTER ALL.

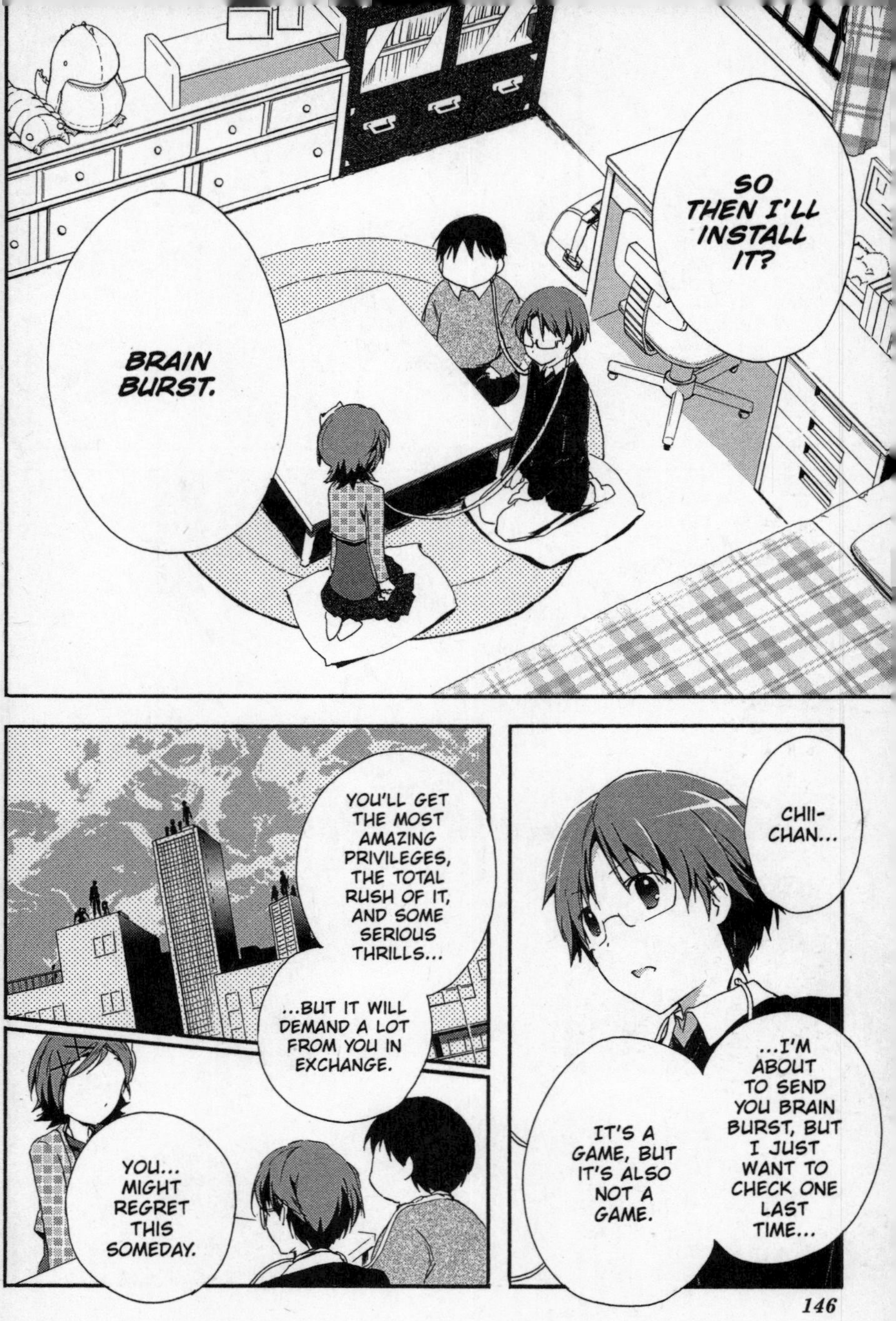
SO THEN I'LL INSTALL IT?
BRAIN BURST.
CHII-CHAN...
...I'M ABOUT TO SEND YOU BRAIN BURST, BUT I JUST WANT TO CHECK ONE LAST TIME...
IT'S A GAME, BUT IT'S ALSO NOT A GAME.
YOU'LL GET THE MOST AMAZING PRIVILEGES, THE TOTAL RUSH OF IT, AND SOME SERIOUS THRILLS...
...BUT IT WILL DEMAND A LOT FROM YOU IN EXCHANGE.
YOU... MIGHT REGRET THIS SOMEDAY.

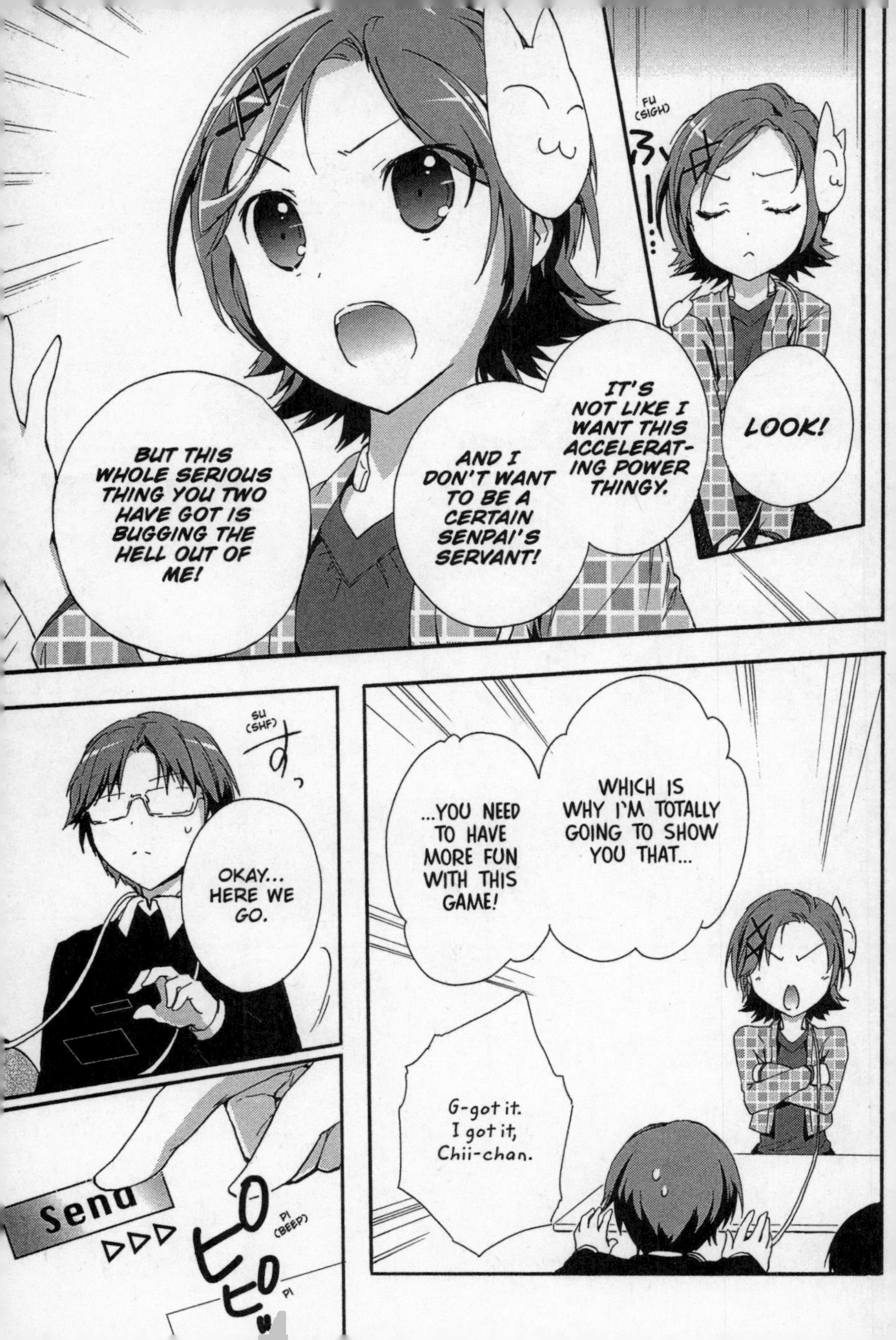
FU (SIGH)
LOOK!
IT'S NOT LIKE I WANT THIS ACCELERATING POWER THINGY.
AND I DON'T WANT TO BE A CERTAIN SENPAI'S SERVANT!
BUT THIS WHOLE SERIOUS THING YOU TWO HAVE GOT IS BUGGING THE HELL OUT OF ME!
WHICH IS WHY I'M TOTALLY GOING TO SHOW YOU THAT...
...YOU NEED TO HAVE MORE FUN WITH THIS GAME!
G-got it. I got it, Chii-chan.
SU (SHF)
OKAY... HERE WE GO.
Send
PI (BEEP)
PI

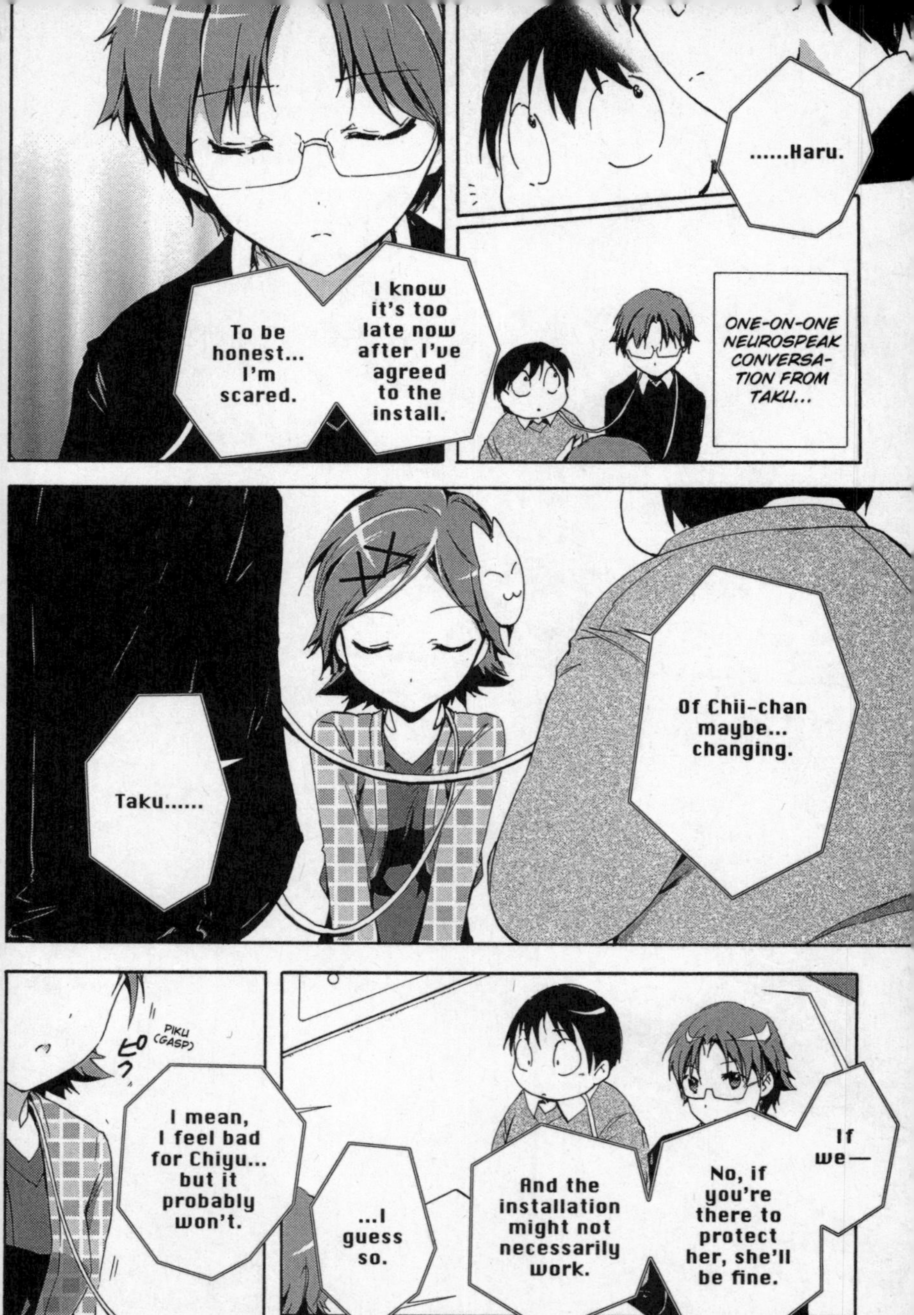
......Haru.
ONE-ON-ONE NEUROSPEAK CONVERSATION FROM TAKU...
I know it's too late now after I've agreed to the install.
To be honest... I'm scared.
Of Chii-chan maybe... changing.
Taku......
If we—
No, if you're there to protect her, she'll be fine.
And the installation might not necessarily work.
...I guess so.
PIKU (GASP)
I mean, I feel bad for Chiyu... but it probably won't.

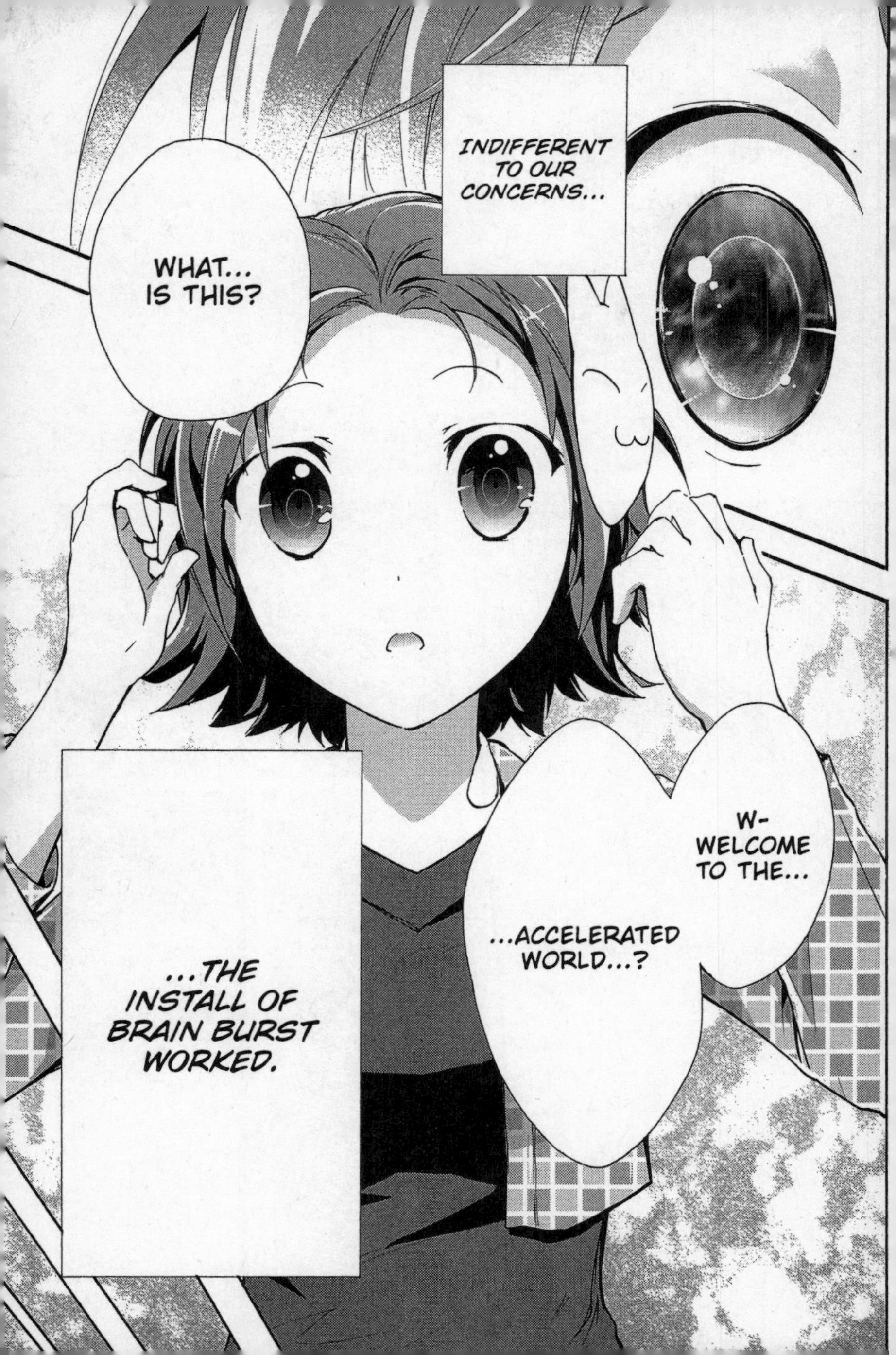
INDIFFERENT TO OUR CONCERNS...
WHAT... IS THIS?
W- WELCOME TO THE...
...ACCELERATED WORLD...?
...THE INSTALL OF BRAIN BURST WORKED.

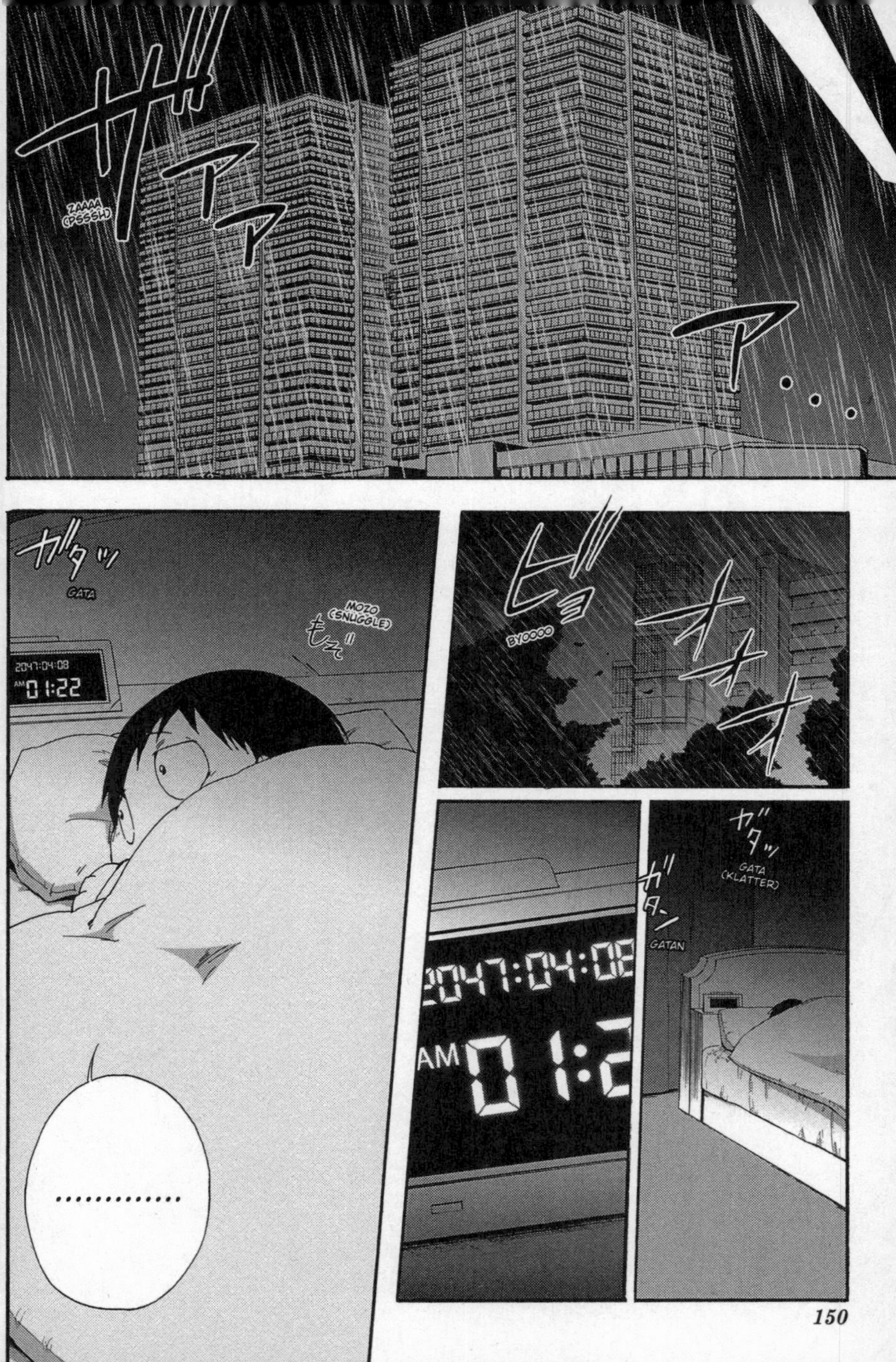
ザァァ
ZAAAA (PSSSH)
ァ...
ビョオオオ
BYOOOO
ガタッ
GATA (KLATTER)
ガタン
GATAN
2047:04:08
AM 01:2
ガタッ
GATA
もぞ
MOZO (SNUGGLE)
2047:04:08
AM 01:22
....

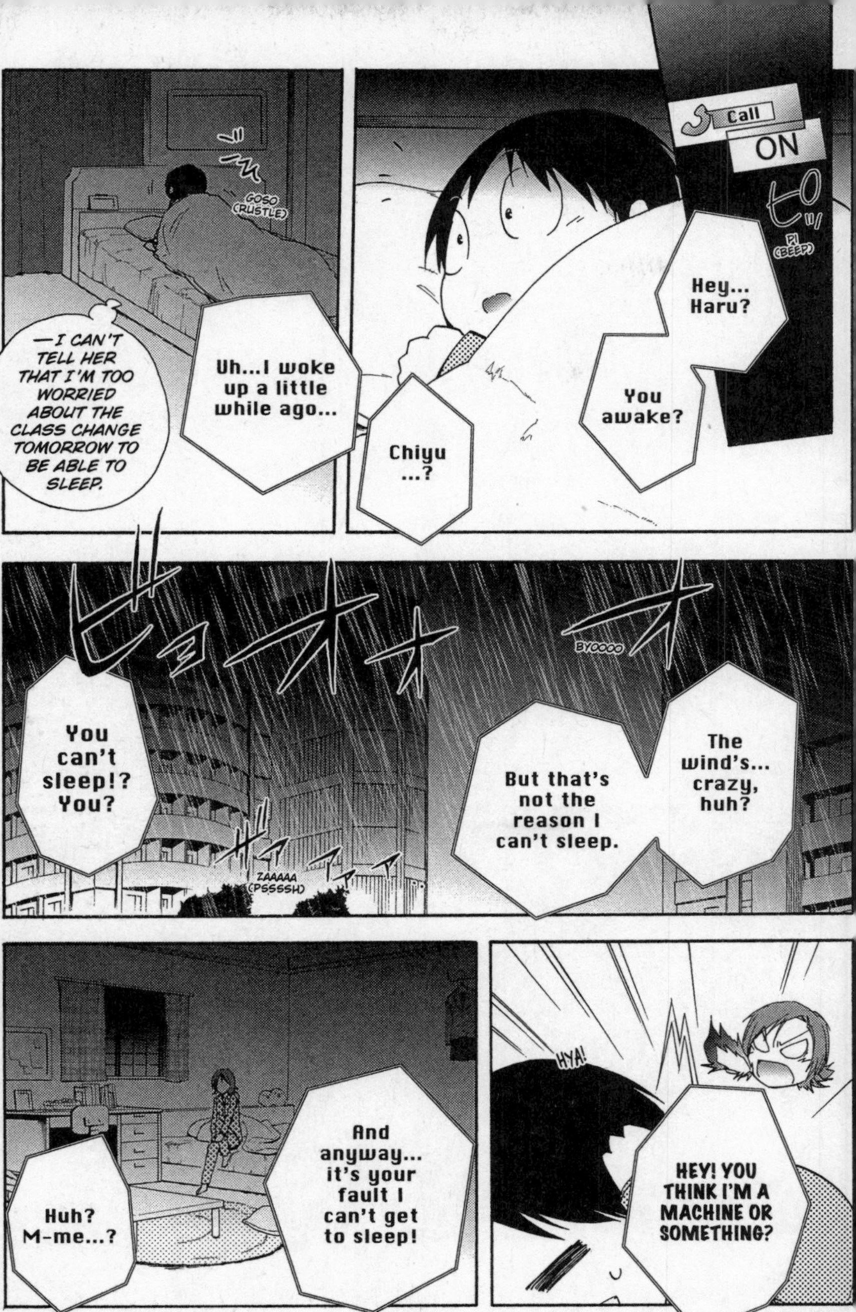
Call
ON
PI (BEEP)
Hey... Haru?
You awake?
Chiyu ...?
GOSO (RUSTLE)
Uh...I woke up a little while ago...
—I CAN'T TELL HER THAT I'M TOO WORRIED ABOUT THE CLASS CHANGE TOMORROW TO BE ABLE TO SLEEP.
BYOOOO
The wind's... crazy, huh?
But that's not the reason I can't sleep.
You can't sleep!? You?
ZAAAAA (PSSSSH)
HYA!
HEY! YOU THINK I'M A MACHINE OR SOMETHING?
And anyway... it's your fault I can't get to sleep!
Huh? M-me...?

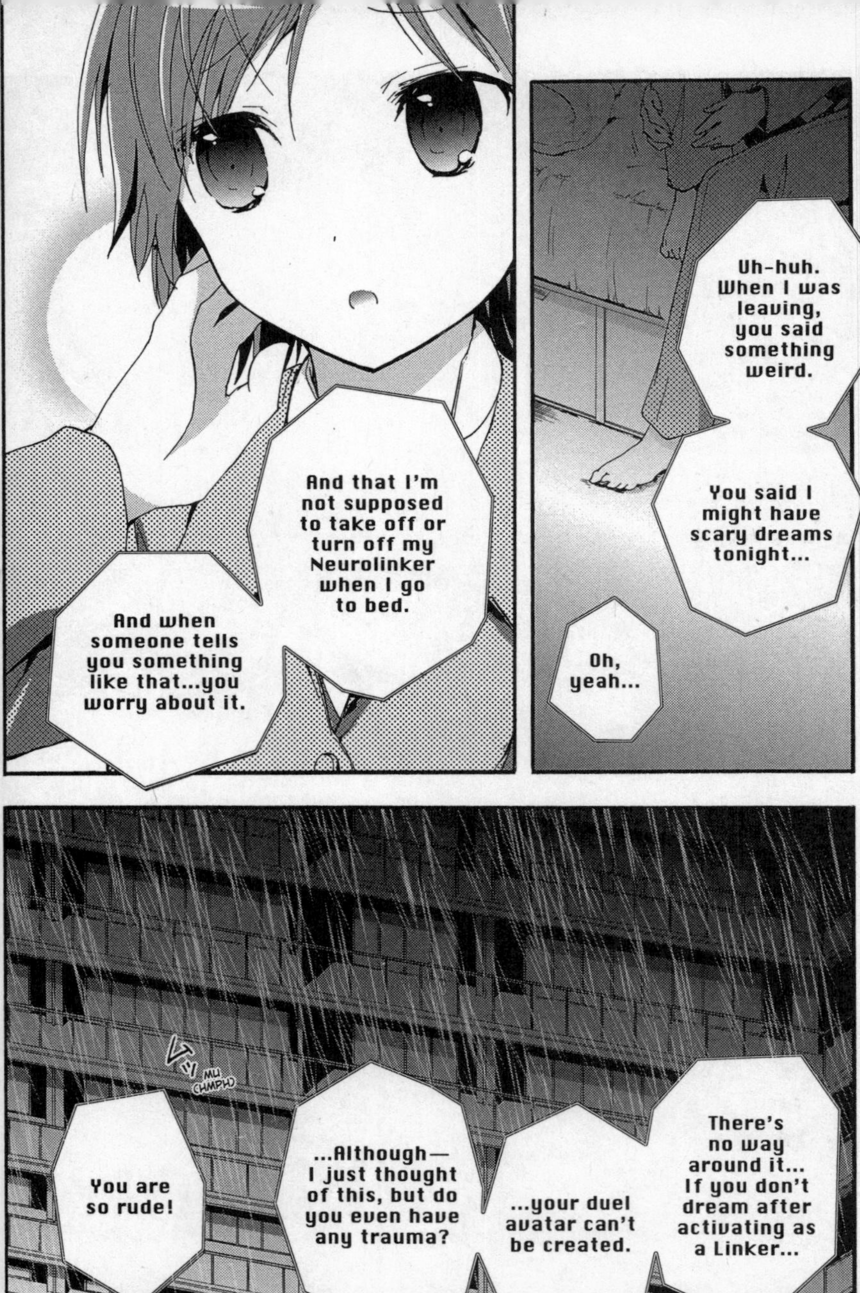

Uh-huh. When I was leaving, you said something weird.
You said I might have scary dreams tonight...
Oh, yeah...
And that I'm not supposed to take off or turn off my Neurolinker when I go to bed.
And when someone tells you something like that...you worry about it.
There's no way around it... If you don't dream after activating as a Linker...
...your duel avatar can't be created.
...Although— I just thought of this, but do you even have any trauma?
ムッ
MU (HMPH)
You are so rude!

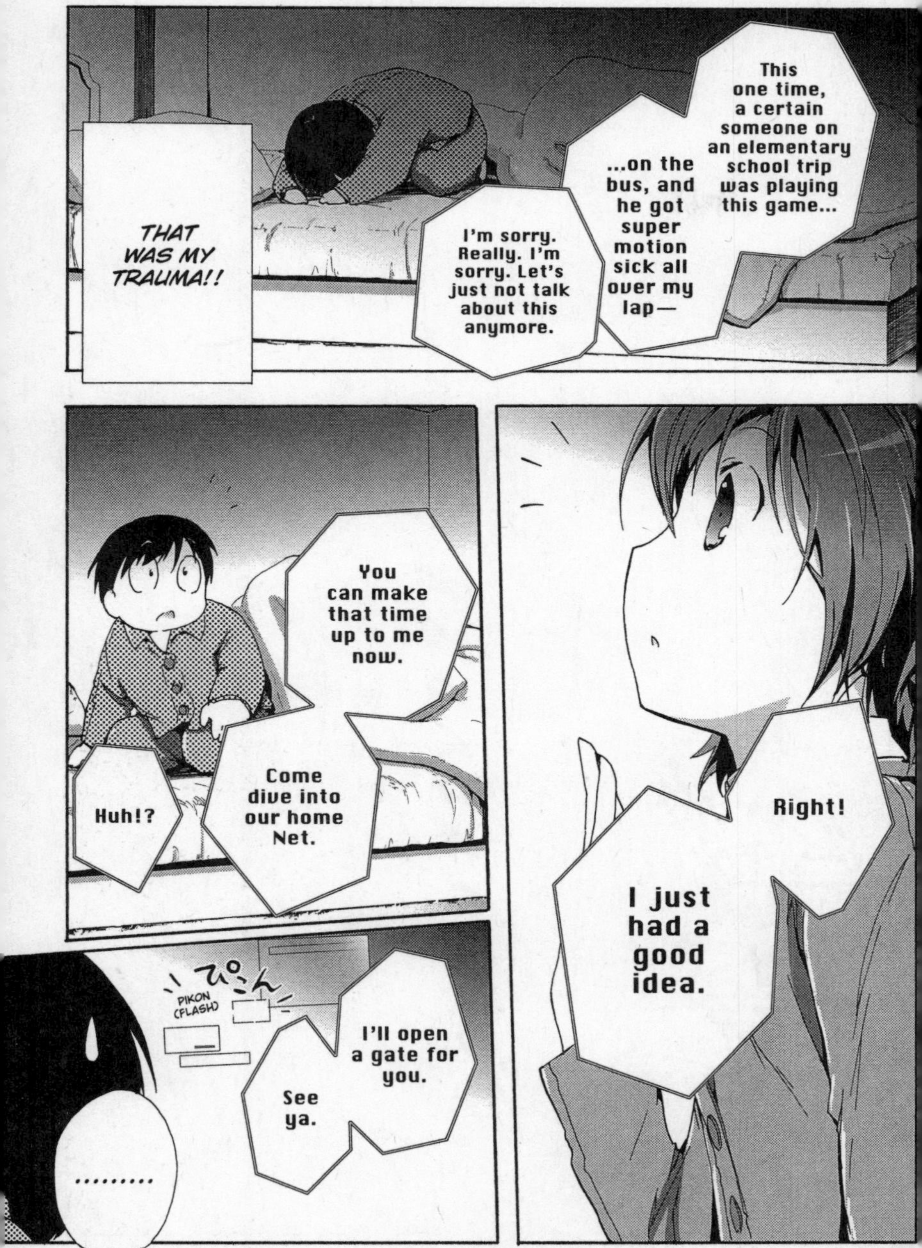
This one time, a certain someone on an elementary school trip was playing this game...
...on the bus, and he got super motion sick all over my lap—
I'm sorry. Really. I'm sorry. Let's just not talk about this anymore.
THAT WAS MY TRAUMA!!
Right!
I just had a good idea.
You can make that time up to me now.
Come dive into our home Net.
Huh!?
ぴこん
PIKON (FLASH)
I'll open a gate for you.
See ya.
....

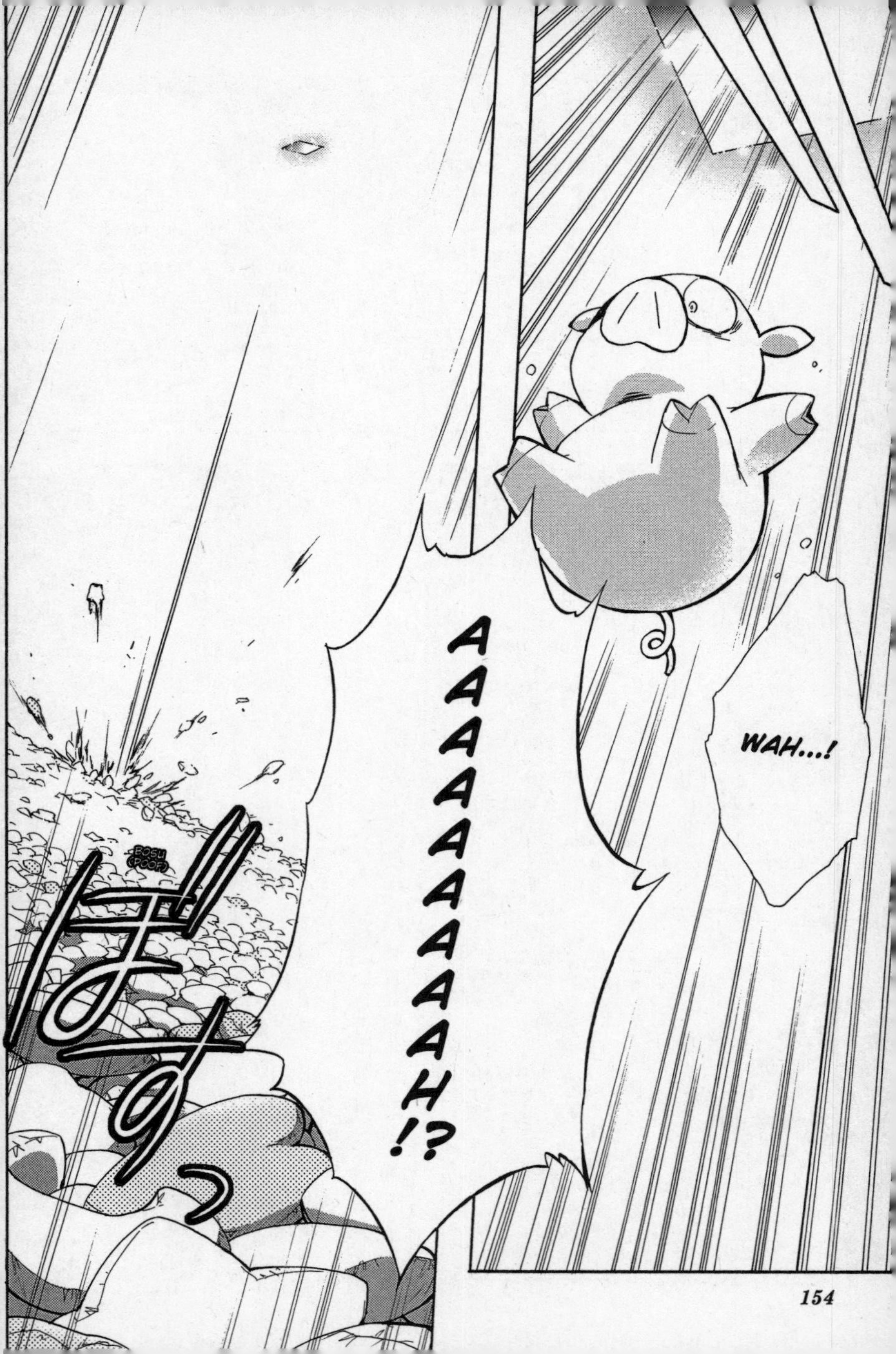
WAH...!
AAAAAAAAAH!?
BOSU (POOF)

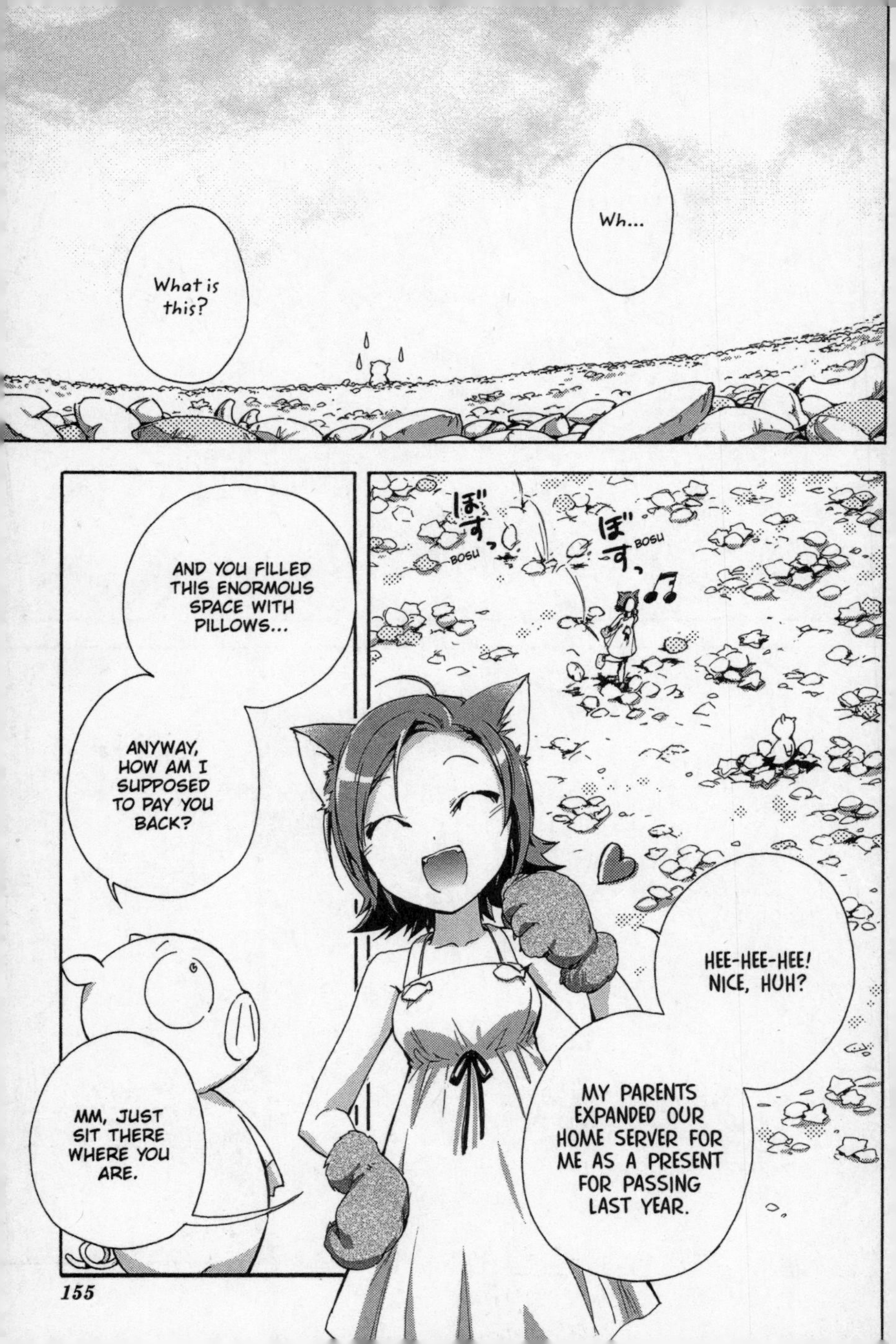
Wh...
What is this?
ぼすっ BOSU
ぼすっ BOSU
HEE-HEE-HEE! NICE, HUH?
MY PARENTS EXPANDED OUR HOME SERVER FOR ME AS A PRESENT FOR PASSING LAST YEAR.
AND YOU FILLED THIS ENORMOUS SPACE WITH PILLOWS...
ANYWAY, HOW AM I SUPPOSED TO PAY YOU BACK?
MM, JUST SIT THERE WHERE YOU ARE.

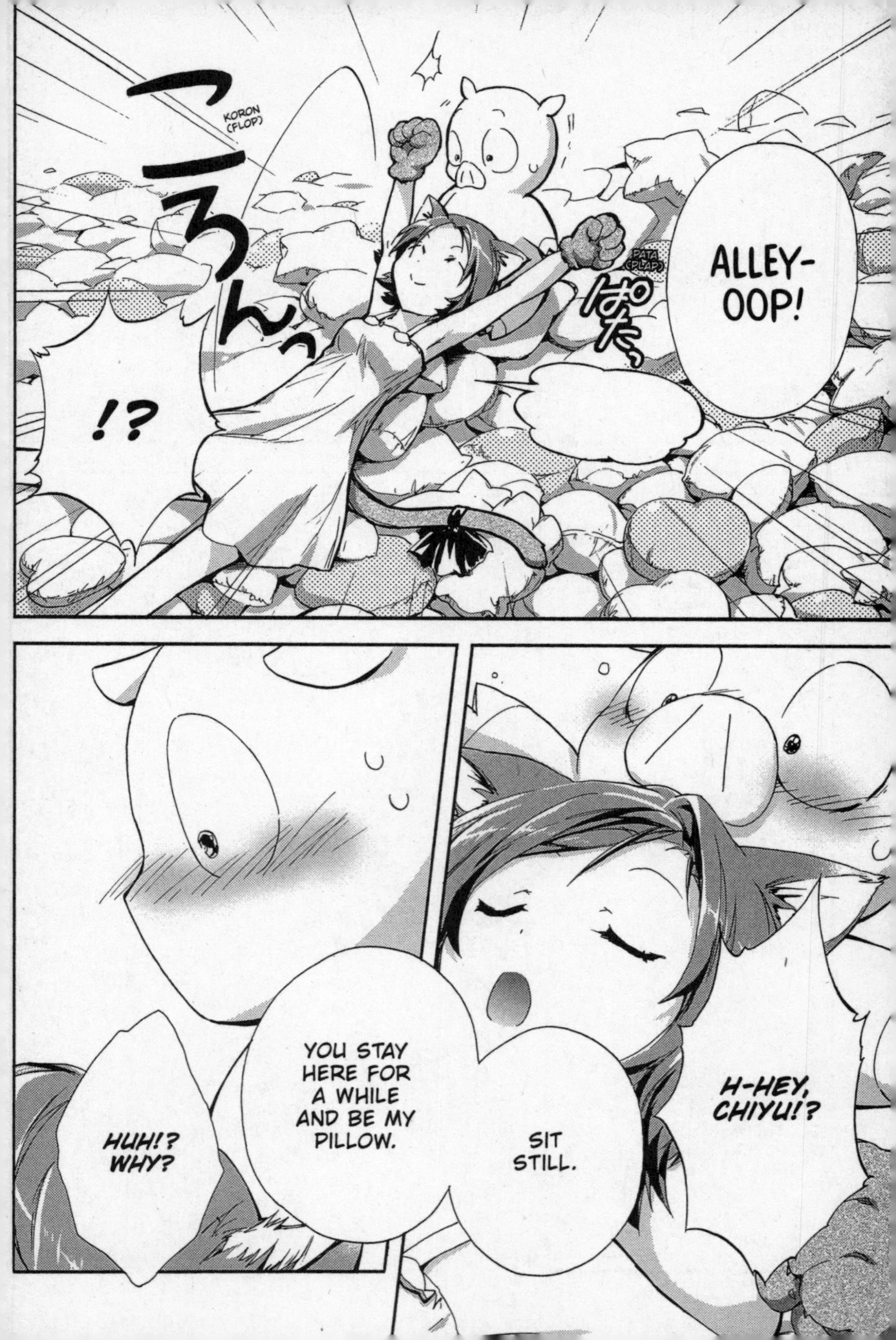
ALLEY-OOP!
ぱたっ
PATA (PLAP)
ころんっ
KORON (FLOP)
!?
H-HEY, CHIYU!?
SIT STILL.
YOU STAY HERE FOR A WHILE AND BE MY PILLOW.
HUH!? WHY?

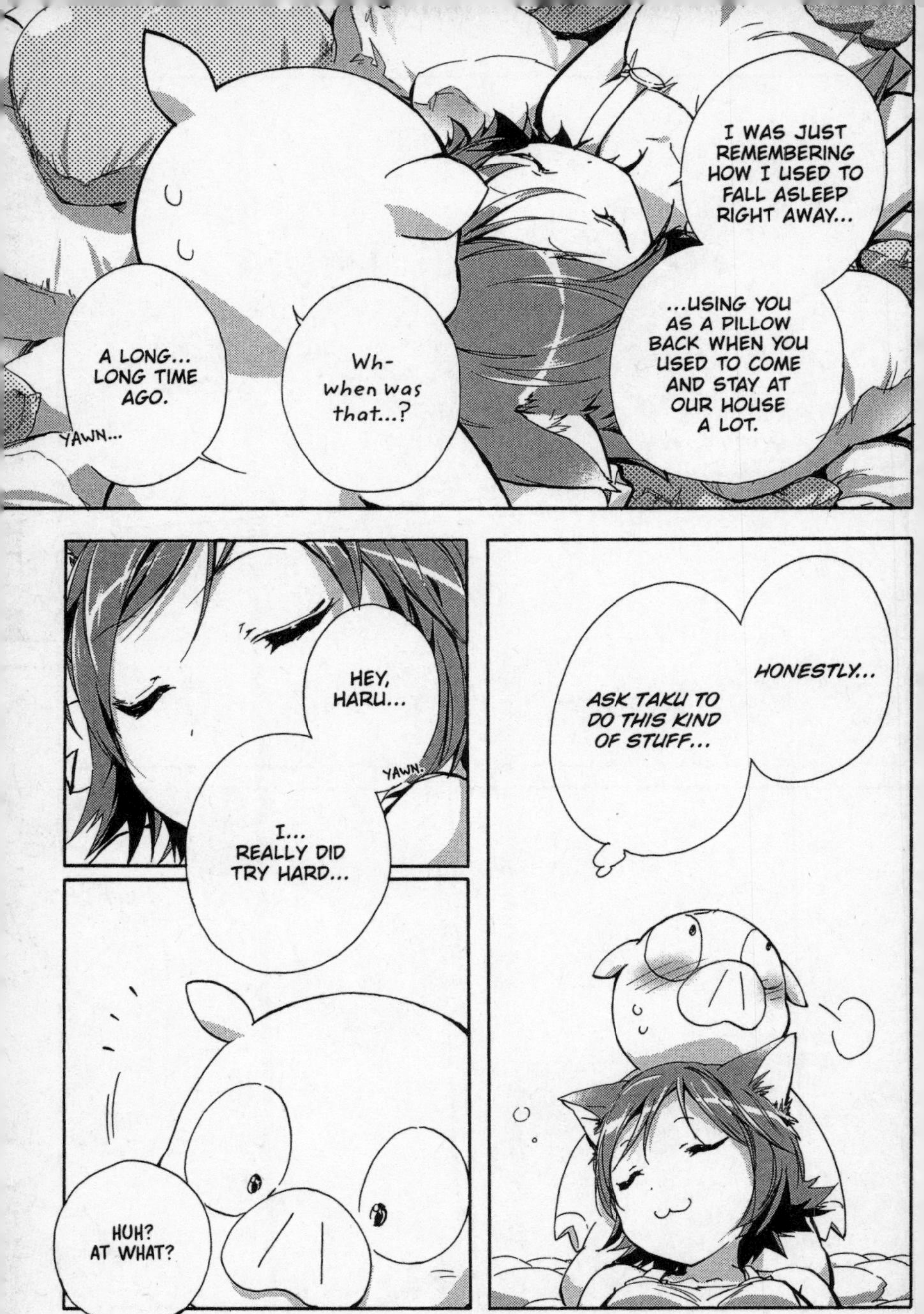
I WAS JUST REMEMBERING HOW I USED TO FALL ASLEEP RIGHT AWAY...
...USING YOU AS A PILLOW BACK WHEN YOU USED TO COME AND STAY AT OUR HOUSE A LOT.
Wh- when was that...?
A LONG... LONG TIME AGO.
YAWN...
HONESTLY...
ASK TAKU TO DO THIS KIND OF STUFF...
HEY, HARU...
YAWN.
I... REALLY DID TRY HARD...
HUH? AT WHAT?

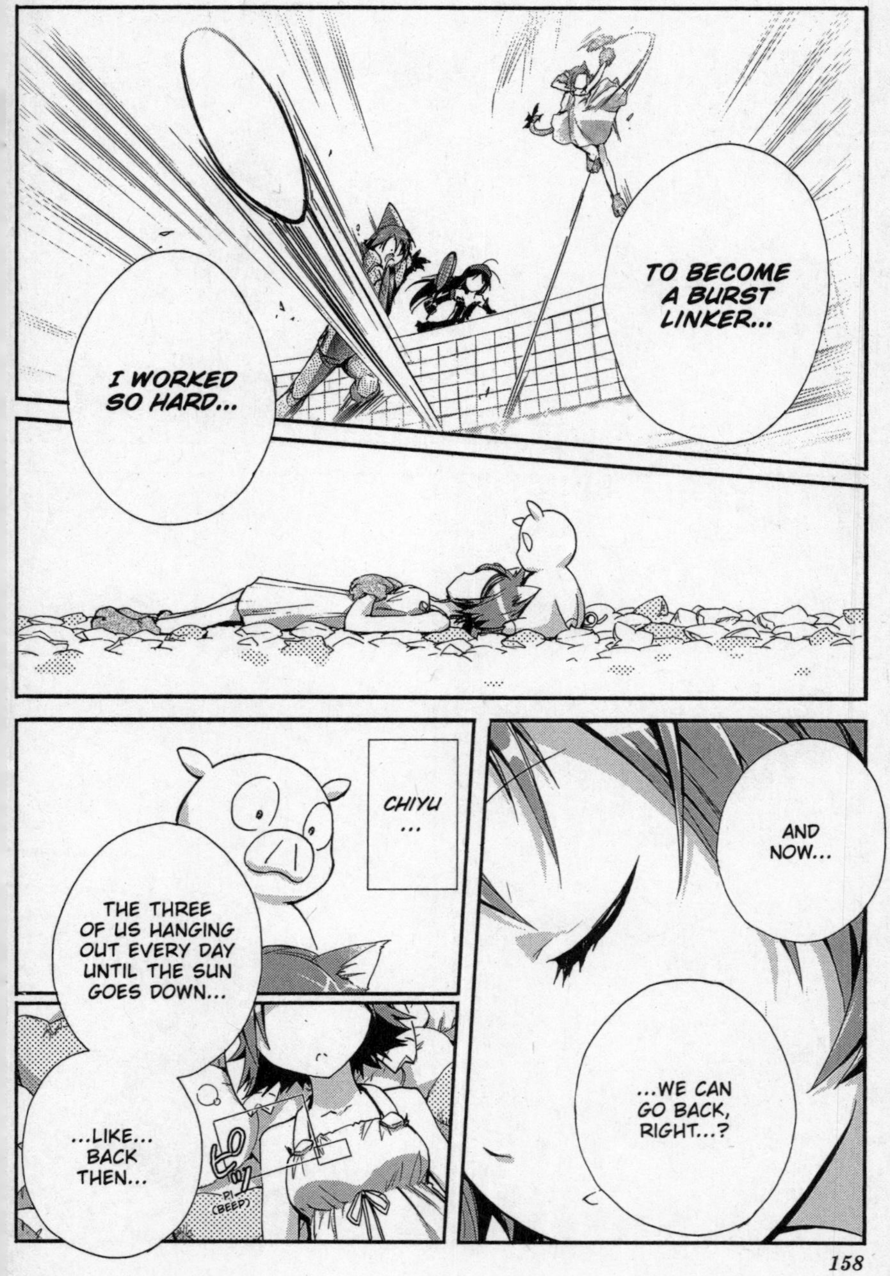
TO BECOME A BURST LINKER...
I WORKED SO HARD...
AND NOW...
...WE CAN GO BACK, RIGHT...?
CHIYU ...
THE THREE OF US HANGING OUT EVERY DAY UNTIL THE SUN GOES DOWN...
...LIKE... BACK THEN...
PI (BEEP)

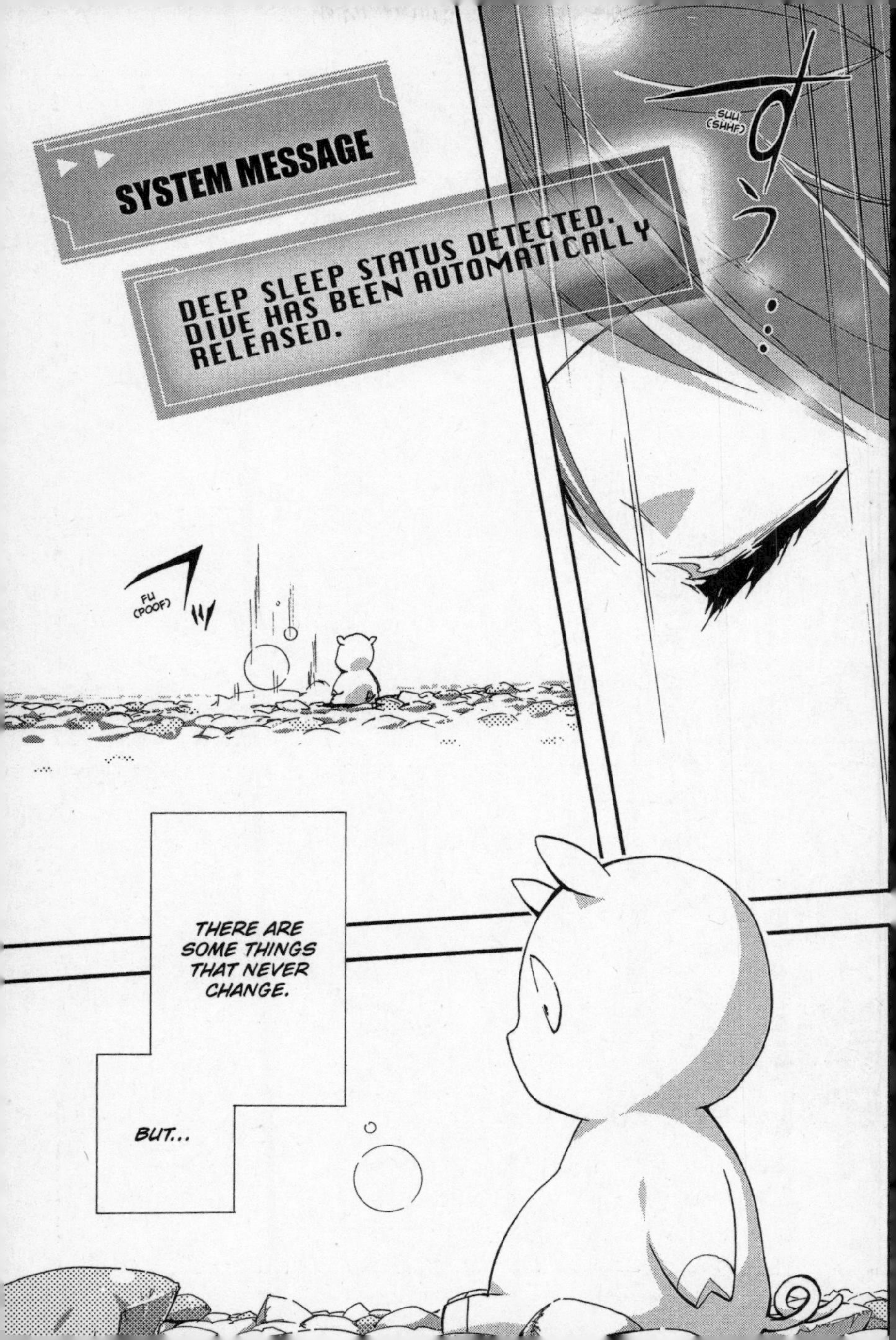
SUU (SHHF)
SYSTEM MESSAGE
DEEP SLEEP STATUS DETECTED. DIVE HAS BEEN AUTOMATICALLY RELEASED.
FU (POOF)
THERE ARE SOME THINGS THAT NEVER CHANGE.
BUT...

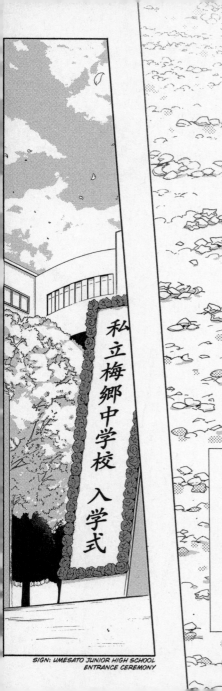

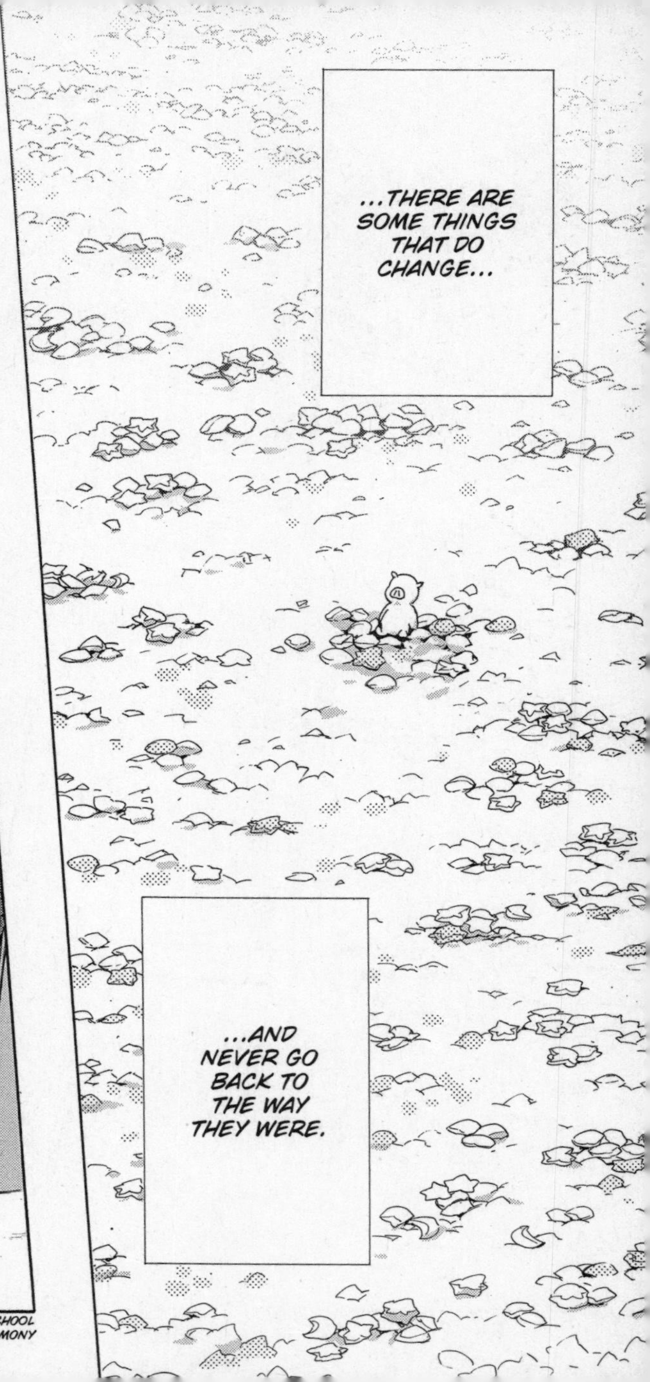
...THERE ARE SOME THINGS THAT DO CHANGE...
...AND NEVER GO BACK TO THE WAY THEY WERE.

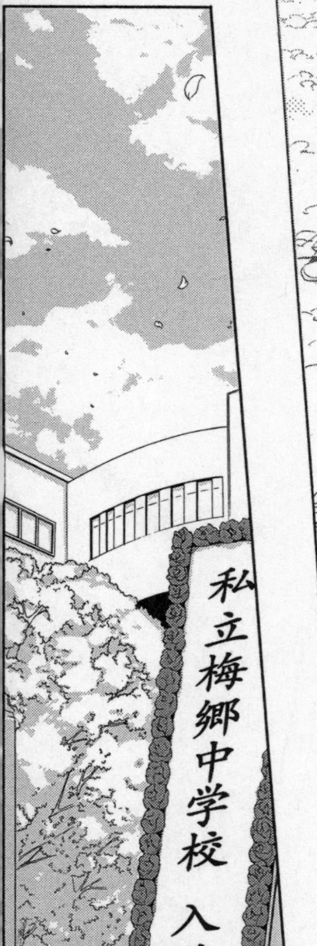
私立梅郷中学校
入学式

SIGN: UMESATO JUNIOR HIGH SCHOOL ENTRANCE CEREMONY

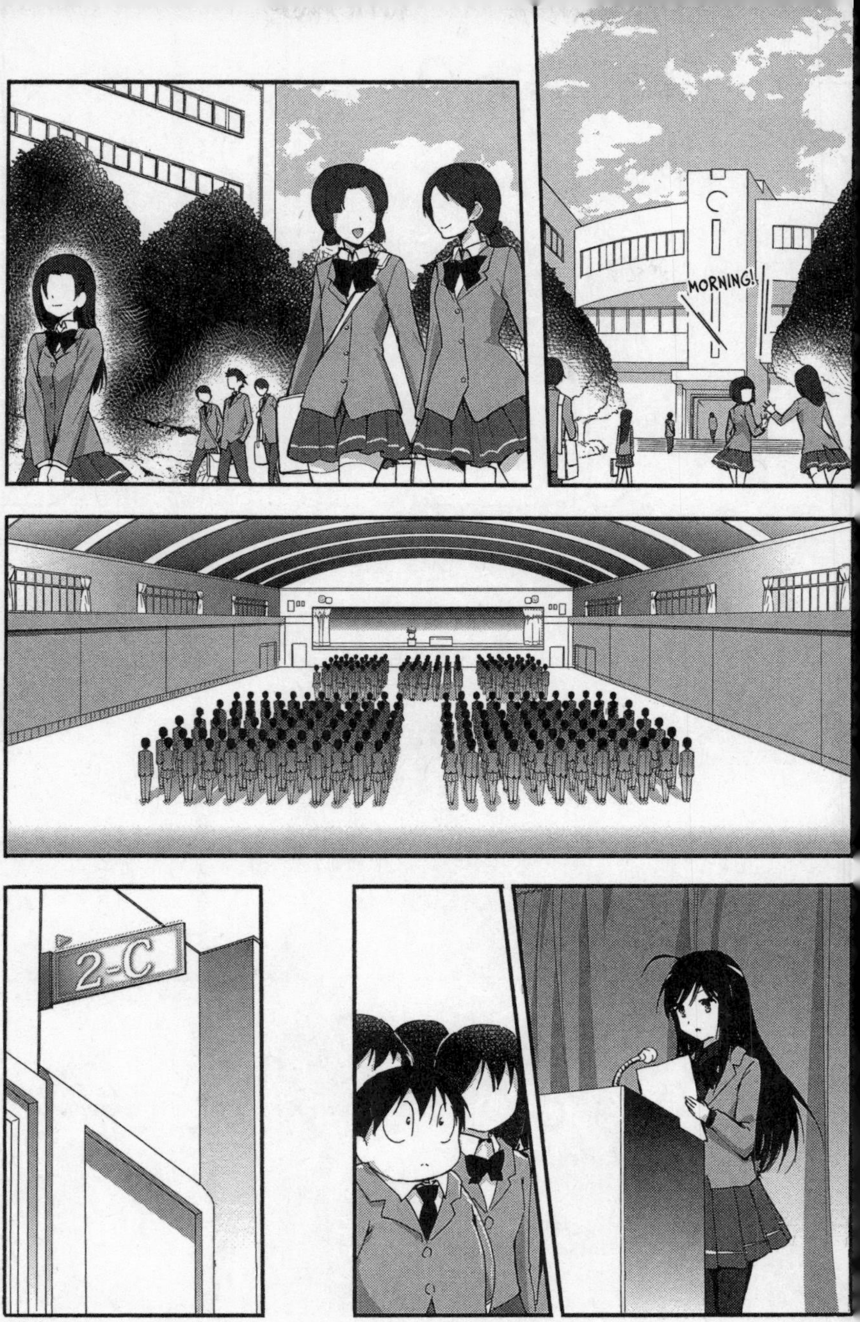
MORNING!
2-C

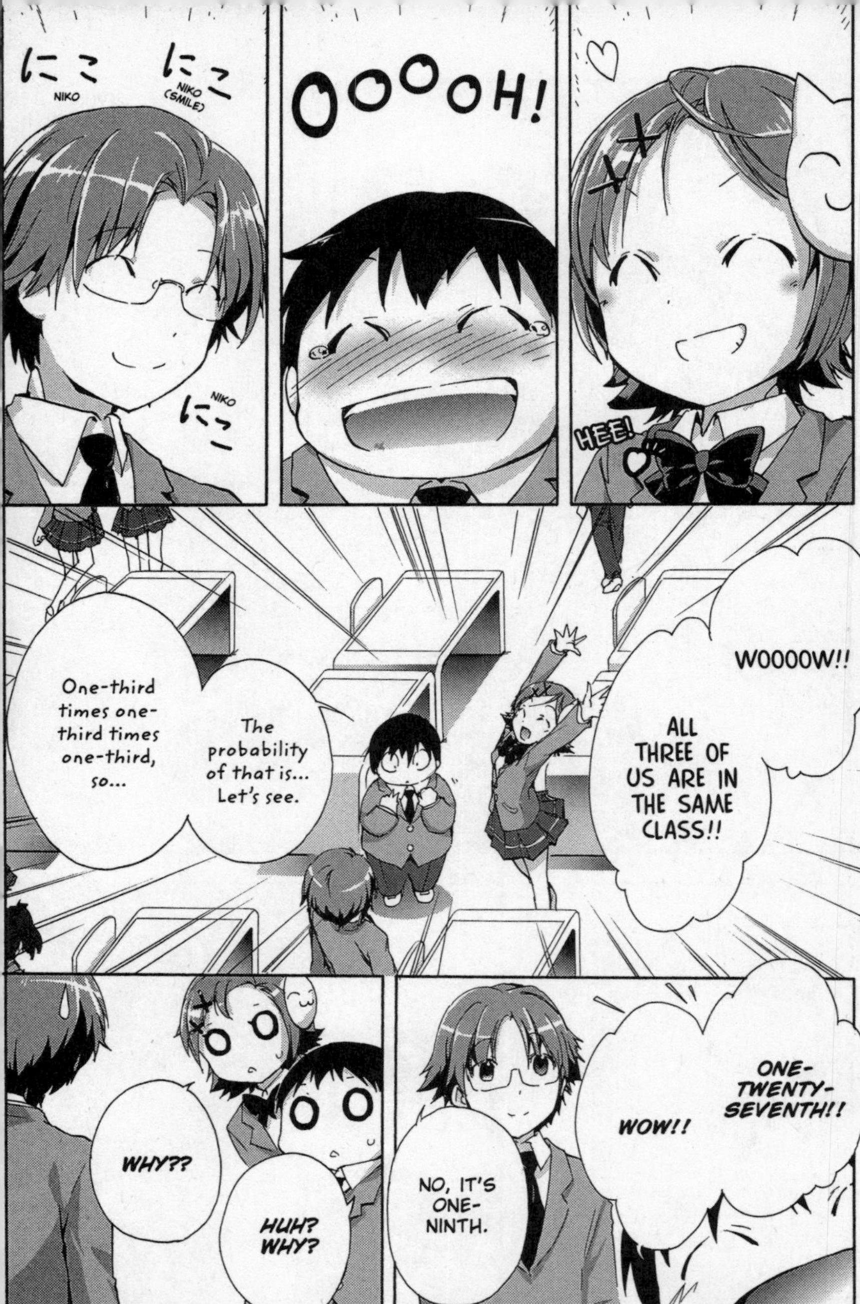
HEE!
OOOOH!
にっこ
NIKO (SMILE)
にこ
NIKO
にっ
NIKO
WOOOOW!!
ALL THREE OF US ARE IN THE SAME CLASS!!
The probability of that is... Let's see.
One-third times one-third times one-third, so...
ONE-TWENTY-SEVENTH!!
WOW!!
NO, IT'S ONE-NINTH.
HUH? WHY?
WHY??

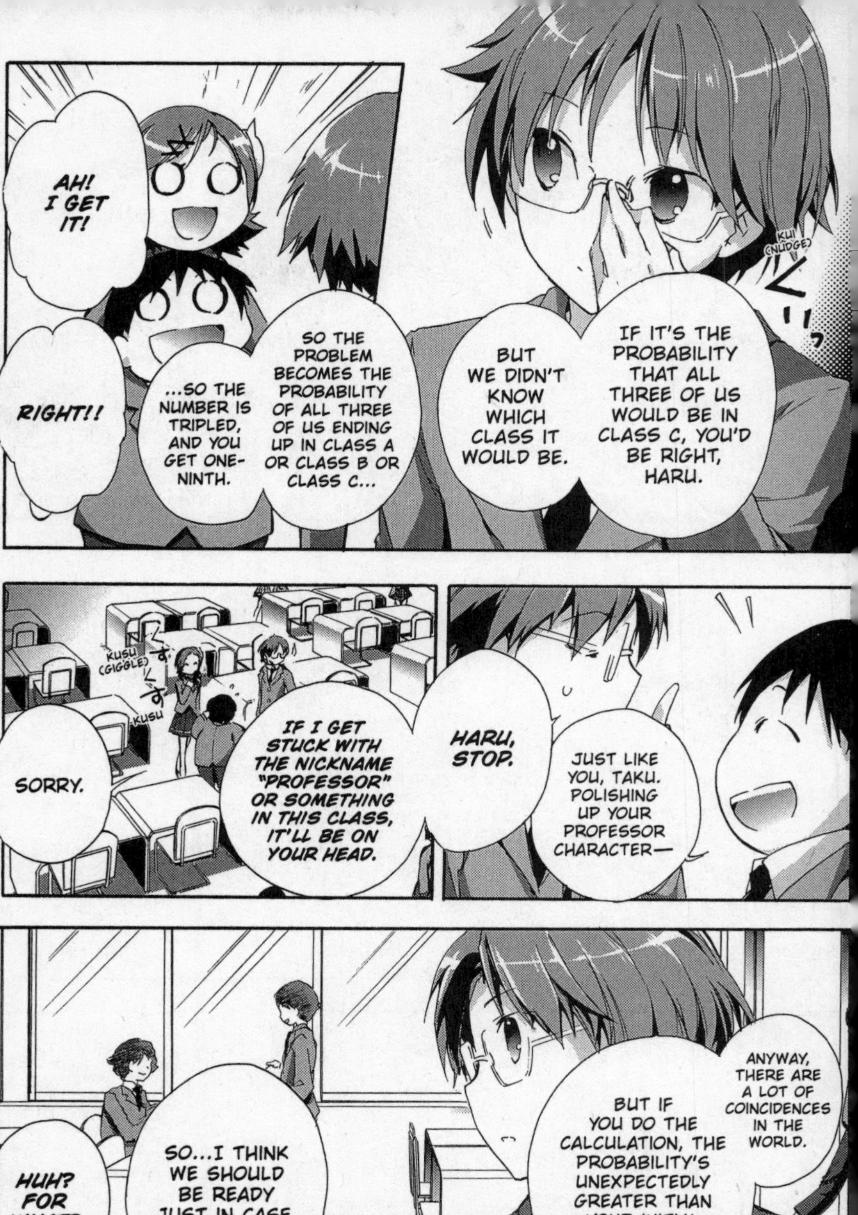
KUI (NUDGE)
IF IT'S THE PROBABILITY THAT ALL THREE OF US WOULD BE IN CLASS C, YOU'D BE RIGHT, HARU.
BUT WE DIDN'T KNOW WHICH CLASS IT WOULD BE.
SO THE PROBLEM BECOMES THE PROBABILITY OF ALL THREE OF US ENDING UP IN CLASS A OR CLASS B OR CLASS C...
...SO THE NUMBER IS TRIPLED, AND YOU GET ONE-NINTH.
AH! I GET IT!
RIGHT!!
JUST LIKE YOU, TAKU. POLISHING UP YOUR PROFESSOR CHARACTER—
HARU, STOP.
IF I GET STUCK WITH THE NICKNAME "PROFESSOR" OR SOMETHING IN THIS CLASS, IT'LL BE ON YOUR HEAD.
KUSU (GIGGLE)
KUSU
SORRY.
ANYWAY, THERE ARE A LOT OF COINCIDENCES IN THE WORLD.
BUT IF YOU DO THE CALCULATION, THE PROBABILITY'S UNEXPECTEDLY GREATER THAN YOUR INITIAL IMPRESSION.
SO...I THINK WE SHOULD BE READY JUST IN CASE.
HUH? FOR WHAT?

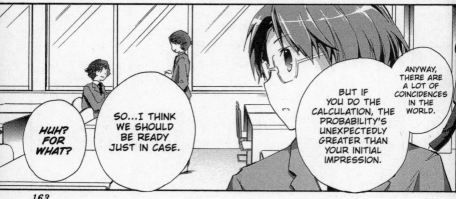

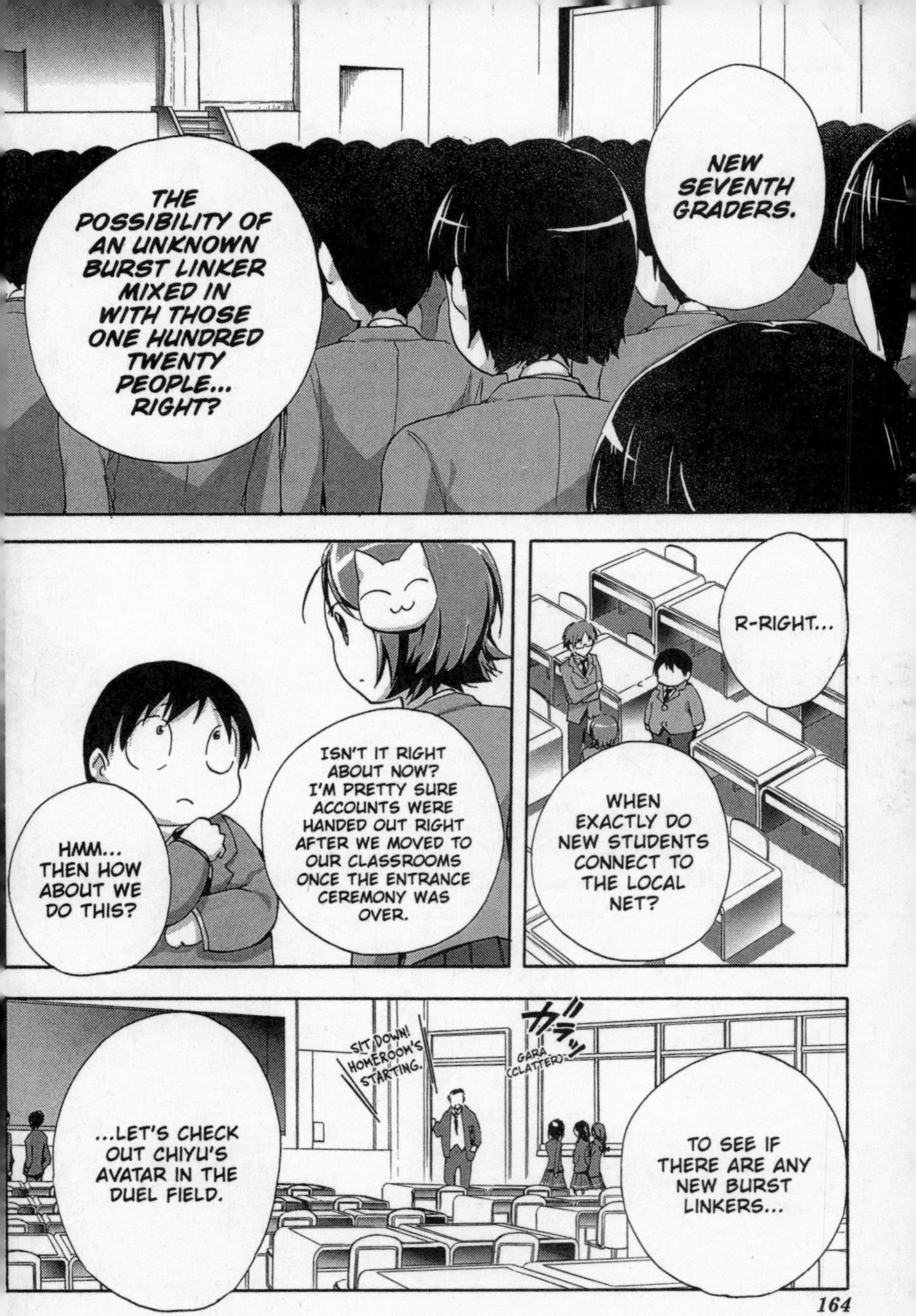
NEW SEVENTH GRADERS.
THE POSSIBILITY OF AN UNKNOWN BURST LINKER MIXED IN WITH THOSE ONE HUNDRED TWENTY PEOPLE... RIGHT?
R-RIGHT...
WHEN EXACTLY DO NEW STUDENTS CONNECT TO THE LOCAL NET?
ISN'T IT RIGHT ABOUT NOW? I'M PRETTY SURE ACCOUNTS WERE HANDED OUT RIGHT AFTER WE MOVED TO OUR CLASSROOMS ONCE THE ENTRANCE CEREMONY WAS OVER.
HMM... THEN HOW ABOUT WE DO THIS?
GARA (CLATTER)
SIT DOWN! HOMEROOM'S STARTING.
TO SEE IF THERE ARE ANY NEW BURST LINKERS...
...LET'S CHECK OUT CHIYU'S AVATAR IN THE DUEL FIELD.

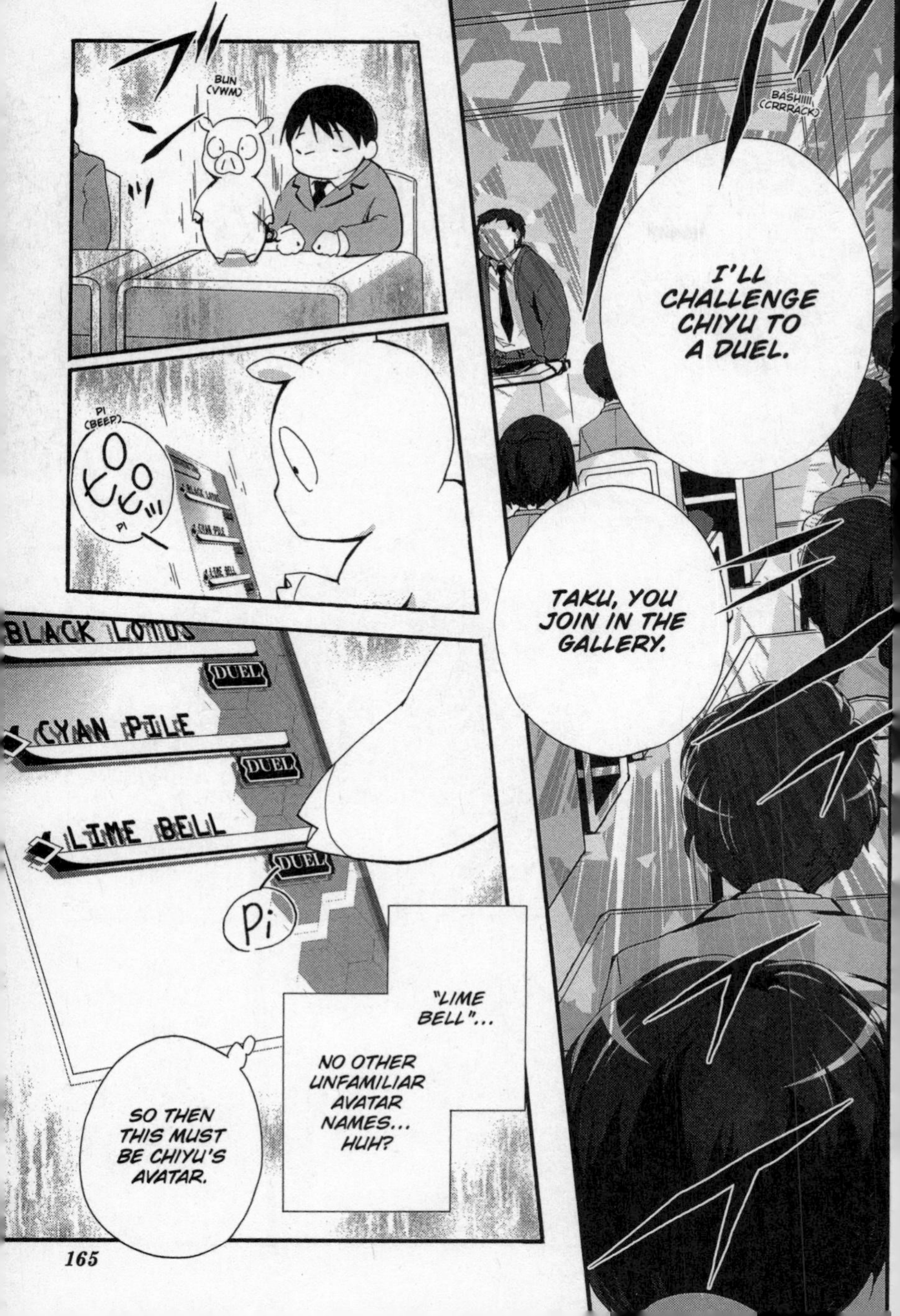
BASHIIII (CRRRACK)
I'LL CHALLENGE CHIYU TO A DUEL.
TAKU, YOU JOIN IN THE GALLERY.
BUN (VWM)
PI (BEEP)
PI
BLACK LOTUS
DUEL
CYAN PILE
DUEL
LIME BELL
DUEL
Pi
"LIME BELL"...
NO OTHER UNFAMILIAR AVATAR NAMES... HUH?
SO THEN THIS MUST BE CHIYU'S AVATAR.

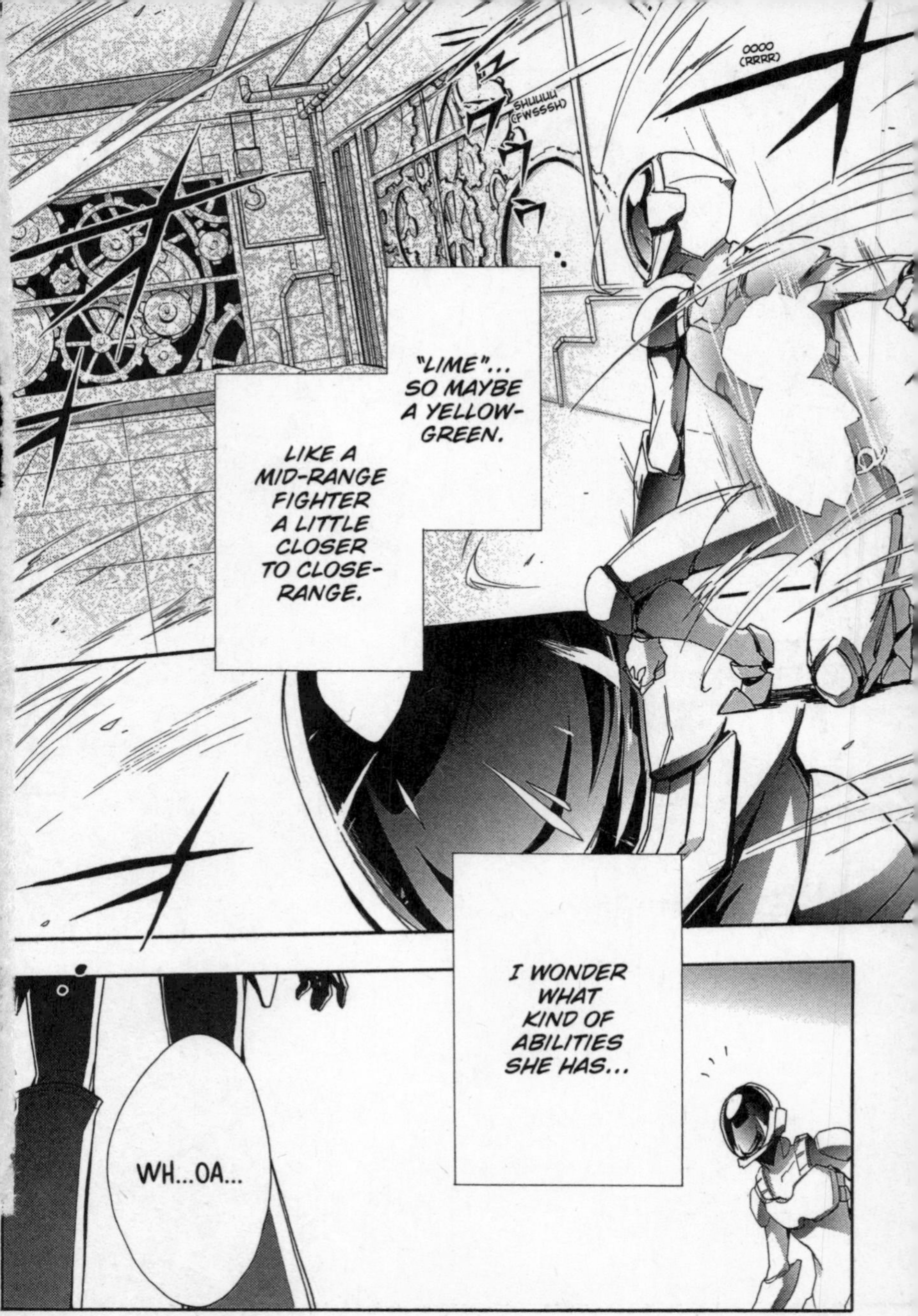
OOOO
(RRRR)
SHUUUU
(FWSSSH)
"LIME"... SO MAYBE A YELLOW-GREEN.
LIKE A MID-RANGE FIGHTER A LITTLE CLOSER TO CLOSE-RANGE.
I WONDER WHAT KIND OF ABILITIES SHE HAS...
WH...OA...

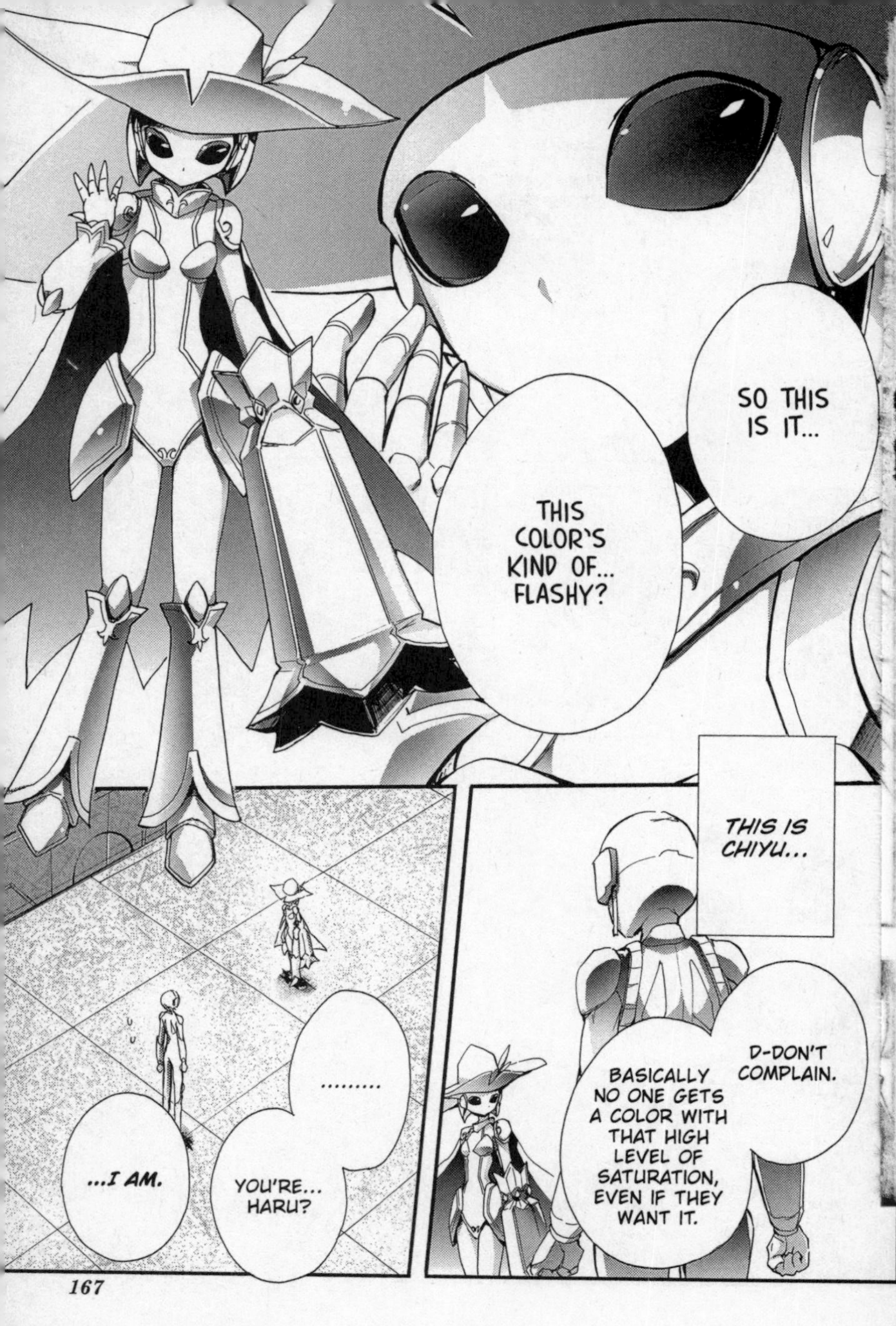
SO THIS IS IT...
THIS COLOR'S KIND OF... FLASHY?
THIS IS CHIYU...
D-DON'T COMPLAIN.
BASICALLY NO ONE GETS A COLOR WITH THAT HIGH LEVEL OF SATURATION, EVEN IF THEY WANT IT.
....
YOU'RE... HARU?
...I AM.

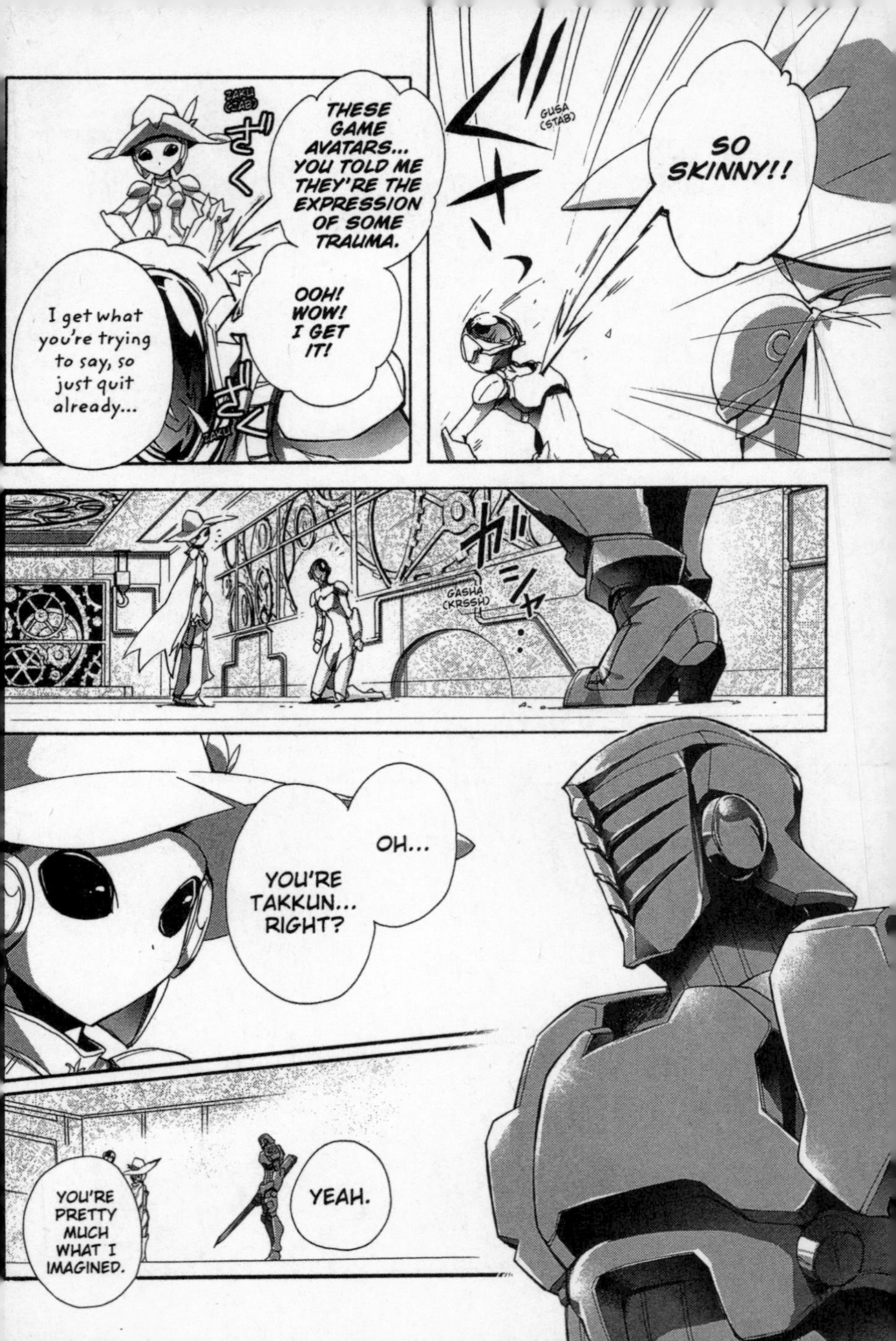
GUSA (STAB)
SO SKINNY!!
ZAKU (STAB)
THESE GAME AVATARS... YOU TOLD ME THEY'RE THE EXPRESSION OF SOME TRAUMA.
OOH! WOW! I GET IT!
I get what you're trying to say, so just quit already...
ZAKU
GASHA (KRSSH)
OH...
YOU'RE TAKKUN... RIGHT?
YEAH.
YOU'RE PRETTY MUCH WHAT I IMAGINED.

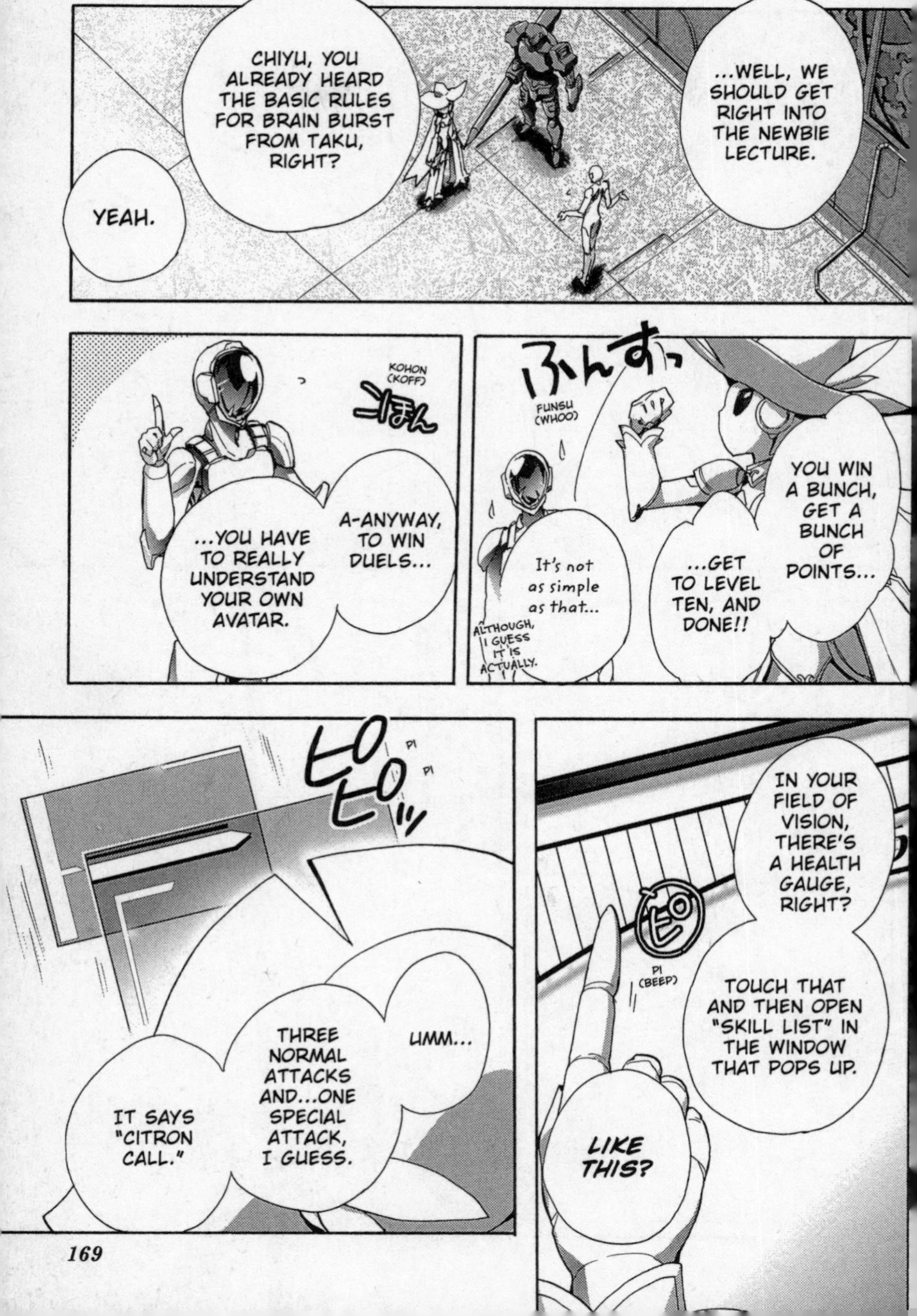
...WELL, WE SHOULD GET RIGHT INTO THE NEWBIE LECTURE.
CHIYU, YOU ALREADY HEARD THE BASIC RULES FOR BRAIN BURST FROM TAKU, RIGHT?
YEAH.
ふんすっ
FUNSU (WHOO)
YOU WIN A BUNCH, GET A BUNCH OF POINTS...
...GET TO LEVEL TEN, AND DONE!!
It's not as simple as that...
ALTHOUGH, I GUESS IT IS ACTUALLY.
こほん
KOHON (KOFF)
A-ANYWAY, TO WIN DUELS...
...YOU HAVE TO REALLY UNDERSTAND YOUR OWN AVATAR.
IN YOUR FIELD OF VISION, THERE'S A HEALTH GAUGE, RIGHT?
TOUCH THAT AND THEN OPEN "SKILL LIST" IN THE WINDOW THAT POPS UP.
ピ
PI (BEEP)
LIKE THIS?
ピピッ
PI PI
UMM...
THREE NORMAL ATTACKS AND...ONE SPECIAL ATTACK, I GUESS.
IT SAYS "CITRON CALL."

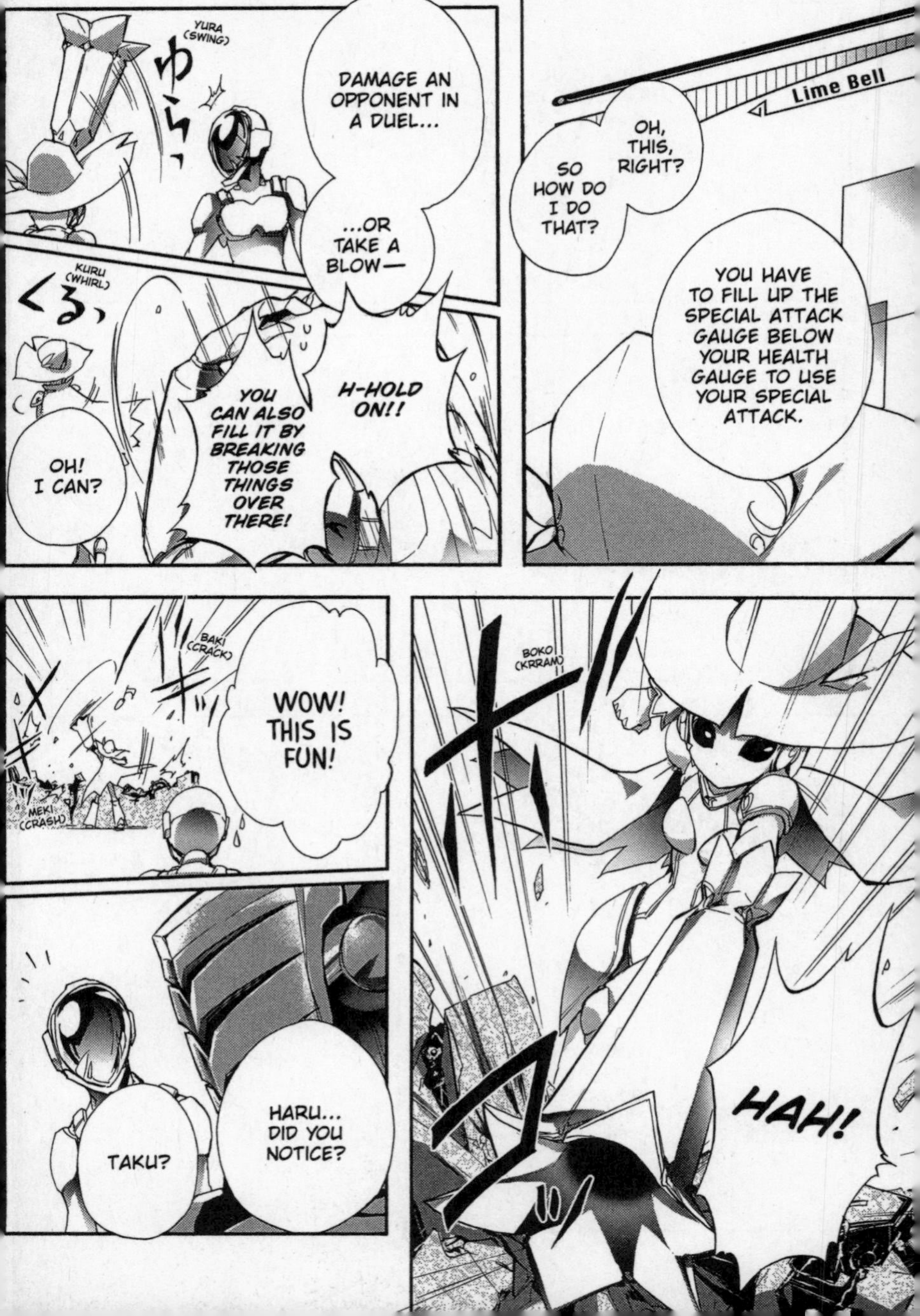

Lime Bell
OH, THIS, RIGHT?
SO HOW DO I DO THAT?
YOU HAVE TO FILL UP THE SPECIAL ATTACK GAUGE BELOW YOUR HEALTH GAUGE TO USE YOUR SPECIAL ATTACK.
DAMAGE AN OPPONENT IN A DUEL...
YURA (SWING)
ゆら
...OR TAKE A BLOW—
H-HOLD ON!!
YOU CAN ALSO FILL IT BY BREAKING THOSE THINGS OVER THERE!
KURU (WHIRL)
くる
OH! I CAN?
BOKO (KRRAM)
HAH!
WOW! THIS IS FUN!
BAKI (CRACK)
MEKI (CRASH)
HARU... DID YOU NOTICE?
TAKU?

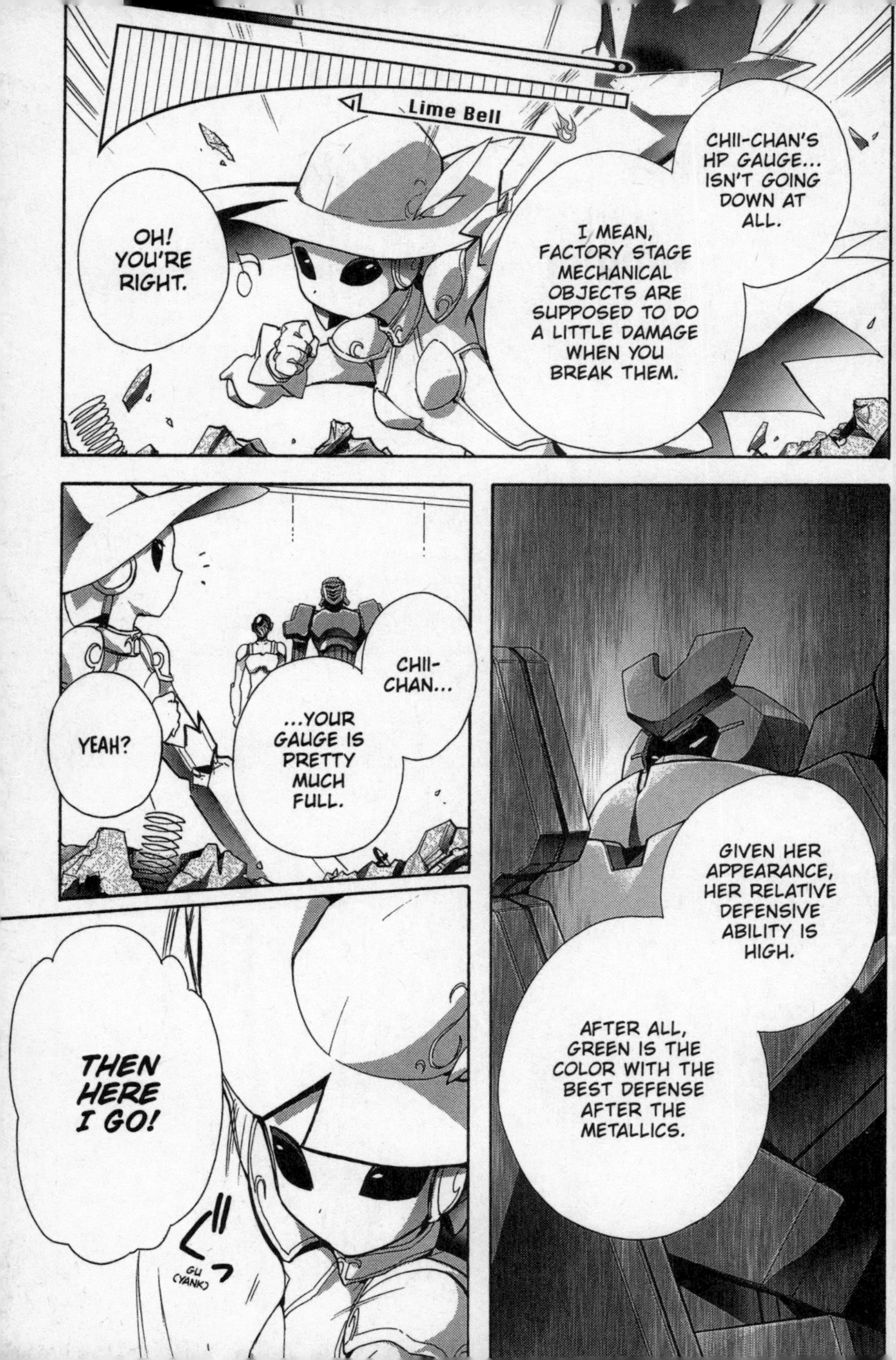
Lime Bell
CHII-CHAN'S HP GAUGE... ISN'T GOING DOWN AT ALL.
I MEAN, FACTORY STAGE MECHANICAL OBJECTS ARE SUPPOSED TO DO A LITTLE DAMAGE WHEN YOU BREAK THEM.
OH! YOU'RE RIGHT.
GIVEN HER APPEARANCE, HER RELATIVE DEFENSIVE ABILITY IS HIGH.
AFTER ALL, GREEN IS THE COLOR WITH THE BEST DEFENSE AFTER THE METALLICS.
CHII-CHAN...
...YOUR GAUGE IS PRETTY MUCH FULL.
YEAH?
THEN HERE I GO!
GU (YANK)

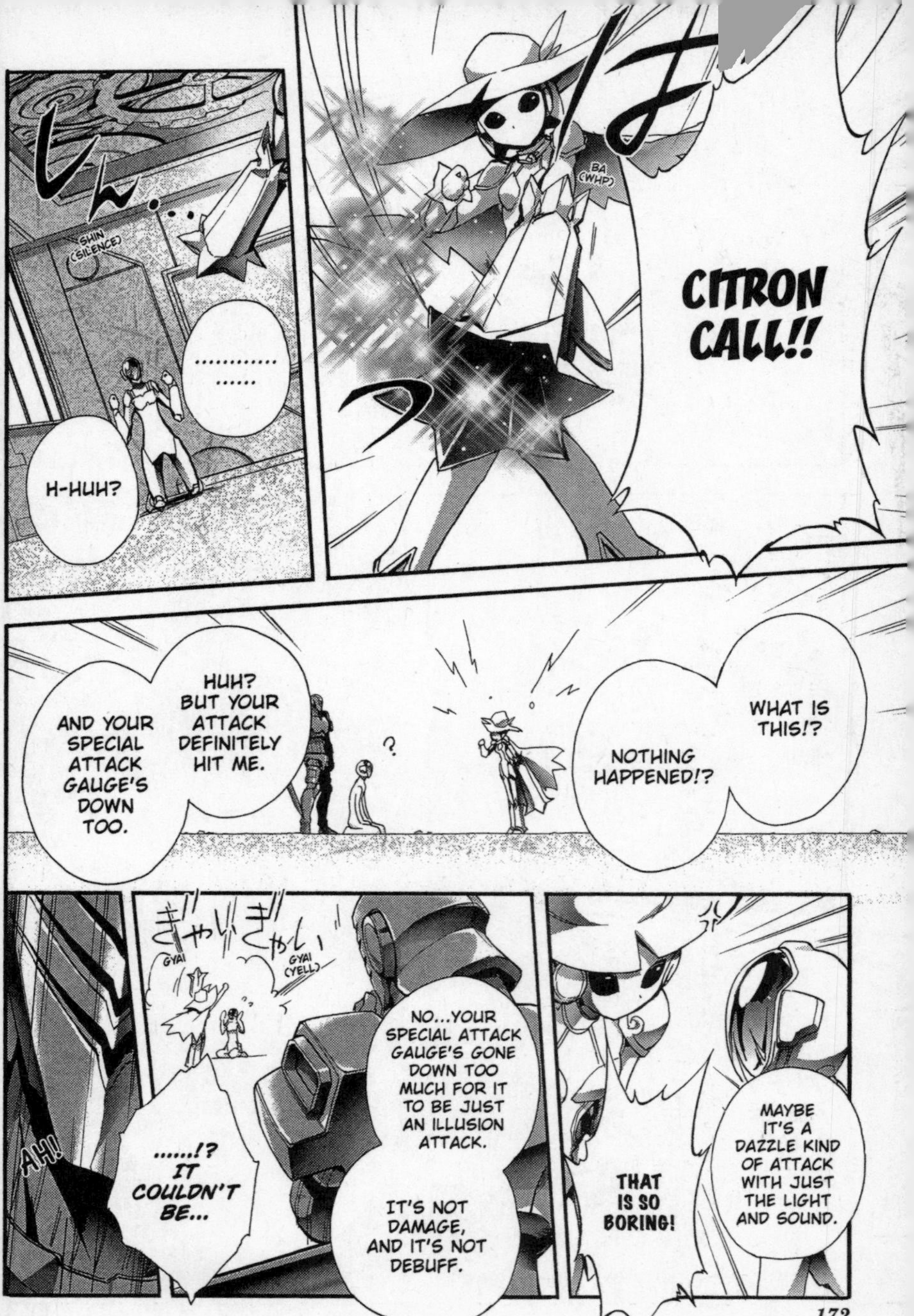
BA (WHP)
CITRON CALL!!
SHIN (SILENCE)
....
H-HUH?
WHAT IS THIS!?
NOTHING HAPPENED!?
HUH? BUT YOUR ATTACK DEFINITELY HIT ME.
AND YOUR SPECIAL ATTACK GAUGE'S DOWN TOO.
MAYBE IT'S A DAZZLE KIND OF ATTACK WITH JUST THE LIGHT AND SOUND.
THAT IS SO BORING!
GYAI
GYAI (YELL)
NO...YOUR SPECIAL ATTACK GAUGE'S GONE DOWN TOO MUCH FOR IT TO BE JUST AN ILLUSION ATTACK.
IT'S NOT DAMAGE, AND IT'S NOT DEBUFF.
......!? IT COULDN'T BE...
AH!

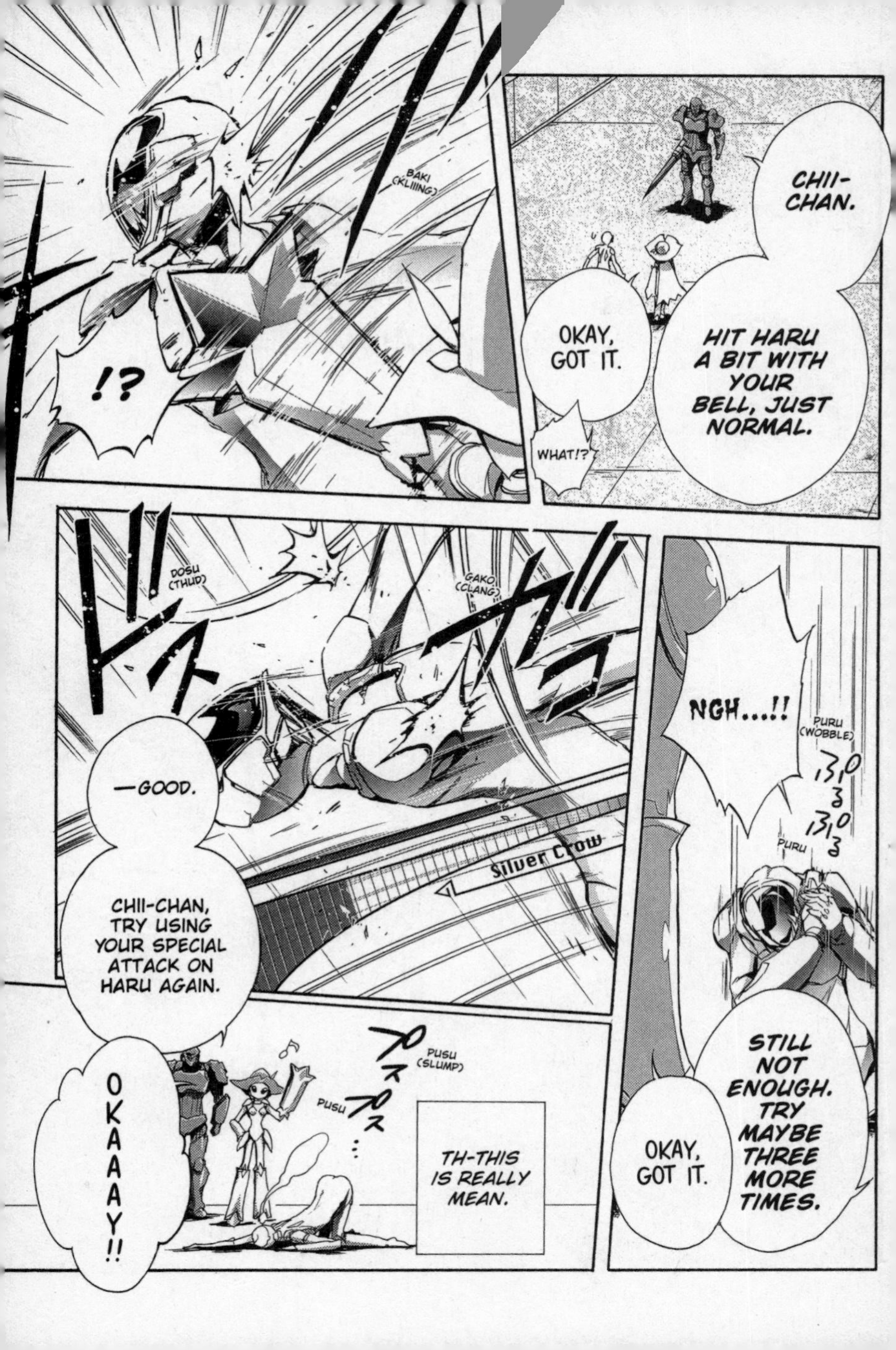
CHII-CHAN.
HIT HARU A BIT WITH YOUR BELL, JUST NORMAL.
OKAY, GOT IT.
WHAT!?
BAKI (KLIIING)
!?
NGH...!!
PURU (WOBBLE)
PURU
STILL NOT ENOUGH. TRY MAYBE THREE MORE TIMES.
OKAY, GOT IT.
DOSU (THUD)
GAKO (CLANG)
—GOOD.
Silver Crow
CHII-CHAN, TRY USING YOUR SPECIAL ATTACK ON HARU AGAIN.
PUSU (SLUMP)
PUSU
TH-THIS IS REALLY MEAN.
OKAAAAY!!

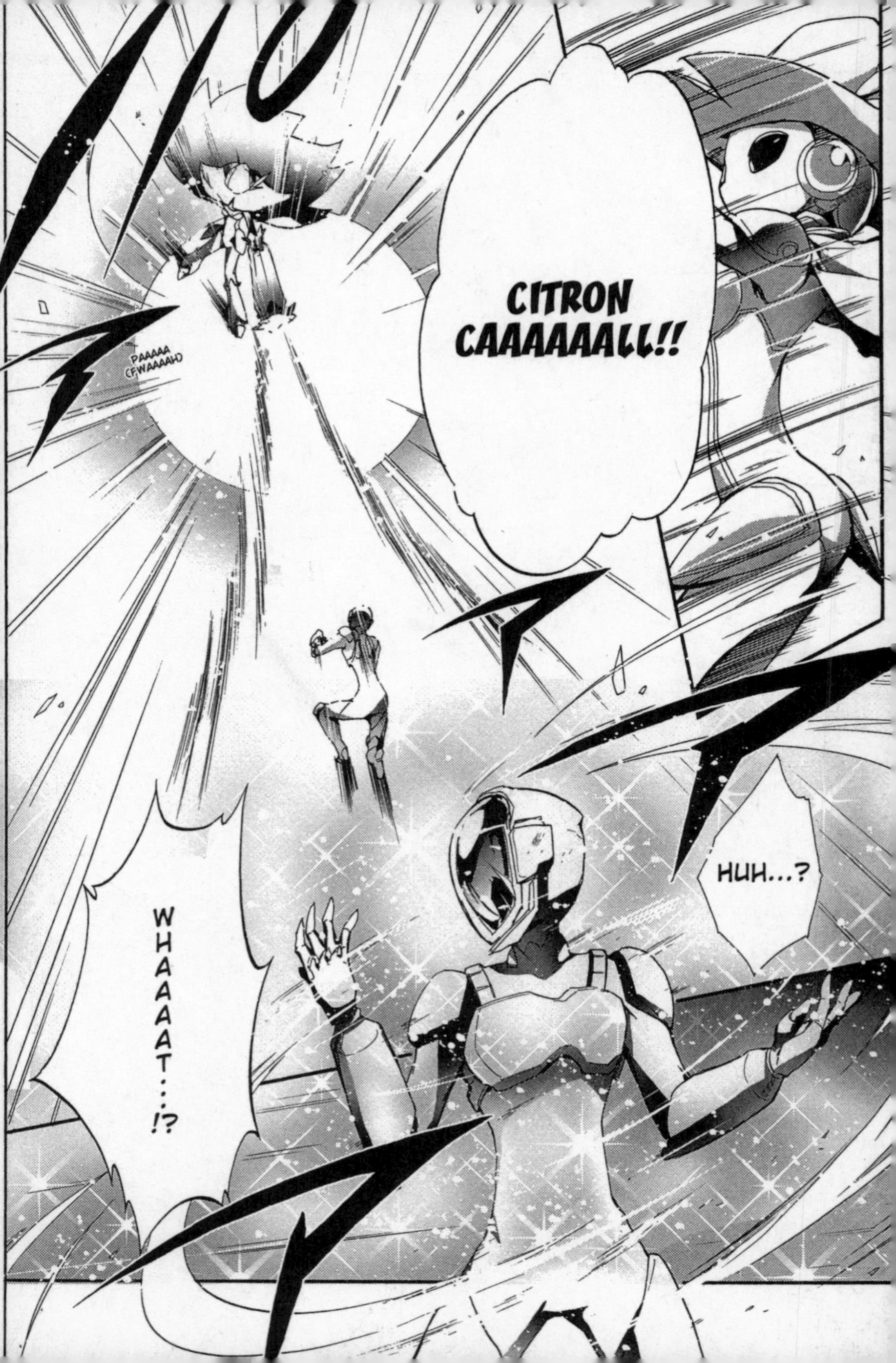
CITRON CAAAAAALL!!
PAAAAA (FWAAAAH)
HUH...?
WHAAAAT...!?

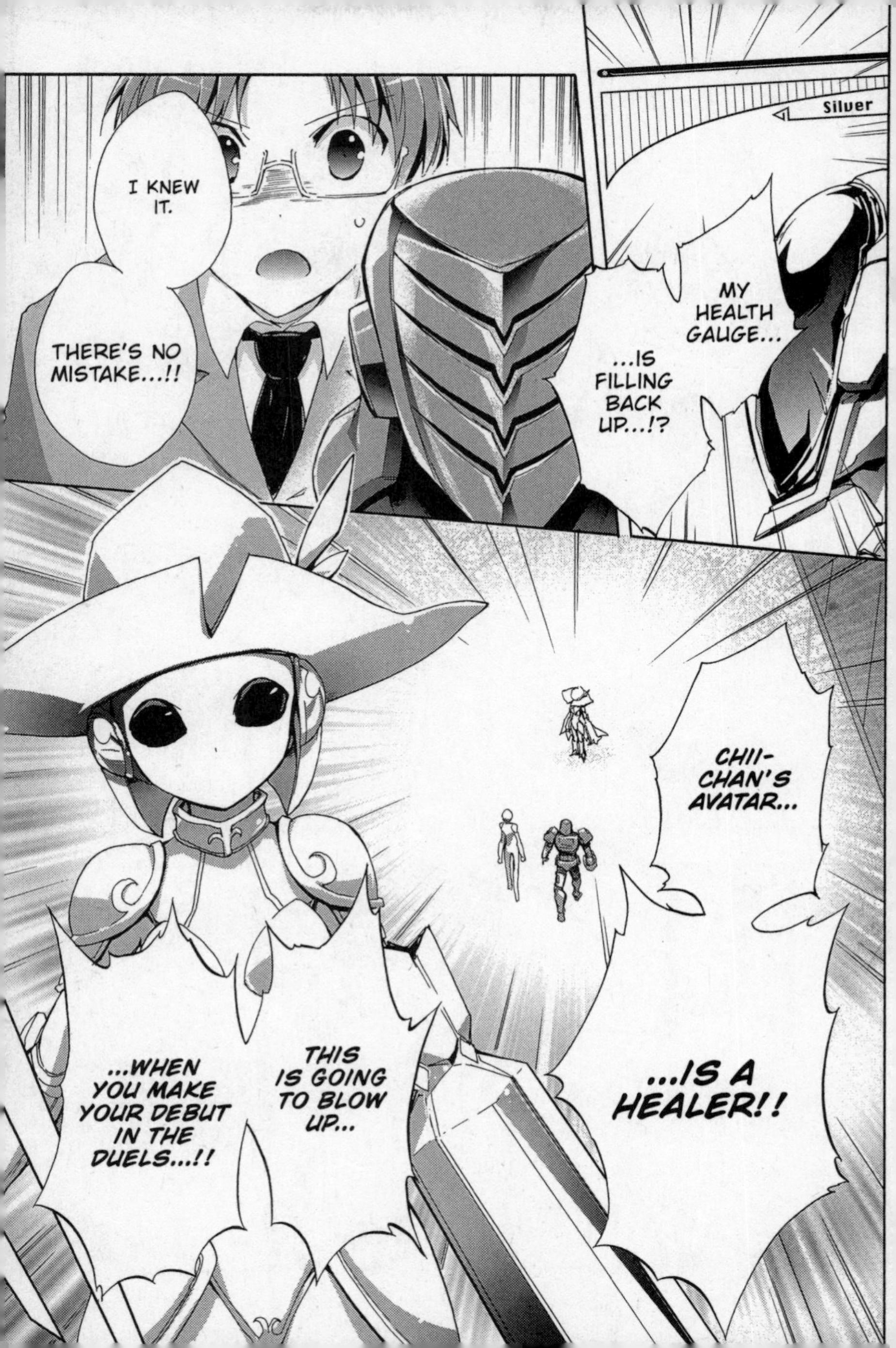
Silver
MY HEALTH GAUGE...
...IS FILLING BACK UP...!?
I KNEW IT.
THERE'S NO MISTAKE...!!
CHII-CHAN'S AVATAR...
...IS A HEALER!!
THIS IS GOING TO BLOW UP...
...WHEN YOU MAKE YOUR DEBUT IN THE DUELS...!!

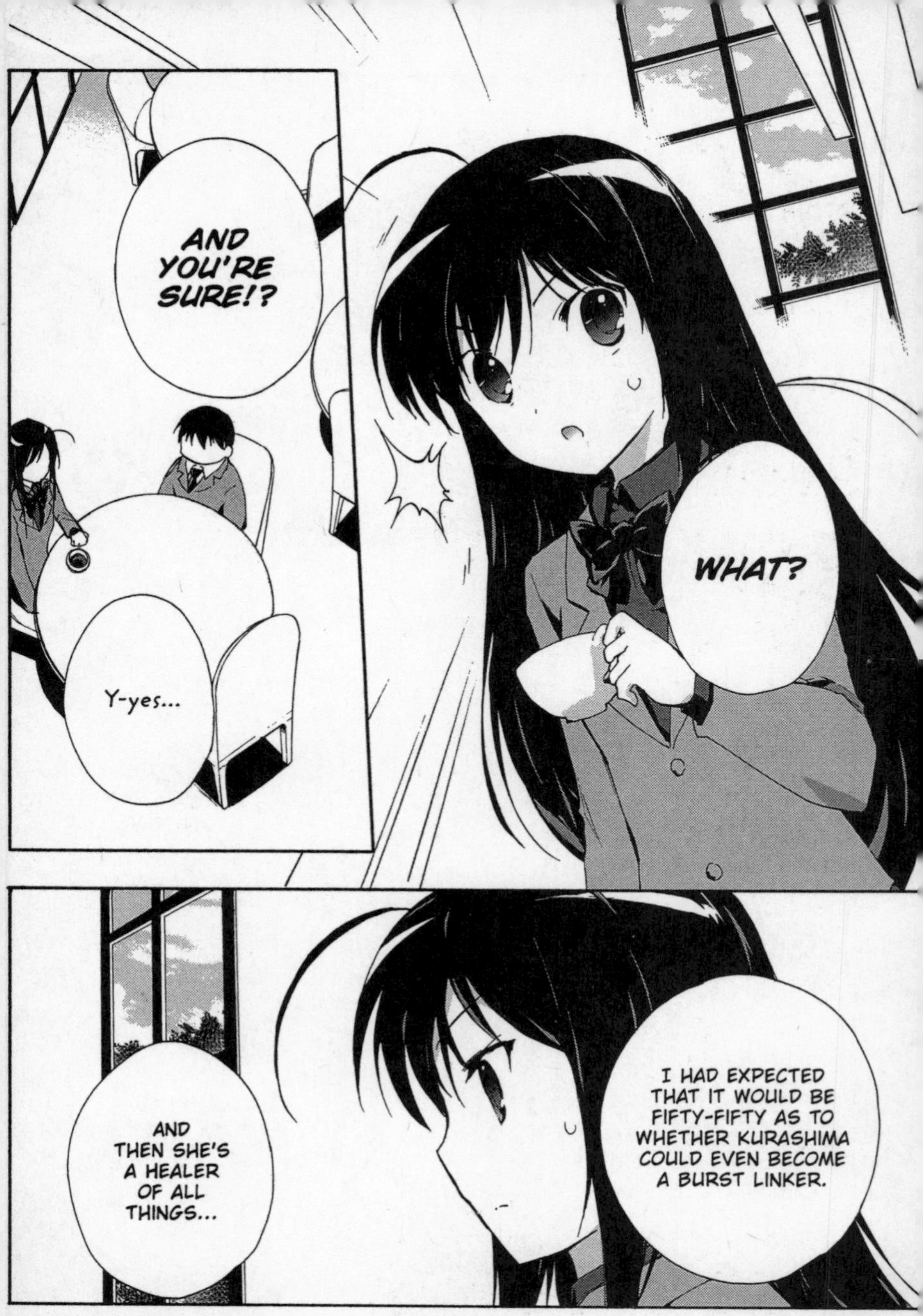
WHAT?
AND YOU'RE SURE!?
Y-yes...
I HAD EXPECTED THAT IT WOULD BE FIFTY-FIFTY AS TO WHETHER KURASHIMA COULD EVEN BECOME A BURST LINKER.
AND THEN SHE'S A HEALER OF ALL THINGS...

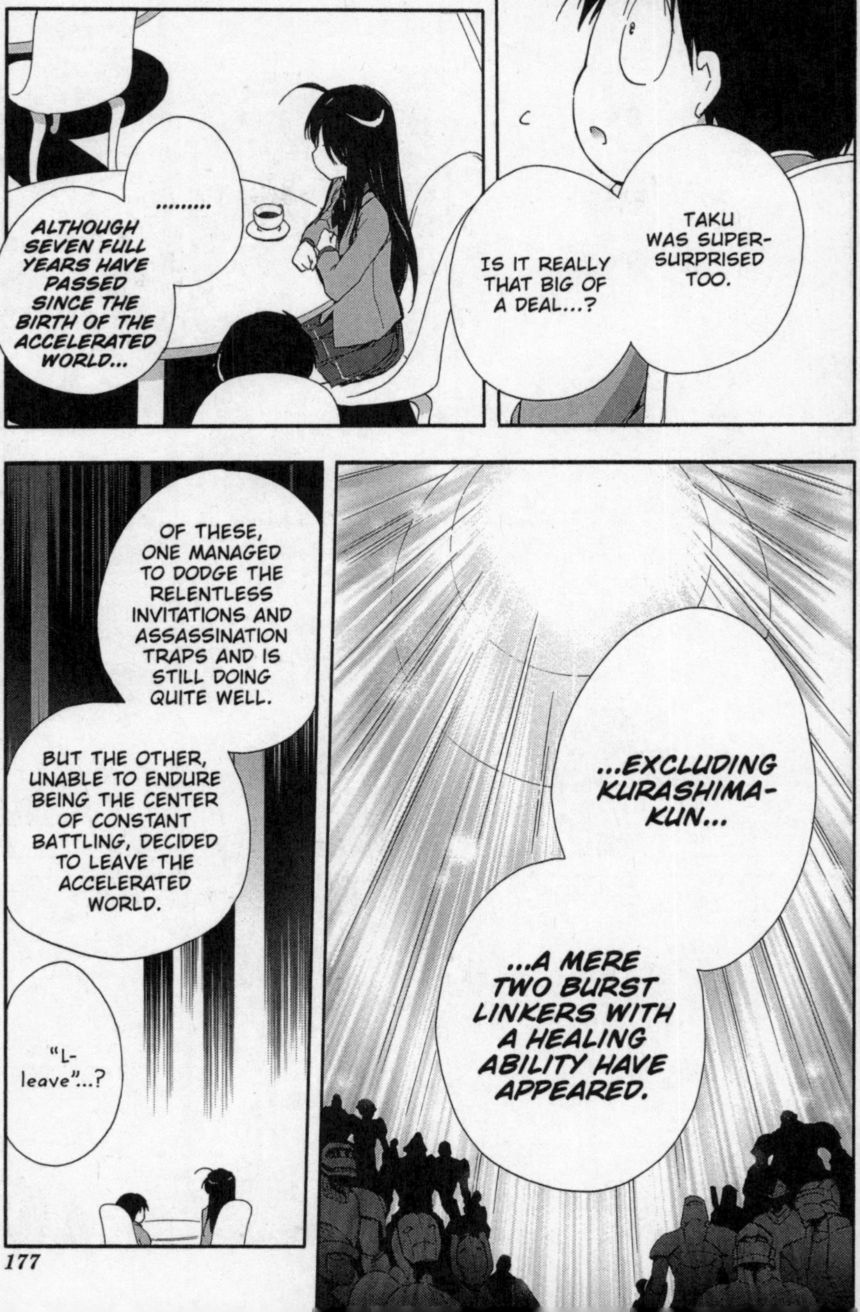
TAKU WAS SUPER-SURPRISED TOO.
IS IT REALLY THAT BIG OF A DEAL...?
....
ALTHOUGH SEVEN FULL YEARS HAVE PASSED SINCE THE BIRTH OF THE ACCELERATED WORLD...
...EXCLUDING KURASHIMA-KUN...
...A MERE TWO BURST LINKERS WITH A HEALING ABILITY HAVE APPEARED.
OF THESE, ONE MANAGED TO DODGE THE RELENTLESS INVITATIONS AND ASSASSINATION TRAPS AND IS STILL DOING QUITE WELL.
BUT THE OTHER, UNABLE TO ENDURE BEING THE CENTER OF CONSTANT BATTLING, DECIDED TO LEAVE THE ACCELERATED WORLD.
"L-leave"...?

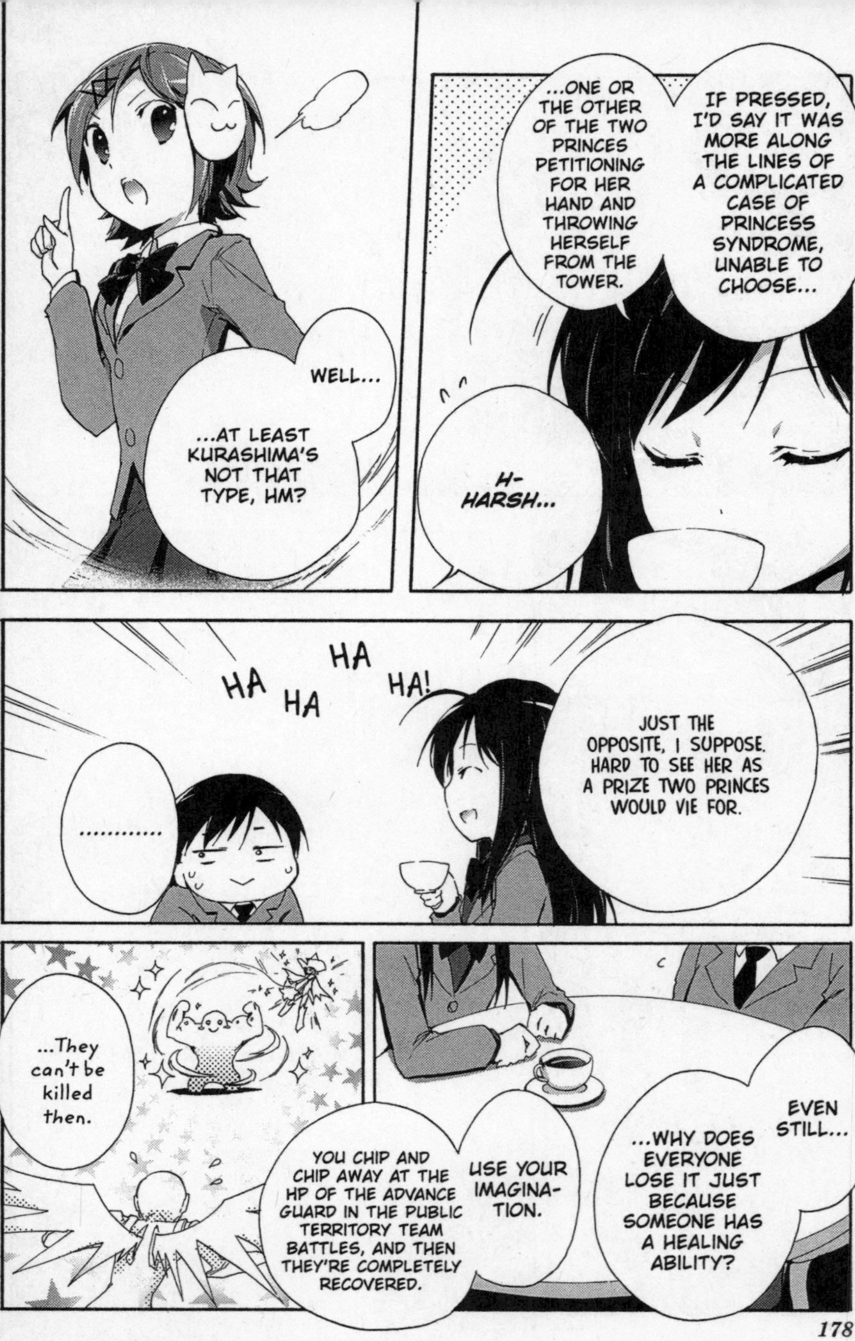
IF PRESSED, I'D SAY IT WAS MORE ALONG THE LINES OF A COMPLICATED CASE OF PRINCESS SYNDROME, UNABLE TO CHOOSE...
...ONE OR THE OTHER OF THE TWO PRINCES PETITIONING FOR HER HAND AND THROWING HERSELF FROM THE TOWER.
H-HARSH...
WELL...
...AT LEAST KURASHIMA'S NOT THAT TYPE, HM?
JUST THE OPPOSITE, I SUPPOSE. HARD TO SEE HER AS A PRIZE TWO PRINCES WOULD VIE FOR.
HA HA HA HA!
....
EVEN STILL...
...WHY DOES EVERYONE LOSE IT JUST BECAUSE SOMEONE HAS A HEALING ABILITY?
USE YOUR IMAGINATION.
YOU CHIP AND CHIP AWAY AT THE HP OF THE ADVANCE GUARD IN THE PUBLIC TERRITORY TEAM BATTLES, AND THEN THEY'RE COMPLETELY RECOVERED.
...They can't be killed then.

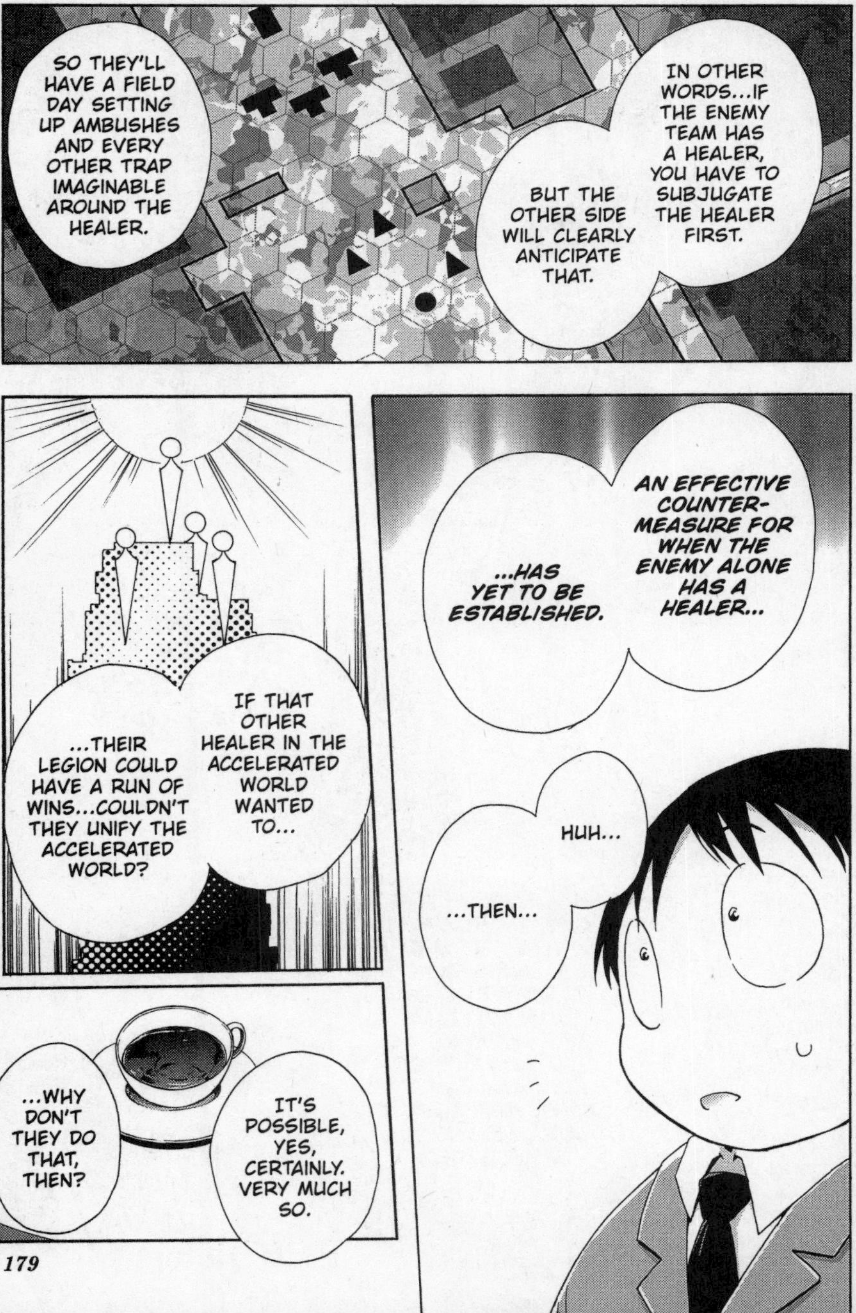
IN OTHER WORDS...IF THE ENEMY TEAM HAS A HEALER, YOU HAVE TO SUBJUGATE THE HEALER FIRST.
BUT THE OTHER SIDE WILL CLEARLY ANTICIPATE THAT.
SO THEY'LL HAVE A FIELD DAY SETTING UP AMBUSHES AND EVERY OTHER TRAP IMAGINABLE AROUND THE HEALER.
AN EFFECTIVE COUNTER-MEASURE FOR WHEN THE ENEMY ALONE HAS A HEALER...
...HAS YET TO BE ESTABLISHED.
HUH...
...THEN...
IF THAT OTHER HEALER IN THE ACCELERATED WORLD WANTED TO...
...THEIR LEGION COULD HAVE A RUN OF WINS...COULDN'T THEY UNIFY THE ACCELERATED WORLD?
IT'S POSSIBLE, YES, CERTAINLY. VERY MUCH SO.
...WHY DON'T THEY DO THAT, THEN?

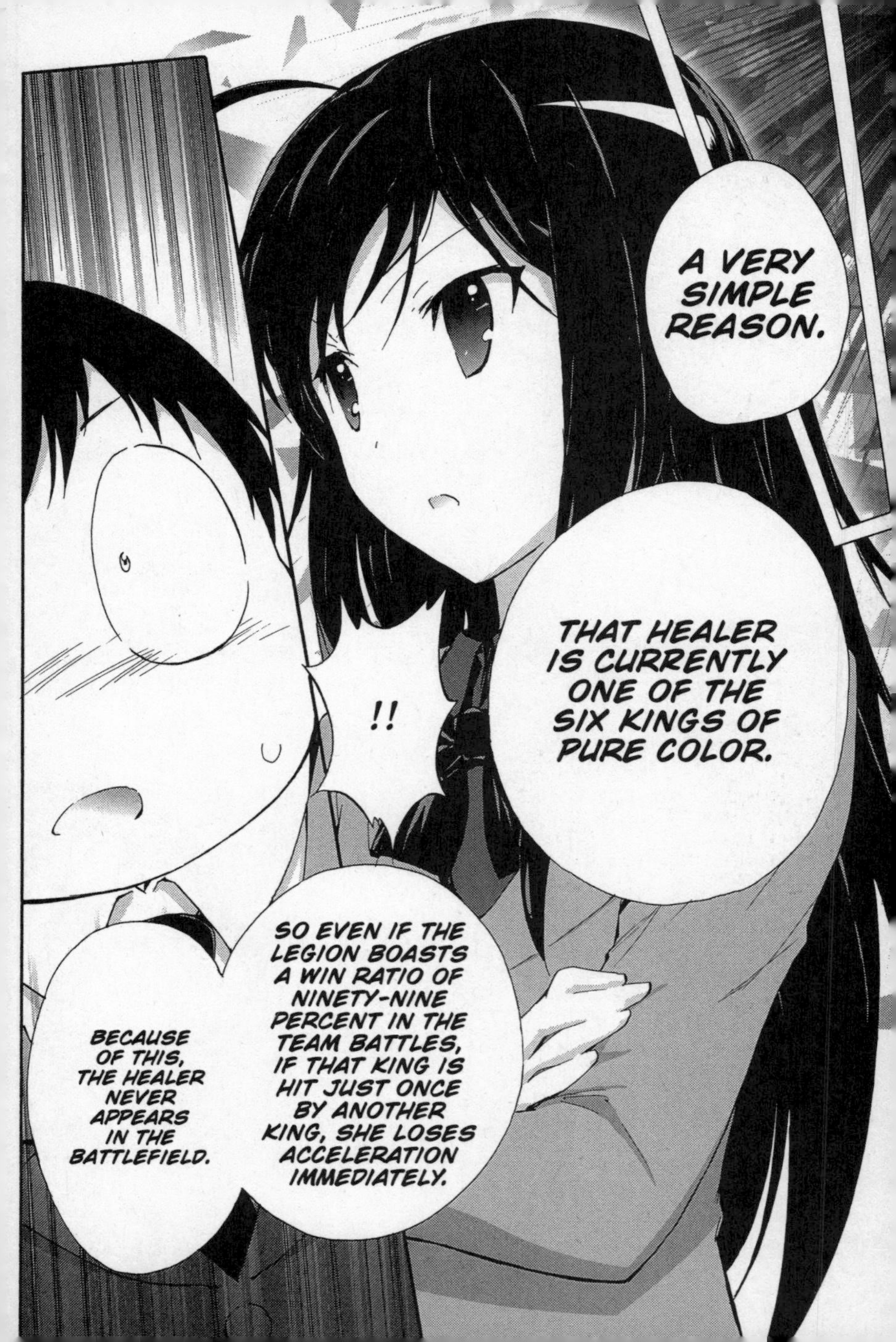
A VERY SIMPLE REASON.
THAT HEALER IS CURRENTLY ONE OF THE SIX KINGS OF PURE COLOR.
!!
SO EVEN IF THE LEGION BOASTS A WIN RATIO OF NINETY-NINE PERCENT IN THE TEAM BATTLES, IF THAT KING IS HIT JUST ONCE BY ANOTHER KING, SHE LOSES ACCELERATION IMMEDIATELY.
BECAUSE OF THIS, THE HEALER NEVER APPEARS IN THE BATTLEFIELD.

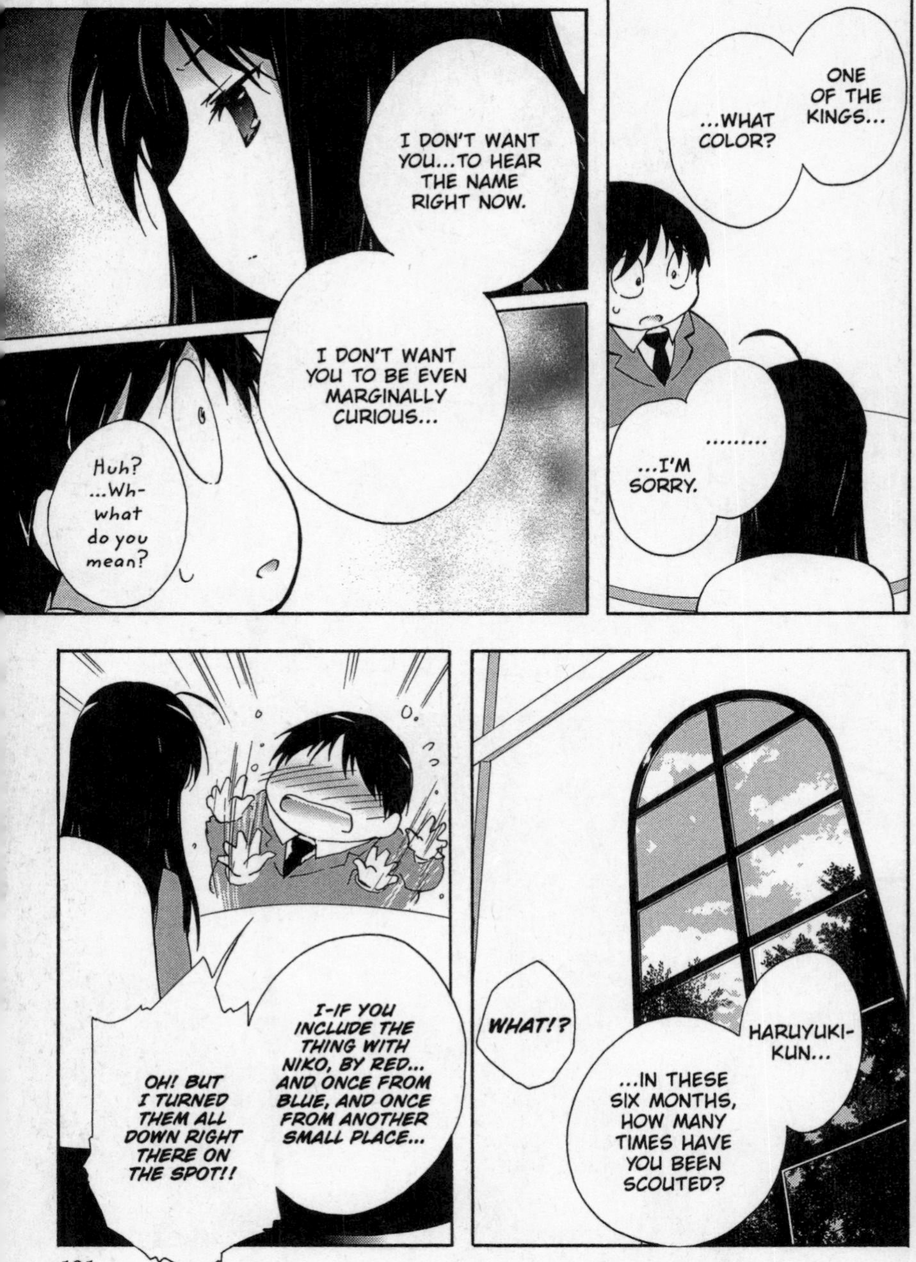
ONE OF THE KINGS...
...WHAT COLOR?
....
...I'M SORRY.
I DON'T WANT YOU...TO HEAR THE NAME RIGHT NOW.
I DON'T WANT YOU TO BE EVEN MARGINALLY CURIOUS...
Huh? ...Wh-what do you mean?
HARUYUKI-KUN...
...IN THESE SIX MONTHS, HOW MANY TIMES HAVE YOU BEEN SCOUTED?
WHAT!?
I-IF YOU INCLUDE THE THING WITH NIKO, BY RED... AND ONCE FROM BLUE, AND ONCE FROM ANOTHER SMALL PLACE...
OH! BUT I TURNED THEM ALL DOWN RIGHT THERE ON THE SPOT!!

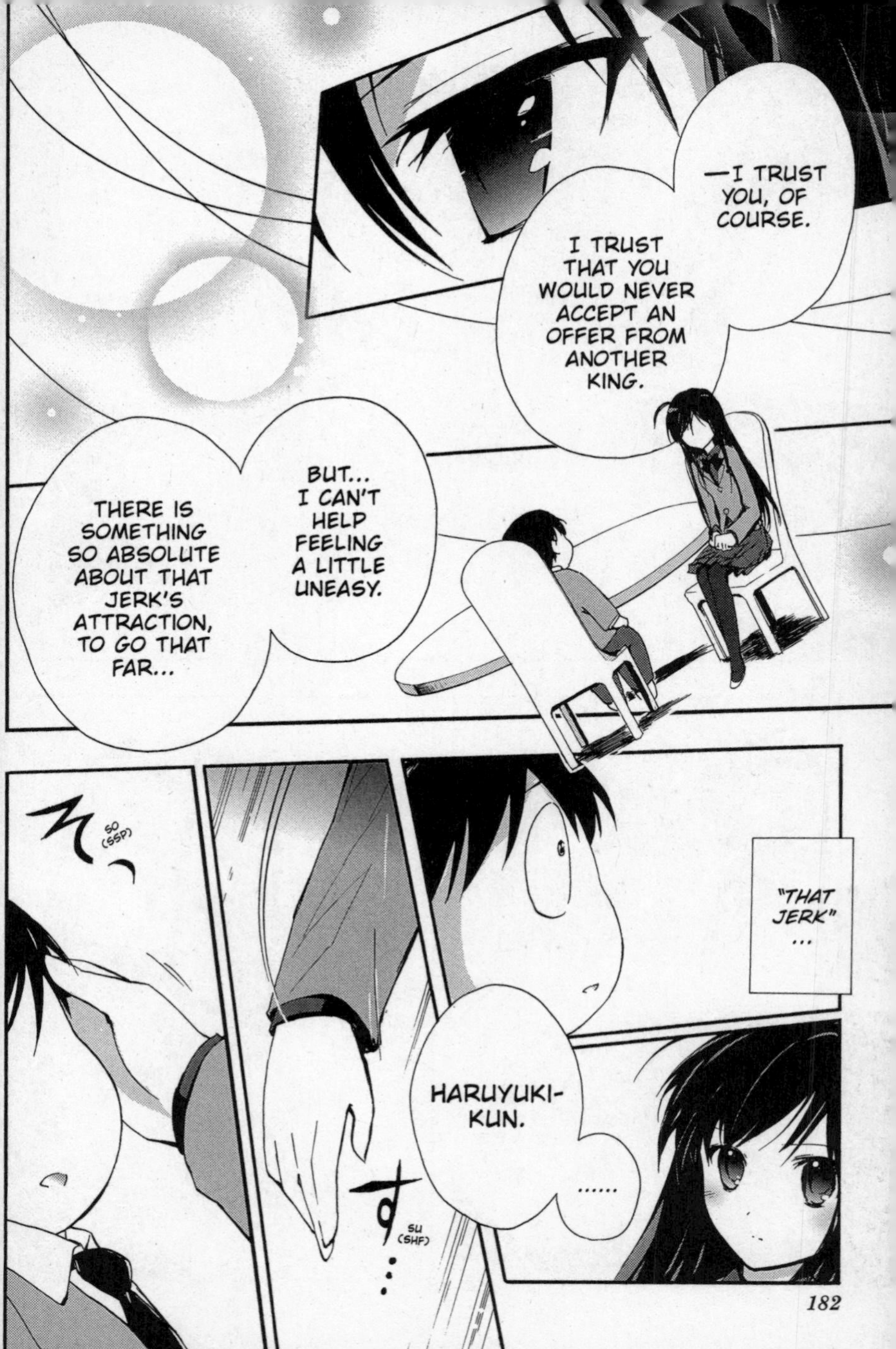
—I TRUST YOU, OF COURSE.
I TRUST THAT YOU WOULD NEVER ACCEPT AN OFFER FROM ANOTHER KING.
BUT... I CAN'T HELP FEELING A LITTLE UNEASY.
THERE IS SOMETHING SO ABSOLUTE ABOUT THAT JERK'S ATTRACTION, TO GO THAT FAR...
"THAT JERK" ...
HARUYUKI-KUN.
......
SU (SHF)
...
SO (SSP)

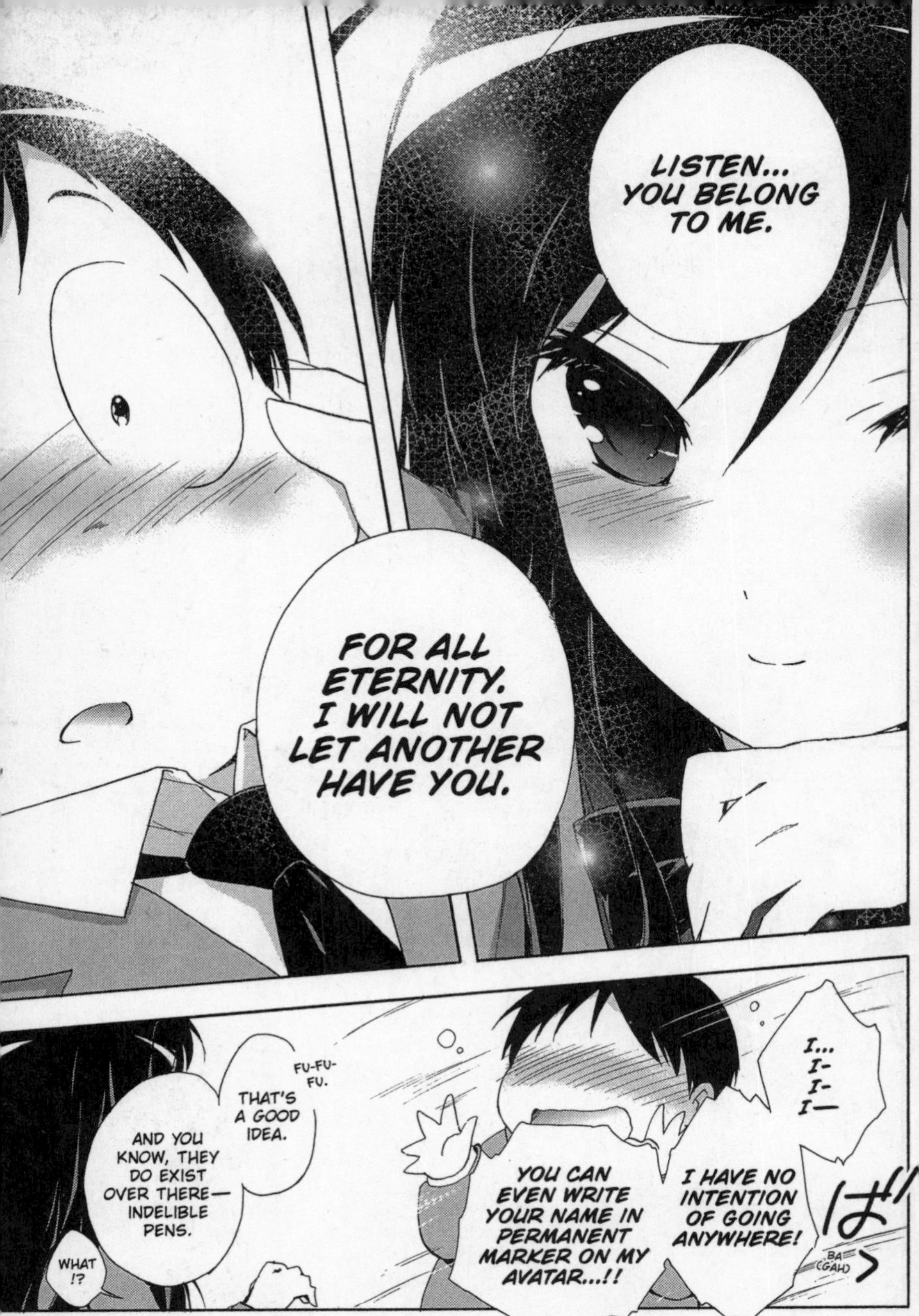
LISTEN... YOU BELONG TO ME.
FOR ALL ETERNITY. I WILL NOT LET ANOTHER HAVE YOU.
I... I- I- I—
ば
BA (GAH)
I HAVE NO INTENTION OF GOING ANYWHERE!
YOU CAN EVEN WRITE YOUR NAME IN PERMANENT MARKER ON MY AVATAR...!!
FU-FU-FU.
THAT'S A GOOD IDEA.
AND YOU KNOW, THEY DO EXIST OVER THERE— INDELIBLE PENS.
WHAT!?

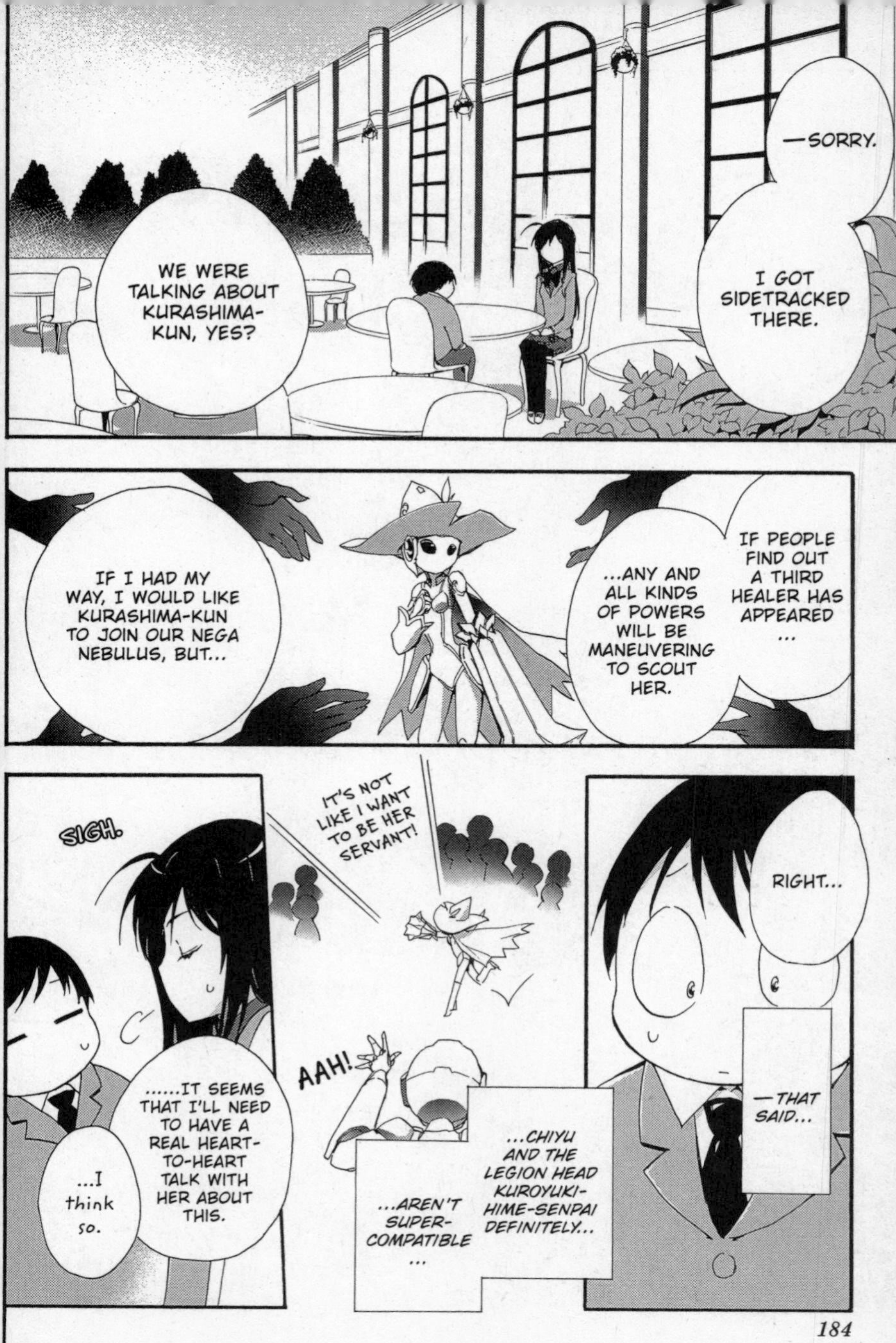
—SORRY.
I GOT SIDETRACKED THERE.
WE WERE TALKING ABOUT KURASHIMA-KUN, YES?
IF PEOPLE FIND OUT A THIRD HEALER HAS APPEARED...
...ANY AND ALL KINDS OF POWERS WILL BE MANEUVERING TO SCOUT HER.
IF I HAD MY WAY, I WOULD LIKE KURASHIMA-KUN TO JOIN OUR NEGA NEBULUS, BUT...
RIGHT...
—THAT SAID...
...CHIYU AND THE LEGION HEAD KUROYUKI-HIME-SENPAI DEFINITELY...
...AREN'T SUPER-COMPATIBLE...
IT'S NOT LIKE I WANT TO BE HER SERVANT!
AAH!
SIGH.
......IT SEEMS THAT I'LL NEED TO HAVE A REAL HEART-TO-HEART TALK WITH HER ABOUT THIS.
...I think so.

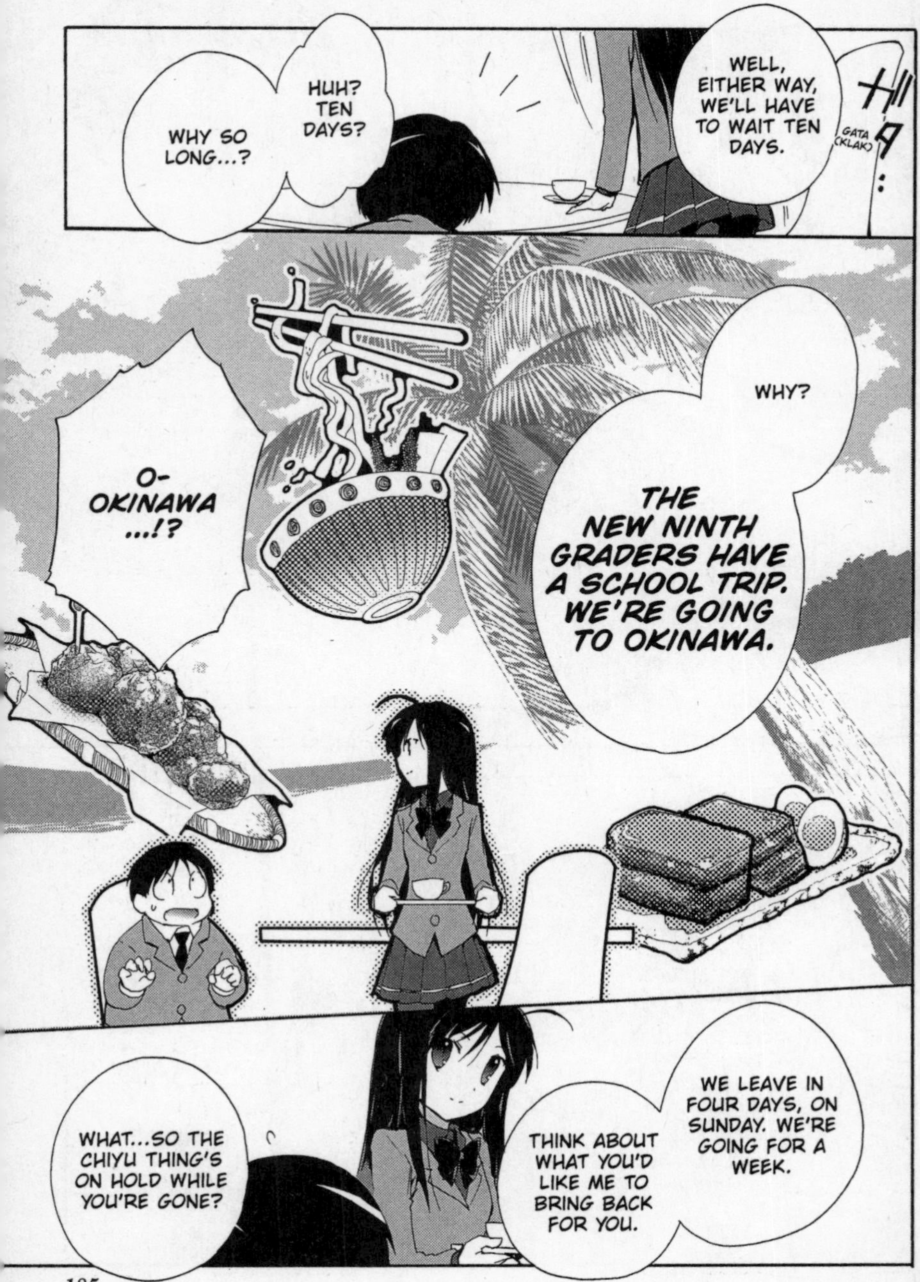

WELL, EITHER WAY, WE'LL HAVE TO WAIT TEN DAYS.
GATA (KLAK)
HUH? TEN DAYS?
WHY SO LONG...?
WHY?
THE NEW NINTH GRADERS HAVE A SCHOOL TRIP. WE'RE GOING TO OKINAWA.
O-OKINAWA...!?
WE LEAVE IN FOUR DAYS, ON SUNDAY. WE'RE GOING FOR A WEEK.
THINK ABOUT WHAT YOU'D LIKE ME TO BRING BACK FOR YOU.
WHAT...SO THE CHIYU THING'S ON HOLD WHILE YOU'RE GONE?

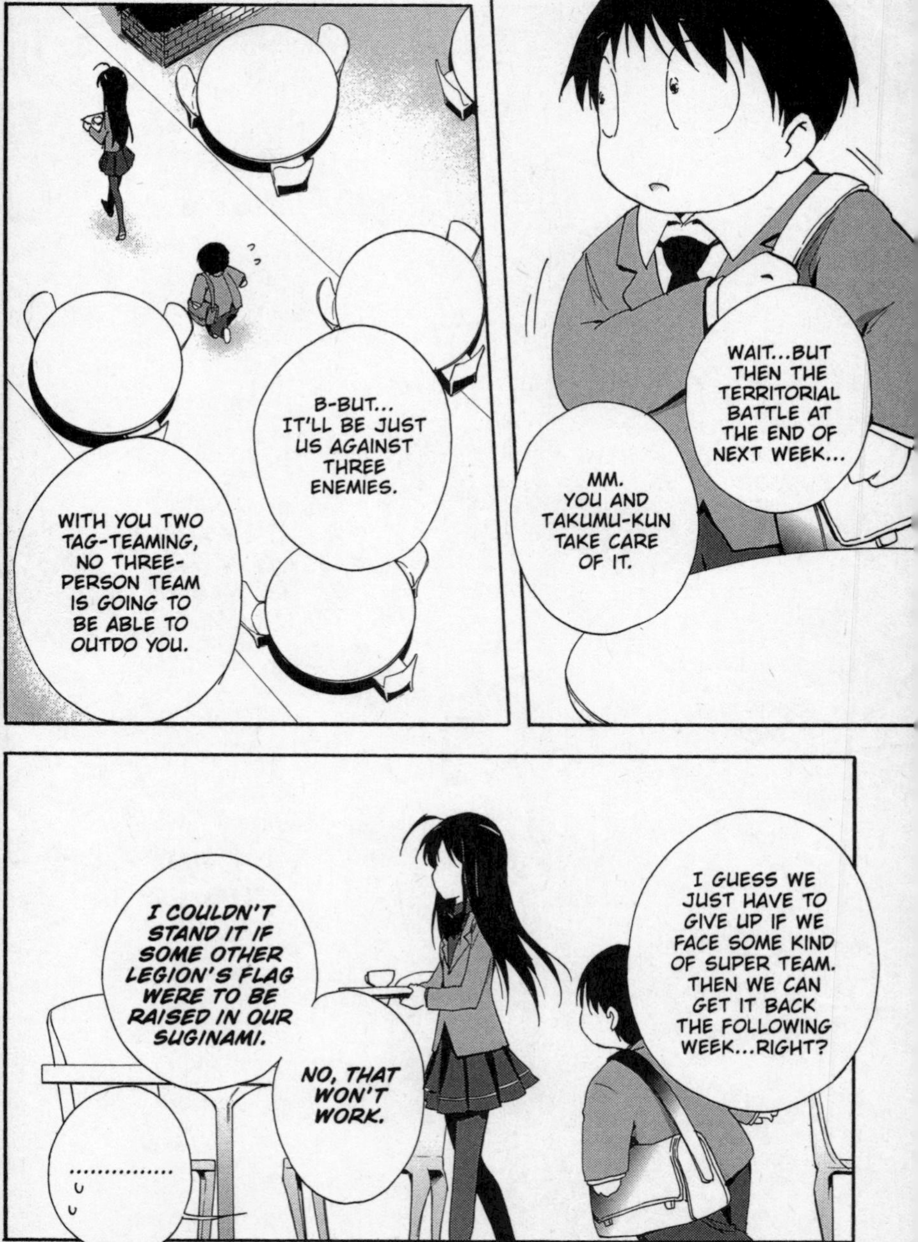
WAIT...BUT THEN THE TERRITORIAL BATTLE AT THE END OF NEXT WEEK...
MM. YOU AND TAKUMU-KUN TAKE CARE OF IT.
B-BUT... IT'LL BE JUST US AGAINST THREE ENEMIES.
WITH YOU TWO TAG-TEAMING, NO THREE-PERSON TEAM IS GOING TO BE ABLE TO OUTDO YOU.
I GUESS WE JUST HAVE TO GIVE UP IF WE FACE SOME KIND OF SUPER TEAM. THEN WE CAN GET IT BACK THE FOLLOWING WEEK...RIGHT?
NO, THAT WON'T WORK.
I COULDN'T STAND IT IF SOME OTHER LEGION'S FLAG WERE TO BE RAISED IN OUR SUGINAMI.
....

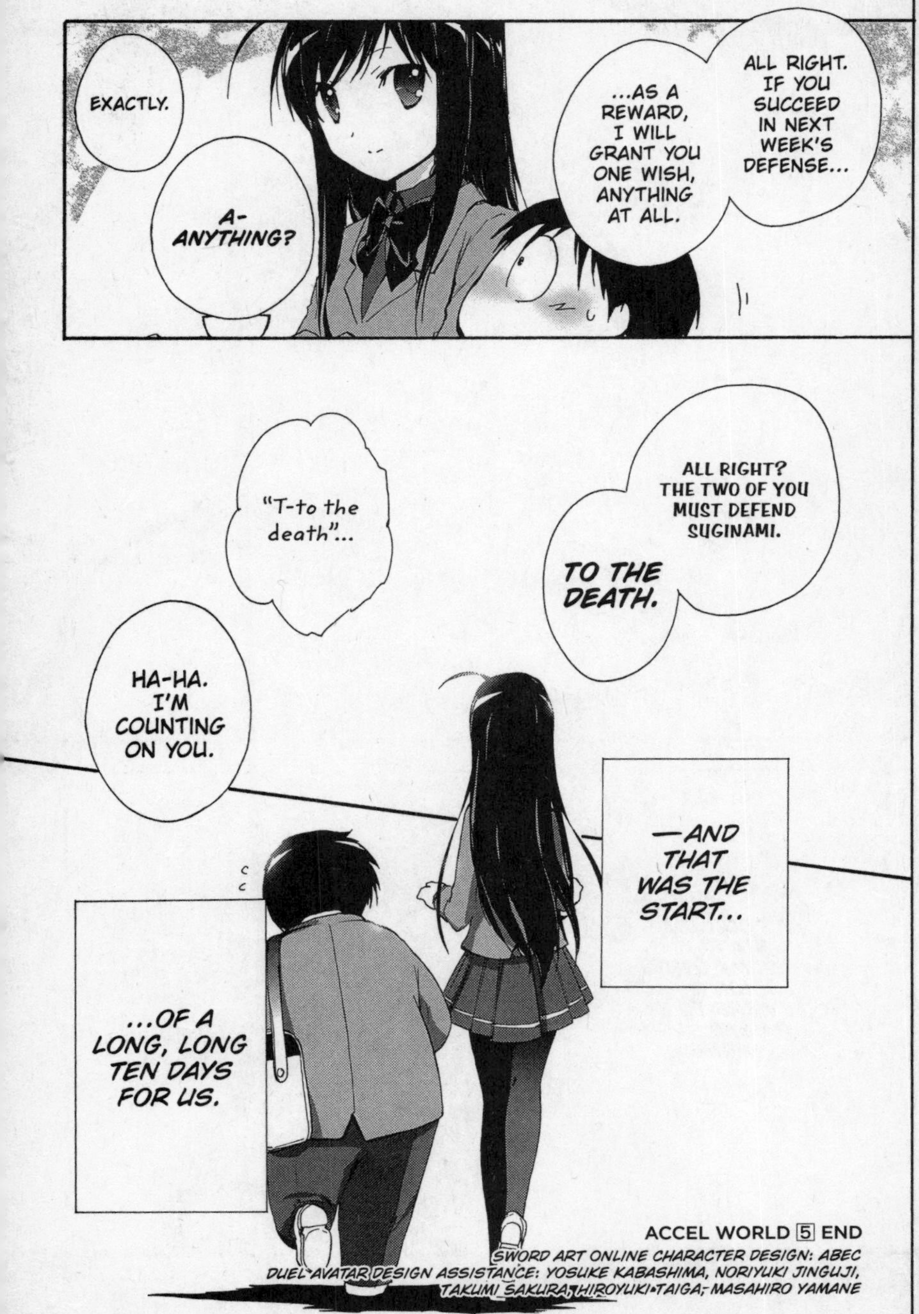
ALL RIGHT. IF YOU SUCCEED IN NEXT WEEK'S DEFENSE...
...AS A REWARD, I WILL GRANT YOU ONE WISH, ANYTHING AT ALL.
A-ANYTHING?
EXACTLY.
ALL RIGHT? THE TWO OF YOU MUST DEFEND SUGINAMI.
TO THE DEATH.
"T-to the death"...
HA-HA. I'M COUNTING ON YOU.
—AND THAT WAS THE START...
...OF A LONG, LONG TEN DAYS FOR US.

ACCEL WORLD 5 END

SWORD ART ONLINE CHARACTER DESIGN: ABEC
DUEL AVATAR DESIGN ASSISTANCE: YOSUKE KABASHIMA, NORIYUKI JINGUJI, TAKUMI SAKURA, HIROYUKI TAIGA, MASAHIRO YAMANE

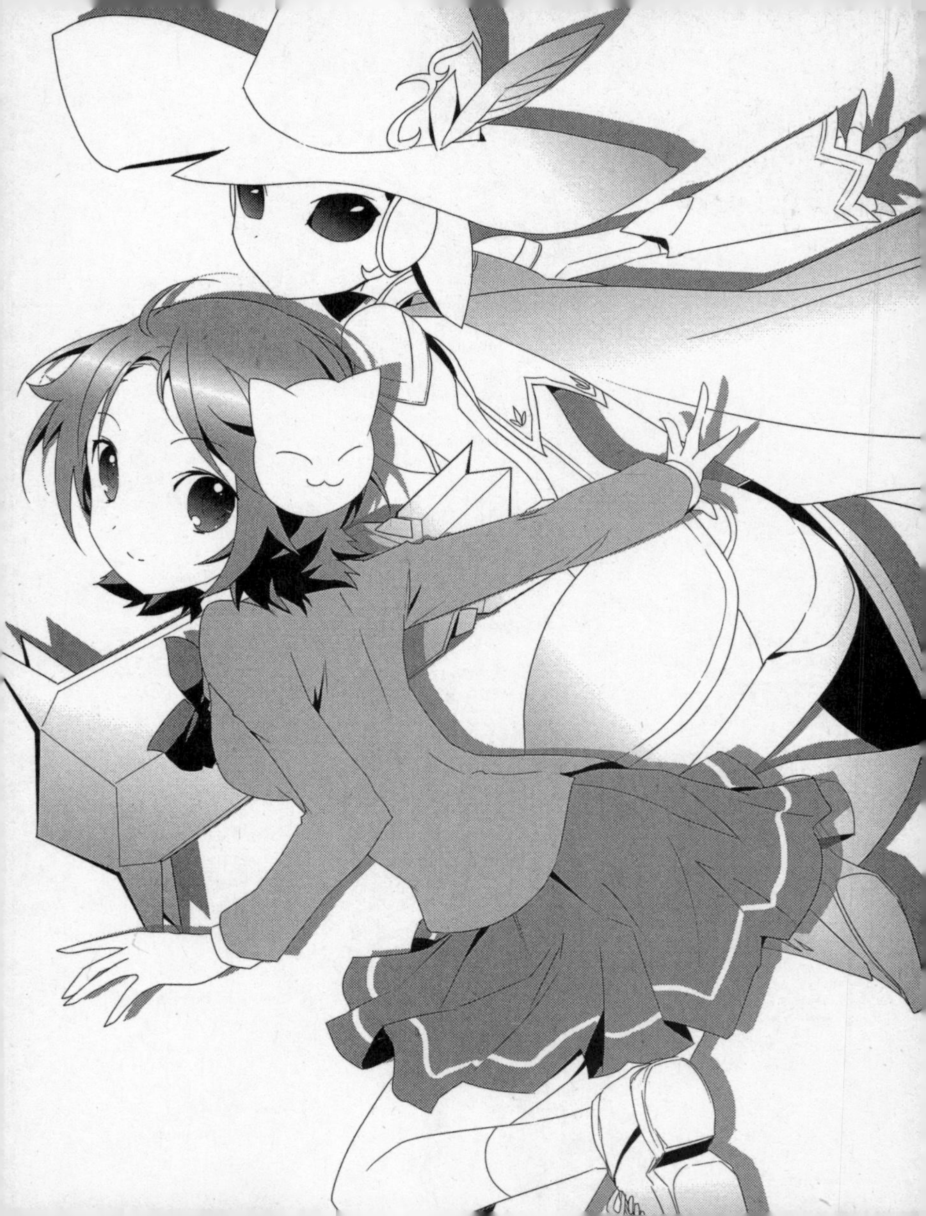

AFTERWORD

Thank you so much for picking up Volume 5 of the manga version of *Accel World*!

This volume features the short story "Versus" included in Book Ten of the original novel series and an episode focusing on Chiyu that connects the second and third novels.

"Versus" is a crossover of Reki Kawahara-sensei's works, a dream matchup between Kirito, the main character in *Sword Art Online*, and Silver Crow. I expect more than a few people were surprised to see Kirito-kun on the cover of this book. With the manga as well, it felt like I had two protagonists, and it was really refreshing to get to draw the story. I hope that AW and SAO fans alike enjoyed it!

The Chiyu chapter that follows is an expansion of an unpublished piece by Kawahara-sensei for some *Accel World* merchandise and tells the story of what happens after Chiyu installs BB until Lime Bell is born. I was the one in charge of the work to expand on the plot from that piece. I've always drawn the manga with the basic principle of staying faithful to the original work, and this was the first time I've gotten the chance to expand on something that wasn't in the original work, so I was pretty nervous about how to do it as I was drawing. Kawahara-sensei was kind enough to agree easily with the plot I proposed, and I was able to feel a bit more at ease in drawing it.
Kawahara-sensei, thank you so much!

And I'd be very happy if we met again in the next volume. This has been Hiroyuki Aigamo.

■ASSISTANT
Hio-sama
Tatsuki Edo-sama
Motoko Ikeda-sama
Sakuraba-sama
Tsukikaname-sama
B-king Ito-sama
Momoto-sama
Hanimaru-sama
Kyosei Yasuda-sama
Ao Esaka-sama
Haru-sama

■SPECIAL THANKS
Reki Kawahara-sama
HIMA-sama
Ryuuryuu Akari--sama
Ayato Sasakura-sama
everyone on the Sunrise Anime staff
abec-sama
Chie Tsuhiya-sama
Kazuma Miki-sama

HIROYUKI AIGAMO

comment in support of "comic" accel world

original story: reki kawahara

DC ACCEL WORLD 05

CONGRATULATIONS ON THE PUBLICATION!

HIMA

character design: hima

comment

Congratulations on volume five of the comic!

Now that the "Niko Assault" (I just decided to call it that now) up to volume four is over, I was wondering what would come next, but I never expected the sudden charge into "Versus"! That the day would come when I could see Kirito as drawn by Aigamo-san... I've been super-excited every month!

With volume five, I had the same thought I've had before, that the slight shonen manga elements in the original novels are expressed much more passionately and much cooler. Which is why I get so worked up, I suppose. I can't wait to see how things turn out going forward.

Aigamo-sensei, I hope you'll keep up the great work!

Reki Kawahara

05

accel world

art:
hiroyuki aigamo
original story:
reki kawahara
accel world 10: elements &
accel world 03: the twilight marauder
character design:
hima

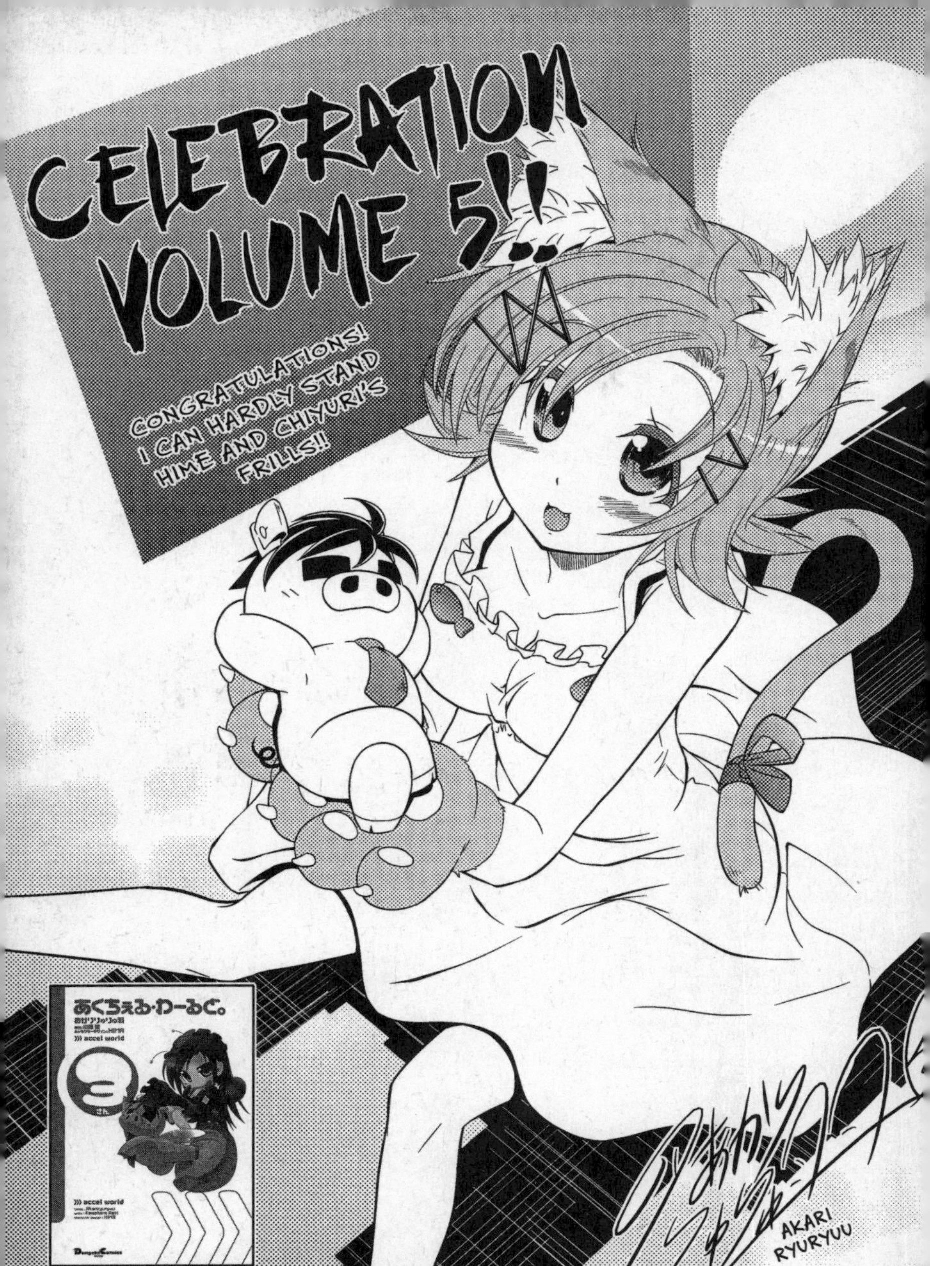
CELEBRATION VOLUME 5!!
CONGRATULATIONS! I CAN HARDLY STAND HIME AND CHIYURI'S FRILLS!!
あくちぇる・わーるど。
accel world
AKARI RYURYUU

Okucheru World by Akari Ryuryuu Vol. 1-3 available in Japan!!
(Story: Reki Kawahara, Character design: HIMA)

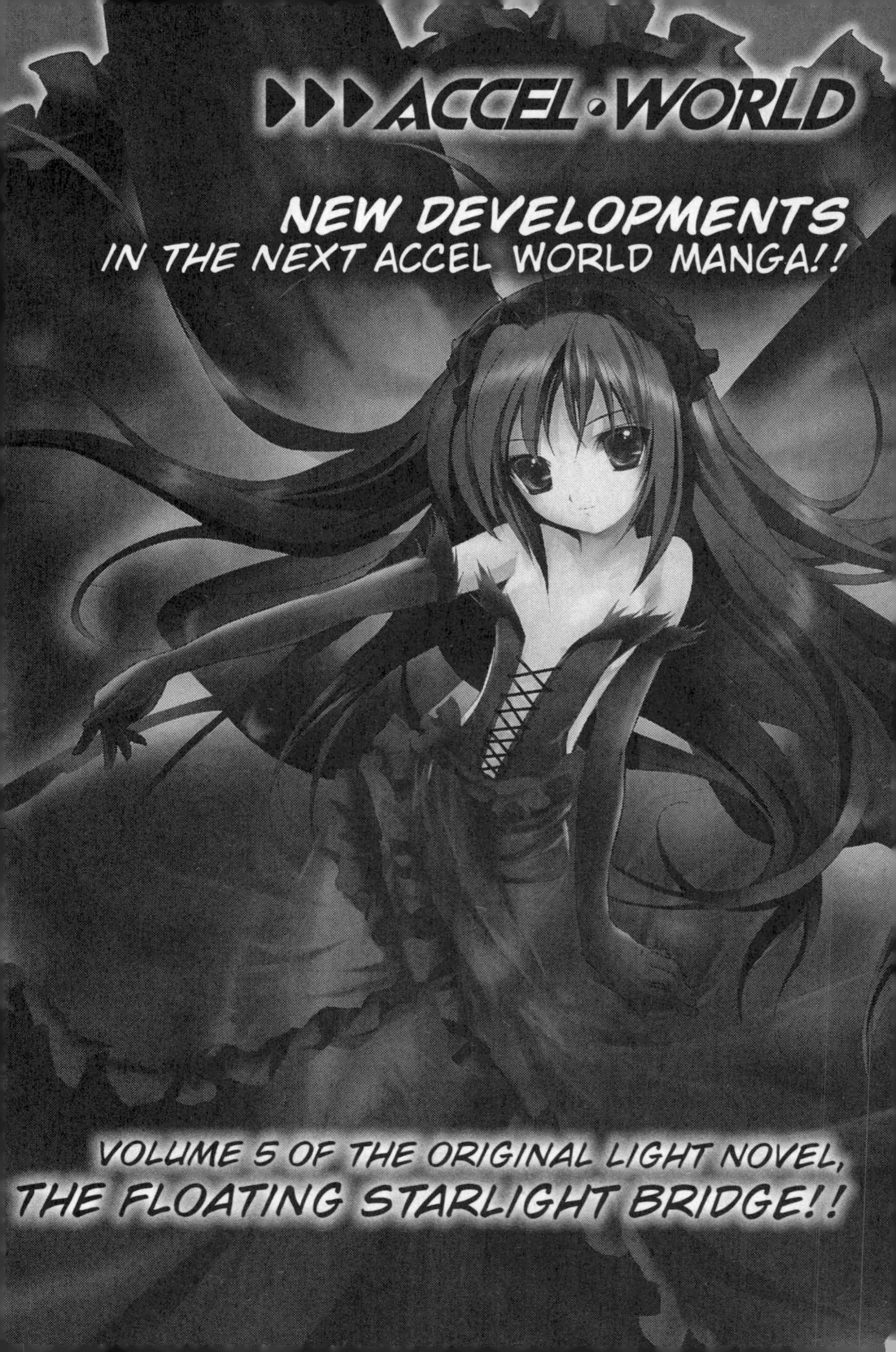
ACCEL·WORLD
NEW DEVELOPMENTS
IN THE NEXT ACCEL WORLD MANGA!!
VOLUME 5 OF THE ORIGINAL LIGHT NOVEL,
THE FLOATING STARLIGHT BRIDGE!!

accel world

THE NEXT VOLUME OF THE MANGA, AW6, HAS EVEN MORE NEW TWISTS AND TURNS!! A NEW BATTLE STAGE APPEARING IN THE SPACE ELEVATOR...HEARING THIS NEWS, HARUYUKI FINDS AWAITING HIM A FIGHT FOR THE SKY TAKING PLACE WITH MEMBERS OF ALL LEGIONS. AFTER SURPASSING COUNTLESS OBSTACLES, WILL THE NEW NEGA NEBULUS WELCOME TWO TRUSTWORTHY COMPANIONS TO WIN OUT IN THIS FIERCE BATTLE!? KEEP AN EYE OUT FOR THE NEXT VOLUME AND A WHOLE LOT OF EXCITEMENT!

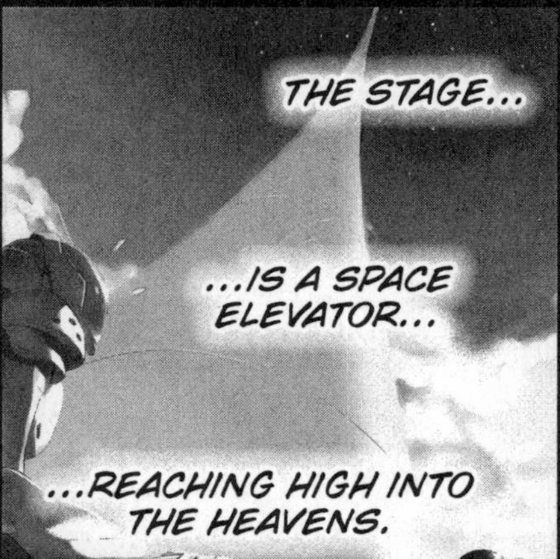
THE STAGE...
...IS A SPACE ELEVATOR...
...REACHING HIGH INTO THE HEAVENS.

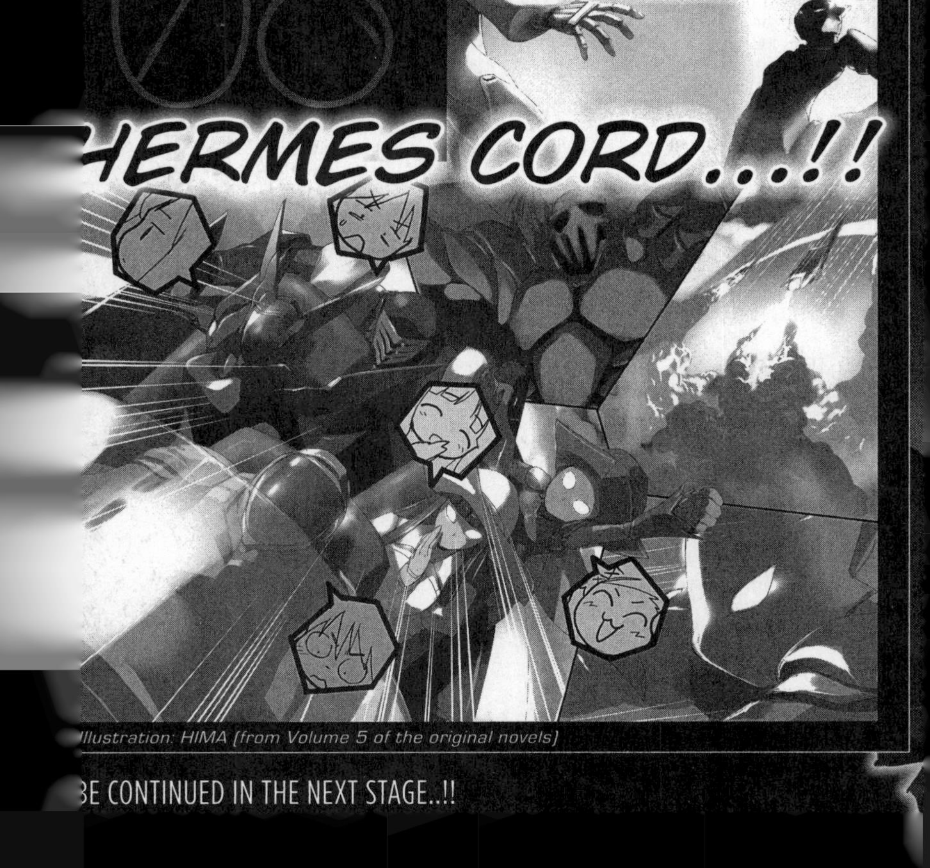
06
HERMES CORD...!!

Illustration: HIMA (from Volume 5 of the original novels)

BE CONTINUED IN THE NEXT STAGE..!!

ACCEL WORLD ⑤

ART: HIROYUKI AIGAMO
ORIGINAL STORY: REKI KAWAHARA
CHARACTER DESIGN: HIMA

Translation: Jocelyne Allen
Lettering: Brndn Blakeslee and Lys Blakeslee

ACCEL WORLD
© REKI KAWAHARA / HIROYUKI AIGAMO 2014
All rights reserved.
Edited by ASCII MEDIA WORKS
First published in Japan in 2014 by KADOKAWA CORPORATION, Tokyo.
English translation rights arranged with KADOKAWA CORPORATION, Tokyo, through Tuttle-Mori Agency, Inc., Tokyo.

Translation © 2015 by Hachette Book Group, Inc.

Yen Press
Hachette Book Group
1290 Avenue of the Americas
New York, NY 10104

www.HachetteBookGroup.com
www.YenPress.com

Yen Press is an imprint of Hachette Book Group, Inc. The Yen Press name and logo are trademarks of Hachette Book Group, Inc.

The publisher is not responsible for websites (or their content) that are not owned by the publisher.

First Yen Press Edition: October 2015

ISBN: 978-0-316-30614-0

10 9 8 7 6 5 4 3 2 1

BVG

Printed in the United States of America